International Political Economy Series

General Editor: Timothy M. Shaw, Professor of Human Security & Peacebuilding, School of Peace & Conflict Management, Royal Roads University, Victoria, BC, Canada

Titles include:

Jomo K.S. and Shyamala Nagaraj (*editors*)
GLOBALIZATION VERSUS DEVELOPMENT

Angela W. Little
LABOURING TO LEARN
Towards a Political Economy of Plantations, People and Education in Sri Lanka

John Loxley (*editor*)
INTERDEPENDENCE, DISEQUILIBRIUM AND GROWTH
Reflections on the Political Economy of North–South Relations
at the Turn of the Century

Don D. Marshall
CARIBBEAN POLITICAL ECONOMY AT THE CROSSROADS
NAFTA and Regional Developmentalism

Susan M. McMillan
FOREIGN DIRECT INVESTMENT IN THREE REGIONS OF
THE SOUTH AT THE END OF THE TWENTIETH CENTURY

S. Javed Maswood
THE SOUTH IN INTERNATIONAL ECONOMIC REGIMES
Whose Globalization?

John Minns
THE POLITICS OF DEVELOPMENTALISM
The Midas States of Mexico, South Korea and Taiwan

Justin Robertson (*editor*)
POWER AND POLITICS AFTER FINANCIAL CRISES
Rethinking Foreign Opportunism in Emerging Markets

Lars Rudebeck, Olle Törnquist and Virgilio Rojas (*editors*)
DEMOCRATIZATION IN THE THIRD WORLD
Concrete Cases in Comparative and Theoretical Perspective

Benu Schneider (*editor*)
THE ROAD TO INTERNATIONAL FINANCIAL STABILITY
Are Key Financial Standards the Answer?

Howard Stein (*editor*)
ASIAN INDUSTRIALIZATION AND AFRICA
Studies in Policy Alternatives to Structural Adjustment

International Political Economy Series
Series Standing Order ISBN 0–333–71708–2 hardcover
Series Standing Order ISBN 0–333–71110–6 paperback
(*outside North America only*)

You can receive future titles in this series as they are published by placing a standing order.
Please contact your bookseller or, in case of difficulty, write to us at the address below with
your name and address, the title of the series and one of the ISBNs quoted above.

Customer Services Department, Macmillan Distribution Ltd, Houndmills, Basingstoke,
Hampshire RG21 6XS, England

Development, Civil Society and Faith-Based Organizations

Bridging the Sacred and the Secular

Edited by

Gerard Clarke
School of the Environment and the Society, Swansea University, UK

and

Michael Jennings
School of Oriental and African Studies, London, UK

Foreword by

Lord Carey

First published in 2008 by
PALGRAVE MACMILLAN
Houndmills, Basingstoke, Hampshire RG21 6XS and
175 Fifth Avenue, New York, N.Y. 10010
Companies and representatives throughout the world.

PALGRAVE MACMILLAN is the global academic imprint of the Palgrave
Macmillan division of St. Martin's Press, LLC and of Palgrave Macmillan Ltd.
Macmillan® is a registered trademark in the United States, United Kingdom
and other countries. Palgrave is a registered trademark in the European
Union and other countries.

ISBN-13: 978–0–230–02001–6 hardback
ISBN-10: 0–230–02001–1 hardback

This book is printed on paper suitable for recycling and made from fully
managed and sustained forest sources. Logging, pulping and manufacturing
processes are expected to conform to the environmental regulations of
the country of origin.

A catalogue record for this book is available from the British Library.

A catalog record for this book is available from the Library of Congress.

10 9 8 7 6 5 4 3 2 1
17 16 15 14 13 12 11 10 09 08

Transferred to digital printing in 2009.

For Adam, Senan and Emma

Contents

List of Figures

List of Abbreviations

ABVP	Akhil Bharatiya Vidyarthi Parishad
ACCESS	Alliance of Concerned Citizens for an Empowered Social System
AHIF	Al-Haramain Islamic Foundation
AMRSP	Association of Major Religious Superiors of the Philippines
APRODEV	formerly the Association of Protestant Development Agencies
ARAM	Arabian–American Oil Company
ARMM	Autonomous Region for Muslim Mindanao
BBC	Bishops-Businessmen conference
BBC	British Broadcasting Corporation
BCC	Basic Christian Community
BEI	Board of Electoral Inspectors
BJP	Bharatiya Janata Party
BMS	Bharatiya Mazdoor Sangh
BUF	Bishops-Ulama Forum
CA	Christian Aid
CAFOD	Catholic Fund for Overseas Development
CARL	Comprehensive Agrarian Reform Law
CBCP	Catholic Bishops Conference of the Philippines
CCSD	Consultative Center for Studies and Documentation
CCT	Christian Council of Tanzania
CFBCI	Center for Faith-Based and Community Initiatives
CFFC	Catholics for a Free Choice
CIDSE	Coopération Internationale pour le Développement et la Solidarité
CIIR	Catholic Institute for International Relations
CLP	Council of the Laity of the Philippines
COMELEC	Commission of Elections
CONCORD	Constitutional Correction for Development
CPP	Communist Party of the Philippines
CSO	Civil society organizations
CWO	Catholic Welfare Organization
DAC	Development Assistance Committee
DFID	Department for International Development
DSWD	Department of Social Welfare and Development

EBF	Ecumenical Bishops Forum
ECOSOC	Economic and Social Council
ELCT	Evangelical Lutheran Church in Tanzania
FBO	Faith-based organisation
FGM	Female genital mutilation
FOCA	Friends of Charities Association
FOMWAN	Federation of Muslim Women's Associations of Nigeria
GAO	Government Accountability Office
GAVI	Global Alliance for Vaccines and Immunization
GRP	Government of the Republic of the Philippines
HDI	Human Development Index
HIPC	Highly Indebted Poor Countries
HRC	High Relief Council
IAF	Islamic Action Front
ICCS	Islamic Center Charity Society
ICG	International Crisis Group
ICSI	Institute of Church and Social Issues
IDB	Islamic Development Bank
IIRO	International Islamic Relief Organisation
ILO	International Labour Organisation
IPPF	International Planned Parenthood Federation
IRDF	India Development and Relief Fund
ICVA	International Council for Voluntary Agencies
JD	Jordanian Dinar
JWU	Jordan Women's Union
MB	Muslim Brotherhood
MDG(s)	Millennium Development Goal(s)
MILF	Moro Islamic Liberation Front
MMA	Muttahaida Majlis-I-Amal
MNLF	Moro National Liberation Front
MU	Mothers Union
MWL	Muslim World League
NAE	National Association of Evangelicals
NAMFREL	National Movement for Free Elections
NASSA	National Secretariat for Social Action
NCC	National Ceasefire Committee
NCCP	National Council of Churches in the Philippines
NCPMC	National Citizens' Peace Monitoring Council
NDF	National Democratic Front
NGO	Non-governmental organization
NMS	Norwegian Missionary Society

NOK	Norwegian kroner
NORAD	Norwegian Agency for Development Cooperation
NPA	New People's Army
NSC	National Security Council
NUC	National Unification Commission
OECD	Organisation for Economic Cooperation and Development
OFAC	Office of Foreign Assets Control
OIC	Organization of Islamic Conference
PA	Professional Association
PC	Philippine Constabulary
PEPFAR	President's Emergency Plan for AIDS Relief
PIRMA	People's Initiative for Reform, Modernization and Action
PPA	Programme Partnership Agreements
PPCRV	Pastoral Parish Council for Responsible Voting
PPMC	Peace Promotion and Monitoring Council
PSL	Personal Status Law
RDO	Research and Documentation Office
RONGO	Royal non-governmental organisation
RSCS	Rapid Social Change Study
RSD	Relief and Service Division
RSS	Rashtriya Swayamsevak Sangh
SDU	Service and Development Unit
SOCAL	Standard Oil of California
SPCPD	Southern Philippines Council for Peace and Development
TANU	Tanganyika Africa National Union
TEC	Tanzanian Episcopal Conference
UDHA	Urban Development and Housing Act
ULP	Ulama League of the Philippines
UN	United Nations
UNDP	United Nations Development Programme
UNFPA	United Nations Population Fund
UNICEF	United Nations Children's Fund
UNOSOM	United Nations Operation in Somalia
USAID	United States Agency for International Development
USCCB	United States Conference of Catholic Bishops
VFA	Visiting Forces Agreement
VHP	Vishva Hindu Parishad
VKA	Vanavasi Kalyan Ashram
VOTE-CARE	Voters' Organisation for Training and Organisation towards Clear Authentic Responsible Elections
WAF	Women's Action Forum

WAF	Women Against Fundamentalisms
WAMY	World Assembly of Muslim Youth
WCC	World Council of Churches
WHO	World Health Organisation
WLUML	Women Living under Muslim Laws
WVI	World Vision International
YCS	Young Christian Students
YMCA	Young Men's Christian Association

Acknowledgements

This book originated in a piece of research by staff of the Centre for Development Studies, Swansea University and the Department of Theology and Religious Studies at the University of Wales, Lampeter, in 2004–2005 for the Department of International Development that looked at DFID engagement with faith-based organizations and the role of faith groups in poverty reduction. We are grateful to all who worked on this research: Tim Bowyer, Sarah James, Alan Rew, Shefali Juneja, Helen Hintjens, Shazad Khan, Alan Thomas, Michael Elliot, Maya Warrier, Mary Grey, Wendy Dossett, Xinzhong Yao, Dan Cohn-Sherbok and Dawoud El-Alami. Outside of the team, we are grateful to a number of people who also helped during the original research and the additional research that shaped this book, including Ian Linden, Martin Palmer, Jonathan Benthall, Jim Manor, Michael Battcock, Heaven Crawley and Mohammed Kroessin. Special thanks to Andy Chaggar for preparing the index.

We are also grateful to a number of publishers for permission to reproduce work which first appeared elsewhere; to Taylor and Francis for material which first appeared in Gerard Clarke, 'Agents of Transformation? Faith-Based Organisations, Donors and International Development', *Third World Quarterly*, Vol. 28, No. 1, 2007; John Wiley and Sons Limited for Gerard Clarke, 'Faith Matters: Faith-Based Organisations, Civil Society and International Development', *Journal of International Development*, Vol. 18, No. 6, 2006; and Ashgate for Christophe Jaffrelot, 'Hindu Nationalism and the Social Welfare Strategy' in A. Dieckhoff and N. Guiterrez (eds), *Modern Roots: Studies of National Identity*, Aldershot: Ashgate, 2001.

Thanks are also due to Jim and Blandina Giblin for comments, advice and a wonderful welcome in Tanzania and especially to Vicky Lewis and Helen Quane for their support and understanding.

Foreword

In 1997, when I was in post as Archbishop of Canterbury I received an unexpected telephone call from Jim Wolfensohn who was then President of the World Bank. He requested an urgent meeting at which he expressed his amazement at the enormous contribution that African churches in particular were making towards development and which were, at that time, almost completely ignored by the World Bank. He cited the example of Tanzania where faith communities, particularly Christian bodies, provided nearly 50 per cent of national education, health care and social provision, yet received no support from the World Bank.

Impressed by the role of religions in areas of health and work among the absolute poor, Jim felt impelled to think outside the box. 'Is it not impossible' he questioned, 'for us to imagine a new relationship between the Bank and the world religions?' He and I co-chaired a historic meeting at Lambeth Palace in 1998 at which senior Board officials met eminent leaders of nine world faiths. From that meeting emerged the World Faiths Development Dialogue which Jim and I founded, and which continues to exist today in facilitating faith-based organizations in their work among the very poor.

This book of chapters by scholars and experts, edited by Gerard Clarke and Michael Jennings, is a major contribution towards understanding the role of religion in development, as well as assisting secular and religious worlds to intersect and challenge each other. As a practitioner in one world religion, and as a person whose faith compels me to care for the poor unconditionally, I am quite convinced that the stand-off between secularism and religion is in no one's best interests, especially the most vulnerable. Hard questions have to be levelled at both sides of this historic conflict.

To all religious communities there is an urgent need to come to terms with modernity. The challenges of science cannot be ducked. Those who claim exclusivity for their particular brand of faith must be prepared to subject their arguments to scrutiny. Those who contend that their scriptures are infallible, and their laws are correspondingly rooted in God's commandments and must take precedence over civil law, must justify this claim before the bar of logic and human rights, if they wish their laws to be normative in civil society.

But secularism cannot be let off the hook. Religion remains a very powerful force for good even if, from time to time, extremists exploit religion for their own ends. Most of the time its role is beneficial in the lives of its adherents, and the failure of some secularists to perceive the positive aspects of religious communities does hinder a true dialogue between those who believe and those who do not. A living religious tradition is far more than a set of beliefs that hold it together; it is a community of faith that fuses belief, faith and action into an indivisible whole and produces what sociologists describe as 'social capital'. Indeed, it is undeniably the case that the religions are involved in development and, in many parts of the world, are enhancing the lives of millions. In the words of Kumi Naidoo, General Secretary of CIVICUS, 'faith based organisations probably provide the best social and physical infrastructure in the poorest countries...because churches, temples, mosques and other places of worship are focal points for the communities they serve'.[1]

The moment we see religion through the distorting lens of 'fundamentalism', 'extremism', 'terrorism' and 'the clash of civilisations' we lose sight of the wider picture and the rich contribution that moderates in all religions make. Cultural condescension, in fact, is a very easy trap to fall into. There may well be times when our instinctive conclusion that 'my way, my culture, my way of looking at reality is superior to yours' is a justifiable conclusion. I firmly believe that with reference to the barbarities of some Muslim practices such as female circumcision or aspects of corporal punishment. On the other hand, Muslim reaction to some aspects of Western secular culture, and religious practices of some Christian groups in America or Britain, may lead them to the opinion that the West is hopelessly decadent. Clearly, the present impasse between secular and religious worlds, as well as between religions themselves, make the quest for a new type of conversation between such different communities a most urgent need.

I have every confidence that this well-argued and well-researched book contains the tools to help create a meaningful dialogue that will allow religious and secular bodies to challenge and learn from each other. If it is very unlikely that argument on its own can convince the believer or unbeliever that his respective conceptual world is wrong, the least we can do is to use our knowledge, experience and compassion to make this world a better place. Faith-based organisations have much to offer, and it may be one of those delicious ironies that encounter with, and openness to, the secular world will enable that contribution to be more effective. Perhaps secularism might even gain something from this encounter too.

LORD CAREY
Archbishop of Canterbury 1991–2002.
Currently: Co-Chair of the Council of 100 of the World Economic Forum.
Chairman of the World Faiths Development Dialogue.
Chairman of the Foundation for Reconciliation and
Relief in the Middle East.

Note

1. Kumi Naidoo, The Charities Aid Foundation, *Alliance*, 5, 1, 2000.

Notes on Contributors

Gerard Clarke is Senior Lecturer in Development Studies in the School of the Environment and Society, Swansea University. The author of *The Politics of NGOs in South-East Asia: Participation and Protest in the Philippines* (1998), his main research interests cluster around NGOs, civil society and development in South-East Asia. He has published the results of recent research on FBOs and development in the *Journal of International Development* and in *Third World Quarterly*.

Janine Clark is an Associate Professor in the Department of Political Science at the University of Guelph, Ontario. Her research interests include religion and politics in the Middle East, civil society and development, women and development, women and party politics, and civil society and democratization. Professor Clark has published two books: *Islam, Charity, and Activism: Middle-Class Networks and Social Welfare in Egypt, Jordan and Yemen* (2004) and *Economic Liberalization, Democratization and Civil Society in the Developing World*, co-edited with Remonda Bensabat-Kleinberg (2000).

Mona Harb is an Assistant Professor at the Department of Architecture and Design at the American University of Beirut (AUB). She has a PhD in Political Science from the Institut d'Etudes Politiques in France. Her research examines Hezbollah's institutions and social networks in the context of the Lebanese political system as well as urban governance. More recently, she has been investigating the cultural dimensions of the 'Islamic sphere' in Lebanon.

Ingie Hovland has recently completed a PhD in Social Anthropology at the School of Oriental and African Studies (SOAS, University of London), entitled *Distance Destroys and Kills: An Anthropological Inquiry into the Nature of Faith in the Lutheran Norwegian Mission Society*. She is currently teaching part-time at SOAS on Women, Men and Christianity.

Christophe Jaffrelot is Director of CERI (Centre d'Etudes et de Recherches Internationales) at Sciences Po (Paris), and Research Director at the CNRS (Centre National de la Recherche Scientifique). He teaches South Asian politics to doctoral students at Sciences Po. His most recent books, all published by Columbia University Press, are *The Hindu Nationalist Movement and Indian Politics, 1925 to the 1990s*

(1996 and 1999); *India's Silent Revolution. The Rise of the Low Castes in North India* (2002); and *Dr Ambedkar and Untouchability. Analysing and Fighting Caste* (2005).

Michael Jennings is Mellon Research Fellow at the School of Oriental and African Studies, University of London. His research examines development processes in Africa with a particular focus on the role of NGOs in development, the links between development and nationalism in post-colonial Africa and on the emergence of African forms of civil society. He has also worked on the role of Christian organizations in the development of East Africa in the colonial and post-colonial period. He is co-editor of *The Charitable Impulse: NGOs and Development in East and North East Africa* (2002).

Mohammed Kroessin works with the Policy and Research Unit of Islamic Relief and is a Research Associate of the 'Religions & Development' research programme at the University of Birmingham where he explores the involvement of faith communities in poverty reduction processes and the role of British Muslim NGOs. A political economist with nearly ten years of experience in development practice, policy and research, he was previously Assistant Chief Executive of Muslim Aid. He has authored a number of articles dealing with Islamic concepts of humanitarianism.

Ian Linden is an Associate Professor at the School of Oriental and African Studies in London. A past director of the Catholic Institute for International Relations, a respected think-tank, which has been linked for 15 years with radical Church groups in Southern Africa, Central America and Philippines, he was awarded a CMG for his work for human rights in 2000. His latest book *A New Map of the World* (DLT) investigates the impact of globalization on the world religions and the growth of a global civil society. He has been engaged in interfaith dialogue for 15 years and works in the Christian–Muslim Forum of Great Britain with paired responsibility for international affairs.

Abdulfatah Mohamed is currently Director of the London-based Al-Muntada Al-Islami Trust. For more than 16 years, he has worked as an advisor to corporations, NGOs and faith-based organizations in Saudi Arabia, the Middle East, Europe and Africa. His contributions have been in quality management, accountability and governance- related capacity building. Post 9/11 he has been actively involved in a number of confidence building projects including the Montreux Initiative, the International Bureau for Humanitarian NGOs in Geneva and Friends of Charities Associations (FOCA) in the United States of America.

Antonio Moreno is a member of the Society of Jesus (the Jesuits) and President of the Ateneo de Zamboanga University in the Philippines. He finished his doctorate in Development Studies in 2003 at Swansea University. Formerly the Dean of the School of Arts and Sciences, (2005–2007), Research Associate of the Research Institute for Mindanao Culture (2003–2007), and Vice President for Social Development at Xavier University (2005–2007), Cagayan de Oro City, he is the author of *Church, State and Civil Society in Postauthoritarian Philippines* (2006).

Ruth Pearson is Professor of Development Studies and Director of the Centre for Development Studies at the University of Leeds. She was one of the pioneers of gender and development scholarship in the United Kingdom, and much of her research has focused on issues of women's employment, identity and empowerment. She is co-editor of *Feminist Visions: Gender, Policy and Analyses* (1998) and author of numerous articles on various aspects of gender and development. Her current research is focused on issues of migration, identity and entitlements of women workers in South-East Asia and the United Kingdom.

Emma Tomalin is a lecturer in the Department of Theology and Religious Studies at the University of Leeds. Her research interests are focused upon gender and religion; religion and international development; and religion and environmentalism, particularly with respect to South and South-East Asia. She is currently contributing to the 'Religions and Development' research programme, based in the International Development Department, Birmingham University. She has published recent research on religion and development in *Progress in Development Studies, Gender and Development* and in *Numen*.

1
Introduction

Gerard Clarke and Michael Jennings

This is a book about positive synergies long neglected and obscured in development discourse and policy. It is about the pivotal role of 'faith-based' or religiously inspired organizations in existing or nascent civil societies, and the commonalities between 'faith' and 'development' as normative ideals and moral discourses concerned with the welfare of humankind. It is about the pivotal role of faith in the identities of both the poor and non-poor, as a bridge that binds them together and links their fates. It is about the role of faith as an analytical lens through which the poor rationalize and often challenge their marginalization.

These synergies have not always been evident in development discourse and policy. Western official donors, for instance, have traditionally been ambivalent about the relationship between faith and development and the activities of faith-based organizations (FBOs). Heavily influenced by the legal separation of Church and state in liberal democracies, they felt that religion was counter-developmental, that religious discourses with strong historical resonance were inflexible and unyielding in the face of social and political change. Reason and faith were constructed as oppositional, mutually incompatible spheres. This antipathy was frequently reciprocated. Faith leaders often saw themselves as the defenders of traditional moral values amid the onslaught of secular modernity, and many were wedded to a paternalistic view of poverty and the poor, ready to advocate the charitable obligations of the faithful but less willing to press for political and social change that benefited the faithful as citizens as much as dutiful believers. With notable exceptions, the main faiths emphasized the spiritual and moral dimensions of poverty at the expense of the material, and representative organizations avoided poverty-focussed social engagement and policy dialogue with governments and donors.[1]

This was not always the case, however. Faith organizations maintained strong connections with the state in colonial economies of the early- to mid-twentieth century, building on linkages and roles created as part of Victorian-era social formations.[2] But as Empires drew to an end, that privileged position was increasingly lost. In Western Europe and North America, too, the decline of the old establishments following the Second World War saw a gradual decline in the place of religion in formal public life.

The connections between the worlds of faith and development, became, as Marshall and Keough argue, 'fragile and intermittent at best, critical and confrontational at worst' (Marshall and Keough, 2004: 1). In little over a decade, however, there has been a gradual movement from estrangement to engagement. FBOs, led primarily but not exclusively by the Christian Churches, have actively sought dialogue with donor agencies, while donors have reciprocated. Much of the impetus stems from the work of former World Bank President James Wolfensohn and former Archbishop of Canterbury Dr George Carey, and a series of conferences of donor representatives and faith leaders (in London in 1998, Washington, DC in 1999, and Canterbury (England) in 2002). The published proceedings of these and related conferences point to the 'faith and development' interface as a significant new theme in development discourse and policy (Marshall and Keough, 2004; Marshall and Marsh, 2003; Palmer and Findlay, 2003; Belshaw et al., 2001).

The Millennium Declaration agreed at the United Nations General Assembly in September 2000, and the associated Millennium Developments Goals (MDGs), lie at the heart of this new engagement.[3] The Declaration is seen in some quarters as a 'covenant', a solemn contract or agreement with quasi-religious or spiritual significance (Marshall and Keough, 2004: 4). In this sense, the Declaration is an inspirational document which generates a moral commitment among signatories and galvanizes the moral energy of the global community. Many years after their approval, however, the MDGs remain poorly understood, much less agreed, on the ground (Ibid: 7). Faith communities and organizations to which they give rise are therefore seen as important actors in galvanizing the moral commitment on which the MDGs depend and in popularizing them in local churches, mosques, temples, and synagogues, translating them into the idioms of the faith and mobilizing support for organizations and community initiatives that contribute to the goals. Two brief examples, separated by thousands of miles and by an equivalent distance in terms of proximity to the levers of political power, help to illustrate this point.

The first example involves the former Chancellor of the Exchequer (UK Minister for Finance) Gordon Brown. In a high-profile ceremony in London in November 2006, Brown launched a £2.1 billion ($4 billion) bond to finance a global immunization programme for under-fives, the first step in a longer-term programme to combat malaria and HIV/AIDS in support of the GAVI Alliance (formerly the Global Alliance for Vaccines and Immunisation). But in an unprecedented gesture of support for a government-funded initiative, the first six bonds were purchased by representatives of Pope Benedict XVI, the Archbishop of Canterbury, the Chief Rabbi (in the United Kingdom), the Muslim Council of Britain, the Hindu Forum of Britain and the Network of Sikh Organizations. Each representative promised their support for an initiative designed to immunize up to 500 million children in the poorest 70 countries in the world and to adapt it to the doctrines of the faith, helping to ease its implementation in a range of complex cultural settings.[4]

The second example involves *Quidan Kaisahan* (Solidarity with the Nameless Ones), a non-governmental organization (NGO) based on the island of Negros in the central Philippines. In January 2007, staff of *Quidan* met with local partners and beneficiaries as part of an evaluation exercise. *Quidan* is a secular organization with no religious objectives, but in a community hall in the middle of a large sugar *hacienda*, the meeting starts with prayers at the behest of a community leader. The members of local Peoples Organizations who have attended the meeting pray keenly and fervently, for this is an area where landless sugar workers, among the poorest of the poor in the Philippines, have organized themselves and expressed their identities through Basic Christian Communities for over three decades. Although secular NGOs now play a key role in supporting the poor in many parts of the Philippines, Basic Christian Communities continue to be a primary and essential unit of social and political organization in the lives of the Philippine poor.[5] Any NGO or development agency that seeks to work in and with this community must engage with its faith identity and the community organizations to which it gives rise.

These two examples underline an important nexus between the sacred and the secular in the context of international development. The second, perhaps, illustrates a more essential truth – that the poor have tended to use the idioms of faith to interpret and respond to the world in which they live, much more so than the language of 'development'. At a minimum, the idioms of faith have a greater historical resonance than the more recent language of development, reflecting older discourses around communitarian values. But the first story illustrates a more recent, yet no less important, 'truth' – that sacred and secular discourses have found common ground around the cause of international development for more than a decade now, around a common concern to improve the lives of the world's hungry and its dispossessed. Organizations concerned with the sacred and the secular alike have had to travel some distance to stake out this common ground. And this journey counts among the most significant innovations in development discourse and policy over the last decade. This volume seeks to explain this journey and to examine its implications.

But this is also a book about antimonies, discordant notes and polar oppositions, including the traditional dissonance between religion and development, and the idea of 'faith-based organizations'. These antimonies frame the discussion that follows and mark our initial point of departure. Religion, for instance, has long been marginalized in development discourse, regarded in some quarters even as the antithesis of development. In this view, religion is a traditional, conservative and counter-development force, dominated by a bleak view of (wo)man's propensity for sin, and primarily concerned with the regulation of individual conduct rather than the promotion of the public good. Historically, the emergence of 'modern' or 'rational' public policy-making has been associated with the constitutional separation of Church and state, the deliberate attempt to displace magic and superstition from the framing of public policy, and the development of specialist, professional skills in the fields of public administration and governance. In recent decades, Western officials have been heavily influenced by constitutional norms on Church-state boundaries and have largely avoided the realms of organized religion. Development discourse and policy in the second half of the twentieth century was largely secular and technocratic in character (although as Linden makes clear in this collection, that secular nature hid strong faith undercurrents). It emphasized the rational at the expense of the spiritual and organized religions were often seen as a significant source of opposition to government and donor policies in critical areas such as HIV/AIDS, gender relations and human rights.

Western donors were more ambivalent on the whole about the role of FBOs. They supported the activities of a small range of FBOs associated with the mainstream Christian Churches but largely because of their perceived quasi-secularism (or because these organizations presented their 'development' work as separate from other aspects of their religious mission). Typically, these FBOs wore their faith lightly – they maintained plural work forces (employing believers and non-believers alike), avoided proselytizing activities (efforts to convert people to the faith) and were non-denominational in their work in developing countries, helping believers and non-believers alike. In many respects, however, this quasi-secularism was largely forced on them, by legislative conventions on Church–state boundaries, by media antipathy to the involvement of overtly religious organizations in public policy debates and by the need for sensitivity in increasingly multicultural and multi-faith societies.

The second area of dissonance that frames the key themes of this book concerns the very idea of 'faith-based organizations' and the implicit tension between the ideas of 'faith' and of 'organizations'. Throughout the book, for instance, we emphasize the distinction between 'religion' and 'faith', even though the distinction is conceptually and operationally difficult to pin down with precision. The term 'religion' is normally associated with the values, rules and social practices that stem from belief in a spiritual and supreme being, usually codified in a sacred text such as the Bible, Quran or Bhagavad Gita. Key world religions include Judaism, Christianity, Islam, Hinduism, Sikhism, Buddhism, Daoism and Shinto. Of these, Judaism, Christianity and Islam share common roots in the Abrahamic tradition of monotheism and originated in the West or Occident. The other world religions are typically polytheistic and originated in South or East Asia. Each sustains a moral system that enables the poor to make claims on the well-off and to challenge their disempowerment or, at a minimum, provides hope of a better future in this or another world.

Used in this sense, however, the term is often criticised for its focus on carefully codified, 'book' religions, to the exclusion of more amorphous and oral traditions, often syncretic in character. The term 'faith' is therefore used here to encompass not only the major book religions mentioned above, but also political philosophies with strong religious elements such as Confucianism or Rastafarianism, modern sects such as the Church of Scientology or the Falun Gong, and belief systems associated with traditional indigenous societies such as shamanism, mysticism or animism. It includes important 'religious' or quasi-religious movements such as the African Independent Churches or the evangelical and Pentecostal Churches of Latin America and parts of East/South-East Asia which combine elements of formal religion and traditional indigenous beliefs. Such faiths are often less rule-bound and ritualized, and less codified in writing but are equally important in enabling people, including the poor, to understand and relate to the wider world.

The term 'faith-based organization' has acquired a political currency for reasons explored further in the chapters that follow, but there is a clear tension between the inclusive and informal nature of 'faith' as understood here and the more formal and hence exclusionary concept of 'organization'. What exactly can, or cannot, be labelled as a faith-based organization? Do we, for instance, exclude Sunday schools, basic Christian Communities, or informal temple committees? The book cannot always offer clear answers and is based on imperfect compromises. We use the term 'faith-based organization' in reference to any organization that derives inspiration and guidance for its activities from the teachings and principles of the faith or from a particular interpretation or school of thought within the faith. Inevitably, therefore, we lay ourselves open to the charge of simultaneously fostering inclusion and exclusion.

Despite its professed concern with 'faith' rather than 'religion', the chapters in this collection focus on three major religions: Christianity, Islam and Hinduism, which claim 1.9 billion, 1.3 billion and 900 million believers respectively, equivalent to almost 70% of the world's estimated population of 6 billion people.[6] Where possible, however, it engages with the overlaps between these religions and other faith traditions. It also focuses on organizations: entities with a formal, rule-based character, clear administrative and regulatory structures, and often with explicit legal recognition. But where possible it encompasses the activities of more informal and spontaneous movements of social and political significance.

In Chapter 2, Clarke presents an overview of the work of faith-based organizations. He examines the growing significance of FBOs against a background of traditional antipathy between 'religion' and 'development', an estrangement which some suggest is illusory in that religious communities have always been concerned about the poverty in their midst and committed to addressing it. He looks at six key factors behind the growing importance of faith-based organizations in international development, including the rise of the US Christian right and of political Islam. He then presents a two-part framework that facilitates an analysis of faith-based organizations in the context of international development. The first part is a typology of faith-based organizations that distinguishes between representative organizations or apex bodies; charitable or development organizations; socio-political organizations; missionary organizations; and finally, radical, illegal or terrorist organizations. This typology, he suggests, points to the different roles that FBOs play in the context of international development, and to the different responses this necessitates on the part of bilateral and multi-lateral donors.

In the second part of the framework, he examines the different ways in which 'faith' manifests itself in the work of different organizations. FBOs, he argues, are varied in their organizational guises but they are also varied in the way they work with beneficiaries, partners or other actors. In particular, they differ in the extent to which faith provides the impulse for action and that the goals for which they strive are rooted in particular teachings and principles of the faith. To this end, he identifies four main ways in which FBOs deploy faith through social or political engagement or link faith to developmental or humanitarian objectives: passive, active, persuasive and exclusive. This typology, he argues, highlights some of the dilemmas for donors and other actors concerned about understanding and supporting the work of FBOs in development contexts, especially the work of charitable and development organizations.

Pearson and Tomlin, while welcoming the increasing convergence of faith and development, add an important cautionary note in Chapter 3. They suggest that one possible outcome of the resurgent dialogue between faith and development communities might be serious reversals in the promotion of gender equity at the centre of development policy. Treating faith communities as monolithic and homogenous, and privileging faith leaders as representatives of entire religious traditions, they argue, risks presenting a normative version of doctrines of faith that are in reality subject to critique and interpretation within those communities.

Drawing on an examination of the work of women's organizations in challenging religious doctrines which undermine women's interests, they explore the tensions arising from dialogue between faith and development communities in two key spheres. The first is the significant tension between the two MDGs concerned respectively with safe motherhood and HIV/AIDS prevention and the 'global gag' on the promotion of abortion and artificial contraception instigated by the predominantly US-based Christian right. This 'global gag', they argue, is promoted mainly through the so-called 'Mexico City Policy' reinstated by President George Bush (in his first day in office in January 2001) and, in turn, through the US$15 billion Presidents Emergency Plan for AIDS Relief (PEPFAR) approved by Congress in 2003. Behind its direct remit, however, the Mexico City Policy has had a far wider impact on women in developing countries, limiting access to a range of sexual and reproductive health services, including pre- and post-natal care.

The second area addressed is the religiously approved use of violence against women and of discrimination against female victims of sexual violence in particular Islamic societies. Pearson and Tomalin focus on Nigeria and Pakistan, and on the incorporation of features of *shariah* law prejudicial to women into civil judicial systems. In both cases, they argue, women's organizations are challenging the conservative interpretation of the *Qur'an* and of the *hadith* (teachings of the Prophet) on which these laws and practices are founded, and in some cases *ulama* (religious scholars) are themselves challenging them, for instance, in Somalia, where Muslim clerics have issued a *fatwa* (or order) condemning the practice of female circumcision/genital mutilation. They present Islamic feminism and secular feminism (secular in the sense of rejecting the union of 'mosque and state', rather than Islamic values *per se*) as coherent responses to problems such as female circumcision in Nigeria or the prosecution of men charged with rape or 'honour' killings in Pakistan.

In Chapter 4, Linden offers a powerful critique of the binary opposition between the sacred and the secular in the discourses of development and of international relations. He notes, for instance, the obliteration from the historical record of the role of religious values in the construction of key pillars of the contemporary world such as the United Nations Charter and the Universal Declaration of Human Rights. In place of a binary opposition, Linden makes the case for a fusion of 'development talk' and of 'God talk', or at least a recognition of profound interconnections between them.

To this end, Linden analyses the development of Church doctrine and teaching which prompted the establishment of leading UK Catholic development agencies in the 1960s, including the Catholic Institute for International Relations (CIIR). He focuses in particular on the Second Vatican Council and the development in Latin America of liberation theology. He writes with great insight of the dilemmas that arose. CIIR's volunteer sending programme, for instance, contained within its structures a non-Catholic department reliant on, and amply funded, by the British government's overseas development ministry. This internal heterogeneity forced on CIIR a translation of language between Catholic and 'secular' discourse, NGO and government policy speak and a perennial struggle over the relative merits and meaning of secularity in development. This was alternatively stimulating and debilitating, in short a microcosm of the wider situation faced by the Catholic Church in 'secular' Europe. Despite the progress of the past ten years, he concludes, 'the gulf between the language and culture of popular religion, be it Christian or Muslim, and the "secular" premises of the majority of developmentalists [remains] large'.

Linden suggests that the 1960s was a critical decade in the history of the Christian Churches' teaching on development and social progress. In Chapter 5, Jennings explores this further, through a study of the Churches engagement with development policy and practice in post-colonial Tanzania. In doing so, he reminds us that the drivers of change (political, ideological or social) do not just occur at the centre – in the ancient halls of the Vatican or the modern corridors of national and international donor organizations – but also take place in the so-called periphery. Jennings argues that the shift from welfare provision in the colonial period (during which time mission-run services formed a piv-otal adjunct to the sparse colonial welfare system) to a more direct engagement in political processes occurred as the Church sought to reformulate its position in newly independent Tanzania, and adopt a more socially engaged understanding of social dynamics and change.

But in a warning to those who assume faith-based organizations' engagement in the politics of development might act as a counterbal-ance to Leviathan, the chapter traces the growing collaboration between Church and State that effectively closed down space for challenges to the powerful state discourse of *Ujamaa*. By the late 1960s, the Christian Churches had been drawn into supporting this policy of rural social-ism, having concluded that *Ujamaa* was compatible with the social teachings of the Church. In doing so, the two main Christian organiza-tions, the Christian Council of Tanzania (CCT) and its Catholic coun-terpart, the Tanzanian Episcopal Conference (TEC), became complicit in the growing authoritarianism of the state and the forced resettle-ment of millions of Tanzanians during the late 1960s and 1970s.

Whilst Jennings provides a counterpoint to contemporary assump-tions that faith-leaders are vital opponents of arbitrary or authoritarian rule, Moreno, in Chapter 6, provides an alternative perspective. The chapter examines the role of the Catholic Bishops Conference of the Philippines (CBCP) in making ruling regimes accountable to citizens and voters, and to promoting their removal from office when they are deemed to have lost popular legitimacy. Moreno focuses on the period from February 1986 to the present, a period characterized by relatively democratic politics in the Philippines. In particular, he examines the events of January 2001 when Church leaders orchestrated popular dem-onstrations which precipitated the removal from office of President Joseph Estrada. Although supported by a minority of its Bishops, the CBCP played a critical role in eroding the legitimacy of the Estrada regime and precipitating its downfall through the timely release of critical statements, the leadership of cross-faith opposition to Estrada (in association with the National Council of Churches in the Philippines (the main representative body of the Protestant Churches) and the Council of Ulama (the main representative body of Islamic scholars), and the mobilization of mass demonstrations centred around Manila's symbolic EDSA Shrine.

In addition to its role in precipitating their removal from office, Moreno's chapter examines the role of the Catholic Church and the CBCP in making ruling administrations accountable to the electorate. He begins by examining the CBCP's role in the promulgation of the 1987 constitution, including its leadership of a campaign to educate voters about the key provisions of the constitution and to encourage them to vote in the referendum that decided its fate. He also examines the CBCP's role in promoting free and fair elections through the establishment of the Pastoral Parish Council for Responsible Voting (PPCRV) and the Voters Organization, Training and Education Towards Clear Authentic Responsible Elections (VOTE-CARE). Both organizations played a critical role in the 1992 and 1998 elections, mobilizing hundreds of thousands of volunteers who monitored voting stations and electoral count centres and who helped educate almost a million voters. Moreno credits these initiatives with contributing to a significant reduction in election-related violence and electoral fraud and an improvement in the transparency and fairness of the electoral system.

In Chapter 7, Clark develops three key points from Chapter 2: that FBOs exist in a number of distinct organizational guises; that FBOs are often highly networked and enmeshed in coalitions that combine many of these distinct organizational forms; and that FBOs differ in the extent to which faith is directly manifest in their activities. The chapter focuses on the Islamic Center Charity Society (ICCS), the charitable arm of the Jordanian branch of the Muslim Brotherhood (MB), and a counterpart of the Islamic Action Front (IAF), the political arm of the MB and one of Jordan's principal opposition parties. While part of a multi-faceted social movement, Clark argues, the three organizations are administratively and financially distinct with separate leadership elections, administrative bodies and sources of revenue. The ICCS was established in 1963 and grew quickly during the 1970s and 1980s, funded by remittances from Jordanian workers in the oil-boom states of the Gulf. Today, it counts among Jordan's largest NGOs, with 3,400 employees.

Clark argues that the ICCS stands outside the mainstream development enterprise, in a Jordanian and international context. It has minimal ties to the Jordanian NGO community, including those NGOs which enjoy royal patronage, and it does not receive, nor solicit, funding from Western donors. Equally, its activities primarily benefit the middle class because its facilities are mainly located in urban areas and because it charges relatively high fees for social services such as primary school education or hospital treatment. Nevertheless, her analysis suggests that the ICCS is an important agent of 'development' for three main reasons. First, many of its social services are targeted at vulnerable social groups including poor families and orphans. Second, the ICCS contributes to many of the Millennium Development Goals, including those concerned with eradicating extreme poverty and hunger, achieving universal primary education, reducing child morality, improving maternal health and combating diseases. Third, although the ICCS belongs to an Islamist movement whose political and social philosophy are conservative by Western standards and opposed to particular Western policies, the movement and its affiliated institutions are neither monolithic nor static. They encompass a range of positions and are open to external as well as internal influences.

In Chapter 8, Hovland tackles one of the most difficult issues addressed in this book – the relationship between donor agencies with a secular mandate and Christian missionary agencies that implement development projects while simultaneously spreading their Christian message and seeking converts to Christianity. Through a case-study of the Norwegian Missionary Society (NMS) and its relationship with the Norwegian Agency for Development Cooperation (NORAD), the chapter raises issues that are relevant in analyses of donor engagement with FBOs throughout Western Europe and North America. The official separation of 'missionary' and 'development' activity within the organizational structure of NMS, is, for many of its staff, difficult to respect in practice, with the result that it frequently breaks down, negating the official line to which NMS and NORAD have subscribed. NMS staff often find it difficult to distinguish between 'evangelism' and 'development' in their everyday work, and the tension between the two often pushes the organization into a schizophrenic stance, placating secular-minded journalists, academics and politicians, yet working to defend the core values of the organization that attract staff and motivate them to work in solidarity with the poor in Sub-Saharan Africa and South-East Asia. Moreover, Hovland suggests, organizations such as NMS provide a distinct 'value-added' to the secular development project and distinctions between secular values and religious values are becoming increasingly nebulous in the context of international development.

In Chapter 9, Kroessin and Mohamed consider one of the most controversial yet poorly understood categories of FBOs – Wahabi- or Salafi-inspired organizations from Gulf states and, in particular, Saudi Arabia, working in countries with a substantial Muslim population in Sub-Saharan Africa and South-East Asia. Such organizations have been widely condemned as promoters of extremist political ideologies and as supporters of terrorism. Yet, following on directly from Hovland's analysis of Christian missionary organizations in Chapter 8, the work of *da'wah*-focused Wahabi or Salafi-inspired organizations appears directly comparable with that of evangelical and Pentecostal organizations.

Kroessin and Mohamed focus on the work of three well-known Saudi-based organizations working in Somalia: the International Islamic Relief Organization (IIRO), the World Assembly of Muslim Youth (WAMY) and the Al-Haramain Islamic Foundation (AHIF). These Wahabi or Salafi organizations have been subject to critical scrutiny (see for example Burr and Collins 2006: 35–43) and tainted with support for *Jihad* on the basis of circumstantial evidence or the misdemeanours of individual staff, leading to the closure of AHIF by the Saudi authorities in 2004 for reasons which remain unclear. This chapter, however, provides an alternative perspective. Each organization has (or in the case of AHIF, had) a distinctive interpretation of the philanthropic message of the Quran and how the responsibility of *da'wah* is to be operationalized, but all three are notable as humanitarian and development organizations, playing important roles in supporting the poor in Muslim countries afflicted by conflict, state failure and/or weak provision of social services. Yet, each was directly and significantly affected by the Western media hype that followed 9/11 and the alleged role of Saudi private organizations in funding terrorist activities. The chapter acknowledges and explains some of the bases for these concerns, for instance, a lack of transparency – due in part to the Islamic tradition of giving to charity discretely – on the part of these organizations. The chapter therefore demonstrates the need to avoid media-driven stereotyping of organizations which seem at odds with Western cultural values and to reach beyond these generalizations to explore the similarities between these and many Western organizations. It demonstrates the need for Western donors to engage in dialogue with their Gulf state counterparts, to involve them in networks and to coordinate aid efforts on the basis of a robust understanding of complimentarities as well as differences.

In Chapter 10, Harb focuses on Hezbollah, the military and socio-political organization which represents the Shi'a (or Shi'i) Muslim community in Lebanese politics and which opposes Israeli intervention in southern Lebanon where the country's Shi'i population is largely concentrated. In opposition to Western views of Hezbollah as a terrorist organization, Harb examines it as a legitimate actor in Lebanese politics and as a provider of vital social welfare and infrastructure in the face of a weak central state. Hezbollah emphasizes a strict or 'authentic' form of Shi'i Islam in its efforts to build a distinct 'Islamic sphere' (*hala islamiyya*) and 'resistance society' (*mutama' al-muqawama*). It seeks to organize, mobilize and represent the *multazimin*, pious Shi'i who are literally 'committed to authentic faith'. Since the conflict of July–August 2006, however, Hezbollah has also attracted support from Sunni Muslims, Maronite Christians and secular socialists. According to Harb, it now maintains a support base of over 300,000 people in Lebanon, a country with a total population of 4 million.

Harb traces many of the reasons for this growing popularity, including its growing electoral strength and its participation in the institutions of local government in Lebanon to a process of internal organizational change and adaptation. She also traces Hezbollah's strengths, however, to the weaknesses of the Lebanese state in providing the infrastructure, services and employment opportunities that voters demand and the role of its faith-based values in enhancing people's sense of dignity, self-worth and belonging amid the degradations brought about by political instability and by sectarian conflict and destruction. Hezbollah, she argues, is not above manipulating its supporters; many of the latter, for instance, have a poor understanding of Hezbollah's funding sources, in particular of the financial support received from Iran. This has done little, however, to hinder its growing popularity, a phenomenon which she explores further in two case studies of Hezbollah-associated organizations. Hezbollah-affiliated FBOs, she argues, responded quickly in the aftermath of the July–August 2006 conflict and used faith values effectively to mobilize volunteers and raise funding. Many of these organizations, she argues, have tentative links to foreign donors but represent distinct foci for further engagement, despite their reputation as components of a terrorist organization and a 'distinct other'.

In Chapter 11, Jaffrelot switches our attention from Christianity and Islam to Hinduism, the world's third largest religion as measured by the number of adherents. He focuses on the activities of the *Sangh Parivar*, a network of organizations committed to the promotion of *Hindutva*, a form of Hindu nationalism variously described as sectarian, chauvinist and racist and led by the para-military *Rashtriya Swayamsevak Sangh* (RSS, Association of National Volunteers). The *Sangh Parivar* counts among the largest FBO networks in the world – the RSS alone has more than 2 million members (and up to 4 million according to some estimates). Jafffrelot provides a valuable account of the historical genesis of *Hindutva* and the growth of the *Sangh Parivar*. His chapter focuses, however, on the elaboration by the RSS of a social welfare strategy designed to inculcate the ideology of *Hindutva* in the minds of lower-caste Hindus and to extend its reach to other Hindus traditionally alienated by Hindu nationalism. This strategy, he argues, has been strengthened by policies of privatization in many Indian states, in which service provision responsibilities are transferred to non-state providers, including affiliates of the *Sangh*, and by the growing wealth and political clout of the Hindu Diaspora in countries such as Britain and the United States, resulting in significant financial and organizational support for the *Sangh's* social welfare strategy. He develops his argument through case studies of two *Sangh*-affiliated charitable or service provision organizations, *Seva Bharti* (Service of India), established in 1989 by the RSS, and *Vidya Bharti* (Indian Knowledge), founded in 1977 to coordinate a network of 700 schools developed by the RSS since the 1950s.

Through careful ethnographic research, he illustrates the ways in which *Seva Bharti*, for instance, deliberately shrouds its explicit allegiance to *Hindutva* in a cloak of charitable activity, yet carefully, almost surreptitiously, inculcates the values of Hindu nationalism. Jaffrelot argues that the charitable activities of RSS and its affiliates are handicapped by significant social cleavages. The culture of low-caste Indians, he argues, is often far removed from the Great Tradition which the RSS seeks to instil in them. These cleavages, he argues, 'can be perceived in the language – often a dialect – used by these strata of society and in their clothes and dietary habits, in short their whole ethos'. But yet despite these handicaps, an influx of funding from overseas affiliates of the RSS has strengthened its social welfare strategy in recent years and made it a significant and controversial element in the rich tapestry of faith-based social engagement in India. Despite the critical analysis here, Jaffrelot acknowledges significant tensions within the *Sangh Parivar* network, based on competing ideologies and organizational mandates. This, in turn, suggests the existence of potential entry points for donors to engage with a network that draws significant support from the poor.

Taken together, these chapters argue that religion, faith and spiritual belief are not idiomatic relics of a pre-modern past. They reflect value systems that have not just endured, but also evolved to meet the new demands of a global economy and society that are increasingly interconnected. These value systems are deeply embedded within development discourse more widely, influencing that discourse as much as it is influenced in turn by that discourse. Human rights, the core values that underscore hopes for political, social and economic justice, have been shaped by clerics of all faiths, as well as by secular humanists. The notion of 'human dignity', and the responsibility of us all as individuals (as well as societies) to assist the weakest, is ingrained in faith texts and oral traditions.

But this collection has not sought to demonstrate that at the heart of faith communities lies a concern with both material and spiritual poverty. Rather, it is to suggest that these values, embedded as they are within faith-based organizations, and linked to their wider faith ethics and values, create in the FBO an institution that (in the best of examples) directly addresses poverty and the marginalization of the poor. FBOs are often controversial, particularly when linked to political manifestations of a faith, or when they operate from within a sectarian or chauvinistic paradigm. But the underlying moral and spiritual values that inform such organizations, this collection argues, are important adjuncts to secular development discourse. Moreover, the 'faith' element of the faith-based organization is not an add-on to its development activity, operating alongside. It is an essential part of that activity, informing it completely. This makes the FBO both distinct (to the extent that faith values imbue its very identity), and yet reflecting the broader non-governmental response to poverty and development, sharing many of the same values.

Donor wariness of FBOs remains a strong undercurrent of development discourse. National governments and international organizations have certainly engaged with a select few – largely those, to adopt the typology presented in Chapter 2, which fall within the active and passive sphere of action. But a fear of engagement with those FBOs that fall within the exclusive/persuasive zone, those that are based upon political forms of faith, and those that call for, or support, radical action (however that 'radical action' is defined), remains. This is where the challenge lies. Faith-based organizations have a set of characteristics that distinguish them from their secular counterparts. The language of faith, the religious idiom, frequently better reflects the cultural norms in which the poor and marginalized operate. They are better able to draw such individuals and communities into global discourses of social justice, rights and development, without recourse to the often distancing language of secular development discourse. World religions (or faiths spreading across local, national, regional, ethnic or other boundaries) draw upon a wide community of support, capable of mobilizing human and capital resources. These organizations are important actors in development and the formulation of development policy. The challenge for donors is to reconcile their secular discourses with the distinct discourses of different faith communities in building a coalition of conviction in the fight for social justice and global inclusion.

Notes

1. According to the former Archbishop of Canterbury, for instance, faith leaders have 'to admit that sometimes we encourage [material] poverty by focusing on spiritual poverty and maybe confusing the two'. (Dr George Carey, opening remarks, Leaders Meeting on Faith and Development, Canterbury, England, October 2002, World Bank transcript. See also Marshall and Marsh (2003: 29).
2. See, for example, Jennings (2007) for the important role missions played in Tanganyika, not just as implementing agencies, but in influencing colonial state policy.
3. For the full text of the Millennium Declaration, see www.un.org/millennium/summit.htm. For details of the MDGs, see www.un.org/millenniumgoals/index.html.
4. 'Brown launches £2.1 bn. bond issues to vaccinate 500 million children', The Guardian, 8 November 2006. 'New bond to save 10 million lives', HM Treasury Press Release 87/06, 7 November 2006.
5. Based on the observations of Gerard Clarke, who attended the meeting.
6. Global estimates compiled on the basis of national figures in Stalker (2004).

Bibliography

Belshaw, D., Cadreisi, R. and Sugden, C. (eds) (2001), *Faith in Development: Partnership Between the World Bank and the Churches in Africa* (Washington, DC: The World Bank).

Jennings, M. (2007), 'A Matter of Vital Importance: The Place of the Medical mission in Maternal and Child Healthcare in Tanganyika, 1919–39' In David Hardiman (ed), *Healing Bodies, Saving Souls: Medical Missions in Asia and Africa* (New York: Amsterdam: Rodopi).

Marshall, K. and Keough, L. (eds) (2004), *Mind, Heart and Soul in the Fight against Poverty* (Washington, DC: The World Bank).

Marshall, K. and Marsh, R. (eds) (2003), *Millennium Challenges for Development and Faith Institutions* (Washington, DC: The World Bank).

Palmer, M. and Findlay, V. (2003), *Faith in Conservation: New Approaches to Religion and Conservation* (Washington, DC: The World Bank).

Stalker, P. (2004), *The Oxford A–Z of Countries in the World* (Oxford; New York: Oxford University Press).

2
Faith-Based Organizations and International Development: An Overview

Gerard Clarke

Introduction

Development studies has traditionally neglected the role of religion and faith and its role in the lives of the poor throughout the developing world. Like other social sciences, it was heavily influenced by 'secularization theory', the belief (in Wilson's classic formulation) that 'religious institutions, actions and consciousness lose their social significance' over time as societies modernize (Wilson 1992: 49).[1] This influence was evident in two key respects: in 'secular reductionism' – the neglect of religious variables in favour of other sociological attributes such as class, ethnicity and gender – and in 'materialistic determinism' – the neglect of nonmaterial, especially religious, motivations in explaining individual or institutional behaviour.[2] In this vein, academics and policymakers perceived poverty as a matter of material deprivation and its elimination a technical undertaking; they systematically ignored the role of faith as an analytical lens through which the poor experienced and rationalized poverty and through which the well-off empathized with their struggles and provided practical support. Donors were not completely immune to variables such as the religious impulse to help the poor. In practice, however, they engaged with a narrow range of faith-based organizations, mainly specialized development organizations associated with the mainstream Christian Churches (Catholic and Protestant), ignoring discourses and organizations from other religious traditions.

Over the past 15 years, however, this situation has begun to change significantly, and sociologists, in particular, have led the way, re-evaluating the link between secularization and modernity. Casanova (1994), for instance, has documented the 'deprivatization' of religion and the rise of public religions in the latter years of the twentieth century. Organized religion, he argues, has traditionally focused on the private sphere, on the moral and spiritual regulation of individual conduct. Since the late twentieth century, however, religious discourse has developed a new concern with the conduct of public life and religious leaders and organizations have become more willing to tread the public stage and to highlight the moral and spiritual import of public policy. Similarly, Juergensmeyer (1993) has documented the rise of religious nationalism, and the implications for the secular state, especially the challenge in reconciling secular and religious nationalism. Since 2000, he has documented the rise of religious violence across the main faith traditions, at a time when it has been linked primarily to one faith (Juergensmeyer 2003).

Academics and practitioners in the development policy community have picked up on these new themes in social science scholarship, and recent literature examines growing engagement between donors and faith communities,[3] and the role of such communities in supporting the poor.[4] Research increasingly examines the relevance of faith in development and the work of faith-based development non-governmental organization (NGOs).[5] The three sections that follow here build on this literature in a number of ways. The first discusses key factors behind the growing salience of faith-based organization (FBOs) in the context of international development, providing a brief historical introduction to the analysis here and in subsequent chapters. The second examines a range of FBOs that are increasingly evident in the context of international development, broadening the narrow focus on development NGOs characteristic of the literature to date. It provides a typology of FBOs and explains the significance of each element of the typology in development contexts. The third section examines the deployment of faith, or particular elements of the faith, in the activities of FBOs and provides a second typology, explaining the significance of each element in debates around international development. The conclusion considers implications that result for donors, civil society organizations and other actors eager to understand, and engage with, FBOs in the context of international development.

The growing salience of FBOs in international development

Despite growing interest in the 'faith and development' interface, donor engagement remains disproportionately focused on the mainstream Christian Churches, especially in Europe. Until 2005, for instance, the

UK Department for International Development maintained Programme Partnership Agreements (PPAs) with Christian Aid, the Catholic Fund for Overseas Development (CAFOD) and with Progresssio (formerly the Catholic Institute for International Relations), but not with organizations from other faiths.[6] Similarly, engagement with faith groups and leaders to date initiated by the World Bank has failed to draw Muslim leaders and organizations in particular into the dialogue and remains disproportionately focused on the mainstream Christian Churches.[7] This record of engagement appears problematic when set against the factors propelling FBOs to prominence in development discourse. These factors are complex and warrant a volume in their own right, but six factors stand out.

The first is the election of Ronald Reagan as US President in 1980, a historic landmark in the rise of US Christian right, centred on evangelical and Pentecostal congregations and their leaders. A born-again (evangelical) Christian, Reagan mobilized the Christian right in support of his domestic and foreign policy, especially his opposition to communism. Over the next two and a half decades, the Christian right grew significantly in response to White House patronage, transforming US politics. By 2003, for instance, an estimated 43 per cent of the US electorate was evangelical,[8] a significant shift away from the mainstream Christian denominations towards a more fervent, and ideologically right-wing, form of faith. In the United States, the Christian right has been influential in the passage of legislation that guides US foreign policy. This influence is exercised in part by charismatic leaders, abetted by significant media access, but organizations that represent the thousands of evangelical and Pentecostal congregations form a vital bulwark. The National Association of Evangelicals (NAE), for instance, had 30 million members in 2005 (up from 2.6 million in 1980s)[9] and has become an important participant in debates around US policy on international development.

Second, the Reagan administration, in alliance with other conservative governments in Western Europe, promoted radical new economic policies at home and abroad in the 1980s, including structural adjustment programmes in developing countries that linked development aid to reduced government spending, privatization and market liberalization. In 'developed' and 'developing' countries alike, FBOs expanded or proliferated as a result of economic neo-liberalism as the faithful responded to growing poverty, inequality and social exclusion. In sub-Saharan Africa, for instance, the World Bank estimates that 50 per cent of education and health services were provided by faith groups and FBOs at the beginning of the millennium (Wolfensohn 2004), a consequence, in part, of structural adjustment and the pivotal role of FBOs in nascent civil societies. In the United States, an ideological revolution further transformed the role of FBOs at the cusp of the new millennium. 'Charitable Choice' provisions in the 1996 Welfare Reform Act and the 2001 Faith-Based and Community Initiatives Act ended discrimination against FBOs in the award of government contracts and funding, provoking concerns about the blurring of church–state boundaries and potential discrimination in favour of FBOs (cf. Dedayan 2004; Bartkowski and Regis 2003: 1–9).

These concerns are magnified in the context of US policy on international development. In December 2002, Executive Order 13280 created a new Center for Faith Based and Community Initiatives (CFBCI) in the United States Agency for International Development (USAID), designed to ensure that provisions of the 2001 Act are reflected in USAID policy. This was followed by a USAID ruling on 'Participation by Religious Orders in USAID Programs', effective from October 2004.[10] The 2004 ruling radically transforms USAID policy on engagement with FBOs, reversing the 'pervasively sectarian' doctrine previously upheld by the US Supreme Court. Under the old doctrine, religious organizations engaging in discriminatory or sectarian practices were barred from government funding. Under the new ruling, however, USAID cannot discriminate against organizations which combine development or humanitarian activities with 'inherently religious activities' such as worship, religious instruction or proselyzation. USAID-funded activities must be separated 'by time or space' from 'inherently religious activities' but commentators fear that such distinctions will be blurred in practice.[11] The ruling, for instance, prevents discrimination against organizations providing social services in a religious setting (e.g. a building characterized by religious iconography) or which engage in discriminatory practices in the hiring of staff (i.e. restricting paid employment to adherents of a particular faith). This means, in practice, that USAID-funded buildings used for the delivery of social services can also be used (but not at the same time) for 'inherently religious activities'. Similarly, FBOs cannot discriminate against nonbelievers in the provision of USAID-supported services, but there is no obligation on them to explain that non-believers can avail of such services on an equal basis. Beyond the general criticism of the 2001 Act, the USAID ruling provokes further concern with its suggestion that less stringent legal standards (than those applicable to domestic programmes) might apply to foreign assistance.[12] Ostensibly designed to equalize the treatment of secular and religious organizations, it effectively tilts the balance in favour of the latter since US or foreign NGOs that provide information on abortion (and which, by definition, are overwhelming secular) are ineligible for USAID funding.[13]

Third, the rise of political Islam, in the Middle East and Gulf regions in particular, has provided a conservative counter-current to the US Christian right. This current was triggered by a number of factors, including the Iranian Revolution of 1979, and the Soviet Invasion of Afghanistan the same year, together representing a significant attack on secular nationalism and on communism, and stimulating the proliferation of charitable and development organizations with a conservative Islamic character throughout these regions. One result was a dramatic increase in Saudi intervention in the affairs of neighbouring countries, including an expansion in the overseas activities of Saudi-based Islamic organizations. Following the election of Roland Reagan, US aid to the Afghan *Mujahidin* increased dramatically, from $30 million in 1980 to $250 million in 1985 (Burke 2004: 60). In the Arab world, however, the *Mujahidin* struggle was seen as a pan-Islamic struggle and Arab, especially Saudi, aid increased dramatically – to support the *Mujahidin,* to counteract growing Western influence over the Afghan conflict and to counter militant Iranian Shiaism, which appealed to disaffected Saudi youth. Official Saudi aid to the *Mujahidin* matched, if not exceeded, US aid but was boosted further by private donations (Ibid.). 'Official' and 'private' funding was channelled through Islamic organizations in Saudi Arabia and other Arab nations, many of which opened offices in Pakistan, paving the way for further activism in other parts of the Islamic world.

Aid to the *Mujahidin* echoed increasing aid from Arab countries to others with a substantial Muslim population. Arab donors are not members of the Development Assistance Committee (DAC) of the Organization for Economic Cooperation and Development (the main 'club' of official donors), and aid flows from the Arab world go largely unnoticed in the international aid community. Arab countries, however, provided an average of 1.5 per cent of GNP per annum as net official development assistance between 1974 and 1994, significantly more than most DAC members (Neumayer 2003: 135). Arab aid is largely provided on a government-to-government basis but significant flows are hidden from public view and channelled through private agencies, including Islamic FBOs at home and in recipient countries. The combination of increased Arab aid flows (in response to the Iranian Revolution and the Afghan war), allied to the adoption of neo-liberal economic policies at home, led to a dramatic growth in the number of FBOs in the Arab world, mostly focusing on domestic issues but with many supporting pan-Islamic causes.

In Saudi Arabia, in particular, a close nexus developed between the Saudi government and organizations or individuals committed to the spread of conservative Islamic currents abroad. A key feature of Saudi foreign policy in recent decades has been the promotion of Wahabism, or Salafism, the dominant strain of Islam in the Kingdom. Members of the royal family, for instance, are represented on the boards of prominent organizations that combine charitable work abroad with *da'wa*, the propagation of the Muslim faith, and, in the Saudi case, its Wahabi/ Salafi doctrines.[14] According to one source, Saudi charities, individuals and government agencies have spent almost $90 billion in the 30 years to 2005 promoting Wahabism/Salafism overseas.[15] Private funding channelled by Saudi charitable organizations or individual donors became a key source of conflict between the United States and Saudi Arabia in the aftermath of the attacks of 9/11 (2001), and in June 2004, the government announced the establishment of the National Commission for Relief and Charity Work Abroad to funnel and filter private Saudi funding for charitable activities overseas.[16]

Fourth, more global forces were at work beyond the confines of United States and Saudi politics. The decline of communism and the end of the Cold War, symbolized by the collapse of the Berlin Wall in 1989, fuelled the rise of identity politics, centred on novel blends of ethnic, cultural and religious identity. Political activists previously enthralled by socialism or communism became increasingly attracted to the oppositional possibilities of faith-based discourse. In many parts of the world, political parties and allied social movements diluted their class character and developed a more multidimensional identity, incorporating a stronger faith dimension. In India, for instance, the *Bharatiya Janata Party* (BJP, Indian Peoples Party) increased its support throughout the 1980s at the expense of the Congress Party by strengthening its allegiance to Hindu nationalism, winning 85 parliamentary seats by 1989. The BJP and associated organizations were instrumental in generating the Hindu nationalist sentiment that triggered the destruction in 1992 of the Babri Masjid mosque in Ayodhya and subsequent riots in which an estimated 1,500 people died in Gujarat. Today, as the Indian case highlights, faith fuels multiple identities, incorporating ethnic and cultural dimensions among others, bolstering the pivotal role of identity politics in both national and international politics.

Fifth, the emergence of a transnational civil society over the past two decades has fostered a growth in faith-based activism in the developed and developing worlds alike, for instance in the Jubilee 2000 campaign for debt relief. Founded in 1996, Jubilee 2000 originated in earlier plans to link demands for debt relief to the old Jewish (and later, Christian) concept of jubilee, a year of celebration in which creditors forgive debtors, slaves are set free and forfeited land is returned to its original owners. Although supported by secular leaders and organizations, the campaign was significant in mobilizing local church congregations in North America, Western Europe and sub-Saharan Africa through faith-based activities and it achieved enormous success. In the late 1990s, for instance, Jubilee 2000 had affiliates in more than 60 countries and by 1999 had collected 17 million signatures,[17] mobilizing pressure on leaders of the G7 countries that led to the Highly Indebted Poor Countries (HIPC) initiative and the cancellation of almost US$100 billion of developing country debt.

The revitalization of civil society is also apparent in the transition to democracy in Asia, Africa and Latin America. Democratic transitions in the 1980s and 1990s were largely driven by the spread of neo-liberal economics, the fall of communism and the end of the Cold War. These factors enabled opposition movements to make headway, often with prominent support from faith leaders and associated organizations, a critical additional ingredient. In South-East Asia, for instance, Christian leaders helped topple the Marcos regime in 1986, Thai Buddhist leaders contributed to the collapse of military rule in 1992 and Indonesian Muslim leaders helped bring down the Suharto regime in 1998.[18] Today, faith leaders and organizations around the world are important participants in struggles to consolidate and expand democratic forms of governance.

Finally, FBOs have become more prominent in development contexts because of immigration. In recent decades, Western nations have become more multicultural and multi-faith as a result of immigration and migrants have developed multiple identities, embracing new nationalities, yet retaining faith identities and familial links to the country of origin. In 2003, for instance, Western Europe and North America hosted almost 100 million migrants,[19] and by the late 1990s, migration had replaced natural increase as the main source of population growth in the European Union (OECD 1998: 23). Developing country migrants remain largely within the developing world, but migration to North America and Western Europe has fuelled the growth of FBOs representing the non-Christian faiths and Islamic, Hindu and Jewish organizations link migrants to the homeland and the pan-national faith community. In the United Kingdom, for instance, Islamic organizations such as Islamic Relief and Muslim Aid institutionalize Islamic traditions of supporting the poor. Hindu organizations such as Hindu Aid channel support from British Hindus on a non-sectarian basis, but others such as *Sewa International* and *Hindu Swayamsevak Sangh* reputedly support sectarian Hindu nationalism (cf. AWAAZ 2004). These FBOs help the faithful to maintain their cultural identity, to help the poor overseas and to provide alternatives to the secular or Christian organizations which dominate aid flows to the developing world.

The complex world of faith-based organizations

These factors have fostered the proliferation and growth of a range of FBOs in different faith contexts. Today, FBOs represent a complex set of actors in development contexts, not least because they come in a variety of organizational guises and have differential effects (both positive and negative) in the context of international development. The key world religions, for instance, sub-divide into different branches, and the ethos of a FBO may derive from one of these. Christianity comes in three main forms (Catholic, Protestant and Orthodox/Coptic), yet each can be further sub-divided (Protestant churches, for instance, can be mainstream or evangelical). Islam divides into the Sunni and Shia traditions, yet further sub-divides into a variety of derivative traditions, depending on allegiance to the teachings of a prophet or an ethno-national grouping, for instance, Hanafi, Maliki, Sufi, Salafi (or Wahabi), Deobandi, Ahmadi or Ismaili. Hinduism, meanwhile, is a diverse religion that includes major traditions such as Vaishnavism, Shivaism and Shaktism but also hundreds of minor traditions, often confined to a specific locality. Similar distinctions can be made between faith/sub-faith systems and associated FBOs on the basis of their commitment to social engagement, their support of the poor or their compatibility with contemporary development discourse. Liberation theology (in the case of Catholicism), the prosperity gospel (in the case of Christian evangelism), socially engaged Buddhism, and civil Islam, for instance, share important similarities with development discourse, while mainstream Catholicism, *Hindutva* (sectarian Hindu nationalism), fundamental Buddhism or Wahabism (in the case of Islam) run counter to it in significant respects.

Clearly then, there are many ways to cut the cake in so far as FBOs as a set of organizations are concerned. Here, the focus is on organizations involved in (1) public policy debates and associated political contests concerned with national and international development; (2) social and political processes that impact positively or negatively on the poor; and (3) direct efforts to support, represent or engage with the poor. In this context, five types of FBO are evident:

1. *faith-based representative organizations or apex bodies* which rule on doctrinal matters, govern the faithful and represent them through engagement with the state and other actors;
2. *faith-based charitable or development organizations* which mobilize the faithful in support of the poor and other social groups, and which fund or manage programmes which tackle poverty and social exclusion;
3. *faith-based socio-political organisations* which interpret and deploy faith as a political construct, organizing and mobilizing social groups on the basis of faith identities but in pursuit of broader political objectives or, alternatively, promote faith as a socio-cultural construct, as a means of uniting disparate social groups on the basis of faith-based cultural identities;
4. *faith-based missionary organizations* which spread key faith messages beyond the faithful, by actively promoting the faith and seeking converts to it, or by supporting and engaging with other faith communities on the basis of key faith principles; and finally,
5. *faith-based radical, illegal or terrorist organizations* which promote radical or militant forms of faith identity, engage in illegal practices on the basis of faith beliefs or engage in armed struggle or violent acts justified on the grounds of faith.

These categories are malleable, and individual FBOs, as the chapters that follow reveal, can straddle more than one. Nevertheless, this typology captures a variety of organizational forms and an equally varied range of impacts in development contexts. *Faith-based representative organizations or apex bodies*, for instance, vary across the main religions or faiths; the mainstream Christian Churches (Catholic, Protestant and Orthodox/Coptic) are hierarchically organized, so representative bodies have an official status and are usually unchallenged by rival organizations, allowing them to speak with authority to the faithful and to represent them in engagement with other stakeholders. Other key religions, however, are less hierarchically organized. Islam, for instance, is based on significant devolution of religious and political authority and no single organization represents the Muslim faith globally.[20] Similarly, Hinduism represents a diverse tradition that lacks a single founder, creed or moral system and, therefore, lacks a coherent political or administrative structure in national or international settings. The absence of representative organizations with a broad-based legitimacy among adherents in non-Christian traditions, therefore, militates against the global mobilization of the faithful in support of international development. It also prevents donors from identifying obvious representative interlocutors, but the need to mobilize the world's faith communities in the battle against global poverty makes it critical that donors work with faith communities to identify such interlocutors and involve them in multilateral fora.

Representative organizations or apex bodies often include subsidiary organizations which promote development or charitable work but which otherwise remained aloof from international development debates until comparatively recently. In recent years, such organizations have become more involved in international dialogue concerned with poverty reduction, debt relief and the global fight against HIV/ AIDS. Leaders of international organizations such as the World Council of Churches (WCC) or national organizations such as the United States Conference of Catholic Bishops (USCCB) were active in the Jubilee 2000 campaign and in the more recent global campaign to 'Make Poverty History'. These processes, and the involvement of such organizations and leaders which they sustain, are critical to the global fight against poverty because they represent and mobilize constituencies traditionally estranged by purely secular development discourse.

The second category, *faith-based charitable or development organizations*, plays a more direct role in tackling poverty and inequality by funding or managing programmes that help the poor and by raising awareness of poverty among the faithful. In the industrialized 'North', FBOs play an important role in providing social services to the poor. In the United States, for instance, an estimated 18 per cent of the 37,000 US non-profit organizations involved in social service provision in 1999 had a faith-based ethos (Wuthnow 2004: 141). These FBOs had estimated assets of $25.5billion and annual budgets of $17 billion in 1999, equivalent to the annual Gross National Income (GNI) of medium-sized economies such as Syria, Sri Lanka or Costa Rica.[21]

Faith-based social engagement at home is mirrored in support for the poor in developing countries. Members of *Coopération Internationale pour le Développement et la Solidarité* (CIDSE, International Cooperation for Development and Solidarity), the largest alliance of Catholic development agencies, had a combined budget of $950 million in 2000, members of the Association of Protestant Development Agencies (APRODEV), the main association of Protestant development agencies,

$470 million, and World Vision International (WVI), the single largest Christian development agency, had a turnover of $600 million in 1999 (Clark 2003: 134–136). Including Caritas International, the second main international coalition of Catholic development agencies, the big four faith-based development agencies had a combined annual income of approximately $2.5 billion at the beginning of the new millennium, or almost two-thirds of the annual budget of the UK Department for International Development (£2.7 billion or $4 billion in 2000/2001).[22] As such, they have become significant players in the international delivery of aid, the equivalent of large bilateral donors.

Faith-based development and charitable organizations have become equally prevalent and significant in developing countries. Across the Arab world, for instance, Islamic charitable organizations proliferated during the 1990s as a result of political reform and economic liberalization (in most cases), or state fragility or collapse (in a minority of cases such as Palestine or Somalia). In Egypt, an estimated 20 per cent of the 12,832 registered voluntary organizations in 1997 were Islamic in character (Clark 2004: 12). According to World Bank research, Islamic NGOs in Egypt are less dependent on state aid than secular NGOs and better able to raise funds locally (Ibid.: 60–61). In Somalia, Islamic NGOs have played an important role in providing social services in the absence of an effective state. Almost all schools, for instance, are privately run and Islamic NGOs have played a vital role in channelling Arab funding to them (Novib, Oxfam Netherlands and WAMY 2004).

The third category, *faith-based socio-political organizations*, is the most diverse, and includes political parties, broad-based social movements, cultural organizations and secret societies. They differ from representative organizations and apex bodies in that they do not normally claim to rule on doctrinal matters or to govern the faithful. Instead, they interpret and deploy faith as a political construct, organizing and mobilizing social groups on the basis of faith identities, but in pursuit of broader political objectives or, alternatively, they promote faith as a socio-cultural construct, as a means of uniting disparate social groups on the basis of faith-based cultural identities. Such organizations have become increasingly important amid the rise of identity politics as a driver of change in national and international contexts.

Throughout the world, for instance, many political parties have a faith-based ethos. Christian democracy, for example, originated as a political ideology in the late nineteenth century when Pope Leo XIII's papal encyclical *Rerum Novarum* acknowledged the suffering of workers and the role of Christian compassion in combating it. Islam has been equally adapted to political purposes, and faith-based political parties are common throughout the Islamic world, including the *Muttahaida Majlis-I-Amal* (MMA), a coalition of six political parties in Pakistan which secured 11.3 per cent of the vote in parliamentary elections in 2002.[23] In Indonesia, the world's largest predominantly Muslim country, Islamic parties garnered 16 per cent of the vote in the 1999 general elections, support which they have retained in subsequent elections and opinion polls.[24] Faith-based political parties draw significant support from sections of the poor and are therefore important stakeholders in the framing of national strategies to reduce poverty. Overseas donors, therefore, face challenges in engaging with the discourses of such parties and developing constructive forms of engagement. Islamic political parties have been central to the rise of political Islam as a potent force in national and international politics, but broad-based social movements have arguably played a greater role. Political Islam is most closely associated with the Muslim Brotherhood, founded by Hassan El Banna in Egypt in 1928 and which has branches today in over 70 countries and a membership of many millions, mostly in the Arab world. In a number of Arab states, it has been associated with armed struggle against colonial rule or against the nationalist but secular regimes which replaced it. It also functions, however, as a pan-Arab and pan-Islamic social movement which feeds on middle-class resentment at arbitrary state rule and the perceived humiliation of the *ummah* (the community of Muslims) at the hands of Western powers and plays an important role in the organization and delivery of social services to the Muslim poor. A controversial force across the Islamic world, the Brotherhood is attacked for promoting terrorism and exclusive political identities in multi-ethnic and multi-religious societies, yet respected for its social activism and its support (sometimes tactical) for multi-party democracy.[25]

Political Islam is largely concerned with restoring Islam as the organizing principle of political power and social order and the political basis of both the nation-state and the pan-national *ummah*. As such, it challenges ruling secular political parties perceived to have marginalized Islam from political life. Moderate political Islam promotes the gradual Islamization of the nation-state and concedes that the Islamist project must make tactical concessions in pursuit of its strategy. It promotes Islam as the answer to the social, economic and political ills that afflict Muslim societies, effectively that it is the solution (or at least that it frames the solutions), to development dilemmas across the Islamic world. According to Janine Clark, it is partly understood as a reaction against state encroachment on religious authority, including the takeover of mosque-based social services by the state (Clark 2004: 12). In some respects, therefore, moderate political Islam represents the struggle for autonomous civil societies in Muslim countries, where the secular state exists alongside an active community of Islamic FBOs, some of which accept the legitimacy of the state but some of which challenge it. This provides a potential basis for donors to engage with social movements otherwise viewed as opposed to the mainstream development enterprise.

Political parties and social movements are important because of their overt role in mobilizing social groups on the basis of faith and other identities, but secret societies with an explicit faith ethos can have an equivalent influence on the design and implementation of public policy through covert networking among elite social groups. In the West, for instance, the Freemasons derive members primarily from mainstream Protestants and have exercised a shadowy, often corrupt, influence on the functioning of public institutions including the judiciary and police while *Opus Dei*, the secretive Catholic sect, has been accused of supporting right-wing and fascist regimes in the 1970s . In sub-Saharan Africa, political networks are often based on a common allegiance to secret societies that blend mainstream Christianity and traditional African beliefs. Here, according to Ellis and Ter Haar, secret societies of European origin sit easily with indigenous traditions of closed societies, especially in former French colonies influenced by French traditions of masonry (Ellis and Ter Haar 2004: 78). 'A key attraction of secret societies', they write, 'is that membership provides opportunities for doing deals unobserved by the mass of the population and for forming bonds of solidarity that go beyond the ordinary', based on a widespread belief in the omnipresence of spiritual power (Ibid.: 83). Secret societies, however, represent an element of civil society which liberal discourse and donor policy have traditionally ignored. Supporting 'good governance', fighting corruption and expanding the scope of civil society in sub-Saharan Africa, however, depends in part on exposing the activities of such societies, encouraging them to evolve into formal and transparent organizations and supporting institutional alternatives, such as political parties or social movements, based on heterogeneous and public identities.

The fourth category considered here, *missionary organizations*, has long been active in the context of international development, but never more so than today. Missionary organizations associated with the mainstream Christian churches are the forerunners of modern-day development

NGOs in their commitment to the provision of social services and in their support of the local poor. Such organizations, however, have been eclipsed in recent decades by the proliferation of missionary organizations from other faith traditions. In the United States, for instance, the rise of the Christian right has led to a significant expansion in overseas missionary activity by evangelical and Pentecostal congregations.[26] In 2001, an estimated 350,000 Americans travelled abroad with Protestant missionary agencies, and donations to such agencies totalled $3.75 billion, a 44 per cent increase in five years,[27] and significantly greater than the combined annual expenditure of the big four faith-based development NGO networks (CIDSE, APRODEV, Caritas and World Vision).[28] US evangelical missions in Africa, according to Hearn (2002: 33–34), are critical to the implementation of donor, especially USAID, policy yet effectively function as 'invisible NGOs', invisible because they have been ignored in the separate literatures on development NGOs and on African Christianity.

Similarly, the 1990s and early years of the new millennium have seen an increase in the number and reach of organizations committed to *tabligh wa-da'wa,* preaching the message of Allah *(da'wa,* or mission, for short) internationally. Throughout Africa, for instance, Arab organizations, including the World Muslim League (Saudi Arabia), the African Muslim Agency (Kuwait) and the World Islamic Call (Libya) fund local *madrasas* (Islamic seminaries or religious schools), promoting conservative Islamic currents such as Wahabism or Salafism which traditionally have had little purchase in African societies. One significant consequence has been the emergence of a distinct cleavage in many countries between 'African Islam' and 'Islam in Africa', between traditional local forms of Islamic practice and more conservative currents promoted by organizations from the Arab world.[29] Missionary activity characterized by active proselytizing, however, is largely confined to Christianity and Islam. In India, some Hindu nationalist FBOs promote the reconversion of *adivasi* ('tribals'), who convert from Hinduism to escape the oppressive social hierarchy of caste, but otherwise Hinduism lacks the tradition of seeking new converts to the faith, as do other major religions such as Buddhism and Sikhism. Evangelical Christian and Wahabi/Salafi organizations, therefore, represent a particular case for donors concerned to minimize social conflict in complex cultural settings, yet equally concerned to reach constituencies traditionally disenfranchised by secular development discourse.

The fifth and final category, *faith-based radical, illegal or terrorist organizations,* has become important in development discourse and policy comparatively recently, largely as a result of the events of 9/11, and an emerging new nexus between security and development. Such groups typically grow out of two main political phenomena: *religious nationalism* (or communalism) directed against other religious communities and *conservative religious politics* (or fundamentalism) directed mainly against secularists or enemies within the faith tradition (Keddie 1998: 696). Such groups are common to all the major faith traditions, but Islam has been predominantly implicated in the promotion of faith-based violence and conflict in recent years. Loose international terrorist networks such as *Al Qaeda* or *Jemaah Islamiyah* promote a radical and puritanical vision of Islam. At heart, they seek the overthrow of the secular state across the Islamic world and the creation of a pan-national caliphate that unifies the world's Muslims under a single political and religious leader, serving as the direct successor of the Prophet Mohammed. This vision is both utopian and apocalyptic and few Muslims subscribe to it, yet, vulture-like, it feeds off a profound concern across the Islamic world at attacks on the *ummah* in multiple settings; Afghanistan, Bosnia, Chechnya, Iraq, Kashmir, Palestine and so on. From a development discourse and policy perspective, this concern is a real and significant obstacle to broad-based multi-stakeholder partnerships needed to promote international development in a world which is increasingly interlinked and interdependent.

In some settings, however, organizations with a propensity for violence are more socially embedded and represent a stronger case for conceptual and programmatic attention in the development community. In the West Bank and Gaza Strip, for instance, Hamas has emerged as a rival of the secular Fatah party as the principle representative of the Palestinian people.[30] Hamas achieved infamy in Israel and the West for indiscriminate suicide bombings but is widely seen in Palestine, and by some academics, as a social movement that supports Palestinians in the absence of a viable state and government. Until 2005, when Saudi aid was reduced in support of the peace process, Hamas had an annual budget of approximately $70 million, 85 per cent of which came from abroad. An estimated 90 per cent, however, was spent on social services, including schools, health clinics and day-care centres,[31] a significant social safety net given the weakness of the Palestinian Authority. The unexpected victory of Hamas in parliamentary elections in Palestine in January 2006 highlighted the challenge for Western donors posed by this dual character. In the short term, Western governments will cut aid to the Palestinian Authority in the knowledge that Arab donors will make up the short fall, but in the medium term, they face the challenge of engaging with Hamas (or at a minimum, its service provision arm) and both protecting and sustaining their investment in the construction of an embryonic Palestinian state.

The role of faith in the work of FBOs

FBOs are varied in their organizational guises but they are also varied in the way they deploy the teachings of the faith (or a branch of the faith) in mobilizing staff or supporters and in the way they work with beneficiaries and partners. As such, they differ to the extent that faith discourse provides the impulse for action and that the goals for which they strive are rooted in the teachings and principles of the faith or sub-faith. This variation is important in development discourse and policy; multilateral, bilateral and non-governmental donors alike, for instance, are wary of supporting organizations which seek advantage for the faith community, which seek to convert people or which seek to advance one faith discourse at the expense of another. In some cases, it is illegal for them to do so, but more importantly, donors risk promoting conflict and social exclusion by supporting organizations that promote partisan agendas.

This makes it important to distinguish between the different uses of faith in the work of FBOs, a recent focus of academic research. Wuthnow (2004: 142–149), for instance, reviews typologies of the role of faith in the work of US service provision FBOs. Our concern here extends beyond service provision FBOs, so a broader, more encompassing typology is needed. In this vein, we can distinguish between four main ways in which FBOs deploy faith through social or political engagement or link faith to developmental or humanitarian objectives:

Passive: The teachings of the faith (or sub-faith) are subsidiary to broader humanitarian principles as a motivation for action and in mobilizing staff and supporters and play a secondary role to humanitarian considerations in identifying, helping or working with beneficiaries and partners.

Active: Faith provides an important and explicit motivation for action and in mobilizing staff and supporters. It plays a direct role in identifying, helping or working with beneficiaries and partners, although there is no overt discrimination against non-believers and the organization supports multi-faith cooperation.

Persuasive: Faith provides an important and explicit motivation for action and in mobilizing staff and supporters. It plays a significant role in identifying, helping or working with beneficiaries and partners and provides the dominant basis for engagement. It aims to bring new converts to the faith (or a particular branch of the faith) and/or to advance the interests of the faith/sub-faith at the expense of others.

Exclusive: Faith provides the principal or overriding motivation for action and in mobilizing staff and supporters. It provides the principal or sole consideration in identifying beneficiaries. Social and political engagement is rooted in the faith, or a branch of the faith, and is often militant or violent and/or directed against one or more rival faiths.

This typology highlights some of the dilemmas for donors concerned to understand and support the work of FBOs in development contexts, especially the work of charitable and development organizations. The first two variables (*passive* and *active*) present comparatively little difficulty for donors: here, faith motivates action, and, therefore, helps to mobilize staff, volunteers and supporters, but organizations do not expect a faith-based dividend (for instance, converts or greater credibility for the faith among people of other faiths). The other two variables (*persuasive* and *exclusive*) are more problematic, however, because they contain, to varying degrees, a commitment to winning new adherents to the faith (proselytizing), providing support to the faithful to the exclusion of others (i.e. direct or indirect discrimination) or advancing the cause of that faith at the expense of others (potentially generating conflict or social exclusion). Both clearly contain significant risks for donors.

At present, Western donors support *passive* and *active* faith agendas in development contexts and usually avoid support for *persuasive* and *exclusive* agendas.[32] The resulting pattern of engagement and estrangement, when combined with the typology of FBOs above, is captured in Figure 2.1. Four key problems arise, however. First, the four variables are not always clear-cut and exclusive; the policies and practices of an FBO may be *passive* or *active* on one issue yet *persuasive* or *exclusive* on another. Second, FBOs are often highly networked and multi-purpose and constituent parts may have different approaches to the deployment of faith. Third, distinctions between *active* and *persuasive* stances, in particular, are culturally nuanced and give rise to problems of interpretation. For instance, Western organizations (both governmental and non-governmental) working in Islamic cultural settings often work separately yet in parallel with Islamic FBOs which are local or originate in donor countries such as Saudi Arabia or Kuwait. Western organizations may find it difficult to distinguish

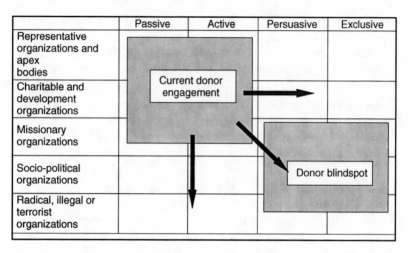

Figure 2.1   Current donor engagement with FBOs and the challenges that arise

between the *passive/active* and the *persuasive/ exclusive* among a range of Islamic charitable, representative or socio-political organizations and miss significant opportunities for productive partnership. Fourth, FBOs which adopt a *persuasive* or *exclusive* stance may help large numbers of poor and command their confidence, in part because of the religious or ethno-cultural bond that unites them. As such, there may be a rationale for donors to engage in dialogue with them and in some cases to fund aspects of their work. Each of these points, for instance, is illustrated by Harb's contribution to this book, which looks at the work of organizations affiliated to Hezbollah, literally 'The Party of God', a military and socio-political organization which represents Lebanon's Shi'a (Shi'i) Muslim community.

These dilemmas become clearer when the work of other FBOs is related to the typology. The *passive* stance, for instance, is most closely associated with development NGOs associated with the mainstream Christian churches. The work of FBOs affiliated to CIDSE, APRODEV and Caritas International, for instance, is inspired by Christian teachings, and these FBOs play an important role in mobilizing the faith community in support of international development. They also rely heavily on church networks to work in developing countries with significant Christian communities. Faith-based principles, however, are secondary to broader humanitarian principles and they support the poor on a non-discriminatory basis in countries with large non-Christian populations, helping Christians and non-Christians on an equal basis.

The extent to which FBOs from other faith traditions adopt a similarly *passive* stance to the deployment of faith in development contexts has traditionally been less clear, although recent research addresses this gap in knowledge. Some studies suggest that charitable and development organizations that ostensibly operate as the counterparts of Western development NGOs in reality function as fronts for more militant causes. Burr and Collins (2006), for instance, offer a detailed account of support for terrorist causes channelled through Islamic charitable organizations. Despite the authors' promise to distinguish clearly between organizations supporting violent *jihad* and 'the many thousands' of Islamic charities supporting peaceful change throughout the Islamic and non-Islamic world, however, the book casts its net over a broad landscape, using media sources of variable quality, and drawing reputable organizations such as Islamic Relief and the Muslim Council of Britain within its critical gaze. The book underlines the clear need for more careful efforts to distinguish between the ways in which FBOs are constituted and through which they deploy faith constructs in their organizational philosophies and their activities on the ground.

Fortunately, we can turn to academic studies with a more focused and methodologically rigorous approach to the study of Islamic charitable and development organizations. Clark (2004) and Wiktorowicz (2001), for instance, suggest that Islamic charitable FBOs wear their faith as lightly and unobtrusively as their Christian counterparts. According to Wiktorowicz, 'the priority [for most Islamic NGOs in Jordan] is the services themselves, not a specific Islamic message or a political agenda': 'What differentiates Islamic NGOs from their secular counterparts is ... not the particular Islamic nature of their activities, but volunteers' belief that they are promoting Islam through their work. It is an insider belief in the mission, more than the activities themselves, that distinguishes them' (Wiktorowicz 2001: 85).

The same is often true of charitable and development organizations from other faith communities in Asia, Africa and Latin America, although government and non-governmental donors alike have much work to do in overcoming the institutional and cultural myopia that hinders engagement with them.

The *active* stance is evident in the work of different types of FBOs, including charitable and development organizations, representative organizations and missionary organizations. Globally, some development NGO networks or mass membership organizations employ a more fervent vision of Christian responsibility to help the poor. The UK-based Mothers Union (MU), for instance, the world's largest Christian women's organization with more than 3 million members, seeks 'to strengthen and preserve marriage and Christian family life' and to 'maintain a worldwide fellowship of Christians united in prayer ... and service'.[33] It runs literacy and development programmes for women in sub-Saharan Africa, working through local MU groups. The MU, however, is committed to ecumenism, rather than conversion. MU staff feel that its overt Christianity helps it to engage with women from other faith traditions, most of whom relate more readily to committed religious belief than to secularism.[34] Organizations such as the MU, therefore, wear their faith on the outside as well as the inside but consequently have a significant ability to mobilize constituencies traditionally unmoved by secular development discourse. For donors, however, this *active* stance is problematic when transmitted through an organization's policies, or where it dictates its approach to partnership. In such cases, dialogue between *active* FBOs and donors is often necessary to overcome misunderstandings or to clarify working assumptions.

Representative organizations and apex bodies necessarily adopt an *active* stance in their use of faith in development debates. To the extent that they represent the faithful, they wear their faith overtly, but they are *active* rather than *persuasive* in working closely with representative FBOs from other faith traditions to build inter-faith dialogue and cooperation. They ask policymakers to acknowledge and respect the faith tradition, and, therefore, play an important role in promoting multiculturalism, but otherwise they seek no advantage for the faith community at the expense of others. As such, organizations such as the United States Council of Catholic Bishops, the Muslim Council of Great Britain or the National Council of Churches in the Philippines (NCCP) are important actors in the development process, educating and mobilizing the faithful in support of development in international, national or sub-national settings and building the bridges to other faith traditions that reduce conflict and produce inclusive, multicultural societies.

Missionary organizations, however, also adopt an *active* stance in development contexts. Missionary orders associated with the mainstream Catholic and Protestant churches, for instance, have reconciled themselves over time to local faith discourses, including syncretism (the blending of established faith principles with local beliefs and customs). As such, they respond to local needs on the basis of faith principles but otherwise avoid proselytizing activities. Despite the proliferation of development NGOs, both secular and faith-based, such missionary organizations remain important actors in development contexts, as providers of social services and as witnesses to the struggles of the poor. Often, they are closer to the poor than development NGOs, because they maintain a long-term presence in local communities and live modestly, sharing in privations that afflict the poor. They are frequently ignored, however, as civil society organizations and as relevant stakeholders in development contexts.

The *persuasive* stance is primarily associated with missionary organizations of a different hue, charitable and development organizations, socio-political organizations and some representative organizations or apex bodies. Evangelical missionary organizations in the case of Christianity or Wahabi or Salafi-inspired organizations in the case of Islam are associated with a fervent form of missionary zeal, an active campaign to win converts to the faith. Such missionary zeal manifests itself in different forms (see, for instance, the contributions from Hovland, Kroessin and Mohamed). WVI, for instance, is evangelical in its ethos and mission. WVI seeks converts to the faith among non-evangelical Christians and people of other, or no, faith; in Zimbabwe, for instance, field staff must sign a 'statement of faith' as part of their contracts and evangelism committees are set up at project sites (Bornstein 2002: 20 and 15). According to Bornstein, such evangelism does not exclude non-Christians or non-evangelicals and brings positive development outcomes through the provision of long-term support to communities, including the empowerment of women trained to speak publicly and to preach (ibid.). WVI attracts significant official donor, especially USAID, funding but aspects of its ethos, including its overt proselytizing and its emphasis on abstinence and faithfulness (at the expense of condom use) in the fight against HIV/AIDS, are problematic for some European donors.

Socio-political organizations and representative organizations and apex bodies, on the other hand, are less interested in winning converts than in advancing the cause of the faith and increasing its political leverage or cultural resilience. Despite their commitment to proselytizing and enhancing the position of the faith at the expense of others, *persuasive* organizations are potentially important partners in development contexts. The National Evangelical Association, for instance, serves thousands of missionaries around the world through the Evangelical Fellowship of Mission Agencies, yet also supports the US 'Make Poverty History' campaign.

Organizations that deploy faith-based teachings in an *exclusive* way are also significant players in the context of development policy and discourse. UK-based World Jewish Relief, for instance, is *exclusive* only in helping Jewish communities in developing or transitional economies and acts as the counterpart of the non-denominational World Jewish Aid (also based in the United Kingdom). At the opposite end of the spectrum are organizations that not only help the faith community but also work to advance the interests of the organization and the faith in a sectarian manner, or to preserve socio-cultural values that isolate the faithful from mainstream society and from development interventions (see, for instance, Jaffrelot's contribution in this book). Such organizations, however, are important in the context of development efforts. *Exclusive* (and *persuasive*) FBOs represent socially conservative religious currents that appeal to large numbers of adherents. Governments and donors face difficulties in connecting with these constituencies, and securing their support for policy initiatives in areas such as health, education and human rights, partly because of their perceived secularism and antipathy to matters of faith. Engagement with *persuasive* and *exclusive* FBOs, however, wherever possible, provides opportunities to extend the reach of policy and practice and to make it more socially inclusive.

In India, for instance, prominent FBOs are committed to *Hindutva,* a sectarian form of Hindu nationalism. Collectively known as the *Sangh Parivar,* they include the BJP, the *Rashtriya Swayamsevak Sangh* (RSS, National Volunteers' Corps, an all-male para-military organization with an estimated 4.5 million members),[35] *Rashtra Sevika Samiti* (a women's organization committed to traditional Hindu notions of femininity) and *Sewa Bharti* and *Sewa International* (the ostensibly charitable arms of the RSS). In practice, *Hindutva* organizations promote inter-faith conflict through their support of sectarian Hindu causes (such as destruction of the Babri Masjid Mosque in 1992) or their sporadic championing of the socially divisive institution of caste. In India, the major opposition to sectarian Hindu nationalism comes from secular nationalism as represented by the Congress Party and moderate Hindus see the electoral system as the primary means of opposing *Hindutva*. Two problems, however, arise for donors. Firstly, *Hindutva* is a malleable ideology and subject to different interpretations, not all of which are overtly sectarian or chauvinist. There is a possible role for donors in supporting these non-sectarian currents, but support of *Hindutva* organizations risks confrontation with federal or state government, as well as alienating Indian secularists and foreign governments. The second problem is the absence of a well-organized middle ground between extreme Hindu and secular nationalism, composed of moderate Hindu FBOs (committed to *passive* or *active* stances as above). Many such organizations exist, mostly based on support for individual gurus.[36] A minority, for instance, actively oppose the institution of caste but most simply refrain from supporting caste-based forms of social organization. Organizations such as the Andhra Pradesh-based Satya Sai Baba Society (led by the guru Satya Sai Baba)[37] can have as many members as the RSS and a significant presence at state or federal level but they lack the networks and commitment to political engagement of the *Sangh Parivar.*

Addressing these problems is not easy. India is defined as a 'secular' republic in the 1949 constitution and both state and federal support of religious organizations are prohibited by law. As such, it is unclear to what extent foreign donors can fund or otherwise engage with FBOs. Nevertheless, in a country where the institution of caste is central to the social construction of poverty and derives much of its legitimacy from religious discourse, the connections between faith and development are accentuated. In these circumstances, the question arises: is there a role for donors to work with state and federal governments to build the capacity of moderate Hindu FBOs as a counterweight to the forces of extreme Hindu nationalism?

Conclusion

This question, of course, illustrates the significant challenges posed by the convergence of faith and development. Donor policy towards FBOs has traditionally rested on established constitutional conventions on the separation of church and state. Since the early 1980s, however, fundamental changes in the conduct of international relations have subjected these conventions to significant strain. In particular, the rise of the US Christian right, of political Islam, of neo-liberal economics and of identity politics and the concomitant fall of socialism, communism and authoritarian regimes have eroded the orthodoxy of secular nationalism across the developing world. Today, FBOs channel large volumes of money to the 'developing' world from Europe, North America and the Middle East; they mobilize the faithful in support of international development and they link migrants to the pan-national faith community. In Asia, Africa and Latin America, they provide vital services to the poor and help to organize, and make governments accountable to them, linking governments and donors to communities alienated by secular discourse. Many FBOs, however, also promote social exclusion and conflict and oppose modern ideas that could help the poor and reduce their vulnerability. The difference between the 'good' and the 'bad' in the work of FBOs is evident in some circumstances yet, often, it is difficult to elucidate, for instance, the difference between *active* and *persuasive* FBOs, or the 'positive' and 'negative' in the work of *persuasive* FBOs.[38]

Many of these phenomena are still not properly understood, largely because the development policy community ignored religion and faith until comparatively recently. The role of FBOs in channelling funding to developing countries, for instance, is still inadequately documented. Funding from the US Christian right or from groups and individuals in the Arab world who support the Wahabi or Salafi form of Islam represent significant financial flows to the developing world. Official Western donors and secular development NGOs, however, have an incomplete understanding of their impact, in particular the respects in which they represent a substantive counter-current to the mainstream development enterprise, or alternatively, the extent to which they represent potential foci for engagement.

To the extent that Western donors (multilateral, bilateral and non-governmental) support FBOs, they currently focus on *charitable and development organizations*, yet a wide range of FBOs act as drivers of change in the developing world, including *representative organizations & apex bodies, socio-political organizations* and *missionary organizations*. Donors face significant challenges in engaging with this broader set of FBOs: of blurring church–state boundaries, of engaging with, or supporting, organizations which engage in discriminatory or sectarian practices and of privileging some organizations at the expense of others. The rise of faith-based activism, however, makes it difficult for donors to ignore the broad range of FBOs examined above, and donors face the challenge of devising strategies to engage with them, where appropriate, to network with them, to fund them, to build their capacity and to engage in joint initiatives with them.

FBOs also differ enormously in the way they deploy faith in their pursuit of developmental, humanitarian, or broader political, objectives. Donors have traditionally engaged with FBOs that deploy faith in a *passive* or *active* manner. Donors now face the challenge of selectively engaging with FBOs that use faith in a *persuasive* or *exclusive* manner, given their importance in channelling funding to developing countries, in providing services to the poor and in representing them in different political fora (see Figure 2.1 above). Donors have traditionally supported the forces of secular modernity over those of religious conservatism in contentious policy areas such as HIV/AIDS, reproductive rights or the empowerment of women. Increasingly, however, they face the challenge of building a middle ground, of moderate faith-based praxis.

Moderate, of course, is a relative concept in different regional or country contexts and one that straddles the *active, persuasive* and *exclusive* categories. Whether European donors can engage with evangelical or Wahabi/Salafi organizations that straddle the *active/persuasive* divide, or with the representatives of political Islam, remains to be seen (the contributions of Hovland and Harb in this book suggest they already do). Whether donors can work with state or federal governments in India to support moderate forms of *Hindutva* through associated FBOs or support moderate Hindu FBOs that respect minority faiths and challenge caste-based social exclusion is similarly unclear.

These predicaments do not necessarily lend themselves to simple policy solutions. In India, for instance, some Hindu nationalist organizations mobilize women in a partially progressive manner, yet for some Hindu nationalists, equal treatment of women is an anti-Muslim weapon (Keddie 1998: 710). Nevertheless, engagement with FBOs which seem sectarian, chauvinistic or exclusionary has become a significant new challenge for development policymakers. In the past, donors with a secular world view often failed to connect with, or even alienated, large groups of intended beneficiaries because of their failure to understand the faith tradition and its political and cultural import or to acknowledge and engage with representative organizations. The challenge posed by the convergence of faith and development is to engage with faith discourses and associated organizations which seem counter-development or culturally exotic to a secular and technocratic worldview, in building the complex multi-stakeholder partnerships increasingly central to the fight against global poverty. Put simply, in development contexts, *faith matters*!

Notes

1. See also Herbert (2003).
2. Terms used in Luttwak (1994) with reference to international relations theory.
3. See, for instance, Belshaw *et. al.* (eds) (2001), Marshall and Marsh (eds) (2003) and Marshall and Keough (eds) (2004).
4. See, for instance, Narayan *et. al.* (2000).
5. See, for instance, *Journal of Religion in Africa,* Vol. 32 No. 1, February 2002 (special issue on Christian and Islamic NGOs in contemporary Africa); *Development,* Vol. 46, No. 4, 2003 (special issue on Religion and Development); Tyndale (2000) or Ver Beek (2000).
6. Since then, however, it has concluded PPAs with Islamic Relief and World Vision.
7. See note 3 for accounts of World Bank dialogue with faith communities.

8. Peter Waldman, 'Evangelicals Give U.S. Foreign Policy an Activist Tinge', The *Wall Street Journal*, 26 May 2004.
9. 'History of the NAE', www.nae.net Accessed June 2005.
10. 22 CFR Parts 202, 205, 211 and 226.
11. The ruling contains a USAID summary of objections received during a consultation stage and the USAID response.
12. See pg. 11, footnote 2, of the ruling.
13. Under the 'Mexico City Policy' (66 FR 17303).
14. Burr and Collins (2006). In particular, see Table 2.1, 'The Saudi Royal Family and Its Charitable Interests', p. 28.
15. Rachel Ehrenfeld, 'Saudi Dollars and Jihad', Frontpagemag.com, 24 October 2005, citing testimony by former Central Intelligence Agency Director James Woolsey before the US House of Representatives' Committee on Government Reform in April 2005.
16. See, for instance, 'Saudi Arabia to fold Al-Haramain and other Charities in National Commission', Press Release, Royal Embassy of Saudi Arabia, Washington DC, 2 June 2004. www.saudiembassy.net. The government announced that a number of prominent organizations, including the Al-Haramain Islamic Foundation, would be closed and their activities absorbed by the new Commission.
17. See Collins, Gariyo and Burdon (2001). On the faith-based character of Jubilee 2000, see Wallis (2005, pp. 272–278) or Marshall and Keough (eds) (2004, pp. 35–48).
18. The Catholic prelate Cardinal Sin, the Buddhist ascetic Chamlong Srimuang and the Muslim cleric and politician Abdurrahman Wahid were significant actors in the democratic transitions in the Philippines, Thailand and Indonesia, respectively.
19. In 2003, Western Europe hosted 56.1 million migrants compared to 40.8 million in North America (IOM 2003).
20. Although the Saudi-sponsored World Muslim League enjoys some support among Sunni Muslims.
21. The 37,000 NPOs had assets of approximately $142 billion and annual budgets of $93 billion in 1999 (Wuthnow 2004: 140 and 325n5). This estimate assumes that FBOs have proportionately similar resources to all NPOs (Ibid.:142). In 2002, Syria, Sri Lanka and Costa Rica had Gross National Income (GNI) of US$ 19 billion, 16 billion and 16 billion, respectively (http://www.worldbank.org/data/dataquery.html).
22. DFID figures: DFID 2001.
23. On the MMA's electoral performance, see *Europa World Yearbook 2004*, Vol. 2, p. 3263.
24. 'Terrorism Undermines Political Islam in Indonesia', YaleGlobal online (www.yaleglobal.yale.edu), accessed 26 November 2003.
25. For summary details, see Kepel (2002) or for country-specific studies, see Wiktorowicz (2001) (on Jordan) or Mishal and Sela (2000) (on Palestine).
26. By the late 1980s, for instance, an estimated 90 per cent of American Protestant missionaries were evangelicals (cf. Hearn 2002:39).
27. Waldman, *op. cit.* See Moreau (2000:45) and Moreau, Corwin and McGee (eds) (2004: 283 and 285) for equivalent figures for 1996–1999. Moreau (2000), for instance, reports income of $2.93 billion in 1999.

28. Although the figures for missionary organizations here include World Vision and other development NGOs associated with the US missionary tradition.
29. See Westerlund and Rosander (1997) and Linden (2004).
30. Hamas translates as 'Zeal' in Arabic, and is the acronym for *Harakat al-Muqawama al-Islamiya* or Islamic Resistance Movement.
31. 'Hamas, Islamic Jihad (Palestinian Islamists)', *Terrorism: Questions & Answers*, Council on Foreign Relations (www.cfrterrorism.org/groups/hamas.html) citing Israeli scholar Reuvan Paz. On the social orientation of Hamas, see also Mishal and Sela (2000: 20–23).
32. Prominent exceptions being the United States and Saudia Arabia. In both cases, significant sums of official funding are channelled through *persuasive* FBOs.
33. Mothers Union website, www.themothersunion.org . Accessed July 2005.
34. Telephone interview with Barbara Laws, Worldwide Projects Officer, the Mothers Union, London, 25 November 2004.
35. 'Analysis: RSS Aims for a Hindu nation', BBC News online, 10 March 2003. www.bbc.co.uk/news.
36. Most gurus derive support from followers who are not formally organized, although the more popular gurus have organized networks of support or oversee formal organizations.
37. Which rejects caste and emphasises the equality of all regardless of caste, creed, race or gender (Burnett 2004: 179).
38. See Bornstein's (2002) discussion of World Vision on the latter dilemma.

Bibliography

AWAAZ (2004), *Bad Faith? British Charity and Hindu Extremism*, London: AWAAZ/ South Asia Watch Limited.

Bartkowski, J. P. and Regis, H. A. (2003), *Charitable Choices: Religion, Race and Poverty in the Post-Welfare Era*, New York: New York University Press.

Belshaw, D., Calderisi, R. and Sugden, C. (eds) (2001), *Faith in Development: Partnership between the World Bank and the Churches in Africa*, Washington DC: The World Bank and Oxford: Regnum Books.

Bornstein, E. (2002), 'Developing Faith: Theologies of Economic Development in Zimbabwe', *Journal of Religion in Africa*, Vol. 32, No. 1, February, pp. 4–31.

Burke, J. (2004), *Al Qaeda: The True Story of Radical Islam*, London: Penguin Books.

Burnett, D. (2004), 'The Satya Sai Baba Society' In Christopher Partridge (ed.), *Encyclopaedia of New Religions: New Religious Movements, Sects and Alternative Spiritualities*, Oxford: Lion Publishing.

Burr, J. M. and Collins, R. O. (2006), *Alms for Jihad*, Cambridge: Cambridge University Press.

Casanova, J. (1994), *Public Religions in the Modern World*, Chicago: University of Chicago Press.

Clark, J. (2003), *Worlds Apart: Civil Society and the Battle for Ethical Globalization*, London: Earthscan.

Clark, J. (2004), *Islam, Charity and Activism: Middle-Class Networks in Egypt, Jordan and Yemen*, Bloomington: Indiana University Press.

Collins, C., Gariyo, Z. and Burdon, T. (2001), 'Jubilee 2000: Citizen Action Across the North–South Divide', In M. Edwards and J. Gaventa (eds), *Global Citizen Action*, London: Earthscan, pp. 135–148.

Dedayan, D. (2004), 'Faith-Based Initiatives: More than Poltics', Washington DC: The Institute for Global Engagement, 2004, downloaded from www.globalengagement.org (July 2005).

DFID. 2001. *Departmental Report 2001*. Department for International Development, London.

Ellis, S. and Ter Haar, G. (2004), *Worlds Apart: Religious Thought and Political Practice in Africa*, New York: Oxford University Press.

Hearn, J. (2002), 'The "Invisible" NGO: US Evangelical Missions in Kenya', *Journal of Religion in Africa*, Vol. 32, No. 1, February, pp. 32–61.

Herbert, D. (2003), *Religion and Civil Society: Rethinking Public Religion in the Contemporary World*, Aldershot: Ashgate.

IOM (2003), *World Migration 2003: Managing Migration – Challenges and Responses for People on the Move*, Geneva: International Organisation for Migration.

Juergensmeyer, M. (1993), *The New Cold War: Religious Nationalism Confronts the Secular State*, Berkeley: University of California Press.

Juergensmeyer, M. (2003), *Terror in the Mind of God: The Global Rise of Religious Violence*, Berkeley: University of California Press, 2nd edition.

Keddie, N. (1998), 'The New Religious Politics: Where, When and Why Do 'Fundamentalisms' Appear?', *Comparative Studies in History and Society*, Vol. 40, pp. 696–723.

Kepel, G. (2002), *JIHAD: The Trail of Political Islam*, London: I.B. Tauris.

Linden, I. (2004), 'Islam, DFID and Poverty Reduction: How to improve the partnership', report to the Department for International Development, London, March.

Luttwak, E. (1994), 'The Missing Dimension', In D. Johnston and C. Sampson (eds), *Religion: The Mission Dimension in Statecraft*, Oxford: Oxford University Press, pp. 8–19.

Marshall, K. and Keough, L. (eds) (2004), *Mind, Heart and Soul in the Fight Against Poverty*, (Washington DC: The World Bank).

Marshall, K. and Marsh, R. (eds) (2003), *Millennium Challenges for Development and Faith Institutions*, Washington DC: The World Bank.

Mishal, S. and Sela, A. (2000), *The Palestinian Hamas: Vision, Violence and Coexistence*, New York: Columbia University Press.

Moreau, S. (2000), 'Putting the Survey in Context' In J. A. Siewert and D. Welliver (eds), *Mission Handbook: US and Canadian Ministries Overseas 2001–2003*, Wheaton IL.: Evangelism and Missions Information Service (EMIS), pp. 33–80.

Moreau, S., Corwin, G. R. and McGee, G. B. (2004), *Introducing World Missions: A Biblical, Historical and Practical Survey*, Grand Rapids MI: Baker Academic.

Narayan, D., Chambers, R., Shah M. K. and Petesch, P. (2000), *Voices of the Poor: Crying out for Change*, Washinton DC: The World Bank; New York: Oxford University Press.

Neumayer, E. (2003), 'What Factors Determine the Allocation of Aid by Arab Countries and Multilateral Agencies', *Journal of Development Studies*, Vol. 39, No. 4, pp. 134–147.

Novib, Oxfam Netherlands and the WAMY (2004), 'Arab Donor Policies and Practices on Education in Somalia/land', Mogadishu: Novib, Oxfam Netherlands and World Assembly of Muslim Youth, September.

OECD (1998), *Trends in International Migration 1998*, Organisation for International Cooperation and Development/SOPEMI, Paris.

Tyndale, W. (2000), 'Faith and Economics in "Development": A Bridge Across the Chasm?', *Development in Practice*, Vol. 10, No. 1, February, pp. 9–18.

Ver Beek, K. A. (2000), 'Spirituality: A Development Taboo', *Development in Practice*, Vol. 10, No. 1, February, pp. 31–43.

Wallis, J. (2005), *God's Politics: Why the American Right Gets It Wrong and the Left Doesn't Get It*, San Francisco: Harper; Oxford: Lion Books.

Westerlund, D. and Rosander, E. E. (1997), *African Islam and Islam in Africa*, London: C. Hurst & Co.

Wiktorowicz, Q. (2001), *The Management of Islamic Activism: Salafis, the Muslim Brotherhood and State Power in Jordan*, New York: State University of New York Press.

Wilson, B. (1992), *Religion in Sociological Perspective*, Oxford: Oxford University Press.

Wuthnow, R. (2004), *Saving America: Faith-Based Services and the Future of Civil Society*, Princeton: Princeton University Press.

3

Intelligent Design?: A Gender-Sensitive Interrogation of Religion and Development

Ruth Pearson and Emma Tomalin

Introduction

Development policy, in terms of international development cooperation, as well as the operations of multilateral, bilateral and mainstream non-governmental development agencies, has tended to focus on the material and political outcomes of development with little reference to the religious structures and belief systems which shape the life worlds in which the majority of the inhabitants of poor countries live. This bias should not be interpreted to deny, as noted elsewhere in this book, that many individuals and organizations have engaged in development work in line with specific commitments from different religious traditions (Alkire 2006). Faith-based organizations (FBOs), particularly in the poor countries of the global South, have increasingly been working in partnership with donor agencies and international organizations, in response, for instance, to calls for greater local accountability and participation of community-based organizations in the development process. Nor can there be any dispute about the fact that faith traditions continue to exert a strong influence upon the lives of many people in developing countries; or indeed that the desired outcome of development practice and policies, in terms of opportunities and services for poor people to enhance their living standards and their overall well-being, coincides with the objectives of most religious traditions. FBOs have been working on a range of development activities, including donor financed projects and programmes, humanitarian and disaster relief and local community development, for many years (Clarke 2006).

46

It is only recently that development analysts and agencies have begun to explicitly acknowledge, if not court, the contributions of FBOs as partners in development. This is partly because of the recognition that the 'global resurgence of religion' (Thomas 2005) has precipitated a political as well as a social role for religious organizations within many nation states in the global South. It is also part of the legacy of the terrorist outrages of 2001, which has propelled Western institutions to a position of positive engagement with religion, or more precisely with faith-based groups in the donor countries as well as in recipient countries.[1]

This ongoing dialogue between the development and religious establishments is broadly welcomed, though there is a level of apprehension amongst the 'gender and development' community. Clearly religious traditions and faith-based organizations present a wide spectrum of ideological, political and philosophical views and practices like any other kind of social or political institutions, including those in the world of development policy and cooperation. However, there is an anxiety that in the rush to engage with a hitherto neglected group of stakeholders, the painful journey over the past 35 years to mainstream development gender equity objectives into overall development strategy (Pearson 2005) is being sidelined, often to the detriment of women within faith communities in developing countries who rely on international standards as a platform on which to base their own struggles for equality within their respective faith communities. This is not an imaginary concern, but it reflects the real situation, since the version of religious authority – political or spiritual – which is represented at international meetings and negotiations invariably reflects those elements which hold political power in any given faith community. The tendency to treat religious traditions as monolithic and as capable of speaking with a single voice can strengthen the ways in which mainstream religious discourse and hierarchies marginalize and reinforce patriarchal power structures. In this chapter we interrogate the concern that the 'religious turn' in development is too frequently adopting the 'let's see what religious leaders have to say' model and that without a gender analysis, with little regard to the hard-won commitments to gender equality within development policy and practice, this will result in further silencing of the range of women's voices within those religions. This danger is particularly acute in countries and contexts where the political rise of both 'fundamentalist' and 'conservative' religious forms has challenged the movement towards the acceptance of universal rights for women.

The ways in which assertion of religious values compromised global consensus about women's rights in the 1995 Beijing Platform for Action has been widely noted (Bayes and Tohidi 2001; Afkhami and Friedl 1997; Afkhami 1995). Indeed, it was the representatives of conservative regimes in Central America, the Vatican and Iran which joined forces in an attempt to veto the use of the term 'gender' in the 1995 Beijing Platform for Action on the grounds that an interpretation of gender roles that were not fixed and 'natural' challenged traditional teachings (Baden and Goetz 1998). The Beijing + 10 Review reports that 'radical attacks on the women's rights agenda have also resulted from the resurgence of religious identities that include the assertion of 'traditional' gender roles and systems of authority that intrinsically violate women's rights' (Molyneux and Razavi 2006: 18). The most commonly cited examples are the Taliban's hostility to women, particularly in the public sphere in Afghanistan, and the patriarchal interpretation of Islam in Iran. But women who currently live within such societies have responded in complex and multiple ways. It is well documented that many feminist activists within the Muslim world 'have set out to provide alternative readings of religious texts supportive of gender-egalitarian practices' (Molyneux and Razavi 2006: 18), seeking to establish the ways in which Shari'ah law can provide the basis for examining the rights of women in certain contexts. But, as Molyneux and Razavi warn, 'when religious authorities become the spokespeople for nations and ethnic communities, and where no guarantees exist for equality, democracy or human rights protection within the political context, there is little scope for contestation and dialogue' (2006: 18).

Indeed, an international network, entitled Women Living Under Muslim Laws (WLUML),[2] was established as far back as 1984 to link women living in countries or states where Islam is the state religion, women living in secular[3] states with Muslim majorities and women from Muslim communities in other states which are regulated by minority religious laws. This network serves as a key reminder that political and religious leaders do not represent the diversity of identities and belief systems of 'Muslim' women and illustrates the importance of recognizing differences within, as well as between, religious traditions in terms of engagement between the development and religious hierarchies. This global network has a particular concern for marginalized women, including non-Muslims in Muslim majority states where the spaces for religious minorities is dwindling, voices which are rarely heard in contemporary interfaith dialogues about and with development institutions.

The MDGs and gender equity

The most recent international statement about the centrality of gender equity in development policy objectives can be located in the Millennium Development Goals (MDGs), which the global community is committed to achieve by 2015. The eight goals are to eradicate extreme hunger and poverty; achieve universal primary education; promote gender equality and empower women; reduce child morality; improve maternal health; combat HIV/AIDS, malaria and other diseases; ensure environmental sustainability; and develop a global partnership for development. Although many gender activists are disappointed that gender equality is only specifically mentioned in objective three, concerning the promotion of gender disparities in education, and that women's human rights are not central to the other MDGs, and not the MDG process as a whole, Noeleen Heyzer, outgoing Director of UNIFEM, has argued that the 'MDGs may represent another change – perhaps the only one – to ... link the goals and aspirations of women to the priorities of governments and development specialists' (2005: 11).

It is in this context that we need to review the current religious turn in development. There is increasing evidence that religious leaders and FBOs are also engaging with the campaign for MDGs, with the active encouragement of the major international development institutions. For instance, the Millennium Campaign[4] website has a separate section on 'Faith-Based Organizations' where Kofi Annan, the General Secretary of the United Nations is cited saying:

> Enlightened religious leaders and scholars of all faiths also have a key role to play. Their advocacy can influence political leaders and ordinary citizens alike ... I encourage religious leaders and scholars to do their part in defeating poverty and hunger, and in delivering the world's poorest and most marginalized people from despair. (2005)

Clarke (2007: 80) argues that faith communities have been actively recruited by the development institutions and are seen as 'important actors in galvanizing the moral commitment on which the MDGs depend'. There is widespread evidence that FBOs and religious communities in donor countries have put their moral weight behind bilateral and multilateral commitments to achieve the overall MDG goals of halving the number of people living in extreme poverty by 2015.[5]

Indeed, there is every indication that important leadership figures from the major world religions are actively buying into the MDGs; but at the same time it is clear that there is an emphasis upon male voices in the expression of various religious responses to the MDGs, as well as a male bias in the articulation of women's roles and needs. For instance, Justitia et Pax Netherlands, a Catholic human rights organization, established in 1968 by the Dutch Bishops' Conference, has produced a document called 'Act Now for Millennium Development Goals – appeals from religious leaders and scholars' (2005). This interfaith booklet (it has contributions from within Islam, Christianity, Hinduism, Buddhism and Baha'i) 'contains 18 personal messages from religious leaders and scholars. In these messages they indicate, from a religious point of view, the need to support the Millennium Development Goals and they encourage communities of the faithful to take a proactive role in their society'.[6] But only 2 of the 18 contributors are women, reflecting the fact that within religious traditions, positions of leadership and scholarship are more likely to be occupied by men.

Another interfaith document, 'Faith in Action: working towards the Millennium Development Goals (an action toolkit for religious leaders and communities)' contains a clear statement of commitment from different religious traditions to many of the values enshrined by the MDGs as well as Gender and Development thinking. Gender equality is explicitly held up as crucial to the eradication of poverty, and the document acknowledges that there are particular challenges to be faced with respect to women's education and the provision of maternal health care (although it does not tell us what they are).

But these documents reveal a problem; the voices which speak about the commitment to the MDGs and general development goals inevitably reflect assumptions and positions of the organizations they represent – religious organizations that typically marginalize and essentialize women's roles. Instead of a critical engagement with the MDGs from the perspective of different religious positions, religious leaders are given a platform to (re)present essentialist views. For example, the Faith in Action document, which purports to introduce the 'MDGs and the key role of faith communities in advocacy and action to advance development',[7] presents (all) women in terms of their divinely ordained biological reproductive roles: 'Mothers appear in the sacred texts and oral traditions of religions all over the world. Their role in giving birth to all children and their contribution to the well-being of their communities are recognized and celebrated' (Religions for Peace 2005: 8).

The document also advocates engaging with women leaders and women's religious organizations since 'women of faith are often on the frontlines of caring for the sick and the neediest in their communities. They are also active agents for positive change in their societies. At the same time, women are often among the most vulnerable to the effects of poverty' (Religion for Peace 2005: 13). This may well be true, but as many feminists have argued, the gender equity issue concerns the ways in which economic and social policy supports these reproductive roles or leaves them the un(der) paid and under valued and invisible work of women (Elson 2004). Statements like this serve to naturalize rather than critically engage with the gender division of responsibilities in developing societies. While it is indeed true that women do tend to shoulder the overwhelming responsibility for the welfare of their families and communities, often in addition to income-generating activity, a critical gender analysis from a religious perspective should also engage with ways in which this inequality can be challenged; it should interrogate the internal dynamics of religious institutions and traditions, which resist any changes in this situation, and it should join forces with those voices within such traditions which are challenging the status quo and working for reform and change from within faith communities. But in spite of the fact that this publication is aimed at women's religious organizations, amongst others, the absence of any acknowledgement of the problems religious institutions and practices pose for women's current and future role in development or of the obstacles to achieving gender equity and empowerment, which stem from the influence of patriarchy, is of concern. This absence raises questions about the accountability of religious leaders who are able to assert their commitment to the MDGs without recognizing that religions, religious institutions and practices can, in practice, be part of the problem as well as the solution.

Other, more recent, documents indicate that these concerns with the marginalization of women's voices are being addressed within some interfaith meetings about key development issues. The international women's network within 'Religions for Peace' makes a much stronger statement about women's role within their communities and with respect to development. This global network of women from across religious traditions (including more than 450 Baha'i, Buddhist, Christian, Hindu, Jewish, Muslim, multi-faith, Indigenous, Sikh and Zoroastrian religious women's organizations) places at the heart of its agenda issues including human rights, domestic violence, conflict resolution and poverty reduction as well as the recognition of the 'marginalization of religious women in faith-based communities and institutions as a key concern and challenge in advancing shared security.'[8] From 24 to 25 August 2006, over 400 women gathered from 65 countries in Kyoto, Japan for the 'Religions for Peace Women's Assembly'. This was an opportunity to meet and prepare for the Religions for Peace Eighth World Assembly that began two days later. The opening session made a number of recommendations, including that 'religious leaders and communities should continually advocate for the importance of studying religious texts carefully and reinterpreting them from a gender perspective and boldly address issues on women's marginalization' and that 'women of faith must reclaim their leadership, status and power in faith communities, and find their voices that will unite across religious and cultural divides' (Religions for Peace 2006: 7). This does represent a more gender aware perspective on issues of gender equity in development, but it is by no means clear to date that these views will modify the conservative patriarchal stance of recognized world leaders of religious traditions.

Part of the difficulty lies in the eagerness of development organizations to treat religious traditions as monolithic and as capable of speaking with a single voice (resembling a broader parallel with the promotion of 'community leaders' in the multicultural policies of the United Kingdom and elsewhere). The failure to deconstruct and understand the range of positions and interpretations of religious prescriptions concerning gender (and other issues) inevitably perpetuates the power of religious (and other hegemonic) discourses to marginalize and reinforce patriarchal power structures and to undermine those dissenting voices that have alternative visions of their religious traditions. If the 'religious turn' in development relies on the uncontested participation of particular versions of religious traditions, then it seems unlikely that their stated commitment to gender equity, even given the limited extent to which this is included in the MDGs, will be advanced by a more active involvement of religious leaders in development. On the contrary, in working with religious traditions and faith-based organizations, development policy makers and practitioners at all levels must be aware of the gender hierarchies within different religions and not only engage with the dominant male perspective.

We are arguing that, from the perspective of gender equity, there is potential both for harmful and for empowering consequences of such engagement. Key to this argument is a discussion of the ways in which organizations (both secular and religious) that are conscious of gender issues, have addressed the patriarchal tendencies of religious traditions through offering competing yet equally plausible interpretations of texts and teachings.

Global development policy: the United States and the Global Gag

The MDGs include commitments to key objectives that can be interpreted as delivering reproductive health for women. Goal number four commits the development community to reduce the mortality rate of children under five by two-thirds; goal number five is a commitment to reduce by three-quarters the ratio of women dying in child birth; and goal number six commits the world to halt and begin to reverse the incidence of HIV/AIDS and other major diseases by 2015. All these objectives require, in the first instance, expansion of reproductive, maternal and child health services which can be accessed by women to protect them and their children from mortality and morbidity related to reproduction and sexual activity.

But in spite of signing up to the UN MDG programme, the government of the United States, under the political influence of the evangelical Christian right, has adopted a position, which, instead of supporting measures to reach these goals, has actually had a negative affect. Development aid policy in the United States, as elsewhere, is shaped by the political forces of the administration that is in government. As Clarke (2007) demonstrates, the shift in domestic welfare policy in the second half of the 1990s heralded an explicit partnership with FBOs in delivering domestic welfare services, similar to the ways in which the UK government is currently proposing a greater role for community and faith organizations in probation, elderly care and other services. The Clinton administration dismantled constitutional barriers to religious organizations receiving funds from federal or state governments, and this was consolidated after President George W. Bush's ascendancy to the White House in 2000. Since 2004, under so called anti-discriminatory regulation, United States Agency for International Development (USAID) cannot discriminate against FBOs in terms of funding of recognized development activities, a move which has paved the way for the increased participation of evangelical and Pentecostal organizations working overseas, particularly in Sub-Saharan Africa.

It is against this background that we have to understand the (re)instatement of the 'Mexico City Policy' (also now called the Global Gag Rule), by George Bush on his first day in office in January 2001 (Crane and Dusenberry 2004; Bayes and Tohidi 2001). The Mexico City Policy was first introduced by the Reagan Administration in 1984, but overturned by the Clinton Administration in 1993. It prohibits any organization in receipt of US funds from providing abortions (except in the cases of pregnancy following rape, incest or when a woman's life is in danger). The prohibition extends to offering advice and information about abortion services, and any lobbying activity for the legalization of abortion. This policy has had a detrimental affect on the provision of reproductive and health services for women, far beyond the apparent curtailment of abortion related services (Rose 2005: 1211; Cohen 2001; Centre for Reproductive Rights 2003). Effectively, key reproductive health service providers, such as Marie Stopes International and International Planned Parenthood Federation (IPPF), were banned from providing family planning services or pre- and post-natal care in countries in Sub-Saharan Africa and Latin America, not because they were transgressing local legislation in those countries on abortion but because in Northern countries – including in the United States of America and the United Kingdom – such organizations offer pregnancy termination as well as other reproductive health services within the legal framework of those states.

The so called 'pro-life'[9] (i.e. anti-abortion) positions on which the Global Gag Rule is based, are rooted in particular interpretations of the Christian tradition, in this case evangelical Christianity. The global impact of this policy has strengthened the position of conservative interpretations of religion which present an anti-reproductive choice position. In March 2005, at a meeting of the UN Commission on the Status of Women, the US delegation were reluctant to sign a declaration reaffirming the 2005 Beijing Platform for Action unless an amendment was included that rejected the right to abortion (Molyneux and Ravazi 2006). Supported only by Egypt and Qatar (out of 130 country representatives), the leader of the US delegation, Ambassador Ellen. R. Sauerbrey, did eventually sign, but made it clear that 'the terms "reproductive health services" and "reproductive rights" do not include abortion or constitute support, endorsement, or promotion of abortion'.[10] This caveat reflects the insistence of the US administration that the term 'reproductive rights' is short-hand for abortion. Similarly, the use of the phrase 'consistent condom use' within UN parlance, as the basis of HIV/AIDS prevention, is taken to indicate tacit approval of under-age sex, with the Bush administration, backed by the right wing evangelical lobby, arguing that the international community does 'not adequately support the promotion of abstinence' (Rose 2005: 1211; Dao 2002). Similarly, at the seven-day Asian and Pacific Population Conference, held in Bangkok in December 2002, US delegates argued that the phrases 'reproductive rights' and 'consistent condom use', in the conference's proposed policy, were opposed to the US position. However, as Rose writes 'when the United States demanded that even the phrase 'reproductive health' be struck from the proposal in order to protect unborn children, critics – even those from highly religious countries like the Philippines and Iran – suggested that US foreign policy had been hijacked by the Religious Right' (2005: 1212).

Sauerbrey's document to the UN Commission on the Status of Women also makes reference to the US position on HIV/AIDS prevention: 'we emphasize the value of the ABC (Abstinence, Be faithful, and correct and consistent Condom use where appropriate) in comprehensive strategies to combat the spread of HIV/AIDS and the promotion of abstinence as the healthiest and most responsible choice for adolescents'.[11] Rose suggests that the emphasis upon abstinence-until-marriage, in which 'fear surfaces as the primary message and tactic to persuade young people to steer clear of sex before or outside of marriage' (2005: 1208; Kantor 1994; 'Teaching Fear' 1996), is inherently problematic, yet has been adopted in the United States as a widespread strategy underpinning sex education. However, to extend a sex education policy that is problematic within a domestic context to the international arena, where the risks associated with unprotected and non-consensual sex are arguably greater in the context of the HIV/AIDS pandemic and the acknowledged disproportionate vulnerability of women (WHO 2006), raises serious concerns. It is too simplistic to assume that women can 'just say no' to sex, in contexts where they are often not empowered to control their fertility and sexuality, even within apparently monogamous relationships (Tallis 2002; Baylies and Bujra, 2000; Marriott and Townsend, no date).[12] AIDS relief funds, announced by Bush in his January 2003 State of the Union Address, promised $15 billion for the 'President's Emergency Plan for AIDS Relief' (PEPFAR). Congress decreed that the funds should be divided as follows: 55 per cent for the treatment of HIV/AIDS; 15 per cent for palliative care; 20 per cent for prevention (of which at least 33 per cent is to be spent on abstinence-until-marriage programs); and 10 per cent for helping orphans and vulnerable children.[13] However, in a document leaked to the Baltimore Sun newspaper, it became apparent that from 2006 a new requirement had come in to play that required at least two-thirds of all government funds for HIV prevention should adopt the AB model ('abstinence' and 'be faithful') with condom provision and promotion are only to be aimed at particularly 'high risk' groups (Kohn 2005).

There is increasing disquiet over such policies. A recent Editorial in *The Lancet* (2006) describes PEPFAR as 'ideologically driven' and that 'a report by the US Government Accountability Office (GAO) suggested that the legal requirement to promote abstinence and faithfulness means that funds for other initiatives, especially prevention of mother-to-child transmission of HIV, have had to be cut. The GAO report is the first analysis to show that workers on the ground are struggling' (Editorial 2006: 1213). It concludes 'what is really needed is a complete reversal of policy. Rigorous implementation of the "C" part of ABC is crucial if PEPFAR is to reach its target of preventing 7 million new infections by 2010' (2006: 1213).

PEPFAR funding is also subject to a number of restrictions that lead to adverse effects on women and counteract efforts to achieve gender equity. In addition to the 'Global Gag Rule',[14] discussed above, the 'Leadership Act', passed in 2003, states that 'no funds made available to carry out this Act, or any amendment made by this Act, may be used to provide assistance to any group or organization that does not have a policy explicitly opposing prostitution and sex trafficking.'[15] This is a controversial policy, which many believe contravenes the notions of gender equity as applied to sex workers as well as being counterproductive in terms of dealing with the spread of HIV/AIDS. As a result, Brazil rejected $40 million in May 2005: 'the Brazilian government and many organizations believed that adopting the PEPFAR condition would be a serious barrier to helping sex workers protect themselves and their clients from HIV'.[16] More recently, in January 2006:

> the BBC World Service Trust abandoned a USAID-funded, multi-million-dollar AIDS awareness campaign in Tanzania because it refused to comply with this anti-prostitution clause. The Trust said it did not want to inhibit its ability to make television and radio programs that discuss sex workers in a non-judgmental way, leaving Tanzania without the funding for a mass media programme to combat HIV.[17]

The implications of such legislation on funding for reproductive and HIV/AIDS health programmes extend beyond bilateral US funding, since they also affect the United States of America's contribution to development agencies such as United Nations Population Fund (UNFPA) and WHO, which are accused of violating America's position by funding and delivering comprehensive reproductive health policies including those of Safe Abortion.[18] In spite of the argument that such policies are based on 'pro-life' interpretations of religious traditions, the reality indicates little concern with women's lives. In October 2006, a new abortion bill, which outlaws even therapeutic abortion in cases of rape, incest and/or danger to the life of mother or foetus, such as ectopic pregnancies, was passed by the Nicaraguan Assembly.[19] The bill, the most conservative in the whole of Latin America, was approved with the support of the now president Daniel Ortega who instructed his formerly left-leaning and radical Sandinista party to vote in favour of it, in a move many believe was aimed at achieving the political support of both the Catholic and the increasingly influential evangelical church in Nicaragua (Llana 2006).

The political influence behind such policies also affects the selection of faith-based partners in receipt of PEPFAR and similar funds. While we would argue that faith traditions and organizations do not all share extreme 'pro-life' and sexually conservative positions (as illustrated by the discussion of dissenting voices and competing positions within religious traditions), there is evidence that the organizations receiving funds are the ones that conform to the dominant US government position. By 2005 23.5 per cent of all PEPFAR partners were FBOs,[20] a rising trend which reflects PEPFAR's explicit position that 'faith-based groups are priority local partners ... In certain nations, upwards of 50 percent of health services are provided through faith-based institutions, making them crucial delivery points for HIV/AIDS information and services.'[21] However, also stressed (but, we argue, not actually taken into consideration) is the suggestion that 'community- and faith-based groups, trained in program management and HIV/AIDS best practices, often design the most culturally appropriate and responsive interventions and have the legitimacy and authority to implement successful programs that deal with normally sensitive subjects'.[22] In this statement, as in so many others, the notion of 'culturally appropriate' is not deconstructed; instead, powerful voices within particular religious communities are allowed to represent the whole range of different views and practices concerning sexual and reproductive health priorities.

In addition to critiques of the encroachment of religion into US foreign policy – from both within and outside the United States (since it challenges the separation of Church and State) – there have also been critiques from within religious traditions (Christianity, in particular) complaining of bias in development policies based on ethics that are 'pro-life' (rather than pro-choice), that are sexually conservative in nature and which do not reflect the views of all Christians. The organization 'Catholics for a Free Choice' (CFFC),[23] for instance, is engaged in both pro-choice and pro-condom campaigns, which it argues are compatible with Catholic religious teachings:[24]

Catholic support for legal abortion is grounded in core principles of Catholic theology, which respect the moral agency of all women. It is bolstered by respect for the religious freedom and rights of people of all faiths and no religious faith, by respect for plural and tolerant democratic societies and, most importantly, by adherence to the Catholic principle of standing with the poor and marginalized of the world who are disproportionately women. Within this context, Catholic[s] worldwide support the right of all women to follow their conscience when deciding about abortion.[25]

CFFC were also signatories to a recent 'Coalition Letter to House and Senate Leaders Urging Review of Abstinence-Only-Until-Marriage Programs' (1/28/2005)[26] highlighting the gender blindness of domestic abstinence campaigns and concerns that similar programmes will be exported under PEPFAR.[27]

Another US organization The Religious Coalition for Reproductive Choice, founded in 1973, describes itself as

the national organization of pro-choice people of faith. The Religious Coalition—comprising Protestant, Jewish, and other denominations and faith groups, the Clergy for Choice Network, and state affiliates throughout the country—works to ensure reproductive choice through the moral power of religious communities. All programs seek to give clear voice to the reproductive health issues of people of color, those living in poverty, and other underserved populations.[28]

This multi-faith coalition, along with CFFC, supports and promotes reproductive choice and is critical of the Global Gag Rule as 'harmful' to women. What interests us here, is the importance of the observations that, first, religious voices are not monolithic and, second, that religious discourse can become an important place for the contestation of restrictive gender identities as well as for the articulation and (eventual) realization of new ones. The final section of this chapter explores these observations with respect to religiously sanctioned violence against women in some Islamic contexts.

Religion and violence against women: the response of 'feminist'[29] organizations

There are various groups from different religious traditions that are supportive of women's rights, yet acknowledge potential for interpretations and practices that respond to the centrality of religion to many women's lives, while at the same time promoting gender equality. For instance, CFFC, the Religious Coalition for Reproductive Choice, WLUML, Women Against Fundamentalisms (WAF) and Sisters in Islam (Foley 2004; Sleboda 2001) are networks of women who oppose repressive and anti-women practices within specific traditions (but which do not reject religion *per se*). In exploring the situation of women's rights in the context of political Islam, we are concerned to look at such examples of 'religious feminism' that, on the one hand, provide alternative interpretations of tradition and, on the other hand, can arguably complement/ enhance 'secular' approaches. The trend to reverse the separation of church and state (anti-secularism) has created new challenges for development policy, particularly in the area of gender equality, given that political control over the personal and sexual conduct of women is a key element in such regimes. The challenge to navigate this difficult territory, in the pursuit of poverty reduction strategies, service delivery or advocacy in low-income countries, is urgent. Unless this 'turn to religion' is accompanied by a gender analysis, then there is a risk that gender and development values will become compromised.

Rather than adopting a politics of empowerment that makes no reference to religion, some women's rights advocates attempt to provide alternative readings of religious texts and traditions that support gender equality. This includes what has been termed 'Islamic feminism' wherein 'examining the rights of women under Shari'a law has been an acceptable terrain for discussion in some settings' (Molyneux and Ravazi 2006: 18; Mir-Hosseini 2000; Afshar 1998). There are different understandings of and usages of the term 'Islamic feminism' (Badran 2002), and the diversity within 'Islamic feminism' suggests that many women living in Muslim contexts draw upon Islam is different ways to support their goals. For instance, it can refer loosely and broadly to the views of women who draw upon egalitarian versions of Islamic teachings in support of women's human rights, but who reject political Islam and the implementation of Shari'a law as state policy as fundamentally oppressive.[30] Or it can be used to refer to women who are supportive of political Islam, yet seek greater gender equality within that system (see Jeenah 2004; Moghadam 2002; Moghissi 2000). For instance, Jamal writes that women activists within the 'fundamentalist' and Islamist Jamaat-e-Islami movement in Pakistan offer a 'vision of Islamic women's rights that questions universalism and secular rights but includes demands for modern education, employment and mobility...These political–cultural activities of Jamaat women are not unlike the strategy of secular feminist groups in Muslim societies' (2005a: 69–70).

Below we discuss three cases of the application of versions of Islam that are oppressive towards women: female circumcision widely (mis) understood as an Islamic practice; punishment for adultery under Shari'a law in Northern Nigeria; and the campaign to repeal the Hudood Ordinances in Pakistan, which discriminate against women who have been raped. This is not to illustrate the undisputed point that these are examples which essentially oppose gender equality and women's rights, but to illustrate the complexity of feminist responses, an understanding of which is crucial if the engagement of northern development donors and agencies with religion does not undermine commitments to gender equality.

Female circumcision

Female circumcision (often known by the pejorative term 'female genital mutilation' (FGM))[31] is predominantly carried out in African countries (Klouman et al. 2005; Caldwell et al. 1997). While the literature on this topic is mainly concerned with 'FGM' as a human rights and maternal and women's health issue (e.g. the operation is often performed in unhygienic conditions, child birth can become very difficult and there is an increased chance of contracting HIV), the belief that it is an Islamic practice is widespread in Africa, as well as elsewhere. [32] Although female circumcision is not condoned in the Qur'an, the practice is advocated in several Hadith (sayings of the prophet, see Wiggins 2001).[33] The practice in fact predates Islam and is deeply embedded within cultural understandings of sex and womanhood – held by both men and women (e.g. the belief that female circumcision makes a woman a better wife or that without it a new born baby can be harmed). Moreover, it is not only carried out by Muslims in Africa, but also by members of other religious traditions in the region.[34]

Nevertheless, many, especially 'Islamic feminists', have sought to challenge the perception that this is an Islamic practice in order to weaken its cultural hold. For instance, El-Gibaly et al. (2002), argue that the persistence of FGM in Egypt reflects widely held views that it moderates female sexuality, that it will ensure a girl's marriagability and the understanding that Islam sanctions it.[35] While many argue that the practice goes against a woman's human rights and should be banned, others (both African and non-African) maintain that circumcision is an important rite of passage for African women (both Muslim and non-Muslim) and that Western feminist condemnation is misplaced (Africa Update 1996). Such appeals to cultural relativity are dangerous (even if they are articulated within an African context). Within a gender and develop-ment perspective, the rights of women not to be subjected to violence is non-negotiable and FGM is understood as a form of violence against women: what is more appropriate for development actors is support for those who are mobilizing against such practices within their own societies.[36]

Explicit condemnation of female circumcision by religious leaders, par-ticularly emphasising that it is a practice that goes against Islamic teach-ing, is widely considered to be an important aspect of campaigns to bring the practice to an end. WLUML reports that in 2005 in Somalia, Muslim clerics issued a *fatwa* against FGM: 'the group of prominent Muslim clerics have condemned the custom as being against the Islamic religion, and say that it should be a punishable offence. One of the clerics was quoted as saying that every girl "suffering this fate" should be able to take their par-ents on in an Islamic court and ask for compensation.'[37] While the author is sceptical that the *fatwa* will be enforced, it is nonetheless suggested that this is a commendable move.[38]

Punishment for adultery under Shari'a law in Northern Nigeria

Since the adoption of Shari'a law in the North of Nigeria in 2000, there have been a number of incidences that reflect the ways in which inter-pretation of Islamic law acts to the disadvantage of women. Kalu (2003), for instance, discusses a recent well-publicized case where a woman found guilty of adultery was sentenced to death by stoning (this has been adopted as an Islamic response to adultery).[39] An international protest letter campaign ensued, and eventually the case was dropped. However, there were accusations that the international campaign, based on a simplistic condemnation of Islamic practices, actually ran the risk of making the situation worse rather than better, illustrating the com-plexity of the relationship between international women's human rights and development networks and those feminists who live and work in contexts dominated by reactionary Islamic authorities. A local organization called 'BAOBAB for Women's Human Rights'[40] made an appeal to stop the campaign, arguing that:

> dominant colonialist discourses and the mainstream international media have presented Islam (and Africa) as the barbaric and savage Other ... Accepting stereotypes that present Islam as incompatible

with human rights not only perpetuates racism but also confirms the claims of right-wing politico-religious extremists in all of our contexts ... when protest letters re-present negative stereotypes of Islam and Muslims, they inflame sentiments rather than encouraging reflection and strengthening local progressive movements.... The point is for us to question who is invoking Islam (or whatever belief/discourse) for what purposes, and also to acknowledge and support internal dissent within the community involved, rather than engaging in a wholesale condemnation of peoples' beliefs and cultures, which is seldom accurate or effective in changing views within the affected community.[41]

They recognize that 'Muslim discourses and the invocation of Islam have been used both to vindicate and protect women's rights in some places and times, and to violate and restrict them in other places and times – as in the present case.'[42] While BAOBAB is an organization that is ostensibly 'secular', other organizations are more pronounced in their commitment to Islam as a personal and political religious force. The Federation of Muslim Women's Associations of Nigeria (FOMWAN) is the most prominent organization utilizing Islamic teachings in pursuit of women's rights. Founded in 1985, it is 'forthright in its belief that Muslim women's rights need to be promoted and fought for – from within the Islamic paradigm' (Jeenah 2004: 3; Bilkisu, 2002). FOMWAN particularly promotes education of women and girls as an Islamic value and has been instrumental in setting up schools and nurseries, as well as campaigning on issues around marriage, inheritance and divorce. FOMWAN faces an uphill battle in demonstrating its Islamic credentials to a male religious elite suspicious that it is a front for Western, secular values (Bilkisu 2002).

Sexual violence in Pakistan

Concerns have also been raised with respect to the treatment of women in Pakistan, under Islamic law. According to Mullally (2005) although the Pakistani constitution supports equal rights for all, the ascendancy of conservative religious values has meant that women's rights have been curtailed. She reports that, 'feminist movements in Pakistan have drawn on a wide range of strategies in seeking legislative and policy reforms for women. Some have adopted 'insider methodologies', appealing to an egalitarian Islam. Others have adopted secularist strategies, refusing to limit their claims to the confines of religious discourse'

(Mullally 2005: 342). Nevertheless, she suggests that

> despite judicial attempts to safeguard women's claims to equal treatment, political expediency and the rise of the religious right continue to deny the possibility of more widespread reforms ... for feminist movements in Pakistan, attempts to promote more egalitarian interpretations of Islam, against a background of increasing polarization of East and West, become ever more difficult (Mullally 2005: 254–355).

This view is borne out by the events following the law passed in December 2004, which made honour killings (*Karo Kari*) punishable by prison or the death penalty. However, in the view of many women's rights organizations, the law did not go far enough, since it did not outlaw the practice of victims' relatives being permitted to take financial compensation as a trade off for the prosecution of the perpetrator. A bill to strengthen the law (which would outlaw the receipt of compensation) was rejected in March 2005, when the government allied with Islamists, declaring the bill as 'unIslamic'.

Recently there have also been moves to reform the Hudood Ordinances under the Protection of Women (Criminal Laws Amendment) Bill 2006. Instigated in 1979, by General Zia-ul-Haq, the Hudood Ordinances aim to implement Shari'a law in Pakistan. They included the Zina ('illicit sex') Ordinance, which makes, among other things, adultery, fornication, rape and prostitution into offences against the state (Jahangir and Jilani 1988). Women who accuse someone of rape, but who cannot provide four witnesses, are liable to be prosecuted for adultery under the Zina Ordinance, leaving many women reluctant to bring charges or to admit to having been raped (Rafiq 2004).[43] The Women's Protection Bill was passed by Pakistan's lower house of parliament on 15 November 2006. Rape was brought under the civil Pakistan Penal Code, the condition for four male witnesses was removed, and convictions could be brought on the basis of forensic and circumstantial evidence (Hadi 2003).

The Islamisation of the state has presented enormous challenges to feminist groups in Pakistan (Jamal 2005b). One strategy – taken by WAF[44] – the Women's Action Forum – was to declare itself 'secular', in the sense of upholding the separation of the mosque and state, with the intention of emphasizing the importance of 'space for heterogeneous definitions of Muslim women's identity and rights' (2005b: 68), as well as to enable the inclusion of religious minorities. But this has led to problems. On the one hand, the *ulemas* (religious leaders) tend to take secular to mean non-religious or anti-religious, and the organization has been condemned as against Islam. On the other hand, the group has faced challenges in 'redefining WAF's stand in matters where the group has utilized the framework of Islam to challenge particular laws' (2005: 68). WAF's self-identification as 'secular' is a response to the political context; however, WAF has adopted religious language and arguments to challenge gender inequality in Pakistan, although this recourse to an 'egalitarian Islam' is clearly framed with reference to notions of universal rights and freedoms. This is illustrated by WAF's campaign against the proposed Law of Evidence (passed in 1984[45]), which included the requirement of two male or one male and two female witnesses as legal evidence of a crime. According to Jamal:

> in their protests against the Law of Evidence women drew attention to the discriminatory and un-Islamic effect of the law. They also invoked the civil and secular role of the (idealized) nation-state in guaranteeing the possibility of heterogeneous interpretations of religion and claimed their rights as both citizens and Muslims to dislodge the monopoly of politico-religious leaders to interpret the Quran. (2005b: 70).

Although 'secular' feminists in Pakistan make recourse to religious teachings in order to support women's rights, they are aware of the challenging contradictions between feminist ideals and the constraints posed by political Islam on the achievement of women's rights and freedoms. They engage with the public voice of Islam through necessity rather than choice. Thus, within Islamic contexts, the term 'secular' typically refers to the relationship between the state and religion, rather than a rejection of religion *per se*, since 'secular feminists' are not necessarily against private religious observance. Jamal reports that secular feminist activist Said Khan:

> despite her long struggle ... for a secular orientation ... admits to doubts that secularist politics are possible given the internalization of religion among legislators and state officials in Pakistan. Said Khan expresses the political and ethical dilemma of feminists in Pakistan with the poignant question: 'Can feminists say that their faith is personal and has nothing to do with the public, while still upholding that the personal is the political?' (Said Khan 1993: x). (Jamal 2005a: 69)

Whilst these issues would appear to be focused on extremist interpretations of religious Islam, they also have development implications, not least because of the impact of violence against women on achieving the development objectives enshrined in the MDGs. But they also illustrate the wider point – that it is often women and feminist groups within such contexts who offer the most reliable partners for development agencies wishing to engage with FBOs in pursuit of positive, gender equitable development goals.

Conclusion

This chapter has signalled some warning notes about the ways in which the newfound enthusiasm of development organizations to engage with FBOs could jeopardize hard won commitments to gender equality. It is important not to lose sight of long-established values of gender equality and gender mainstreaming within development policy and practice. The danger of 'religious authorities (becoming) the spokespeople for nations and ethnic communities, ... where no guarantees exist for equality, democracy or human rights protection within the political context' (Molyneux and Razavi 2006: 18) is real. By ignoring dissenting or different voices within religious traditions and/or by failing to deconstruct representations of dominant 'culture and tradition' espoused by religious leaders, women's voices will be silenced and the progress towards gender equality will be set back.

It is, of course, true that development agencies may be wary of challenging the sexism inherent within much religious discourse and practice, since this could be considered as criticizing deeply held and traditional religious values. But similar objections were made 30 years ago to the engagement with gender equality. If development and FBOs can commit to acknowledge and engage with critical and alternative views about religious values and traditions both sides of this dialogue can contribute to the ongoing pursuit of women's rights within all religious traditions and all communities engaged in development activities.

Notes

1. Pew Forum on Religion and Public Life, interview with Katherine Marshall, Director, 'Dialogue on Values and Ethics' at the World Bank 06/03/2006 (http://pewforum.org/events/index.php?EventID=100), accessed 21 August 2007.
2. www.wluml.org, accessed 21 August 2007.
3. The term secular can be used to draw attention to different things at different times, for example, secular as the separation of church and state; or secular as a broader rejection of the relevance of religious modes of belief and practice. Here, it refers to the former meaning.
4. The campaign, which was launched in October 2002 is led by a secretariat at the United Nations Development Programme (UNDP) headquarters in New York.
5. See the Department for International Development (DFID) response to a submission by small NGOs to the International Development Select Committee, November 2003, which stated: 'We agree that it can be helpful to link defined constituencies in the UK with the developing world. DFID has engaged with faith groups in various ways in delivery of its objectives over many years. For example, we collaborated with UK Sikh, Jewish and Muslim groups to produce the 2015 booklets, which were designed to help publicize the MDGs in those

communities. We have also now initiated a programme of work to develop greater clarity on how faith groups can in future contribute to development objectives' (http://216.239.59.104/search?q=cache:orF63Oy1sHYJ:www.bond.org.uk/pubs/groups/smallngos/dfid_response_04nov03.doc+dfid_response_04nov03.doc&hl=en&ct=clnk&cd=1&gl=uk&lr=lang_en), accessed 21 August 2007.

6. www.millenniumcampaign.org/site/pp.asp?c=grKVL2NLE&b=260481, accessed 21 August 2007.

7. Ibid.

8. http://www.wcrp.org/initiatives/women/kyoto, accessed 21 August 2007.

9. The terminology of 'pro-life' has been disputed by feminists who see the 'pro-choice' position, which supports a legal option for abortion, as prioritizing women's lives over that of a foetus. The disregard for the lives of women implicit in the anti-abortion position is highlighted by recent events in Nicaragua.

10. United States Mission to the United Nations, 'Explanation of Position by the United States Representative to the Commission on the Status of Women Ambassador Ellen Sauerbrey, at the 49th Session of the United Nations Commission on the Status of Women, March 4, 2005' (www.un.int/usa/05_039.htm), accessed 15 March 2007.

11. Ibid.

12. It is increasingly recognized that married women, who behave monogamously are extremely vulnerable to infection. Islamonline reports that six out of seven new cases of HIV inflection in Arab countries are of married women infected by their husbands (www.islamonline.net/livedialogue/english/Browse.asp?hGuestID=g21n4y), accessed 21 August 2007.

13. Source: www.avert.org/pepfar.htm, accessed 21 August 2007.

14. The situation with the Global Gag Rule remains confusing. In response to considerable protest 'in August 2003, President Bush released an Executive Order specifically exempting HIV/AIDS funds from restrictions under the Global Gag Rule ... there remains confusion about how the Global Gag Rule relates to HIV/AIDS funding, and some organisations may be denied funds as a result. Moreover, the policy is a significant obstacle to the integration of HIV prevention with reproductive health services' (www.avert.org/pepfar.htm), accessed 21 August 2007.

15. United States Leadership Against HIV/AIDS, Tuberculosis, and Malaria Act of 2003, PL108-25. (www.avert.org/pepfar.htm), accessed 21 August 2007.

16. www.avert.org/pepfar.htm; Boseley and Goldenberg (2005), accessed 21 August 2007.

17. www.avert.org/pepfar.htm; Gill (2006), accessed 21 August 2007.

18. See Lobe (2005), who reports on the US Administration's denial of funding to UNFPA – on the (erroneous) grounds that this agency continues to fund programmes in China, which include coerced abortions and sterilizations. The United Kingdom was one of several European countries that have increased their contributions to make good this deficit. In 2006, the United Kingdom's DFID initiated a new donor fund specifically to replace funds lost by the US imposition of the Global Gag Rule, particularly to increase safe abortions (Lobe 2005).

19. See www.nicanet.org/hotline_jan312007.php, accessed 21 August 2007.

20. PEPFAR: Community and Faith-Based Organizations (September 2005), Report to Congress (www.state.gov/s/gac/progress/creports/54316.htm), accessed 21 August 2007.
21. Ibid.
22. Ibid.
23. www.catholicsforchoice.org, accessed 21 August 2007.
24. This includes a campaign to 'Ask Pope Benedict XVI to Lift the Ban on Condoms' (www.catholicsforchoice.org/actioncenter/alerts/default.asp), accessed 21 August 2007.
25. www.catholicsforchoice.org/topics/abortion/default.asp, accessed 21 August 2007.
26. www.aclu.org/reproductiverights/sexed/12757leg20050128.html
27. www.pepfarwatch.org, accessed 21 August 2007; see also The Content of Federally Funded Abstinence-Only Education Programs (www.democrats. reform.house.gov/Documents/ 20041201102153-50247.pdf), accessed 21 August 2007.
28. www.rcrc.org/pdf/global_gag_rule.pdf
29. Many women activists working within an Islamic frame of reference as primary are often wary of the term 'feminism' owing to its associations with the Western values that they consider stand opposed to Islam.
30. In this context, they could also be referred to as 'secular feminists' since they reject political Islam. See the discussion of Women's Action Forum below.
31. Some commentators also prefer to use the term 'female genital cutting' (FGC), arguing that 'female circumcision' is problematic since it implies that the practice is similar to male circumcision and downplays the more serious consequences of FGC for women.
32. See Kelly and Hillard (2005); Abu Daia (2000); Amnesty International (1997); Robinson (1998); Hicks (1996); Dorkenoo (1995); Dorkenoo and Elworthy (1992).
33. However, many Muslims consider these to be 'weak' Hadith (Muslim Women's League 1999).
34. FGM is also practiced in parts of the Middle East (i.e. Yemen, Oman, Iraqi Kurdistan); amongst some Bedouins in Israel; amongst Bohra Muslim populations in parts of India and Pakistan; amongst Muslim populations in Malaysia and Indonesia; and within parts of the Diaspora, (http://www. forwarduk.org.uk/key-issues/fgm), accessed 21 August 2007.
35. They also suggest that the campaign against FGM, which gained momentum after the 1994 UN population conference in Cairo, has corresponded with a decrease in the practice in Egypt.
36. See www.gmu.edu/student/mrrc/FGM%20PROJECT, accessed 21 August 2007.
37. www.wluml.org/english/newsfulltxt.shtml?cmd%5B157%5D=x-157-412165, accessed 21 August 2007.
38. See also 'West Africa: Religious leaders denounce FGM', 25/01/2006 (www. wluml.org/english/newsfulltxt.shtml?cmd%5B157%5D=x-157-500609), accessed 21 August 2007 and 'Al-'Azhar University Scholars Argue over the Legitimacy of Female Circumcision Practiced in Egypt', 2/12/2007 (http:// memri.org/bin/articles.cgi?Page=countries&Area=egypt&ID=SP148307), accessed 21 August 2007.
39. See also Adamu (2004); Miles (2003); Benedek et al. (2002).

40. 'BAOBAB For Women's Human Rights is a not for profit, non-governmental women's human rights organization, which focuses on women's legal rights issues under the three (3) systems of law – customary, statutory and religious laws in Nigeria.' BAOBAB For Women's Human Rights hosts the Nigeria wing of the organization Women Living Under Muslim Laws (www.baobabwomen. org/history.htm), accessed 21 August 2007.
41. www.whrnet.org/docs/action-03-05-07.html, accessed 21 August 2007.
42. Ibid.
43. In July 2006 President General Musharaff passed the "Law Reform Ordinance 2006" that allowed women convicted of zina offences to be released on bail, rather than held in prison (ACHR 2006; IRIN 2006; Rehman 2006; Khan 2003).
44. To cover 'all cases other than those covered by the Hudood Ordinance and any other "special law"' (Mumtaz and Shaheed 1987: 106).
45. WAF (Women's Action Forum, or Khawateen Mahaz-e-Amal), was founded in 1981 during one of the worst eras of political oppression in the name of Islamisation (and indeed following the implementation of the Hudood ordinances).

Bibliography

Abu Daia, J. M. (2000) 'Female Circumcision'. *Saudi Medical Journal*, 21 (10), pp. 921–923.

ACHR (2006), *Appeasing the Mullahs: Protection of Women (Criminal Laws Amendment) Bill 2006 of Pakistan*, Asian Centre for Human Rights, http://www.achrweb.org/Review/2006/132-06.htm, accessed 21 August 2007.

Adamu, F. L. (2004) 'Household Politics, Women and Shariah Courts in Sokoto, Northern Nigeria'. *Peripherie*, 24 (95), pp. 284–305.

Afkhami, M. (ed.) (1995) *Faith and Freedom: Women's Human Rights in the Muslim World*. London: Tauris.

Afkhami, M. and E. Friedl (eds) (1997), *Muslim Women and the Politics of Participation: Implementing the Beijing Platform (Gender, Culture & Politics in the Middle East Series)*. Syracuse: Syracuse University Press.

Africa Update (1996) *Female Circumcision in Africa*, 3 (2), http://www.ccsu.edu/afstudy/upd3-2.html#Z1, accessed 21 August 2007.

Afshar, H. (1998) *Islam and Feminisms: An Iranian Case Study*. Basingstoke: Macmillan.

Alkire, S. (2006) 'Religion and Development' In D. A. Clark (ed.) *Edgar Companion to Development Studies*. Cheltenham: Edward Elgar, pp. 502–510.

Amnesty International (1997) 'What is female genital mutilation?' http://web.amnesty.org/library/index/ENGACT770061997, accessed 21 August 2007.

Baden, Sally and Anne Marie Goetz (1998) 'Who Needs (Sex) When You Can Have (Gender)? Conflicting Discourses on Gender at Beijing,' In Cecile Jackson and Ruth Pearson (eds) *Feminist Visions of Development: Gender, Analysis and Policy*. London: Routledge, pp. 19–38.

Badran, M. (2002) 'Islamic Feminism: What's in a Name?', *Al-Ahram Weekly Online*, Issue No. 569, 17–23 January, http://weekly.ahram.org.eg/2002/569/cu1.htm, accessed 21 August 2007.

Bayes, Jane H. and Nayreheh Tohidi (eds) (2001) *Globalization, Gender, and Religion. The Politics of Women's Rights in Catholic and Muslim Contexts.* Basingstoke: Palgrave.

Baylies, C. and Bujra, J. (2000) *AIDS, Sexuality and Gender in Africa; the Struggle Continues; Collective Strategies for Protection Against AIDS in Tanzania and Zambia.* Routledge: London.

Benedek, W. Esther Kisaakye, and Gerd Oberlietner, (eds) (2002) *The Human Rights of Women: International Instruments and African Experiences.* London: Zed Books.

Bilkisu, H. (2002) *The Veil and Male Chauvinists* (www.africasource.com/content/view/42/68, accessed 21 August 2007.).

Boseley, S. and Goldenberg, S. (2005) 'Brazil Spurns US Terms for Aids Help', *Guardian*, 4 May, http://www.guardian.co.uk/brazil/story/0,12462,1475966,00. html, accessed 21 August 2007.

Caldwell, J. C., Orubuloye, I. O. and Caldwell, P. (1997) 'Male and Female Circumcision in Africa from a Regional to a Specific Nigerian Examination'. *Social Science and Medicine*, 44 (8), pp. 1181–1193.

Centre for Reproductive Rights Factsheet (2003): 'The Global Gag Rule's Effects on NGOs in 56 Countries', www.reproductiverights.org/pub_fac_ggreffects. html, accessed 21 August 2007.

Clarke, G. (2006) 'Faith Matters: Faith-Based Organisations, Civil Society and International Development'. *Journal of International Development*, 18 (6), pp. 835–848.

Clarke, G. (2007) 'Agents of Transformation? Donors, Faith-Based Organisations and International Development'. *Third World Quarterly*, 28 (1), pp. 77–96.

Cohen, S. (2001) 'Global Gag Rule: Exporting Antiabortion Ideology at the Expense of American values'. *The Guttmacher Report on Public Policy*, 4 (3) http://www.guttmacher.org/pubs/tgr/04/3/gr040301.html, accessed 21 August 2007.

Crane, B. B. and Dusenberry, J. (2004) 'Power and Politics in International Funding for Reproductive Health: The US Global Gag Rule'. *Reproductive Health Matters*, 12 (24), pp. 128–137.

Dao, J. (2002) 'Over U.S. Protest, Asian Group Approves Family Planning Goals'. *New York Times*, 18 December, http://query.nytimes.com/gst/fullpage.html?sec=health&res=9D02EFD7153DF93BA25751C1A9649C8B63&n=Top%2FReference%2FTimes%20Topics%2FSubjects%2FA%2FAbortion, accessed 21 August 2007.

Dorkenoo, E. (1995) *Cutting the Rose – Female Genital Mutilation: The Practice and Its Prevention. Minority Rights Group.* London: Minority Rights Publication.

Dorkenoo, E. and S. Elworthy (1992) *Female Genital Mutilation, proposals for change.* London: Minority Rights Group.

Editoral (2006) 'HIV Prevention Policy Needs an Urgent Cure'. *The Lancet*, 367 (9518), 15–21 April, p. 1213.

El-Gibaly, O., Ibrahim, B., Mensch, B. S. and Clark, W. H. (2002) 'The Decline of Female Circumcision in Egypt: Evidence and Interpretation'. *Social Science and Medicine*, 54 (2), pp. 205–220.

Elson, D. (2004) 'Feminist Economics Challenges Mainstream Economics' In Special issue of the *Newsletter of the International Association for Feminist Economics*, Bina Agarwal (ed.), 14 (3), pp. 6–8.

Foley, R. (2004) 'Muslim Women's Challenges to Islamic Law: The Case of Malaysia'. *International Feminist Journal of Politics*, 6 (1), pp. 53–84.

Gill, P. (2006) 'BBC Backs Off from Bush in Africa', *The Guardian*, 23 January, http://media.guardian.co.uk/mediaguardian/story/0,,1692457,00.html

Hadi, S. (2003) 'Women's Rights in Pakistan: A Forensic Perspective'. *Medicine, Science and the Law*, 43 (2), pp. 148–152.

Heyzer, N. (2005) 'Making the links: Women's Rights and Empowerment are Key to Achieving the Millennium Development Goals'. *Gender and Development*, 13 (1), March, pp. 9–12.

Hicks, E. (1996) *Infibulation: Female Mutilation in Islamic Northeastern Africa*. New Brunswick; London: Transaction Publishers.

IRIN News (Integrated Regional Information Networks) (2006) *Pakistan: Over a Thousand Women Freed Under Change in Law*, 7 October, http://www. politicalaffairs.net/article/articleview/3790/1/196/

Jahangir, A. and Hina J. (1988) *The Hadood Ordinances: A Divine Sanction*. Lahore: Rhotac Books.

Jamal. A. (2005a) 'Feminist 'Selves' and Feminism's 'Others': Feminist Representations of Jamaat-e-Islami Women in Pakistan'. *Feminist Review*, 81 (1), pp. 52–73.

Jamal, A. (2005b) 'Transnational Feminism as Critical Practice. A Reading of Feminist Discourses in Pakistan'. *Meridians: Feminism, Race, Transnationalism*, 5 (2), pp 57–82.

Jeenah, N. (2004) *Muslim Women Cultures and Movements in Sub-Saharan Africa*, http://naeemjeenah.shams.za.org/Muslim%20women%20cultures%20 and%20movements.pdf

Justitia et Pax Netherlands (2005) *Act Now for Millennium Development Goals – Appeals from Religious Leaders and Scholars*, http://www.millenniumcampaign. org/atf/cf/{D15FF017-0467-419B-823E-D6659E0CCD39}/faith_justiciapax_ manual.pdf

Kalu, O. U. (2003) 'Safiyya and Adamah: Punishing Adultery with Sharia Stones in Twenty-First-Century Nigeria'. *African Affairs*, 102 (408), pp. 389–408.

Kantor, L. (1994) Attacks on Public School Sexuality Education Programs: 1993–1994 school year. SIECUS Report. 22: 11–16.

Kelly, E. and Hillard P. J. A. (2005) 'Female Genital Mutilation'. *Current Opinion in Obstetrics and Gynecology*, 17 (5), pp. 490–494.

Khan, S. (2003) 'Zina and the Moral Regulation of Pakistani Women'. *Feminist Review*, 75 (1), pp. 75–100.

Klouman, E., Manongi, R. and Klepp, K. I. (2005) 'Self-reported and Observed Female Genital Cutting in Rural Tanzania: Associated Demographic Factors, HIV and Sexually Transmitted Infections'. *Tropical Medicine and International Health*, 10 (1), pp. 105–115.

Kohn, D. (2005) 'More HIV Funds to Promote Abstinence: Researchers Call Policy Misguided', *Balitmore Sun*, 10 December, http://www.actupny.org/ reports/bush_abstinencefunding.html

Llana, S. M. (2006) 'Evangelicals Flex Growing Clout in Nicaragua's Election' *Christian Science Monitor*, 2 November, (http://www.wwrn.org/article. php?idd=23241&sec=57&cont=all)

Lobe, J. (2005) 'Bush Denies UNFPA Grant for Fourth Year', *People and Planet*, 28 September, http://www.peopleandplanet.net/doc.php?id=2542\

Marriott, A. and Townsend, C. (eds) (no date) Gender and HIV/AIDS, Dossier, Bridge, http://www.eldis.org/gender/dossiers/index.htm

Miles, W. F. S. (2003) 'Shari'a as De-Africanization: Evidence from Hausaland'. *Africa Today*, 50 (1), pp. 51–75.

Mir-Hosseini, Z. (2000) *Islam and Gender: The Religious Debate in Contemporary Iran*. Princeton, NJ: Princeton University Press.

Moghadam, V. (2002) 'Islamic Feminism and Its Discontents: Toward a Resolution of the Debate'. *Signs: Journal of Women in Culture and Society*, 27 (4) (Summer), pp. 1135–1171.

Moghissi, H. (2000) *Feminism and Islamic Fundamentalism: The Limits of Postmodern Analysis*. Oxford: Oxford University Press.

Molyneux, M. and Ravazi, S. (2006) *Beijing Plus 10: An Ambivalent Record on Gender Justice*. NRSID Occassional Paper 15. www.unrisd.org/UNRISD/website/document.nsf/ab82a6805797760f80256b4f005da1ab/4ee168779e57e924c125 71ca003c2295/$FILE/opgp10.pdf

Mullally, S. (2005) 'As Nearly as May Be: Debating Women's Human Rights in Pakistan'. *Social and Legal Studies*, 14 (3), pp. 341–358.

Mumtaz, K. and Farida S. (1987) *Women of Pakistan: Two Steps Forward, One Step Back?* London: Zed.

Muslim Women's League (1999) *Position Paper on Female Genital Mutilation/ Female Circumcision*, pp. 1–5. www.mwlusa.org/pub_fgm.html

Pearson, R. (2005) 'The Rise and Rise of Gender and Development' In Uma Kothari (ed), *A Radical History of Development Studies*. Capetown; London: Zed Press, pp. 157–179.

Rafiq, S. (2004) *Justice and Equality for Women*, www.onlinenews.com.pk/articledetails.php?id=52986, accessed 21 August 2007.

Rehman, S. (2006) Women's Legislation: Gap between Musharraf Regime's Promises and Action, 2 September, Pakistan Peoples Party, www.ppp.org.pk/Party/Party%20Issues/P_articles48.html, accessed 21 August 2007.

Religions for Peace (2005) *Faith in Action: Working Towards the Millennium Development Goals (an Action Toolkit for Religious Leaders and Communities)* www.millenniumcampaign.org/atf/cf/{D15FF017-0467-419B-823 E-D6659E0CCD39}/FINAL%20ENGLISH%20AFRICAN%20RFP%20MDG%20 TOOLKIT.PDF, accessed 21 August 2007.

Religions for Peace (2006) Empowering Women as Agents of Social Change, report April 1st 2005 through March 31st 2006, www.wcrp.org/files/AR-WomensProgram-2006.pdf, accessed 21 August 2007.

Robinson, B. A. (1998) Female Genital Mutilation (Female Circumcision) in Africa, the Middle East and Far East, www.religioustolerance.org/fem_cirm.htm

Rose, S. (2005) 'Going too Far? Sex, Sin and Social Policy'. *Social Forces*, 84 (2), pp. 1207–1232.

Sleboda, J. (2001) 'Islam and Women's Rights Advocacy in Malaysia'. *Asian Journal of Women's Studies*, 7 (2), pp. 94–136.

Tallis, V. (2002) *GENDER and HIV/AIDS Overview Report*, Bridge, http://www.bridge.ids.ac.uk/reports/cep-hiv-report.pdf, accessed 21 August 2007.

Teaching Fear (1996) *The Religious Right's Campaign Against Sexuality Education*, People for the American Way, http://www.pfaw.org/pfaw/general/default.aspx?oid=2012, accessed 21 August 2007.

Thomas, S. (2005) *The Global Resurgence of Religion and the Transformation of International Relations*. London; New York: PalgraveMacmillan.

WHO (2006) AIDS Epidemic Update, http://www.who.int/hiv/mediacentre/2006_ EpiUpdate_en.pdf, accessed 21 August 2007.

Wiggins, D. (2001) 'Islamic Texts and Circumcision', *Africa Update*. 8 (4), http://www.ccsu.edu/AFSTUDY/upd8-4.htm#Islamic, accessed 21 August 2007.

4
The Language of Development: What are International Development Agencies Talking About?

Ian Linden

Introduction

It is commonplace today to find the categories 'religious' and 'secular' dealt with as two givens indicating an important distinction. A sub-set of this binary opposition between two – usually undefined – categories is to be found in the growing interest in 'faith-based' organizations (FBO) and their differences from what are thus necessarily described as 'secular' organizations. I would like to investigate just how 'given' this distinction is with particular reference to the field of development.

As a relatively new designation, 'FBO' draws sustenance from a binary narrative that emerged historically, in the Marxist sense, as a classic ideological construct; in other words, it became 'common sense' to view aspects of the world as divided into religious and secular antinomies, and this entailed a systemic distortion of history in the interests of a dominant discourse. It is not difficult to find instances of this ideology at work.

To give two examples, the founding of the United Nations and the writing of its Charter and Declaration of Human Rights was significantly influenced by the thinking and advocacy of Protestant Christians – American, British and Lebanese to mention the most prominent – working either as official representatives of Churches or of their states. Their allies included an effective Jewish lobby. Their primary concerns with creating a lasting peace with religious liberty were the proximate cause of their commitment to the wider contemporary promotion of human rights.[1]

Because the United Nations (UN) needed support and signatories from, most notably, Muslim and atheistic communist governments, the historic role of these Christians had to be lost in the telling. The dilemma was how to deal with pluralism in the context of a struggle for consensus around a 'thick' version of the liberal human rights check-list. This would provide ideally the necessary foundations for a just, democratic and non-totalitarian society. An imagined secularity in the discourse of human rights was the only practical way forward. The problem was otherwise insoluble.

No conspiracy of silence was required. Mislaying the Judaeo-Christian roots of the UN Charter and Declaration was not a difficult endeavour. The Enlightenment had already successfully finessed the origins of human rights in the Christianity of early modern Europe. In this second example, the concept of human rights became the fruit of the overthrow of the tyranny of superstition by Reason and the corollary, an emergent individualism. So ran the story. There was supposedly a rupture, a hiatus between the Christian discourse of Natural Rights in the Middle Ages and the Rights of Man imagined as bursting forth *de novo* from the French Revolution and *philosophes*. That the language of human rights had begun to emerge in modern form amongst the school of the Salamanca Dominican theologians, men such as Bartolomeo de las Casas and Francisco de Vitoria, reacting to the shock of the *conquistadores'* claims and barbarities in the New World was ideologically ruled out.

Thus, what it meant to be a human being was not first a theological question fought over the seas from Rome to Mexico, but a secular question fought over in the streets of Paris. We learnt about Tom Paine purportedly as the pioneer of human rights and receive a skewed version of what John Locke was trying to say, neglecting his religious premises and accentuating his individualism and liberalism (Ruston 2004: 191–251). In much the same way Benedict Spinoza and Mulla Sadra are taught in the separate worlds of Shi'ite Islamic philosophy and Western philosophy ignoring the fact that in many respects they both lived during the seventeenth century in a common intellectual world and were answering the same questions (Wilson, www.muslimphilosophy.com).

The obfuscation was worsened by the willingness of the Roman Catholic Church to buy into the binary opposition. This was hardly surprising. The Rights of Man had meant in practice no rights for the Church. During the nineteenth century, Popes, as is much rehearsed, fulminated anathemas. Anything sounding like a liberal account of human rights was ruled out in the face of anti-clerical liberal governments. This defensive 'anti-modernism' was put to rest only in 1963 with Pope John XXIII's encyclical *Pacem in Terris*, which on the basis of natural law fully adopted the modern discourse of human rights, and by the Second Vatican Council's Decree on Religious Liberty which gave up on dreams of the mediaeval confessional state obedient to the one Church.

The primary ideological role of this religious–secular opposition was to achieve the goal of excluding religious institutions, leaders and committed believers as much as possible from public space. They had shown themselves unsuited to its occupancy in the debilitating and prolonged Religious Wars of the seventeenth century. Put in a more positive way, that religion is a personal and private matter, not under the jurisdiction of the state beyond the needs of public order, became enshrined in liberal laws; and the supposition behind such laws was, and is, precisely that religion is *private* and *personal*. The key to effective religious freedom is a clear account of what states *cannot* do with regards to religion, and, reciprocally though sometimes implicitly, what religion cannot do with regard to the state and public space.

The contemporary context is notable in a number of different regards. The impact of liberation theology and the rise of Pentecostalism from the 1970s onwards, the growth of Wahabi and Salafi forms of Islam and their pernicious mutation into *jihadist* movements, each in their very different ways have dissipated the mirage of a world tidily divided into private religious and secular public space. Forms of religious organization have emerged from the shadows as political forces to be contended with. Faced with a plethora of such organizations, the modern state has rapidly discovered that it needs to know more about them, how they differ from 'secular' organizations in civil society, and how they relate to a pluralist project and the current understanding of 'development'. On the one hand, a process of redefining and negotiating the legitimate access of religions to the public sphere is underway; on the other, several parts of the Middle East are disintegrating under the impact of imprudent military intervention. Overall, to paraphrase William Cavanagh 'one senses that religion in public is to be treated like a paroled convict in the workplace; he should be given a second chance to be a productive citizen, but the letter openers should be kept in locked drawers'.[2]

Some problems of definition

This process of recolonization of public space by world religions prescinds from a number of fundamental questions. One preliminary question is what the state means by 'faith-based' and how this differs from its understanding of the 'secular'. Moreover, the concept 'secular' is more multivalent and complex than normally indicated. Does it convey the ideological meaning of the marginalization of religion, its exclusion from public space? And how can this today include the corollary: the claim that religion is a private matter, something that goes on 'inside' people, or inside places of worship, rather than outside in society. Or does it mean the abandonment of religious explanations for how things are in the world? Or simply the loss of beliefs about human transcendence, God, or different spiritual beings. Or rather a turning away from institutional expressions of religion? Britain is a secular society in one sense not another. The United States is secular in an entirely other sense.

Of course, secular constitutions may be the solution to the problems of dealing with a high level of religious diversity in society, as India illustrates, rather than an expression of a society which is secular. So agreeing on a definition of 'secular' can be very important in avoiding sterile debate about what is going on, the problem of social cohesion and national development, and the way forward for pluralism.

Nor does any useful single definition encompass the uniqueness of each of the world's faiths. 'Behaviour appropriate to the mystery of God, or the power of the spirit world, or the quest for human transcendence' is more of an *insider* description than a definition. Though it does potentially allow for the practice of 'development' as a religious behaviour. No monolithic account of each religion does justice to the diversity within it, the difference between how people live and express their religion, and *normative* accounts describing how things ideally ought to be for a *true* believer.

That said, the world religions share many common features. First, they are not simply a matter of beliefs, values or 'worldviews'. Religions are embedded in cultures and communities (an idea developed in Thomas 2005). Indeed many people in rural parts of the world, unaccustomed to urban diversity, would not find the distinction between 'culture' and 'religion' meaningful. And the distinction between Arabic culture and Islam is often elided even amongst better educated urban people (Rosen 2002: 108–129). An assertive religious identity most often is the product of a competitive multi-cultural, multi-faith environment in which a religion is challenged or threatened. The past two decades in the north of Nigeria, for example, would give credence to this hypothesis.

Even under challenging circumstances religions do not become closed and static systems. Their boundaries are fluid. They can absorb new ideas and practices. Elements within them change. People who talk about Islam, Buddhism, Judaism, Christianity, for example, 'resulting in', 'causing', 'saying and 'showing' this and that, as if they are monolithic systems, are talking at best about abstract ideas, not real people in communities. At worst, they are taking the first steps that lead to stereotyping people and the denial of a diverse, lived reality, respect and understanding. Contemporary concerns about different forms of fundamentalism, violence and exclusivity, while entirely understandable from a human rights and security perspective, easily compound the problem. Religions become judged by the attitudes and actions of small and aberrant minorities.

Religious cultures and communities are shaped by their specific histories, particularly by their founding stories and texts, by *narratives*. Together these generate practices, rituals, institutions, resonant symbols, and different ways of doing things, praying, fasting, worshipping. Most importantly, they underpin ethics, values, politics and provide a framework for moral decisions: what it means to be a human being, How to organize society, the possibilities of human transcendence and spirituality, and, with the exception most notably of Buddhism, relationships to a God or to a Spiritual Being or beings. All of these components of religions have implications for what is understood by the term human development and, by extension, what might be a desirable form of justice, law and political dispensation.

But more often than not the world religions vie with local religions, and entrenched cultural patterns, to guide individual behaviour and social norms. For example, neglect of cultural and religious patterns that predated the arrival of the world religions in Africa is a recipe for failed preventative work on HIV/AIDS. World religions do not displace but are often juxtaposed to earlier forms of religious consciousness focused on the fertility of the land and of women.[3]

Development talk and God talk

The concept of development began to take shape in the first five decades of the nineteenth century in a particular context: the impact of the industrial revolution notably in serious economic crises that threatened the social and political fabric of European states. It emerged as part of a complex of interrelated problems and allied concepts: progress, corruption, continuity and change, evolution and revolution, organic versus inorganic. 'The inorganic has one final comprehensive law, GRAVITATION', wrote Chambers. 'The organic, the other great department of mundane things, rests in like manner on one law, and that is DEVELOPMENT' (Chambers, cited in Cowen and Shenton 1996: 3).

The irony was that the idea of development was to be carried forward by Marx with an emphasis on capital as the driving force of development, perhaps mundane but certainly not organic, and on the other, by John Henry Newman with an emphasis on the development of doctrine, conscience and God. It was Newman though, grappling with the problem of continuity and change in Catholicism, rather than Marx grappling with capital accumulation and the trusteeship of the bourgeoisie over development in India, who was to deliver something very close to the modern understanding of development and tease out its diverse meanings. The term was used, he analysed in his 1845 *Essay on the Development of Christian Doctrine,*

> in three senses indiscriminately, from defect of our language; on the one hand for the process of development, on the other for the result; and again generally, for a development true or not true (that is faithful or unfaithful to the ideas from which it started), or exclusively for a development deserving the name. A false or unfaithful development is called a corruption. (Newman, cited in Cowen and Shenton 1996: 94–95)

Shenton and Cowen make an interesting comparison here with Gunder Frank's concept of underdevelopment, and explore the historical questions about the role and identity of the 'Trustees' of development (Cowen and Shenton 1996: 4–5, 25–27, 42–56, 60–115; Goulet 1980).

Newman managed to present development not merely as a problem for the doctrines of the Roman Catholic Church but as a positive feature of its commitment to the truth. From this starting point it was not difficult to conceptualize development as a positive dynamic that would remedy the depredations of progress: social disorder, unemployment, immorality, old and new corruption and the destructive consequences of immanent change. Though, for Newman, such a dynamic would have to be in the hands of some responsible Trustees, while for Marx the helmsman was, when it was not the internal dynamic of capital accumulation, the Proletariat.

Newman's attention to the process of development as well as its result, and his pervasive emphasis on history, were to re-emerge as core antecedents to the Second Vatican Council. But his thinking was far more extensive in its impact. 'Is it not a remarkable thing', wrote Mark Pattison, a clergyman and supporter of the Social Sciences Foundation, in 1878, 'that you should have first started the idea – and the word – development, as the key to the history of Church doctrine, and since then it has gradually become the dominant idea of all history, biology, physics, and in short has metamorphosed our view of every science, and of all knowledge' (Chadwick 1957: ix–x). This adulation may have been excessive, but Newman's influence in the Victorian intellectual world was prodigious (Cowen and Shenton 1996). It does give some indication of the close link between God-talk and the origins of development talk, a third example of ideological forgetfulness.

My purpose in beginning with this preamble is simply to open up the possibility that the invention of the key concepts of development and human rights that inform the thinking of development agencies do not easily allow for any simplistic division into religious and secular, least of all when it comes the question of the Trusteeship of development . And, to suggest that what may be problematic is not the retention by FBOs of a link between God-talk and development talk, but the ideo- logical *tours de parole* repeatedly played out by development agencies that believe themselves to be, usually for unspecified reasons, some- thing called 'secular', and neglect this link. For it is far from clear if the available ethical frameworks of secularity permit coherent accounts of either development or human rights, as, I would argue, is the case with some theological accounts.[4] Since this chapter attempts to address the experience of the sector of UK's international Catholic development agencies, I will briefly set out the roots of the thinking that makes up their tradition and informs their action.

Creatureliness and human dignity

The roots of the Christian understanding of human dignity, which underlies the promotion of both human rights and human develop- ment, lie in the doctrine of creation found in the first book of Genesis. This contains the account of how human beings, mankind (*adam*), while being creatures created by God are nonetheless made 'in the image and likeness of God'. Since in the contemporary Middle Eastern ideology of kingship only kings were viewed in this way, the Genesis account was an unprecedented and revolutionary revelation.

The explanation of what is meant by the *imago dei* still remains chal- lenging for any Christian anthropology. The theme provides a vital underpinning for the moral theology of St. Thomas Aquinas in his *Summa Theologiae*, and it is this stream of Catholic thinking that has been most influential over the centuries.

Intelligence, free will and virtuous action, human moral agency, are understood by Thomas as the essential qualities that define human beings as God's creatures, and separate them from the rest of the living world in a position of dominion over other created things. And with this status and 'right' of dominion goes the duty of stewardship over creation in the model of God's own maternal loving nurture. This provides a framework for an ecological ethic. In the Syriac tradition, Theodore of Mopsuestia, one of the Antiochene Fathers, presented humanity as a vice-regency of God in the sense of forming the bond, *syndesmos,* and pledge of friendship, *philias enekhyron,* for the whole of the living world, a position of great responsibility and solidarity with creation (Kerr 2002: 124; Murray 2000: 51).[5]

Thomas makes it clear that human beings are not made as images *of* God rather they are made *ad imaginem* (<u>to</u> the image of God). This cannot, of course, be a question of *physical* likeness. So a rather poor analogy would be the head of an emperor on a coin, or, a better one, a work of art subtly bearing the particular impress of the artist. The analogy is further developed in the Christian expression 'artisans of a new humanity' used increasingly from the 1960s to describe Christians' co-operation with God's work of liberating redemption. And in undertaking this work human beings draw within themselves on traces of God's own – utterly different and loving – creativity and redemptive power.

Nonetheless the Christian concept of 'the image of God' in no ways underestimates the degree to which sin flaws human beings as God's works of art, and thus flaws their work as artisans of a new humanity. The second Vatican Council is insistent that the *imago dei* cannot be understood outside its full realization in the relationship to divinity found in Jesus Christ, to pursue the analogy, God's perfect self-portrait as *the* craftsman and exemplar of a redeemed new humanity (Ruston 2004: 55).[6]

For Christians, then, God's plan of creation can, therefore, never be divorced from the plan of redemption.[7] The attribute of human dignity is both the product of having been created *and* redeemed – in both cases as the recipients of a loving gift – and the resulting capacity to seek, encounter and ultimately know God.

Thomas Aquinas himself still retained a mediaeval, hierarchical use of the word 'dignity' which was applied as an attribute to a limited number of 'persons' who were 'dignitaries'. This quality referred particularly to their supposed endowment with superior wisdom used in, what today would be called, 'governance' of Church, State and Society. In short, God's providential dispensation of 'dignity' made its recipients 'fit for purpose'. As such, this special attribute had to be honoured by all. The word for this honouring was *observantia.*

After Europe's discovery of the New World in the sixteenth century, and its stimulus to ideas of human equality and 'universality', by extension this objective requirement to honour came to include *all* human beings and nations. It was their due. Obedience to God, based on humanity's unique God-given nature as a creature, now required that human dignity be observed universally. Correspondingly the duty of religious *observantia*, observance towards God was a universal duty, a feature shared with Islam. In the words of Cardinal Renato Martino, addressing the ILO in 2005: 'In the age-old history of the Church, the concept of a common humanity, stretching to the extreme limits of the earth, introduced to human civilization a dynamism raising the dignity of the individual and at the same time expanding this dignity beyond any boundary or border'. What was entailed in recognition of this universal dignity was spelt out for states by Pope John XXIII in *Pacem in Terris*, and applied to conduct of the international community, under the heading of the 'universal common good'.[8]

Integral human development

This is not the place to chart the elaboration of the idea of human dignity in Catholic Social Teaching over the centuries. But it is important to mention some seminal documents that have profoundly informed the work of Catholic development agencies, indeed stimulated their creation in the 1960s. The conciliar document, the *Pastoral Constitution of the Church in the Modern World* (*Gaudium et Spes*), with which the second Vatican Council in fact ended in 1965, is an attempt at reading the 'signs of the times', in particular the Church's grappling with the key issues of modernity. It takes the form of a dialogue with the modern world, as it were, an essay in a contextualized Christian anthropology.[9] 'Hence the pivotal point of our total presentation', declares *Gaudium et Spes*, 'will be man himself, whole and entire, body and soul, heart and conscience, mind and will'. Hence *integral*. And because humanity exists in time and history, and should not be a static, abstract concept, this vision of an integral humanity raises immediately the question of integral development.

But perhaps because classic 'natural law' is, and was then, often misunderstood as a static and biological account of being human, and is, and was, thus frequently rejected, the Pastoral Constitution does not attempt to link believers and unbelievers by the traditional means of starting with 'natural law', accessible by Reason, as previous Popes had done. The starting point is rather the faith of the Church that 'in her benign Lord and Master can be found the key, the focal point, and the goal of all human history'.[10] This, of course, does create a problem of language, translation and explanation for non-Christians.

Gaudium et Spes presents a subtle and realistic Christian anthropology that takes culture seriously. It rejects spiritual dualism by defending equally the dignity of the *body* which, by definition, embodies the uniqueness of the human person, while underlining that the human spirit transcends the material universe. Moreover, it is well in advance of its time in emphasizing the importance of what it calls "human interdependence", what today is increasingly analysed in terms of globalization. In keeping with earlier Catholic Social Teaching, the profound characteristic of the human person is seen to be that human beings are essentially social and, in consequence, human dignity forms the non-negotiable bedrock of society. This sociability was taking on a new global dimension to which the Church wishes to address itself. 'Today the principal fact we must all recognize is that the social question has become worldwide', Pope Paul VI begins in somewhat arcane Vaticanese.[11] And the official teaching of the Church henceforth goes on to say with increasingly clarity, that these universal social bonds of the human family, being of an ontological and moral nature, are most fully realized in the virtue of *solidarity*.

This is not left as a vague moral exhortation. The context of these assertions in the late 1960s was the newly independent nations, admitted to the United Nations, and beginning to make powerful claims on the richer countries for international justice. The vision was soon to develop and be formulated in terms of the need for a New International Economic Order. In 1964, the United Nations Conference on Trade and Development had its first meeting in Geneva. The representatives of the assembled nations gave two prolonged ovations; one was to Che Guevara, the other was to Louis-Joseph Lebret, a Breton Dominican priest sent by Pope Paul. Lebret was a developmentalist and adviser to a number of governments in Latin America and Africa, who as a young man had learnt from the struggle of Breton fishermen against powerful fishing lobbies. He was one of the earliest proponents of a right to development. 'In a humanity which realises solidarity', Lebret said, 'the right of all peoples to development must be recognized and respected'.[12]

On his return to Rome, Lebret was asked by the Pope to draft for him an encyclical on international social justice, to encompass the complexity of the relationship between rich and poor nations. The resulting Progress of Peoples (*Populorum Progressio*) appeared as a necessary development of the Church's reflection on the requirements of human dignity in the context of contemporary, Western-directed international development, an incipient new wave of globalization and the dominance of modernization theory. It was to be the charter for all the European Catholic development agencies.

The second Vatican Council had fully acknowledged the autonomy of science, economics, culture and politics: 'created things and societies themselves enjoy their own laws and values which must be gradually deciphered, put to use, and regulated by men'.[13] Again, as in Islam, this made the pursuit of knowledge and the use of reason, an integral part of the Christian vocation and human development, not as it were part of some 'secular' and non-religious domain. In *Populorum Progressio* is found just such a critical preliminary decipherment, notable in that the Pope attempted to analyse causes before proposing solutions. And prominent amongst the causes are those in the realm of structures. Pope Paul VI demands structural changes, 'bold transformations in which the present order of things will be entirely renewed or rebuilt' (Dorr 1983: 139–143). In this sense any radicalism in Catholic development agencies does not require explanation outside of official Church teaching, and should not be misinterpreted, as it frequently was, as a result of socialist or communist infiltration. The rationale behind such changes was simply that 'the economy should be at the service of man', and that 'the universal social bonds of the human family requires everyone to commit themselves to the promotion of development'. Schumacher, a Buddhist, reflected this theme in his catchy phrase 'economics as if people matter' (Schumacher 1973).

What makes *Populorum Progressio* a seminal document is that it sets out unequivocally the responsibility of the Christian community to work for development, and critically repudiates false contemporary approaches to development such as economism. The response to this green light was immediate: the growth of Catholic development agencies and justice and peace commissions, what was to become a widespread and global lay movement. These bodies, many founded at the beginning of the 1960s – the Catholic Institute for International Relations took its name in 1965 and developed from the wartime Sword of the Spirit – gained momentum and popular support gradually influencing the life of the Church by promoting and enacting, rather than merely teaching, Catholic Social Doctrine.

Populorum Progressio was 'political' in a number of matters. There is a clear rejection of colonial and neo-colonial solutions to problems of poverty and injustice. All peoples and nations have the right to be 'artisans of their own destiny'. Pope Paul VI directly quotes Lebret: 'We do not believe in separating the economic from the human, nor development from the civilizations in which its exists' (Lebret 1961). Life itself is described as a 'vocation' to development and fulfilment – but always in particular cultures and societies. In other words, *people* develop themselves; others cannot do it for them, and for this they need literacy and education. Thereby the notion of trusteeship is smuggled back in and not, as first seems, done away with; the educated elite is clearly seen as leading the process of development – something that was in the process of being actively challenged around the world in national democratic revolutions.

The core Catholic understanding of integral development is set out somewhat clumsily in paragraphs 14–23 of the encyclical and is called 'transcendent humanism'. The meaning of this is spelt out in concrete examples that describe 'less human conditions' and 'more human conditions' presenting integral development as a journey of transformation for individuals, peoples and nations. The end and purpose of this journey, its teleology, is clear. 'By reason of his union with Christ, the source of life, man attains to a new fulfilment of himself, to a transcendent humanism which gives him his greatest possible perfection: this is the highest goal of personal development'. Marx's idea of 'free development' has an analogical teleology. Both have a clear sense of the instrumental and the final in human development (Cowen and Shenton 1996: 449–450).[14]

Much of specific content of *Populorum Progressio,* for example, its emphasis on unequal power relations and fair trade, seems uncontentious today. Indeed, the recent campaign by all the development agencies for fair trade, *Make Poverty History,* takes up precisely these issues. Bearing in mind that 30 years have since elapsed, the Pastoral Constitution's emphases have proved remarkably well judged. Where the document remains most prophetic is in its reiteration of the Catholic tradition of an economics of 'enough', the theme that there can be too much as well as too little. 'Less than human conditions?' the encyclical lists: 'The material poverty of those who lack the bare necessities of life, and the moral poverty of those who are deformed by selfishness'.[15] In one instance what this challenge means in practice is spelt out rhetorically in unusual detail. 'Are we ready to pay higher taxes, are we ready to pay more for imported goods which are fairly traded?'[16]

Aquinas' notion of *superflua,* surplus wealth that is owed to the poor by right- (because *ta koina,* the common goods of creation, are for all) forms the basis of this call to redistribution. It is reflected in the repeated reference to the 'common heritage of all mankind' and 'the universal destination of the goods of the earth' in Catholic writing, and forms a radical limitation in Catholic tradition to any absolute right to private property (Linden 2004: 151–152). Echoes of 'enough' are found in Pope John Paul II's concept of 'superdevelopment': 'an excessive availability of every kind of material goods for the benefit of certain social groups'. This 'easily makes people slaves of 'possession' and of immediate gratification, with no other horizon than the multiplication or replacement of the things already owned with those still better'.[17]

No less important for the evolution of the thinking of Catholic development agencies has been the influence of Latin American theology. An important contribution of the Catholic Institute for International Relations (CIIR) was to promote this theology as an ideology of development from the 1970s. Its most important official elaboration came in the form of the deliberations of the Latin American Bishops at Medellin in 1968 and Puebla in 1979. Their pastoral priority to draw closer to the poor in charity and solidarity, not least by denouncing injustice and oppression, was highlighted in the famous phrase of the Puebla Conference that echoed around the world: 'We affirm the need for conversion on the part of the whole Church to a preferential option for the poor, an option aimed at their integral liberation' (CIIR 1980). This preferential love rooted in imitation of Jesus of Nazareth's life, ministry and teaching amongst the excluded of his day, demanded both resistance to what John Paul II calls 'structures of sin' and the eradication of poverty by positive local measures and programmes.[18]

Attempts to work for the universal common good and human development necessarily involved as their primary dynamic a process of 'integral liberation' that was partly political because of the oppressive conditions under which huge numbers of people were suffering. Evangelization therefore made specific demands on the Church that included and subsumed 'the duty to proclaim the liberation of millions of human beings ... the duty of assisting the birth of this liberation, of giving witness to it, of ensuring that it is complete', an agenda set out in the encyclical *Evangelii Nuntiandi* in 1975. The theological concept of development was incontrovertibly political.

Despite the ambivalence, not to say hostility of Pope John Paul II – his experience of eastern Europe is obviously critical here – to some of the proponents of liberation theology, his contribution to thinking on development has not been negligible. One important contribution has been to elaborate some of the moral implications of the theme of interdependence. Reflecting on the low price of goods imported by the industrialized North he underlines the moral responsibility of the consumer. Using the metaphor of the 'indirect employer' who shares responsibility for the low wages of the worker employed – by a 'direct' employer – in the product's country of origin, he raised fundamental trade issues.[19] But it is the idea of solidarity that gets the most extended treatment:

> When interdependence becomes recognised in this way, the correlative response as a moral and social attitude, as a 'virtue' is solidarity. This then is not a feeling of vague compassion or shallow distress at the misfortunes of so many people, both near and far. On the contrary, it is a firm and persevering determination to commit oneself to the common good; that is to say to the good of all and of each individual, because we are really responsible for all.[20]

Solidarity is thus a *habitus* in Aquinas' sense, amongst other things, the habitual practice of resistance to structural sin, a significant ethical underpinning to the quest for development.

Solidarity is demanded not with some abstract universal 'humankind' but with persons in societies with different cultures and religions. So solidarity necessarily entails dialogue. The often heard plea that the Church must be 'the voice of the voiceless' is fine as far as it goes; but amongst some Catholic organizations in the past it sometimes went too far. The poor have perfectly good voice if they are enabled to express it and to adopt a platform of sufficient strength to be heard and heeded. And when the 'poor' are asked, rather than told, what they need, the answer is often not what development Trustees and practitioners wish to hear. The World Bank project 'Voices of the Poor' which attempted to listen to the needs of diverse poor communities evoked responses that surprised many in the World Bank. Poor, rural Muslim women, for example, wanted as their top priority 'health' and 'to learn how to pray'. For many it will be surprising that this shocked the development establishment, and some measure of the impact of the prevailing ideological blinkers (Alkire 2004: 90).

In summary the Catholic concept of integral development is constituted both by human rights based and directly theologically based discourse, by faith and by reason. It can be described in terms of working for the common good, in a personal, social and political morality – the 'ethical action' of Maurice Blondel who influenced Maritain and the French theologians at the Second Vatican Council – and as a spirituality of justice, articulated most notably by liberation theologians such as Gustavo Gutierrez and drawing on deep biblical roots. It is a rich vein in contemporary Catholic faith and life, and essential to understand in any evaluation of Catholic development agencies.

It also entails precise – 'autonomous' – prescriptions about process: how development might best be achieved in different societies, whether, to give some examples at random, by the elimination of the crippling burden of national debt, reform of financial institutions, and/or by promoting the central role of women as agents of change and development. Such prescriptions for action form the substance of development theory and practice and are obviously shared with the 'secular development community'. The Catholic agencies, notably the Catholic Fund for Overseas Development (CAFOD), have played a positive, pioneering and relatively successful role in advocacy for debt reduction internationally but, with some notable exceptions, lagged behind 'secular' agencies in the promotion of women as leaders of development. Likewise, the emphases of liberation theology have tended to be anarchist in the sense of neglecting any elaborated theory about the role of the state and political parties in development, and assuming, in practice though not in theory, a Trusteeship role for a non-governmental elite. This anti-statism in the United Kingdom has partly been a consequence of the legal charitable status of development agencies.

What is incontestable is that the development agencies of the Catholic Church around the world have played a major role in development in the mainstream cultures of their countries, not to mention witnessing to the Church's option for the poor in a striking way. Their vision, of course, has not invariably been shared throughout the Catholic Church. This important political role is jeopardized today more by the proliferation of 'emergencies' and disaster relief, skewing the priorities of work, than by the increasingly warm embrace of government.

Theory and practice 1980–2006

The Catholic development agencies did not sit down and read papal encyclicals and then decide on their priorities and how to talk about their work. But there is nonetheless a remarkable interaction between theory and practice. CIIR, for example, was not formally within the hierarchical structures of the Catholic Church – except for the Presidency constitutionally held by the Cardinal Archbishop of Westminster – but managed to sustain a degree of creative ambivalence in its relationship to it that was a little reminiscent of the Christian Institute in South Africa. Its aims were to promote international understanding of social justice and, to this end, create educational study programmes within the framework of the Church, and to promote volunteer service overseas in developing countries. The latter involved becoming part of the secular British Volunteer Programme and the former was interpreted in an activist mode by its small young staff and underpinned by its first General Secretary, Mildred Nevile whose training had been in the Cardijn methodology of the Young Christian Students (YCS) , known often simply as 'See-Judge-Act'. As the 'Catholic contact' with the British government and sending agencies, CIIR was given Central America as its special region though many volunteers were sent to Africa, and several other countries in an original non-governmental programme. CIIR, therefore, inherited Nicaragua where many of the theological ambivalences of Catholicism were worked out with dramatic political clarity. It also inherited the experience from Sword of the Spirit days of having been a recruitment service for Catholic schools in Africa, and had served on the UK national committee of the 1962 inter-governmental Freedom from Hunger campaign (Walsh 1980).

Its distinction from the other major 1960s Catholic initiative, CAFOD, founded in 1962 around a Catholic national family fast day promoted by Catholic women's organizations, is significant. CAFOD's governing body is chaired by a bishop appointed by the Catholic Episcopal Conference of England and Wales as are its board of trustees. Its goal is to promote social justice and human development as an institutional Church witness to Christian faith and Gospel values. As such it initially acted primarily as a bridge for development aid between the Catholic Church in United Kingdom and the Church in developing countries (Nevile 1999: 99–121).

CIIR on other hand described itself as an *independent* lay organization – in other words, it had no formal institutional Church role – and was not involved in the transfer of aid overseas. It formed a bridge with a wide variety of non-governmental organizations (NGOs), many of which were Catholic, for example, Justice and Peace commissions, selected on the basis of their commitment to social justice and development. These included organizations more overtly political in nature than would have been possible for, say, CAFOD, and indeed for most of the other European international agencies in the Catholic grouping, Coopération Internationale pour le Développement et la Solidarité (CIDSE). This was not simply a matter of their status in the Church but also their relationship with government; MISEREOR, for example, received substantial state funding in Germany and believed it had to remain broadly within the framework of German foreign policy on sensitive issues.

CIIR in its volunteer programme also contained within its structures a non-Catholic department reliant on, and amply funded by, the British government's overseas development ministry. This internal heterogeneity forced on CIIR a translation of language between Catholic and 'secular' discourse, NGO and government policy speak, and a perennial struggle over the relative merits and meaning of secularity in development. This was alternately stimulating and debilitating, in short a microcosm of the wider situation faced by the Catholic Church in 'secular' Europe. For those with a 'sacramental imagination' secularity meant simply a Catholic acknowledgement of the 'autonomy' of development as a process, not an assertion of a hybrid identity for CIIR (Hanvey 2005: 63–65). Those who wished to leave out the second half of St Therese of Lisieux's famous saying, 'we must act as if everything depended upon us and then believe that all the success came from God', were at liberty to do so.

CIIR pioneered political advocacy and engagement with government policy making during the 1970s. In April 1974, during the fascist Caetano regime, the Portuguese Ambassador to London complained to the Cardinal Archbishop about publications in CIIR's *Comment* series on Portuguese Africa. But on the whole the Catholic bishops were happy to have an 'unofficial' semi-detached and radical Catholic voice that they could claim or denounce as they saw fit. By the 1980s many of the development agencies were building up their own 'policy departments' and CAFOD, led by a former CIIR Latin America desk specialist steeped in liberation theology, Julian Filochowski, was no exception drawing on biblical and papal sources to legitimize and promote highly effective campaigns amongst its Catholic constituency.

The particular advantage of the Catholic agencies was that they had the elaborated corpus of Catholic Social Teaching to draw on, as well as biblical sources, as their language of development and transformation. So the movement from the thinking of the 1950s to that of the 1960s, essentially one from a charity-led to biblical justice-led forms of action could be – though not always effectively enough – strongly and officially underpinned by theology and authoritative teaching. This journey was less easily charted by the Protestant agencies such as Christian Aid that had to rely solely on the interpretation of biblical sources while answering to a wide range of interpretative theological traditions in the ecumenical movement.

The Catholic agencies could situate themselves in relation to an organic body of teaching, some key elements of which are sketched out above. And an organization such as the CIIR, on the margins, could within the framework of liberation theology, handle building bridges with liberation movements in Latin America, Asia and southern Africa, where official Church teaching and action was sometimes more 'political' in the sense of wishing to sustain relationships with unjust and tyrannical governments in order to safeguard the Church's institutional interests, thus vacillating on the merits of revolutionary activity. Nicaragua is a notable example (Mulligan 1991).

Conclusion

The spirituality of charity and justice that informed, and informs, the development discourse of the Christian agencies was, and is, more in tune with that of the majority of poor recipients of development aid from governmental and NGO donors, than the secularity of other agencies. It is doubtful if development is a particularly meaningful concept for the rural and newly urbanized poor, and issues of poverty are often debated within the idiom of religious symbols, narratives and duties, particularly those relating to justice in the divine dispensation. This is no less true of the Muslim development agencies such as Islamic Relief, Muslim Aid and Muslim Hands in the United Kingdom, perhaps more true. For an increasing number of staff of Christian agencies, particularly in policy departments, are not believers, while this is not the case for the Muslims.

Where Catholic development thinking has been less successful since the 1970s is in elaborating its tradition theoretically, perhaps because of its fraught history of difficulty with liberal concepts of freedom. The innovative work of Amartya Sen, now reflected in the annual UN Human Development Reports, has rested in his vision that human development is essentially a process of expanding human freedoms and capabilities, rather than supplies of commodities, and his keen sense of evaluating the instrumental means to this end. This sets an agenda for the developmental state as provider of entitlements. In different populations, different bundles of entitlements, though, make possible different activities, 'functionings' and abilities. Moreover, a person's entitlements in practice depend crucially on their labour power, in other words, whether they can get a paid job. The major implication of the capabilities approach is thus a particular set of priorities for the state directed at raising the level of employment. It goes without saying, though, that particular forms of paid labour, child labour, sweat shops and so on, drastically *reduce* human freedoms and capabilities. So the Trusteeship question has not gone away. Catholic Social Teaching, strong on the role of work and trades unions, also with a clear understanding of what are instrumental and final goals of development, has some interesting resonances with Sen's understanding of human well-being based on expanding capabilities (Sen 1980).

This is perhaps not surprising. While Sen develops some of Marx's ideas about 'free development' he is nonetheless influenced by Martha Nussbaum's Aristotelianism. Catholicism with its Thomist synthesis of Aristotle still underpinning much of its teaching draws from the same wells. In this sense, the fact that Sen is a 'secular' thinker is probably the most trivial point to be made about his seminal work. For there is much evidence that Sen's 'freedom' is not a freedom of self against others rather an openness at critical stages of development to the freedom to seek the good of the other, and some final good, as an evolving capability, or what Aquinas would call a virtue (Sen 1999).

The tendency by the developmentalist elites, the Trustees of development, to consider 'secular' language as normative rather than instrumentally specialized, and faith-based development agencies as, therefore, interesting or irritating marginal players in the struggle for human emancipation from poverty and necessity is thus an ideological device that is being increasingly challenged today. Historically there has been a process of translation between God-talk and development talk, in both directions, a creative dialogue.

But in a fast moving globalized economy neither is adequately dealing ethically with the question of what is being destroyed and what is being put in its place in the global process, and how this process can be controlled in the interests of peoples and populations. The governmental Trustees of development are in systemic failure. Despite a rhetoric of cultural sensitivity, they neither allow those whose cultures are suffering severe losses in the name of development to decide what those losses should be, nor implement effective and comprehensive formulas for alleviating poverty and tackling ecological crisis. FBOs have a special responsibility in this regard. And, of course, the contemporary vision that development must now urgently rectify the impact of technological progress, man-made climate change, is one that would be entirely comprehensible to our religious Victorian forebears.

The gulf between the language and culture of popular religion, be it Christian or Muslim, and 'secular' premises of the majority of developmentalists is still large despite a decade of pleas to take religion seriously. There is a dearth of 'analogical imagination' and sympathy that can see complementarity and similarity in pluralist difference (Tracy 2000). After the secular madness of the twentieth century expressed in different forms of totalitarianism, humiliation, anger, violence and militarism are now clothing themselves in exclusive religious languages, negating all possibilities of development. The place of religious development FBOs and secular NGOs is now rightly together in a joint enterprise of advocacy of a different and radical meaning of human development. The categories 'religious' and 'secular', here as elsewhere, relate to forgetfulness not to commonality of purpose.

Notes

1. John Nurser (2005) cites Otto Frederick Nolde, Charles Malik, Max Warren, Eleanor Roosevelt, John Foster Dulles and Joseph Proskauer as amongst the key players.
2. William Cavanagh, unpublished paper, 'Violence, Religion and the State', 2003.
3. James Putzel and Alex Munthali 'HIV/AIDS and Leadership in Malawi', Report for DFID in Malawi makes the case for a focus on 'primal' religions.
4. Zizek Slavoj (2005) gives one such interesting critique. My experience in NGOs is that the incompatibility of the Trustees' prescriptive development with forms of cultural relativism, the denial of cultural loss in the process of development, allows the retention of incompatible goals and creates incoherent ethics.
5. St John Chrysostom wrote of the 'gentleness and mildness' of God as being the key qualities understood in the *imago*. *Homilies on Genesis* 8:6–8 translated R.C. Hill in *Fathers of the Church* Catholic University of America Press, 1990, 109. Pope Benedict XV wrote of not compromising 'the equilibrium of nature, the fruit of order in creation, rather to take care to pass on to future generations a world capable of feeding itself', see Message to the Director-General of the FAO on World Food Day, 2005. Comparable verses from the Holy Qur'an: Al-Rahman, 16; Loqman, 20; Al-Ja thiath 13; Baqarah, 22; Ghafer, 64; Naba, 6; Hud, 61; Nisa, 1.
6. Rowan Williams (2005) takes up the theme from the position of the artist's openness to transcendence.
7. *Evangelii Nuntiandi* 31 'one cannot dissociate the plan of creation from the plan of redemption. The latter plan touches the very concrete situations of injustice to be combated and justice to be restored'. Paul VI, 1974.
8. This did not, of course, gain universal assent. It was strongly attacked as naïve in the United States of America in the right wing Catholic *National Review* and seen by some to be an assault on national sovereignty in its call for a world authority seen as open promotion of the United Nations. This fierce opposition to the United Nations is found in powerful dispensationalist and Pentecostal groups influential in the Christian Right in the United States of America today.
9. Cardinal Walter Kaspar 'The Pastoral Constitution 'Gaudium et Spes'', paper presented at Worth Abbey, Conference on Gaudium et Spes 40 Years On, 4–7 July 2005.
10. Ibid.

11. *Populorum Progressio* Pope Paul VI, 1967, 3.
12. *Paroles de l'Eglise catholique sur le developpement*, French Justice and Peace Commission, 1990, 75.
13. Gaudium et Spes, 36.
14. Populorum Progressio, 21.
15. Ibid.
16. Ibid., p. 47.
17. *Sollicitudo Rei Socialis* John Paul II, 1987, 28.
18. Ibid., 36.
19. *Laborem Exercens* John Paul II, 1981, 17.
20. Sollicitudo Rei Socialis, 38.

Bibliography

Alkire, S. (2004), 'Culture, Poverty and External Intervention' in V. Rao and M. Walton (eds) *Culture and Public Action* (Stanford, California, Stanford University Press).

Chadwick, O. (1957), *From Bossuet to Newman: The Idea of Doctrinal Development* (Cambrige, Cambridge University Press).

CIIR (1980), *Puebla Conclusions. Evangelisation at Present and in the Future* (London, Catholic Institute for International Relations, CIIR), No.1134.

Cowen, M. P. and Shenton, R. W. (1996), *Doctrines of Development* (London, Routledge).

Dorr, D. (1983), *Option for the Poor* (London, Gill and Macmillan).

Goulet, D. (1980), 'Development Experts: The One-Eyed Giants', *World Development*, 8, pp. 481–489.

Hanvey, J. (2005), *On the Way to Life: Contemporary Culture and Theological Development as a Framework for Catholic Education, Catechesis and Formation* (London, Heythrop Institute for Religion, Ethics and Public Life), pp. 63–65.

Kerr, F. (2002), *After Aquinas: Versions of Thomism* (Oxford, Blackwell).

Lebret, L-J. (1961), *Dynamique concrete de developpement* (Paris, Paris).

Linden, I. (2004), *A New Map of the World* (London, DLT).

Mulligan, J. (1991), *The Nicaraguan Church and the Revolution* (Kansas City, MO, Sheed and Ward).

Murray, R. (2000), 'The Image of God: Delegated and Responsible Authority', *Priests and People* February, pp. 49–54.

Nevile, M. (1999), 'The Changing Nature of Catholic Organisations' In Michael Hornsby-Smith (ed.) *Catholics in England 1950–2000 Historical and Sociological Perspectives* (London, Cassell), pp. 99–121.

Nurser, J. (2005), *For All Peoples and Nations: Christian Churches and Human Rights* (Geneva, WCC Publications).

Rosen, L. (2002), *The Culture of Islam Changing Aspects of Contemporary Muslim Life* (Chicago, University of Chicago Press).

Ruston, R. (2004), *Human Rights and the Image of God* (Canterbury, SCM Press).

Schumacher, E. F. (1973), *Small is Beautiful: A Study of Economics as if People Mattered* (London, Blond and Briggs).

Sen, A. (1980), 'Equality of What', In S. McMurren (ed.) *The Tanner Lectures on Human Values* (Salt Lake City, University of Utah Press).

Sen, A. (1999), *Development and Freedom* (Oxford, Oxford University Press).

Slavoj, Z. (2005), 'Against Human Rights' *New Left Review*, July/August, pp. 115–131.

Thomas, S. M. (2005), *The Global Resurgence of Religion and the Transformation of International Relations* (New York, Palgrave Macmillan).

Tracy, D. (2000), *The Analogical Imagination, Christian Theology and the Culture of Pluralism* (New York, Crossroads).

Walsh, M. (1980), *From Sword to Ploughshare: Sword of the Spirit to Catholic Institute for International Relations 1940–1980* (London, CIIR).

Williams, R. (2005), *Grace and Necessity: Reflections on Art and Love* (Harrisburg: Morehouse; London, Continuum).

Wilson, C. 'Knowledge and Immortality in Spinoza and Mulla Sadra' www.muslimphilosophy.com

5
The Spirit of Brotherhood: Christianity and Ujamaa in Tanzania

Michael Jennings

Introduction

Looking at Africa today, it is hard to imagine that in the early 1960s, the place of Christianity in Africa was believed by some to be under threat. As Paul Gifford has written, 'Thirty years ago, it was commonly thought that Christianity in independent Africa would become ever less significant, because it was associated so closely with colonialism' (Gifford 1994: 514). At the end of Empire, the place of the Christian Churches in sub-Saharan Africa was far from secure. Its identification with the colonial regime left it vulnerable to charges of complicity with the excesses and authoritarian tendencies of Empire. Its dominance in social welfare provision was about to be challenged by the nationalist drive of the post-independence governments. The European-dominated upper echelons of the Church seemed increasingly vulnerable to charges of failure to Africanize.[1] These dire predictions seem almost absurd today in the face of the massive rise of Pentecostal Churches across sub-Saharan Africa, the role played by Christian leaders in pro-democracy movements in the continent and the increasing global strength of African Christian leaders.

The Christian Churches in many developing countries of the nineteenth and up to the mid-twentieth centuries played an important role in building up the infrastructure of a modern state through their participation (and in some cases dominance) in social welfare provision. The significance of their role has diminished since the 1960s, as the state, and then private and voluntary secular agencies scaled up their action in service delivery. Nevertheless, the Churches remain active in this area, but this reality has been largely obscured by development discourse.

This chapter examines the role of the Churches in Tanzania in the 1960s, arguing that this was a critical period both for relations between the African state and the Christian Churches (and faith communities and organizations more widely), as well as for the emergence of a distinctly development-oriented (rather than welfare-focused) approach. In this decade, as Linden notes in his chapter, the Churches started to redefine their social mission in relation to the new post-colonial world which was starting to emerge, and to the growing development discourse signalled by Kennedy's announcement of the first decade of development. However, whilst Linden focuses on theological and doctrinal debates at the centre, this chapter takes as its focus the periphery – the Church in the field, as it were. It argues that attempts to redefine the role of the Church in society took their lead not just from a new discourse emerging from, for example, the Vatican, but from the very real and practical dilemmas of how the Church should manage the transition from colonial-era institution to post-colonial partner of a new, Africanized government.

However, in the case of Tanzania, this transition came at a cost. In this period, both Catholic and Protestant Churches were able to redefine their relationship with the government, ensuring a position of trusted 'partner'. Both saw the philosophy of rural socialist development, *Ujamaa*, as reflecting a renewed Christian social mission. But in doing so, they became complicit in its implementation, and in the gradual, yet unmistakable, creeping authoritarianism of the state. Far from acting as guardians of civil society – a voice challenging the state – they became part of a broader development front that effectively closed off avenues for dissent and opposition.

During the colonial period, Christian faith organizations played a major role in social welfare and social development (see, for example, Jennings 2007). The bulk of medical services to Africans were provided by mission-run clinics and hospitals. Even at the end of the colonial era, mission dominance in health provision was clear. At the end of 1961, missions ran 287 hospitals, dispensaries and clinics across Tanzania, compared to just 73 government centres.[2] Mission dominance of education was overwhelming. As well as such services, missions also offered training in industrial skills, agriculture, hygiene and so forth. They acted as refuges in times of disaster, distributed food relief and provided medical care during major epidemics. Without the work of the missions, Imperial claims to be meeting the social needs of their territories would have rang even more hollow.

The strength of the Churches in welfare provision reflected, in part, their capacity to reach down to the individual through the networks of missions, dioceses and parishes. The colonial state could never hope to replicate this reach. It also rested upon a sense that Christian leaders, whether European, or increasingly African, held a degree of cultural and social authority in their areas that created a sense of local legitimacy.

But whilst the power of the missions in their local communities, and their dominance over social welfare position, gave them a certain power within the colonial administration, it was not a power that could be taken for granted, nor was it complete. Missions were viewed with suspicion, with scepticism over their claims to represent their communities, and with concern over their claims for ever-greater shares of territorial funds. The dominance of the Church in colonial society, limited as it was, had been fought for, and continued to be struggled over. In the 1920s and 1930s, despite a recognition of the role played by missions in health-service delivery, the colonial regime remained wary of providing state-funding for fear that it would create unwanted precedents (Jennings 2007). In the early 1950s, plans were drawn up by the Colonial Office in London to consider nationalizing health and education services: 'hospital services ... will evolve on a similar pattern to that in the UK where hospitals, originally created and maintained exclusively by charitable institutions, were eventually absorbed into a unified national hospital service'.[3] It was a long-term aim, but one nevertheless that challenged the dominance of the Church in this hitherto protected space. The privileged position of the Church in colonial Tanganyika was, then, by no means unassailable.

The coming of independence did not, then, signal the beginning of the Church's involvement in development. It had been involved in aspects of social development for at least 60 years (and in some cases significantly longer). Nor had its relationship with the colonial state been as clear-cut as has often been assumed. It was neither a colonial stooge, nor a champion of African nationalism, but occupied a space of its own (albeit one that overlapped considerably with the colonial re-gime). The arrival of independence inevitably changed the nature of that space. The Church could no longer function in the same way. It needed to look to a new form of participation in the social and political life of Tanzania in order to maintain the privileged (but not unchal-lenged) position it had enjoyed during the colonial period.

From welfare to social change: the shifting role of faith engagement in development

From the beginning of the post-colonial era, the Churches were deeply involved in Tanzanian development: they ran small-scale projects;

provided funding for services and schemes in their dioceses; channeled funding from external (international) agencies (largely Christian, but increasingly from the 1970s from secular sources too) into local development; sat on local and central government committees planning development. A brief snapshot of activity in 1963 gives some indication of the scale of activity. In Mbeya Region, south-west Tanzania, some 40,232 adults were being taught in literacy classes run by Catholic, Moravian and Swedish missions. The missions also ran domestic science schools and provided technicians for village-based projects. One bishop in the region funded the construction of a road, whilst the White Fathers paid for a qualified nurse/midwife to work in a newly constructed clinic. In Mara Region in the north, Catholic, Mennonite, Seventh Day Adventist missions and the Church Missionary Society ran adult literacy classes, women's groups (in collaboration with the government Community Development Department) and promoted and organized 'self-help' small-scale projects. The Catholic Church in Mara worked closely with the local government Regional Development Committee, proposing schemes to establish a domestic science school; a training facility for agricultural work; and the establishment of community loan groups to make credit available to small-scale producers.[4] The same story was being repeated across the country. Churches and missions were organizing local development, participating in official schemes, and providing assistance in the villages and scattered settlements across rural Tanzania.

With the coming of independence, the Christian Churches were faced with a new challenge: how to adapt their long-tradition of service to their new political masters and perhaps more importantly, how to re-forge links to the state broken with the departure of the colonial regime?

In 1962, the Christian Council of Tanzania (CCT)[5], the umbrella organization of member Protestant Churches (primarily Anglican, Lutheran, Mennonite and Moravian), launched the Rapid Social Change Study (RSCS). The study was intended to serve as a platform from which a major shift in Church policy on its engagement in society and with the state could be launched. It was an attempt to fundamentally reshape the nature of the Church's engagement with society as it sought to create a new role for itself in the changed environment of post-colonial Tanzania. Entitled 'The Christian Responsibility in the Midst of National Development', the study was to consider Church policy across six areas: the Christian contribution to society; the responsibility of the Church to support national economic development; the response of the

Church to urban poverty and social problems; the role of the Church in rural and agricultural development; the response of the Church to changes in the roles of women and the family; and lastly the impact of social change on the Church itself.[6]

Three main themes run through the RSCS' focus of study. First, the nature of society, and the Church's role within it. Moving from an understanding of the 'theological and biblical basis of the Christian responsibility for society', the study sought to uncover 'the present attitude of the Churches in Tanganyika towards community, society and social change', and undertake a fundamental re-examination of the appropriate form of 'Stewardship' the Church should hold. Second, the study examined 'the various ways of understanding the relationship between the Church and state'. In particular, it called for consideration of 'the Christian responsibility in political life'; 'the Christian responsibility in legislation'; and the 'churches' cooperation with government in the economic effort'. Third, it called for 'an examination ... of Christian work in rural areas', reflecting a concern that the Church needed to devise a new form within which to achieve its social ambitions. Such examination should include, it continued, a focus on 'the churches cooperation with Area and Village councils' and 'new forms of Church action in ... technical assistance'.[7]

By 1963, the CCT was ready to call upon its member Churches to reappraise the way they conceived their role in society. The preliminary report on 'The Christian Contribution to a Dynamic Society in Tanganyika' noted the need to move beyond the traditional focus on 'individual ethics and morality' towards engagement with the 'great range of social problems':

> In the past the Churches have engaged in medical, educational and various welfare services in which they have demonstrated their concern for man but generally they have regarded these as secondary to the work of evangelism. Today in our situation we need to widen the scope of Christian concern and action to match the new opportunities for showing forth the love of God to our neighbours in the midst of a new nation.[8]

The old colonial models of welfare service provision had to be replaced with a more engaged model of service, one more closely linked to the government's commitment to social development and social change.

This shift to a broader-based response was reiterated in 1968: 'Traditionally, the Churches have built and maintained schools and hospitals.... Now the time has come to help equip our people for rural development.'[9] CCT member Churches, its Relief and Service Division reported, were now designating increased numbers of personnel and capital resources to rural development and training a rural-based leadership in the villages.[10]

But the RSCS was not just about reshaping the response of the Church to the needs of Tanzania's citizens and their own parishioners. It was also part of a strategy of defining how the Church should respond to the new government. It reflected a perception of the need to formulate a new role for the Church in relation to both the people and the state. As part of the study group looking at 'the Christian contribution to a dynamic society', key questions it sought to address included 'the various ways of understanding the relationship between the Church and state', 'the Christian responsibility in political life' and its role in 'legislation'. The RSCS also sought to understand in what way the Church should cooperate with the government in economic policy (particularly over the issue of socialism).[11] The relationship between Church and state was not only understood at the central level: it also considered how to ensure effective cooperation with local government structures, especially village and district council level.[12]

The response of the CCT to independence was, then, to attempt a root and branch re-definition of its role in Tanzania: to move away from colonial models of welfare-based service in collaboration with the state, towards a broader and deeper connection with the state's national developmental objectives. In other words, faith-based organizations (FBOs) in Tanzania sought not to distance themselves from the government, but to further entrench their linkages with it, to tie their policy more explicitly to that of the state (an effort that was to have important consequences for the notion of the Church as civil society actor, as will be discussed later). This was reflected at two levels: the day-to-day engagement of faith-based groups with development at the local level; and at the organizational level of the Church – the creation of specific instruments for supporting that development, and the attempt to create a common (within the specific denominational structures) ideology of development.

Promoting social development

In 1966, the CCT noted that the involvement of the Church in development in Tanzania was 'both heartening and astounding'.[13] There was much to validate this assessment. The Church was the largest of the non-official agencies working in social and economic development.

The Churches at all levels were participating in local schemes, funding small projects and undertaking a range of interventions across the country. In 1972, the CCT was running three cattle projects in villages across the country, a youth farming scheme in Msalato, constructing a Medical Assistant training centre at Bumbuli Hospital, undertaking several water projects, as well as seeking funding for the establishment of six chapels in new Ujamaa villages. In addition, a list of new projects agreed to in that year included: ten schemes for constructing, extending or rehabilitating dispensaries and clinics across the country; five projects setting up training and education facilities (two dedicated to agricultural training, and two for business and commerce); four water-supply projects in rural villages (bringing water pipes to over 15 villages and over 35,000 people); three post-school level skills training; and the construction of three community centres, amongst other schemes.[14] In Northern Tanzania the YMCA was assisting the Maasai cultivate over 800 acres of wheat and maize. In 1975, the CCT was running 124 development projects, and had received an income of Tanzanian Shillings (Tsh) 33,894,724 for its development work from its donor agencies ($4,691,764).[15] The Evangelical Lutheran Church in Tanzania (ELCT – one of the major actors in the CCT) was running 65 projects in 1973: 27 medical, 18 educational, 14 'social', and 6 agricultural schemes.[16] The Catholic Church was similarly deeply engaged in development activity. In the decade following 1969, with financial support from the international Catholic organization International Cooperation for Socio-Economic Development (CIDSE), Catholic Churches in Tanzania ran 1,217 projects, supported by $30,310,300.[17]

This represents, importantly, only those projects overseen by the main Church organizations. Much Christian-based development activity, especially in the 1960s and early 1970s, was not, in fact, run through the central coordinating agencies of either the major Protestant or Catholic Churches. Thus, the scale of faith-based activity was substantially higher than official records suggest. Religious and lay officials sat on local village or district official development committees, set up local training centres or agricultural schemes, supported construction of roads, schools, hospitals and community centres, provided outreach and extension services. In Moshi, in the shadows of Mount Kilimanjiro, Bishop Joseph Sipendi set aside 450 acres for the creation of an agricultural training centre in 1974. The centre was to train local villagers in best agricultural practice and nutrition; and agricultural extension officers to follow-up former students and provide outreach work in the diocesan villages. The scheme also envisioned the establishment of a small-scale industries centre.[18] The Development Office of the Catholic Archdiocese of Tabora, sought funding in 1977 for a project to construct 20 wells to provide clean water for villages across 2 parishes. In 1981, the scheme was expanded to construct an additional 100 wells. The Archdiocese's 3 Year Development Plan (1976/79) planned for 21 projects across 4 main sectors: water projects (in addition to the 20 wells, the construction of a water reservoir in Kaliua, provision of a clean water supply to Ushirombo, and 4 other projects to provide piped water); health projects (the construction of three dispensaries and one Maternity and Child Welfare clinic); eight education projects (mainly training centres); and three industrial/agricultural production schemes.[19] In 1970, the Sisters of St Theresa developed a cooperative farm on mission land near to Bukoba township, whilst the Diocese of Kigoma set up a carpentry training workshop to boost the livelihoods opportunities for rural dwellers in 1972.[20]

Creating an infrastructure for development intervention

Throughout the 1960s and 1970s, faith-based development work was largely based upon the initiative and activities of individual Churches and parishes. It was they who set up schemes, provided the funding (or sought external funding), established management and oversight structures and so forth. Nevertheless, the authorities and central structures increasingly sought, in this same period, to establish a degree of conformity and coordination over 'Church-based' development. Both the Protestant Christian Council of Tanzania, and the Catholic Tanzanian Episcopal Conference (TEC) created specific departments within Church structures to coordinate development activity, and attempted through these structures to create an ideology of development, a set of principles to which all constituent elements could subscribe to.

During the colonial period, no dedicated central structure for coordinating Church-based development within the Protestant Church community existed. In 1961, the Project Planning Committee was formally established as part of the CCT administrative structure to fill this gap. Its membership consisted of representatives from all member Churches, but a degree of central control was assured by placing the Chair with a representative of the CCT administration, and appointing the Executive Secretary from the Evangelical Lutheran Council of Tanzania. The General Secretary of the CCT served as an advisor without vote.

The Committee did little in its first two years to impose central control over Church-based development, issuing little in the way of policy directives, and limiting its role to the formulation of vague guidelines and principles that might influence project selection.[21] As Church-based activity increased, the lacunae created by such a weak mechanism became increasingly apparent, and in 1963 a new structure was created: the Relief and Service Division (RSD) (Figure 5.1). Its role was both more clearly defined, and more pro-active than its predecessor, and represented a stronger assertion of the centre over the periphery in the question of who should be shaping faith-based development policy. Its task was to create a 'common ministry of service' through action across six key areas: to identify the needs of the people and the Churches; to advise members on available resources; to act as the fulcrum around which relationships between development agencies (Tanzanian and international) and the Church revolved; to establish a degree of conformity between the various initiatives and efforts of CCT members; and to provide assistance to Church-based projects in initiating and organizing schemes.[22] It was to receive project applications from individual Churches and recommend them for approval by the General Secretariat. It was also to take a more pro-active role in seeking to devise schemes and suggest individual Churches take them up.

Critical to the ability to establish dominance over the development planning process was the control the RSD could exert over securing and distributing funding from international donors. As early as 1961, the CCT recognized the importance of this. In response to a series of grants made to a number of missions made by the German Christian development agency, Bread for the World, the CCT called for all development funds to be channelled through itself.[23] By the mid-1960s, the World Council of Churches (WCC) and its member organizations were committed to funding only those projects which had been approved by the RSD and CCT General Secretariat, and to providing those funds through

Individual Church/Parish
↓
CCT Relief and Service Division
↓
CCT General Secretariat
↓
World Council of Churches
↓
WCC Member Agencies

Figure 5.1 CCT development structures, 1963–1975

Source: Michael Jennings, *Surrogates of the State: Oxfam and Development in Tanzania, 1961–79*, PhD thesis, London University, 1998, p. 156.

the CCT's structures. Whilst this did not prevent Churches seeking (or securing) external funding without recourse to the structures established by the CCT, it did narrow the opportunities for doing so. The British NGO Christian Aid, a member of the WCC, for example, noted that whilst it supported in principle a scheme submitted by the Diocese of Zanzibar and Dar es Salaam, 'as it had not had the blessing of the Council, we ought not to do anything about it'.[24]

The TEC had been established in 1957 as the official central organization for the Catholic Church. However, whilst Catholic Churches and missions, like their Protestant counterparts, were deeply involved in development activity throughout the period, no dedicated development agency was created within the TEC until 1971 when Caritas Tanzania was established. In common with the RSD, it was intended to function as a national coordinating body shaping the Catholic Church's overall development strategy, and to serve as an intermediary between individual dioceses and overseas donor agencies. It was charged with securing funds for development activity, to provide training, advisory and information services for the Catholic Church, and to promote development, welfare and relief activities within the Church.[25]

Unlike the CCT, which was an umbrella organization for a number of independent member Church organizations, Caritas functioned within a more rigid hierarchy of control. Operating from within the TEC, with its formal authority over diocesan and Church authorities, gave it a greater and firmer reach than the CCT enjoyed. This control was enhanced from 1973, when the Caritas structure was extended down to diocese (and even individual parish) level. The first such sub-national Caritas Committee was established in Tabora Diocese in 1976 (Figure 5.2).

What had propelled the Catholic Church to create a more rigid and professional structure for the coordination of development activity in

Tanzania Episcopal Conference
↓
Caritas Tanzania ←—→ Caritas Executive Committee
↓
Diocesan Caritas ←—→ Diocesan Caritas Committee
↓
Parish Caritas ←—→ Parish Executive Committee

Figure 5.2 Catholic development structures, 1976

Source: Adapted from 'Report on a Development Survey', Tabora Diocese, July–August 1976, p. 51. OxA Tan 136a.

the 1970s was not to boost the level of activity. The Church (of all denominations) was already the most significant non-official development actor in Tanzania by this stage. Rather it was a perceived need to more firmly establish control and direction over faith-based development. Moreover, this determination to increase the control of the centre was echoed in administrative reforms to CCT's own systems. In 1975, a second agency was created to operate alongside the RSD, the Service and Development Unit (SDU) (Figure 5.3). The Unit was to function as project manager from inception to completion: individual Church projects were to be sent to the SDU for advice and help in drafting funding applications; and the Unit would also act as project supervisor on behalf of the donor. The RSD under this new structure took on a more policy-oriented focus, responsible for drafting a national CCT development plan (closely linked to the government's own Five Year Development Plan objectives), and ensuring that individual Church plans were effectively coordinated to create this national strategy.[26]

Thus, during the 1970s, one can detect a Church-wide concern over the levels of control over development activity within the faith (or more specifically, Christian) sector. But why the concern? Other than the efficiencies of coordination of activity and maximizing the use of relatively scarce resources, was the concern to establish central control and dominance anything more than inter-institutional power-broking? Power was certainly an issue, but securing control at the centre mattered less for power-relations between the centre and periphery of Church structures, than for the implications it carried for the place of the Church within Tanzanian state and society. Development was not just an appropriate form of social ministry, it was a currency of power (just as welfare service provision had been for the mission sector in the

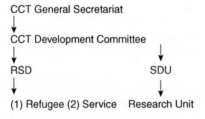

Figure 5.3   CCT development structures from 1975

Source: Michael Jennings, *Surrogates of the State Oxfam and Development in Tanzania*, 1961–79, PhD thesis, London University, 1998, p. 156.

colonial period), and a currency the Church was determined to utilize in re-establishing its position in the post-independence era.

Working with the state: the challenge of socialist development

The challenge for the Church (or rather, Churches) was not just how to impose a tighter central control over their constituent parts (looking down, as it were), but also to turn their gaze upwards, and consider how best to reformulate the relationship with the state. The coming of independence undermined the links between Church and state that had been present under colonial rule (links largely shaped by the Church's claim to be the main social welfare provider). The mission-based model of the colonial era was no longer appropriate to the changed conditions in which the new African government was determined to rid the country of its reliance on the former Imperial power. The Church was, then, in danger of losing its prestigious position in society. The RSCS, the attempts to create national Church development plans, and the discussions at all levels of the appropriate response of Christianity to the government's socialist development policy, were all part of the same process: the redefining of the place of the Church in independent Tanzania.

The links between the Church and post-independence government were not, of course, newly established following 1961. Although some senior members of the Church were wary of the nationalist movement and its leaders, fearing 'anti-white and communist elements in it'[27], close bonds between the new leadership and senior Church officials had been established during the colonial period, through the mission-education nationalist leaders had received, and through the role individual clerics played in the nationalist struggle. Nyerere, educated at a Catholic school in Tabora, where he later taught, forged close links with Catholic officials, and received financial and other supports from the Church prior to independence. The national Catholic newspaper, *Kiongozi*, was an unapologetic supporter of the Tanganyika Africa National Union (TANU – the main nationalist movement) in the late 1950s.[28]

But whilst close bonds existed, it is clear that the moment of independence defined a clear changing point in the relationship between the broad institution of the Church and the state. The departure of the British administration raised two immediate, and linked, questions: what role should the Church play in society (what, in other words, the notion of a 'social ministry' meant in the context of a nationalist government and newly independent nation?) and what were the risks to the Church of the increasing socialist rhetoric of that government? To a large extent, the answer to the second question shaped the response to the first: in reconciling itself, if not to socialism, then to the specific form of socialism offered by Nyerere's conception of Ujamaa, the Church sought to define its social ministry in terms of support for the government's development policy. To be a good Christian, by the mid-1960s, was to work with the government in developing the nation.

Nyerere's socialist principles were well known long before the official adoption of Ujamaa in 1967. Promulgated through speeches and publications, and through the support given to socialist experiments in the early 1960s (Jennings 2003), it was clear to Church officials that the spectre of socialism had to be confronted. Thus, even before the adoption of Ujamaa, the Church had begun the process of seeking to reconcile socialism and its own principles. The RSCS, for example, was in part an attempt to ask whether, and how, the Church could participate 'in building a socialist pattern of society.'[29] Van Bergen has characterized the response of the Church in the 1960s as a 'fear of a development towards communism'. Westerlund similarly notes an ingrained suspicion of Ujamaa within the Church, suggesting that Sunni Muslims were significantly more supportive of Ujamaa than Christians.[30]

It is true that Church officials in Tanzania in this period were concerned over the possibility of a rising Marxism, but as Sivalon notes, the political and social role of Catholic officials (and one could extend this across the Christian faith organizations more generally) was 'complex, ambiguous and at times contradictory'.[31] The Mennonite Church in Musoma, for example, was divided in the late 1960s between Church elders who remained suspicious of cooperative settlement schemes, and younger members of the Church who were enthusiastic supporters of Ujamaa Villagisation.[32] The Secretary-General of the TEC, Father Robinson, found in 1963 no contradiction in warning of the dangers of socialism, whilst concluding

> Never has the Church found itself in a position more favourable for fulfilling its divine mission in a pluralistic society. Ujamaa seems to be in complete conformity with the principles of natural law as applied to society and ... it is in complete conformity with the social teaching of the Church.[33]

The Catholic Bishops Pastoral of 1968, 'The Church and Developing Society of Tanzania', endorsed the socialism of Ujamaa, finding in it Christian notions of justice and equality:

No-one should doubt that in the [Arusha] Declaration we can find restated in a way that is really practical for men here and now in Tanzania, the true principles of human living and human society. We can see very well how closely it agrees with the true spirit of Christ and the Church which is a spirit of brotherhood, of sharing, of service and of hard work.[34]

In the mid-1970s, the Catholic Tabora Archdiocesan development office similarly sought to emphasise the commonalities between Christian faith and Ujamaa: 'The Church must help the Christians to understand the relationship between the political ideology of Tanzanian socialism and the practice of Christian religion. There is a real relationship there'.[35] No doubt the Catholic faith of Nyerere helped the Church more widely to accept Tanzanian socialism, and made the trick of portraying it as somehow different from secular (in particular Chinese) forms of socialism easier. Many Church officials, indeed, went further in their support for socialism, seeing in the Arusha Declaration a form of liberation theology.[36]

By 1967, the Church as a whole backed Ujamaa, regarding it as a form of socialism that could be reconciled with Christian teachings. Certainly that support was not universal, nor unequivocal, but it was prominent at all levels and across all denominations. Thus, having reconciled itself to the foundations of government development policy, the Church now had to define the role it wished to play in the promotion and support of that development policy.

Both the Church and the State believed that Churches were important partners in the official development plans of the government. The official First Five Year Development Plan (1963/1967) for Nachingwea District planned for local missions to contribute Tsh 5,000 over the period for the purchase of agricultural equipment. The Tukuyu District Community Development Division Officer reported in 1963 that Catholic, Moravian and Lutheran missions Churches 'are ready to participate in almost all activities' of the official development plan.[37] In 1969, a priest at the Kirando Mission wrote to a British NGO:

[the] Tanzanian Government work hand in hand with the Church. As you know much more has been done by the Church and all mostly

for the Government ... Our Bishops ... are moved to work side by side with the Government to fight against the enemies – the common enemies of Governments: ignorance, poverty and disease.[38]

The Church's perception of this close role was mirrored by the state. Voluntary Agency (essentially, in this period, faith organizations) participation in local development committees and planning processes was not only encouraged, but expected. At the national level, members of the RSD sat on the government's Emergency Aid sub-committee.[39] The *Baraza la Wazee* – an informal advisory Committee consisting of three Catholic Bishops, one Anglican Bishop and a representative from the Lutheran Church – regularly met with President Julius Nyerere to discuss Church–State relations, including the role of the former in development.[40]

The close relationship with the state forged in this period saw the Church become in effect an arm of government policy: it deliberately shaped its response to the development needs of the country in line with government policy, and acted increasingly as a forthright defender and promoter of the government's aims. This role is perhaps most clearly seen in the reaction of the Church to the Government's policy, announced in 1967, of resettling the entire rural population in newly established Ujamaa villages. In 1972, with the onset of the government's Operation Kigoma designed to villagise the region, Fr Georg Leisner of Mulera Parish wrote in his parish newsletter of the importance of supporting the government's campaign: 'My Fellow Christians, now you have heard the plan of "Kigoma Operation". In our parochial we shall have four village.... Do not delay in joining these villages as soon as possible'.[41] Anticipating the upheaval, he exhorted his parishioners to do their duty to both the nation, and the Church:

'Operation' means 'kupasua' (split, tear, rend). It hurts, and the Government realises that: but it hurts people in order to help them to progress. Provinces which are behind are like sickness in the body of our Nation. It is like the Church: Christian who does sin is hurting the body of the Church, he is hurting his fellow Christians. In the same way it is in our Parochial. We can't be contented with a Christian who has rebelled.[42]

By explicitly linking the notion of the sinful Christian to that of the poor citizen, the message was clear: good Christians were those who accepted the Government's plans. Fr Leisner was prepared, for this greater good, to accept the use of coercion against those who resisted: whilst he explained 'we shall not use power first', he added, ominously, 'we have been permitted to trouble them. But we shall respect their humanness [sic]'.[43] The 'we' he referred to was the power of both Church and State, unified in the effort to develop the nation against the resistance of those too ignorant or sinful to accept it.

Fr Leisner may have been unusual in the fervour with which he supported government policy and, in particular, the use of coercion where necessary.[44] But his ardent commitment to the government-vision of development was not unusual. Across the hierarchy, members of the Church sought to work closely with the state, helping implement the vision of Nyerere and his government, and designing their own projects to fit in with that vision. The CCT noted that its Five Year Plan in the early 1970s was 'to a great extent a complement to the Government of Tanzania Five Year Development Plan ... typifying Church participation in planned development'. Moreover, efforts were made to ensure 'the Church's contributions are really in tune with what the government is considering.[45] A Mennonite Church in Musoma sought to create an Ujamaa Village settlement in Tarani in 1969.[46] The Diocesan Office of Kigoma set up a carpentry training scheme in 1972, to ensure sufficient skilled carpenters were available for house construction when Operation Kigoma started.[47] The Anglican Diocese of Zanzibar and Tanga worked with the government in the late 1960s to establish an Ujamaa Village on diocesan land at Kiwanda on the Tanzanian mainland.[48]

By the mid-1960s, then, Church authorities across all denominations had reoriented their social mission to fit in with the development policy and objectives of the state. Projects and schemes were explicitly designed to fit in with official national development plans. Parish, diocesan and national faith organizations sought to assist the government in implementing its plans as much as it could (be that through support in the form of projects, or admonishments to the faithful to comply with government demands). The result was a dramatic shift in the conceptualization of the place of the Church in society.

The new government was determined to nationalize welfare services, thereby undermining the central claim of the Church to power within the state. But by the mid-1960s, the Church had created for itself a new claim to be a member of the political elite, a new reason why it deserved a privileged status within the establishment – its role in promoting and supporting national development. It had access to funds from external donors; it had a network that stretched far beyond the reach of national and local government; and it had a long-standing authority amongst its faithful that the new government was yet to establish.

Both the Church and the state had much to gain from the establishment of a close relationship. The Church maintained a privileged position in society, its officials represented in the formal institutions of the state at local, regional and national level, its counsel sought, and views respected. Tanzanian political leaders were careful not to criticize faith or pursue anti-clerical secular policies. In return, the state gained the support of the largest and most pervasive group of non-official organizations operating in Tanzania. It was able to count upon an organization, and individuals within that organization, which held a natural authority amongst its faithful. The result was more than just a partnership for development, however. As the state became increasingly authoritarian from the late 1960s, the Church was complicit in this process through the support it gave to development processes that withdrew power from below and concentrated it at the centre. Villagisation had become divorced by 1972/1973 from the its ideological roots of the mid-1960s, and become a mechanism for establishing the control of the state over the rural sector. It was used as justification for abolishing the cooperatives; it extended state and party structures down to sub-village level; it had become a tool for the government to seek to control levels and types of production through the use of by-laws, village development plans and state pricing and purchasing mechanisms. It was a massive extension of state power, and organizations supporting it (whether they were Church or international non-governmental organization) were complicit in that exercise of power.

Conclusion

During the 1960s, Christian faith-based organizations were seeking to redefine their role in society. It came to be a role defined primarily through development. Just as the government sought to create a national identity and notion of citizenship through recourse to a powerful rhetoric of developmentalism, so too the Church found it an ideal trope through which to claim authority and power in Tanzania. But the result was a profound shift in the nature of the relationship between the Church and state. In the colonial period, the missions had functioned as both supporters of the colonial state, and as effective challengers to some aspects of its policy. It functioned, in many ways, as a proto civil society organization. It is true that it was controlled by a mostly non-national elite, and patrician in its control over parishes and individual Churches.

The upper echelons were often in conflict with lower-ranking officials and lay-members (complaints over salaries and conditions, and even strikes by mission school teachers were a relatively common phenomenon). The European-elite negotiating with the government could hardly be said to be representative in any meaningful sense of the wishes of the African grassroots. The interests of the mission were often allied to those of the colonial state. But nevertheless, the Church in some important ways did function as a form of civil society, albeit one that was frequently divided and contradictory in its perspective. The institutions set up to mediate between missions and colonial state did serve to challenge the authority of that state, in particular over the paucity of its provisions for social welfare. Support from elements within the Church for the nationalist movement was a more credible claim to its civil society function.

In the post-colonial period, the Church seemingly abandoned this role, tentative as it was. Rather than focusing on representing the interests of the grassroots, it transformed itself into a set of institutions bound to the state. Moreover, this decision to ally itself completely with the state – to become, indeed, part of that state – was not one forced upon it. Whilst the government was seeking to undermine civil society, co-opting or abolishing voices of opposition within the country, the Church in effect supported this rising authoritarianism. Certainly, from its privileged position within the state, individual officials did react against government coercion and human rights abuses. But it did not make such criticisms public, nor did it seek to challenge the fundamental policy of Ujamaa and Villagisation itself. The Church had fully committed to the government's development policy, and was determined to be a faithful partner in providing all the support it could.

In the mid-1980s, the Church across Africa underwent a similarly dramatic shift in the conceptualization of its role. As democracy movements began to spread across the continent, Church leaders were at the front of such movements, taking on the mantle of challenger to the over-mighty state, rather than as part of that state. Across west and central Africa, national conferences calling for democratization were chaired by senior Church officials: Benin (Mgr Isidore de Sousa, Archbishop of Cotonou), Gabon (Mgr Basile Mve Engone, Bishop Oyem), Togo (Mgr Sanouko Kpodzro, Bishop of Atakpame), Congo (Mgr Ernest Kombo, Bishop of Owando) and Zaire (Mgr Laurent Monsengwo Pasinya, Archbishop of Kisangani). Mgr Isidore, indeed, served as President of the Haut Conseil de la Republique, in effect Benin's highest authority, during the 13 month transition to democracy (Gifford 1994: 513). In Kenya, a 1995 pastoral letter from the Catholic Bishops accused the government of human rights abuses, corruption and of eroding judicial independence, signalling a shift to opposition to the state on the part of the Church. The National Council of Churches of Kenya was a prominent player throughout the decade in agitating for a transition to multi-party democracy and reform to the country's constitution. In Madagascar, the Catholic Archbishop of Antananarivo denounced the government in 1991, calling for the President's resignation, and the Council of Churches was part of the Forces Vives that ousted President Ratsiraka in 1992 (Africa South of the Sahara 2006: 599–600, 683–684).

What underlay this shift from support for, to opposition to, the state in Africa? John Iliffe suggests that at the heart of this transformation lay a long-standing concern over power: 'The democratization movements of the 1990s were in part attempts by professionals to regain their lost leadership. The prominent role in them taken by clergymen from historic churches ... witnessed another declining status group seeking to recover its position' (Iliffe 2005: 344–345).

By the 1990s, it was clear that the decision to work closely with the government, rather than act as a counter-balance to its strength and power, had undermined the Church's claim to leadership in Africa. It had become passively complicit in some of the excesses of state power, had neglected its responsibility to speak up for the powerless and represent the interests of the marginalized. It was in danger of becoming, as Adrian Hastings puts it, 'fundamentally marginal' to social and political realities in Africa (Hastings 1990: 208). The Church gradually (and imperfectly) moved from a position of being a part of the state, to a conceptualization of its place as distinct and outside that state, more akin to the civil society sector.

This shift in the role the Church created for itself should not be surprising. As an institution, it had showed itself to be eminently capable of reinventing its place in society. Fearing it could lose power and authority in a newly independent Africa wishing to divest itself of all reminders of colonial occupation, the Church sought to ally itself to the new governments by showing itself to be supportive of their aims and objectives. In Tanzania, that meant support for its development objectives and for Ujamaa. Loyalty to the government was a means to ensure Christianity retained its significance in post-colonial Africa.

This assessment is not intended to be unduly cynical about intentions. There is no doubt that many, if not most, Church officials truly wished to assist development processes and eradicate poverty, just as the commitment to democracy and human rights in the 1990s was not just about seeking to re-establish a diminishing authority. But to dismiss such concerns is to miss an important part of the story, and to assume a Whiggish approach to understanding the evolution of institutions and their policies. Power *was* an important consideration, even if it was not the only one.

The consequence of such conclusions raise further questions about current links between Christian faith organizations and civil society. Those who argue that faith groups by their very nature cannot be considered as civil society actors are ignoring the history of the Church acting in precisely this manner (the support for nationalist movements in the 1960s; the moral and financial support, and leadership, given to democratization movements in the late 1980s and 1990s). But if the actions of the Church in this regard are, as Iliffe suggests, at least partly driven by a desire to regain a lost leadership, are Christian faith organizations acting from faith or opportunity? Such considerations raise at the very least a note of caution against blindly assuming faith-based organizations are inherently vital parts of civil society, or forces capable of countering the over-mighty state. That the Church has come to occupy this position is important, but its place there must not be assumed to be permanent.

The 1960s remain a critical decade in the history of faith engagement with development discourse. It was during this period that the Churches radically reinterpreted their role and their understandings of how to engage with that discourse and process. Yet, whilst this liberalizing step was taking place, in Tanzania at least, the Churches gradually moved into the constricting orbit of the state. What would occur in the late 1980s and 1990s was no less profound a sea-change, as this relationship was fundamentally re-examined and found to be wanting.

Notes

1. Whilst senior Church officials remained largely European, the bulk of Church officials overall by the 1960s were African (indeed, by the early twentieth century, contact with Christianity for most Africans was more likely to be an African, rather than European, experience).
2. Tanganyika Government, Annual Health Report, 1961 (Dar es Salaam, Government Printer, 1962), pp. 12–15, 24.
3. Secretariat Minutes, Director of Medical Services (A. T. Howell), 18 April 1952, p. 1. TNA 42293.
4. Community Development Division Mbeya Region, Annual Report 1963, p. 3, 7. TNA 465 D3/18; Mbeya Regional Development Committee minutes,

27 July 1965, p. 2. TNA 471 C5/44/2 v.1; District Commissioner Chunya to Administrative Secretary Southern Highlands Region, 6 June 1962. TNA 465 D3/24; Community Development Assistant i/c North Mara, Annual Report 1963. TNA SI/III; Community Development Division, Mara Region, Annual Report 1963, pp. 2, 4. TNA 544 SI/III; Regional Development Committee minutes, Mara Region, 26 August 1963. Author's translation from Kiswahili. TNA 544 P/30.

5. The name 'Tanzania' was adopted after the union of Tanganyika and Zanzibar in 1964. The Christian Council of Tanganyika changed its title accordingly. In this chapter, the term 'Tanzania' will generally be used to for the post-Independence period.

6. CCT Standing Committee unconfirmed minutes, 5–7 February 1963, appendix G. Christian Aid archive (CA), CA/A/6/8.

7. Ibid.

8. CCT RSCS, Preliminary Report Study Commission A: 'The Christian Contribution to a Dynamic Society in Tanganyika', May 1963, p. 18. CA/A/6/7.

9. CCT AGM minutes, 20–21 June 1968, 'Report of the Relief and Service Division', p. 1. CA/A/7/2.

10. Ibid., pp. 2–3.

11. Ujamaa ('Rural Socialism') was adopted as official national policy until 1967, although its ideas began to take root from the early 1960s.

12. CCT Standing Committee unconfirmed minutes, 5–7 February 1963, appendix G. Christian Aid archive (CA), CA/A/6/8.

13. CCT Minutes, 9–10 June 1966, 'Relief and Service Report', appendix J. CA/A/7/1.

14. CCT Five Year Plan, 'Report on Listed Projects, New Projects', 30 April 1972, pp. 4–24. CA2/A/26/6.

15. 'Report of the General Secretary' (Stanford A Shauri), CCT Annual General Meeting, 21–23 May 1975, p. 3. CA2/A/26/6. The income is equivalent to almost $26 million in 2005 money. Calculation based on nominal GDP per capita, using Relative Value Calculator at http://www.measuringworth.com/calculators/compare accessed on 1 November 2006.

16. Joel Ngeiyamu, 'The Impact of Church Development in Tanzania', 18 May 1973, p. 2. CA2/A/26/6.

17. John C. Sivalon, Roman Catholicism and the Defining of Tanzanian Socialism, 1953–1985: An Analysis of the Social Ministry of the Catholic Church in Tanzania, PhD Thesis, University of St Michael's College, 1990, p. 156. This figure does not include funds from religious institutions working within Tanzania, non-CIDSEE funds or funds from US sources.

18. Brian Polkinghorne, 'Proposal for the establishment of Kilacha Production and Training Centre', 14 August 1974; Diocese of Moshi, Application for a Grant', 11 October 1974. OxA Tan81 v.I.

19. Project Application, covering note, January 1977; Oxfam Field Director to Oxfam-UK, November 1981; Rev. Fr John B. Kabeya and Rev. Fr Tony Byrne, 'Report on Development Survey Archdiocese of Tabora Tanzania, July – August 1976', p. 52. OxA Tan 92.

20. OxA Tan 49. Kigoma Diocese, Grant Application, 5 May 1972. OxA Tan 57.

21. CCT Standing Committee unconfirmed minutes, 5–7 February 1963. CA/A/6/8.

22. CCT Standing Committee unconfirmed minutes, 15–17 October 1963. pp. 21–23. CA/A/6/8.
23. CCT Chairman to World Council of Churches (Cooke), 18 September 1961. CA/A/6/7.
24. Dudbridge to Harris, 26 January 1967. CA/A/6/9.
25. Mwakahesya, *Caritas Tanzania after 25 Years*, unpublished draft report, 1996.
26. Report of the General Secretary to the CCT Annual General Meeting, 21–23 May, 1975, pp. 1–2. CA2/A/26/6.
27. Sivalon, *Roman Catholicism*, p. 74.
28. Ibid., pp. 86–95.
29. CCT Standing Committee unconfirmed minutes, 5–7 February 1963, appendix G. Christian Aid archive (CA), CA/A/6/8.
30. Jan P. van Bergen and D. Westerlund, cited in Sivalon, *Roman Catholicism*, pp. 20–21.
31. Ibid., p. 12.
32. Oxfam Field Officer, to Oxfam-UK, 28 February 1969. OxA Tan 30.
33. Cited in Sivalon, *Roman Catholicism*, p. 125.
34. Bishops Pastoral, *The Church and Developing Society of Tanzania*, pp. 2–3, cited in Ibid., p. 145.
35. Fr Kabeya and Fr Byrne, Report on Development Survey, Archdiocese of Tabora, July – August 1976, p. 45. OxA Tan 92.
36. According to one Catholic priest, two American priests were actually deported from Tanzania in the 1970s for criticizing the government for not going far enough in implementing socialism. Interview with Fr Riddle, Dar es Salaam, 11 June 1997.
37. Nachingwea District Development Committee, 'Five Year Development Plan', appendix C, 'Capital Requirements', pp. 1–5; Community Development Division, Tukuyu, to Regional Community Development Officer Mbeya, 9 September 1963. TNA AN320 CD1/3/1.
38. Fr Kalukula to Oxfam, 1 March 1969. OxA Tan 45.
39. CCT Standing Committee Minutes, appendix J, November 1966. CA/A/7/1.
40. Sivalon, *Roman Catholicism*, pp. 167–168.
41. Fr Georg Leisner, Parochial of Mulera: Plan for the Month of February, 1972, p. 2. OxA Tan 69.
42. Ibid.
43. Ibid., pp. 1–2.
44. He may equally, of course, have been entirely typical. However, the documentary record on this is limited.
45. Shauri, Second Consultation of the CCT Five Year Plan, London, 20–21 June 1972, Paper 3, pp. 4, 7. CA/A/26/6.
46. OxA Tan 30.
47. Grant Application, Socio-Economic Development Coordinator, Kigoma Diocese, 5 May 1972. OxA Tan 57.
48. P. Mntambo to Church Province of East Africa, 1 September 1969. CA2/A/28/14. The Church started working with the government in establishing a village settlement at Kiwanda in 1964, initially as part of the ill-fated Village Settlement Programme. When the government adopted Ujamaa as official policy in 1967, the diocese shifted the emphasis of the settlement to the new Ujamaa model.

Bibliography

Africa South of the Sahara (London and New York: Routledge 2006).

Adrian Hastings (1990), 'Christianity in Africa' In Ursula King (ed.) *Turning Points in Religious Studies* (Edinburgh: T & T Clark), pp. 201–210.

John Iliffe (2005), *Honour in African History* (Cambridge: Cambridge University Press).

Michael Jennings (2003), 'We Must Run While Others Walk: Popular Participation and Development Crisis in Tanzania, 1961–9', *Journal of Modern African Studies*, 41, pp. 163–187.

—— (2007), 'Missions and Maternal and Child Health Care in Colonial Tanganyika, 1919–1939' In David Hardiman (ed.) *Healing Bodies, Saving Souls: Medical Missions in Asia and Africa* (Amsterdam: Clio Medica Press), pp. 227–250.

Paul Gifford (1994), 'Some Recent Developments in African Christianity', *African Affairs* 93, 373, pp. 513–534.

6

Engaged Citizenship: The Catholic Bishops' Conference of the Philippines (CBCP) in the Post-Authoritarian Philippines

Antonio F. Moreno

> We knew what we were against, and we opposed that fairly effectively. It is not nearly so easy to say what we are for and so we appear to be dithering, not quite knowing where we want to go nor how to get there.
>
> Archbishop Desmond Tutu (Quoted in Kassimir 1998: 77)

In speaking of the mainline African Churches above vis-à-vis democratization, Archbishop Desmond Tutu seems to portray accurately a prevailing impression of the Church leadership's role in the transition to democracy and a continuing search for strategic directions in the post-authoritarian milieu. The Church leadership in many instances, particularly its moderate and progressive hierarchical ministers, demonstrated its capacity to oppose authoritarian regimes, but there appears to be an ambiguity in its position in the newly found democratic space. The experience of the African Churches appears to suggest that while many Churches were against political tyranny, it needs to be convincingly demonstrated that they are for democracy in the post-authoritarian period (Ranger 1998: 22). The Church in this context refers to the ordained ministers (bishops, priests and deacons) as they interact with lay people.

This chapter argues that the Philippine Catholic Church leadership represented by the Catholic Bishops' Conference of the Philippines (CBCP) *was* an actor in promoting democracy through engaged citizenship. Engaged citizenship is not simply a matter of asserting legal claims

117

as provided for by the State. Neither does it merely entail affiliation to a particular national identity. Rather, citizenship is a claim to legal status (comprising affiliation, rights and obligations) *and* active engagement (Jones and Gaventa 2002: 5). Engaged citizenship goes beyond the assertion of rights. It includes the exercise of responsibilities towards the realization of collective dreams. These collective aspirations need not confine themselves to a national territory, but could well extend to the global sphere. This brand of citizenship is often shaped by class and gender relations, political identities, ethnicities and other such factors. This idea of citizenship formation appears to be the single most important contribution of the CBCP in the post-authoritarian Philippines.

The beginnings of the CBCP's social involvement

The CBCP started as the Catholic Welfare Organization (CWO) in 1945 (Santos 1997, 395). In 1968, CWO was renamed CBCP as the official body of the Philippine hierarchy, headed by one of its member bishops (Ibid.: 424). In the Philippines, where eight out of ten people are Catholic, the CBCP is the most influential Church body in politics. A crucial point of departure for the CBCP's social involvement was its sponsorship of the National Congress for Rural Development in 1967, two years after Vatican II. The Congress, convened a year before the Latin American Conference in Medellin in 1968, officially endorsed the Basic Christian Communities (BCCs). This shows that, as Bishop Francisco Claver (1988: 26) puts it, the Philippine BCCs are 'wholly indigenous and not.... copy-cat imitations' of Latin American BCCs, although influences from the latter affected the former subsequently.

The CBCP periodically issued pastoral letters and statements responding to key faith and moral issues affecting not only the faithful but also of the whole citizenry. The CBCP established its own social arm: the National Secretariat for Social Action (NASSA). It formed linkages with sectors of society and national religious organizations which shared their interests in promoting the participation of marginalised groups, peace building, social development and inter-religious dialogue. The Bishops-Businessmen Conference (BBC),[1] CBCP-National Council of Churches in the Philippines (NCCP)[2] Joint Committee, Bishops-Ulama (Muslim religious leaders) Forum (BUF)[3] [later known as the Bishops-Ulama Conference] are a few partnerships that were set up for these purposes.

The CBCP and authoritarian rule

During the authoritarian period (1972–1986), the bishops were classified according to three main tendencies: progressives, moderates and conservatives.[4] The role of the CBCP in democratization evolved from adaptation and ambivalence with regard to the *status quo* to outright active resistance. The evolving roles were shaped by the Church's struggle to renew itself along the lines of Catholic social teaching and Vatican II principles (e.g. human dignity, social involvement, development).

The Church hierarchy's initial position regarding martial law was one of cautious acceptance that masked internal divisions. Five days after its declaration, the Administrative Council of the CBCP, while cautioning the government to respect human dignity, exhorted the people 'to remain calm and law-abiding' (CBCP 2003a). Shortly after the CBCP statement, 17 bishops and 17 members of the Association of Major Religious Superiors of the Philippines (AMRSP) issued a statement of concern against possible State abuses and sought the lifting of martial law within months (Carroll 1999: 19). Nonetheless, the pastoral letters of the CBCP from 1972 to 1975 plainly showed a cautious leadership which neither categorically denounced nor endorsed martial law (Santos 1997: 428). Sustained persecutions of the Church marked the beginning of the consolidation of the critical position of its leadership. From 1977 to 1981, during the presidency of Jaime Cardinal Sin, the CBCP leadership adopted 'critical collaboration' as its attitude with regard to the authoritarian State (ibid.: 429). The CBCP criticized the government particularly when injustices were done by the authoritarian regime, but otherwise it generally tolerated the state.

On 21 August 1983, former Senator Benigno 'Ninoy' Aquino, thought to be the political leader who could best unify the opposition, was assassinated on arrival at Manila International Airport (later renamed Ninoy Aquino International Airport) under the custody of military guards. His death marked a sea change in the progressive deterioration of Church–state relations. It sparked the biggest mass protests in the postcolonial Philippines. When the subsequent snap presidential election was marred by significant fraud, the CBCP on 14 February 1986 declared that the Marcos government had 'no moral basis' to govern (CBCP 1990: 61–63). The CBCP was the first among the national organizations to issue a statement challenging the legitimacy of the government. Before long, Marcos was ousted from office.

The CBCP in post-authoritarian Philippines

The Church leadership was well positioned in post-authoritarian Philippine society following the accession of President Corazon C. Aquino to power. The Philippine Church (comprising the ordained ministers and laity) enjoyed a huge trust margin in surveys of popular opinion posting, +65 ('big trust' minus 'small trust') in September 1988 and +66 a year later (Mangahas 1991: 1–2). Church–state relations during the Aquino administration were anchored on 'constructive critical collaboration' that largely stressed partnership. The Church leadership backed Aquino generally. Similarly the state sought help from the Church particularly in strengthening the fragile democracy. The CBCP issued a statement on 14 July 1987 insisting that peace could be achieved through genuine land reform (CBCP 1990: 117–121). In 1988, in follow up, Cardinal Sin urged the Aquino administration to push for land reform as mandated in the 1987 Constitution (Mangahas 1988: 1 and 8). Church–military relations during the Aquino administration remained tense particularly with regard to the latter's counter-insurgency campaigns and human rights abuses (Youngblood 1989). The persecution of some lay people continued, and human rights violations persisted despite institutional commitment to uphold human dignity.

The CBCP's support for the 1987 Constitution

President Aquino spared no time in abolishing the 1973 Constitution, the legal foundation of authoritarianism. She convened a 48 member Constitutional Commission to write a constitution. The draft constitution received full backing from the CBCP when it secured its own interests: a pro-family stance, anti-abortion, anti-divorce and anti-death penalty provisions openness to religious instruction in government schools, human rights protection, social justice provisions, and safeguards against declaration of martial law (Carlos 1986: 2; Santos 1997: 435). Cardinal Sin was particularly elated with the draft, although some Church leaders had some misgivings about it (Youngblood 1989: 17). The CBCP in their pastoral letter of 21 November 1986, appealed for an educational campaign to inform people about the new constitution and recommended its ratification (CBCP 2003b). On 2 February 1987, the constitution was ratified overwhelmingly by 76 per cent of the 22 million voters – amid an extremely high turnout of 90 per cent of registered voters (ibid.). Philippine Churches, particularly the Catholic Church, could claim a fair share of this victory as they campaigned vigorously for its ratification. The Left and some radical elements in the Church (both its leaders and members), on the other hand, rejected it.

The 1987 Constitution underpinned people's sense of citizenship in the post-Marcos era. First, it attempted to mainstream people's participation in a restored democracy. To this end, the constitution declares, 'The State shall encourage non-governmental, community-based, or sectoral organizations that promote the welfare of the nation' (The 1987 Constitution of the Republic of the Philippines, n.d.: 3). In addition, '(t)he State shall respect the role of independent people's organizations to enable the people to pursue and protect collective interests and aspirations through peaceful and lawful means' (ibid.: 49). Second, the 1987 Constitution enshrined key provisions that attracted organized groups and marginalised sectors to participate in framing social policies affecting their lives. This is particularly true in the case of human rights and social justice provisions (e.g. agrarian reform).[5] If at the heart of citizenship is the exercise of legal claims and active engagement, the proliferation of these organized groups provided a mobilizing structure for expressing one's citizenship. In a way, the 1987 Constitution enlarged the discourse and practice of citizenship to promote people's participation and press state accountability as a new mode of 'people power' in the post-authoritarian context.

The Church and elections

In the Church's electoral involvement, one can discern how people claimed and articulated their citizenship. In this, the Church leadership played a critical role. Post-authoritarian elections had generally lower violent and death-related incidents (Linantud 1998: 298–318). John Linantud claims that the deployment of the military in its increasingly depoliticized State and the active involvement of the Church in electoral reform were important developments in curbing electoral violence (ibid.). The Church's participation in restoring confidence in the post-authoritarian electoral processes particularly in the 1992 and 1998 elections was, indeed, a significant factor in democracy building.

The 1992 elections

The 11 May 1992 synchronized (national and local) elections were extremely crucial in the consolidation of democracy. Since July 1991, the CBCP issued four pastoral statements on the 1992 elections to underscore the significance of the event in the life of a fledgling democracy (Claver 1992: 8–9). President Aquino endorsed the candidacy of

Fidel V. Ramos, her former Defence Minister. Ramos, a Protestant in a dominantly Catholic nation, was feared by some conservative members and leaders of the Catholic fold. He was a key enforcer of martial law in the 1970s as chief of the Philippine Constabulary (PC). This was still fresh in the minds of people, especially Cardinal Sin (Tasker 1992: 18). Although the CBCP did not endorse particular candidates, Cardinal Sin was perceived to have led a 'whispering campaign' for Ramon Mitra who finished in the 4th place (ibid.). When it was clear that the *Iglesia ni Cristo* (INC)[6] with its two million voting members was supporting Eduardo Cojuangco, Sin released a pastoral letter on 19 April citing issues militating against certain unnamed candidates (ibid.). Ramos won, collecting 23.58 per cent of the votes cast in a six-way contest.

The Church-based electoral movements

The 1986 presidential snap elections saw a massive reactivation of the electoral watch group National Movement for Free Elections (NAMFREL) after the Catholic bishops formalized an alliance with business and professional groups.[7] NAMFREL, however, was tainted with partisan politics when its head, José Concepcion, was appointed as Secretary of Trade and Industry, a Cabinet position in the Aquino government. Further, allegations that it favored government candidates in NAMFREL's Operation Quick Count in 1987, tarnished its image as non-partisan (Callahan 2000: 88–129). This, among other factors, prompted Church leaders involved in NAMFREL to form their own electoral movement (ibid.). Consequently, two important Church-based electoral movements surfaced in the 1990s: the Pastoral Parish Council for Responsible Voting (PPCRV) and Voters Organization, Training and Education toward Clear, Authentic, Responsible Elections (VOTE-CARE).

Although initiated by the Archdiocese of Manila, with full backing from Cardinal Sin, PPCRV became a national electoral arm of the Philippine Church, covering some 54 dioceses throughout the country (ibid.). Henrietta T. de Villa, then chairperson of the Council of the Laity of the Philippines (CLP), headed PPCRV.[8] The major activities of PPCRV included pre-election preparations such as the organization of coordinating councils (e.g. arch/diocese, district, parish) to recruit trainers and volunteers; voter's education; and an information campaign (ibid.). On election day, PPCRV assumed many tasks such as helping voters, assisting members of the Board of Electoral Inspectors (BEI), ensuring and protecting electoral returns, assisting NAMFREL's operation quick count and keeping watch during the canvassing of votes in designated places. PPCRV was able to recruit 346,688 volunteers for the 1992 elections (ibid.).[9] Printed educational materials which were distributed reached 899,435 copies (ibid.). Public approval of PPCRV was relatively high after the 1992 elections. With a 69 per cent level of awareness, in September 1992, PPCRV gained a satisfaction margin of +45 ('Social Weather Report Survey', n.d.).[10]

VOTE-CARE was conceived in October 1991, eight months after the celebration of the Second Plenary Council of the Philippines (PCP II), when the bishops and the social action directors committed to the 1992 elections. Some 550,000 volunteers were recruited by NAMFREL, PPCRV and VOTE-CARE for the 1992 elections (Callahan 2000: 90). Many volunteers in the 1992, 1995 and 1998 elections assumed double affiliations (PPCRV and VOTE-CARE) or triple memberships including NAMFREL. VOTE-CARE's primary goal along with that of PPCRV was voter's education (Guyano 1995a: 17). Voter's education aimed not only to make the electoral exercise peaceful, clean and honest, but meaningful by enabling the voters to shift from patronage-based to issue-based politics (Callahan 2000: 89).

The 1992 elections were relatively peaceful compared with the elections during the authoritarian period. Some 87 violent incidents and 60 deaths were reported, a significant improvement on the 296 violent incidents and 153 deaths in the 1986 elections or the 1984 elections where 918 counts of violence and 154 deaths were recorded (Linantud 1998: 301). Thanks to PPCRV's candidates forum, the programme of the candidates were scrutinized by the voting public (PPCRV 1992: 4). The signing of 'peace covenants' among candidates was institutionalized by electoral watch movements making the candidates promise to desist from using violence and respect the electoral outcome. Honouring the covenants was another thing, but at least they sealed their intent under the watchful eyes of the citizenry. It is difficult to ascertain the impact of PPCRV and VOTE-CARE's education campaign. Nonetheless, the information campaign did create an alternative venue of debate and discussion to the campaign issues raised by the candidates themselves. Poll watching was the main task for PPCRV and VOTE-CARE on election day itself. Voter's assistance desks were set up in polling places making PPCRV's presence visible and assistance readily available when voters were in need of help. In many cases where members of the BEI were not around, PPCRV volunteers assisted (ibid.). Unfortunately, however, the momentum of citizenship formation was not sustained beyond the election period.

The 1998 elections

The political education conducted by both PPCRV and VOTE-CARE in the 1998 elections did not seem to make an impact since the voting public still elected a number of people on the basis of personal popularity and not in terms of the programme they represented.[11] This appears to be a significant limitation of the PPCRV and VOTE-CARE campaigns, but given the political machineries, deeply entrenched political base of many traditional politicians, and the resources that sustained their political clout, personality-based politics was still the order of the day. In addition, PPCRV and VOTE-CARE were reactivated when the election period was getting close (around six months before the elections). This meant that they needed more time to launch their pre-elections activities. Further, given the time constraint, the success of voter's education was uneven and largely dependent on the skills and knowledge of the staff giving the seminars. The voter's seminars were often conducted in a non-participatory way.

Nevertheless, PPCRV and VOTE-CARE in general were involved in a systematic and extensive way in the 1998 presidential elections. PPCRV sent volunteers to 57 out of 79 (72 per cent) (arch)dioceses (PPCRV 1998). VOTE-CARE supported 42 out of 79 (53 per cent) of the [arch] diocesan social action centres with a total of $156,100 in financial assistance or an average of $3,700 per local Church (Guyano 1995b: 14–15). In February 1998, PPCRV garnered a relatively high +49 trust rating while VOTE-CARE had +26, which showed positive recognition in what they were doing ('Social Weather Report Survey', n.d.). These Church-based electoral movements enabled and mobilized the people to exercise their citizenship, not simply by casting votes but by ensuring that the votes are properly registered, counted and protected. Further, by participating in the conduct of the elections and campaigning for electoral reform, clearly the people were hoping to realise their collective dream: strengthening electoral integrity and confidence.

The Church's peace advocacy

Soon after assuming office as President, Aquino sought assistance from the Church in a bid to end the conflict with the Communist Party of the Philippines–National Democratic Front–New People's Army (CPP–NDF–NPA) (Youngblood 1989: 19). The NDF is an aggregation of organized sectors and groups that adhere to the nationalist democratic principles largely espoused by CPP chairman Jose Ma Sison. The CPP is a vital and controlling body in the NDF. The NPA is the armed wing of the CPP. The insurgency in the Philippines led by the CPP–NDF–NPA is one of the longest running in the world. Shortly after the CPP was established in 1968, the NPA was formed and mobilized against government forces. During the Marcos period, no peace negotiation with the CPP-NPA was attempted. Aquino's invitation, however, coincided with the Pope's exhortation to the bishops in the wake of the February revolution to be ministers of reconciliation (*L'Osservatore Romano* 1986). The CBCP (2003c) enjoined the people to promote 'national reconciliation, unity, and peace'. Striking a peace settlement with the CPP–NDF–NPA was extremely precarious and difficult. In May 1986, preliminary discussions between the two groups (Government of the Republic of the Philippines (GRP) and NDF) led to a 60-day ceasefire agreement with effect from 10 December 1986 (Coronel-Ferrer and Raquiza 1993: 5–6). Two military coup attempts in July and in November 1986, the killing of trade union leader Rolando Olalia in November and Enrile's unyielding criticisms of Aquino's 'kid-glove approach' to communism jeopardized the initial talks between GRP and NDF (Wurfel 1988: 311–313). Despite the turn of events, a ceasefire agreement was signed on 27 November 1986 while talks were going on (ibid.). Bacolod Bishop Antonio Y. Fortich chaired the National Ceasefire Committee (NCC) which monitored and supervised the ceasefire agreement. Subsequently, 14 regional and 7 local ceasefire committees were formed (Coronel-Ferrer and Raquiza 1993: 6). For the first time since the beginning of the insurgency movement in 1969 a ceasefire was in place despite some cases of reported violations.[12] Maria Serena I. Diokno (1994: 70), a member of the GRP panel, remarks: 'The ceasefire could not have been implemented without the cooperation of the bishops, priests and other religious who served in the national and local ceasefire committees.'

The military coup attempts that plagued the first year of the Aquino administration undermined the peace process as distrust between the military and the NDF heightened. On 22 January 1987, 18 demonstrators were killed by government forces while protesting in Mendiola Street, near the Presidential Palace (Coronel-Ferrer and Raquiza 1993: 70). This prompted the immediate withdrawal of the NDF from the peace talks. In an address to graduating cadets of the Philippine Military Academy on 22 March 1987, Aquino vowed to 'unleash the sword of war' against the insurgents (ibid.: 11).

This policy shift elicited divided reactions from the Church. Cardinal Sin threw his support behind a military solution to the insurgency, arguing that 'after compassion, justice should now be dispensed', although the CBCP remained consistently leery of such a campaign (Youngblood 1989: 58–59; see also Villacorta 1991: 166). Still, the CBCP did not oppose the policy shift of the government. While some conservative elements in the Church hierarchy concurred with Aquino 'that perhaps sterner measures against the left were necessary', they nevertheless condemned violence (Youngblood 1989: 60). Progressive bishops and clergy members were quick to highlight the dangers of employing a predominantly military approach to the crisis (ibid.: 59). This all-out war against the rebels had devastating effects in the military's 'Operation Thunderbolt' in Southern Negros Occidental in April 1989 resulting in a severe criticism by the local Church, AMRSP and several Church leaders.

Following the coup attempts of 1989, the clamour for peace was all the more intensified. Upon the suggestion of peace advocates and the Churches, Aquino proclaimed 1990–2000 as the Decade of Peace (NCCP–RDO 1992: 96). Peace, she claimed, was not simply the 'absence of conflict' but must be coupled with 'authentic development with justice, whose fruits benefit all' (ibid.). By way of a follow up to the EDSA Shrine gathering, on 1 January 1990, the bishops of Manila in a pastoral letter categorically declared that 'to seize power through a coup d'etat is a sin' (Sin and the Auxiliary Bishops of Manila 1989: 1 and 13). The pastoral letter urged the people to resort to non-violent ways of rectifying the problems of Philippine society. While the bishops of Manila admitted 'abuses and incompetence, graft and corruption' in the government, the people must use the existing grievance mechanisms provided for in the constitution (ibid.). The Manila bishops also urged the government to undertake social reforms while soliciting people of 'solidarity, collaboration and self-sacrifice' to defend constitutional democracy (ibid.: 13). On 31 January 1990, the CBCP (1990: 219–227) issued a pastoral letter following the basic lines of the bishops of Manila in December 1989. Echoing the government's declaration of a 'Decade of Peace (1990–2000)', the bishops proposed a ten-point peace agenda which had a significant influence on government policy on peace (ibid.: 224–225). The Research and Documentation Office (NCCP–RDO 1992: 153) maintains that this was the CBCP's 'most concrete agenda for peace'. In October 1990, more than 100 Catholic Protestant and Muslim organizations crafted a declaration 'Towards a National Vision for Peace' – the broadest consensus and synthesis on issues affecting peace (Abueva 1992: 16). Despite many attempts to initiate exploratory talks to re-open negotiations during the Aquino period, however, peace remained elusive.

Immediately after his accession to power, President Fidel V. Ramos renewed calls for peace and reconciliation. He granted amnesty to those who applied for it during the time of the Aquino administration, released 13 NDF leaders, established the National Unification Commission (NUC) and lobbied for the repeal of the Anti-subversion Law (Republic Act No. 1700), which would legalize the CPP and other underground movements (ibid.). The NUC was an executive-legislative body created on 1 September 1992, headed by former COMELEC Commissioner Haydee Yorac and Bishop Fernando Capalla, a CBCP representative, who was later elected as its Vice-chairperson. Although political persecutions continued, the repeal of the Anti-Subversion Law was an opening for many communist rebels to relinquish the armed revolution and enter political life or join civil society movements (Abueva 1997: 26). The CBCP issued a pastoral statement on 25 January 1993 manifesting its all-out endorsement of the peace process, and the NUC in particular, amid threats of withdrawal from peace talks from the Left (Quitorio 1995: 786–789). Although the NUC succeeded in negotiating a peace deal with the military rebels, however, it failed to reach a settlement with the NDF.

President Joseph Estrada's commitment to peace was dismal, despite the rhetoric. He resumed a thoroughgoing military approach to the Moro Islamic Liberation Front (MILF), thus dampening hopes for a peace settlement in Mindanao during his watch. Eager to win over the NDF, Estrada set a deadline in his peace talks with the rebels. When the peace talks were suspended, Cardinal Sin (1999a: 511–512) in a pastoral letter of 1 March 1999, offered to mediate between the two parties but the offer went unheeded. The peace talks were finally shelved on 27 May 1999 after the ratification of the Visiting Forces Agreement (VFA), because the letter legitimized the presence of American troops in the country, a presence to which the NDF was implacably opposed.

Church peace initiatives in Muslim Mindanao

In Mindanao, there was little headway in peace building during the time of President Aquino, despite efforts to strike a deal with the Moro National Liberation Front (MNLF) in 1986 and 1987. The MNLF was founded by Nur Misuari in the 1970s to wage a struggle leading to the creation of an independent Moro (Muslim) homeland otherwise known as *Bangsamoro* (comprising of Southern and Western Mindanao, Sulu and Palawan).[13] During the watch of President Ramos, the MNLF initially rejected the creation of the Autonomous Region for Muslim

Mindanao (ARMM) as mandated by the 1987 Constitution. The MNLF claimed that this was not what the Tripoli Agreement in 1976 had envisioned (Abueva 1997: 41). In this peace agreement, full autonomy would be granted to 13 provinces in Mindanao. In a plebiscite on 17 November 1989, only 4 out of the 13 provinces voted to be included in the ARMM. Along with the ARMM was the creation of the Southern Philippines Council for Peace and Development (SPCPD) which was originally intended as a 'transitional structure and mechanism' to implement the Tripoli Agreement (Vitug and Gloria 2000: 54).[14] The SPCPD declared 14 (originally 13) provinces and 10 cities as 'Zones of Peace and Development' and Consultative and Development Councils in Mindanao (ibid.). Muslims and Christians opposed SPCPD for different reasons. As the opposition among the priests in Mindanao stepped up, the CBCP likewise aired its concerns and lamented the lack of consultation regarding the creation of SPCPD. Nonetheless, after some dialogue, the CBCP supported it (ibid.: 54–55). The CBCP raised fears about the possible Islamization of schools, threats against religious freedom, separation of Church and state and the issue of equal representation in the Consultative Assembly (Carroll 1999: 60).

In another development, the concerns expressed by both Christians and Muslim leaders arising out of a series of drafts of the GRP-MNLF agreement gave impetus to the coming together of some Catholic bishops and members of the Ulama League of the Philippines (ULP), headed by Lanao del Sur Governor Mahid Mutilan. Nonetheless, some of the *ulama* members of the MILF who did not belong to Mutilan's group rejected the ULP branding it 'as a counter-insurgency tool of the government' (Vitug and Gloria 2000: 153). This dialogue eventually led to the creation of the Bishops-Ulama Forum (BUF) on 29 November 1996. Aside from Governor Mutilan, some key figures in BUF included Archbishop Fernando Capalla (former chairperson of the CBCP Episcopal Commission on Inter-religious Dialogue), and Bishop Hilario Gomez, Jr of the Protestant NCCP. The Bishops-Ulama Conference (BUC) was established to rediscover and foster the 'spiritual foundation for peace from both Christian and Muslim religious traditions' (Ledesma 2005: 23). It emerged at the height of the heated debates concerning the SPCPD. It received a strong backing from Secretary of Defence, Renato de Villa. President Ramos supported this group and donated some $100,000 from the NUC fund (Vitug and Gloria 2000: 151). The BUF met quarterly, exploring the spiritual foundations of inter-religious dialogue and issues that threatened the peace process (Ledesma 2005: 24). The BUC, for instance, pronounced its position and peace agenda at critical times (e.g. the killing of Bishop Ben de Jesus and Fr Rhoel Gallardo) and during the counter-insurgency campaign waged by President Estrada against the MILF in 2000 (ibid.).

Over time, the BUF became the BUC. Although the CBCP did not play a critical role in BUF, individual Catholic bishops were key figures in it. The BUF conducted peace education and advocacy, and supported inter-religious dialogue. To dramatize the peace issues, the NCCP and CBCP, NASSA and BUF organized a peace caravan from Cotabato to Zamboanga and back again to Cotabato in Mindanao collecting some one million signatures from both Christians and Muslims supporting the peace process.

In sum, despite limitations, the Church leadership (the CBCP or as individual bishops) made some inroads in the formation of a engaged citizenship that privileged the peace agenda. Starting with the unprecedented 60-day ceasefire, the 10-point peace agenda of the CBCP, the crafting of 'Towards a National Vision for Peace' – the broadest consensus of more than 100 CSOs on peace issues – and BUF peace caravan that collected more than one million signatures, all these are indications of a vibrant citizenship founded on peace and justice. The peace constituency did not simply assert its right and claimed spaces for their collective aspiration but actively proposed ways and means to rectify systemic political, economic and social ills that bred violence. Peace in this sense as intimately linked to authentic human development was undoubtedly a Church mission in keeping with Catholic social teaching (e.g. *Pacem en terris* and *Populorum Progressio*), Vatican II and post-Vatican II documents. Sustaining this peace constituency and the energy for peace building remained a challenge for this kind of citizenry.

The Church and charter change (cha-cha) campaigns

Between 1995 and 1999, charter (constitutional) change campaigns were launched by the Ramos and Estrada administrations. Both were widely perceived as attempts to undermine the democratic features of the 1987 Constitution. In both cases, perhaps more intensely during the Ramos administration than during the Estrada government, the Church, including conservative elements and pro-democracy civil society groups, stood shoulder to shoulder to oppose the cha-cha campaigns. In effect, the CBCP became the voice of citizens and advocated accountability in these state-led campaigns.

Ramos's bid for charter change

In September 1995, a draft constitution (to replace the 1987 Constitution) was exposed by constitution expert and Jesuit priest Joaquin Bernas (Riedinger 1999: 203). The draft was believed to have been the handiwork of the National Security Council (NSC) headed by General José Almonte, a close adviser of President Ramos (ibid.). The draft contained anti-democratic elements such as the weakening of accountability of the executive branch to the Congress, the suspension of *habeas corpus* in cases when public safety is threatened and the absence of provisions curtailing periods of martial law (ibid.). The constitutional reform debate then centred on contentious provisions in the 1987 Constitution which curbed the duration of office for the members of the executive and legislature. The 1987 charter did not allow the president to extend his or her single six-year term of office. The spirit and intent of this prohibition was based on a lingering 'fear of a repetition of the Marcos phenomenon' (Bernas 1999: 7). Members of the Senate were limited to two consecutive terms, with six years per term while members of the House of Representatives were allowed three terms of three years each.

Ramos successfully projected himself as a hardworking economic manager and enjoyed relatively high public satisfaction levels (Pinches 1997: 112–113). Proponents of cha-cha argued on the strength of Ramos's achievements as an economic manager. The People's Initiative for Reform, Modernization and Action (PIRMA, also a Filipino term meaning to sign or signature) led the movement to amend the constitution. PIRMA led the Alliance of Concerned Citizens for an Empowered Social System (ACCESS), a movement of 40 pro-cha-cha non-governmental organizations (NGOs) (Go 1997: 38). On 23 June 1997, PIRMA initially submitted to the COMELEC some 5.6 million signatures in aid of the 'initiative and referendum' clause in the constitution so that an amendment could be pursued (ibid.; Riedinger 1999: 204).

The CBCP on 20 March 1997, issued a pastoral statement declaring the 'inopportuneness' of charter change (*The CBCP Monitor* 1997a: 3). The CLP likewise believed that charter change initiatives were 'suspect of political and governmental manipulation' (*The CBCP Monitor* 1997b: 3). A much stronger CBCP statement was released in August claiming that the real motive of charter change was 'addiction to power' (*The CBCP Monitor* 1997c: 12). Suspicions abounded that Ramos was orchestrating the movement covertly (Thatcher 1997). While he denied he was seeking another term of office, the key leaders in PIRMA, in the legislative and executive branches supporting the move, were closely identified with him. In addition, he did not attempt to dissuade them from pursuing it nor did he categorically state that there would be no constitutional amendment before the 1998 elections.

PIRMA's petition to the COMELEC seeking its assistance for a signature campaign was rejected by the Supreme Court on 19 March 1997 and subsequently confirmed on 10 June 1997 (Go 1997: 39). The rules for 'initiative and referendum' based on the 1987 charter had not been passed by the Congress, and so the legal mechanism was inadequate for this purpose (Bernas 1999: 194–196). Despite the Supreme Court's ruling, the campaign shifted to convoking the Congress making it into a Constituent Assembly (Alegre 1997: 43–44). Public opinion of various sources was largely against charter change. Two separate surveys indicated 60–69 per cent opposition (Baretto-Lapitan 1997: 25).

The Churches (Catholic and Protestant) along with pro-democracy civil society groups intensified their campaign nationwide. Cardinal Sin issued two pastoral letters. The first one released on 3 July 1997 warned against convoking the existing Congress as a Constituent Assembly as this merely showed 'aggrandizement of certain persons and political dynasties' (Sin 1999a: 444). The other letter was an appeal to support the mobilization on the National Day of Protest, 21 September 1997, the 25th anniversary of the declaration of martial law (Sin 1999b: 462–463). The AMRSP joined the chorus that rejected cha-cha and supported the 21 September mobilization ('AMRSP and Mission Partners' statement against charter change', 1997). Despite a heavy downpour, some 600,000 people gathered in Rizal Park, Manila, led by former President Aquino and Cardinal Sin, two prominent figures of People Power I (Pinches 1997: 104 and 116). This was the biggest protest assembly and the broadest representation of political groups in the post-Marcos era (Alegre 1997: 45). To dramatize their formation, 50 representatives (including former President Aquino and Cardinal Sin) coming from 12 sectors, 10 national social movements and 8 political parties signed a 'Multisectoral Covenant for Freedom and Democracy', but unfortunately the unity fizzled out subsequently (Ibid.; *The CBCP Monitor* 1997d: 3). Similar gatherings nationwide were also held to protest the cha-cha campaign. In Cebu, Cardinal Vidal, convenor of the 5th Visayas Region Pastoral Assembly, issued a statement rejecting cha-cha and raising fears of a 'new oligarchy and of another dictatorship' in the offing (Vidal 1997). Sixty-five dioceses nationwide held some form of mass protest (*The CBCP Monitor* 1997c). These rallies involving a million people merely confirmed the strong opposition registered in public opinion. President Ramos was left with little choice. Hours before the massive 21 September rally in Rizal Park, Ramos categorically assured the public that there would be no cha-cha before 1998 (ibid.). Thus, Amando Doronila (1997: 9) concludes that '(t)he rallies (anti-cha-cha protests) further proved that outside of the state, the Church is the only social force capable of mobilizing public opinion and protest against any regime'. Indeed, the Church (i.e. ordained ministers interacting with the laity) appeared to be the only organization which could fill the political gap created by a bankrupt party system, but only when it was allied with civil society.

Estrada's constitutional correction for development (CONCORD)

President Estrada likewise attempted to tamper with the charter, but using the economic development card. In his State of the Nation Address on 26 July 1999, Estrada openly declared his intention to change the constitution to accelerate economic development. Estrada initially planned to convene the Congress into a constituent assembly for the approval of economic provisions and then set up the constitutional convention to address the political reforms. This was interpreted to mean removing the 'Filipino-First Policy' in the constitution (Bagares 1999: 1 and 5).[15] For others, the economic motivation was simply a veneer over a dreaded political intent: lifting the presidential term cap (Doronila 2001: 45).

Opposition to Estrada's CONCORD was generated quickly by the Protestant and Catholic Churches and civil society actors including the Left. CBCP President Archbishop Oscar V. Cruz declared that the charter amendment 'does not augur well for the redemption of Filipinos as a people' (*The CBCP Monitor* 1999: 3). The Archdiocese of Manila, led by Cardinal Sin, mobilized its flock in a multi-sectoral rally on 20 August 1999 (Sin 1999b). The timing was significant as 21 August marked the assassination of Benigno 'Ninoy' Aquino in 1983. Corazon Aquino and Cardinal Sin once again led this grand mobilization (Araneta 1999: 1 and 6). Meanwhile, Ricardo Cardinal Vidal and 58 bishops from the Ecumenical Bishops Forum (EBF), consisting of Catholic and Protestant bishops were united in resisting moves to amend the constitution (Gallardo and Rivera 1999: 1 and 14). Cardinal Vidal urged the faithful to show their opposition on 20 August in unity with other Churches (ibid.: 14).

On 20 August, rallies were held across the country. In Manila, some 70,000 people led by ex-President Aquino and Cardinal Sin congregated at the heart of Makati, the business hub in Manila (PDI 1999a: 1 and 18). Outside Metro Manila, around 160,000 people demonstrated (PDI

1999b: 6). The Diocese of Bacolod held the biggest provincial protest, with about 60,000 participants led by Bishop Emeritus Fortich (ibid.). On 21 September, the 27th anniversary of the proclamation of martial law, further demonstrations led by militant groups and Church-supported organizations took place in Metro Manila and in 31 provinces and cities (PDI 1999c: 1 and 16). The Church in partnership with civil society was a key protagonist in the campaign against CONCORD. In Manila, following instructions from Cardinal Sin, the pealing of the Church bells signalled a noise barrage to protest Estrada's CONCORD (ibid.). Meanwhile, Estrada's popularity (net performance) in opinion polls plunged from +60 in September to +28 in October to an all-time low of +5 in December 1999 (Mangahas 2000). A Social Weather Station survey in June showed that 86 percent of the people polled were against constitutional amendment (Marfil and Lujuan 1999: 1 and 18).[16] With mounting opposition to CONCORD and declining personal popularity, Estrada shelved the project.

The mobilizations were a clear indication of people's determination to articulate their voice and to press for accountability – thanks in great measure to the CBCP, and individual bishops. This speaks of the capacity of the Church leadership to instill the notion of engaged citizenship among the people, despite differing political persuasions.

The Church and People Power II

The ousting of President Estrada (between 15 and 20 January 2001), dubbed 'People Power II' by some political observers, was a more complex phenomenon than the 'People Power I' that prompted regime change in 1986. First, Estrada, unlike Marcos, had a significant electoral mandate (winning nearly 40 per cent of the vote in a ten-way contest with significant support, mostly from the poor). Second, there was a broader elite consensus in People Power I compared with People Power II. Estrada had strong backing from key elements of the business elite including former Marcos-linked business magnates Eduardo Cojuangco and Lucio Tan, but the bulk of the business elite opposed him. Third, the Church, from its leaders down to its members, was fragmented on the issue. And fourth, CSOs were likewise divided. The anti-Estrada civil society forces were typically middle class while the pro-Estrada organized groups mainly came from the urban poor.

Estrada had impressive net satisfaction ratings in his first year of office: +61 net satisfaction in November 1998, +67 in March 1999 and +65 in June 1999 (Mangahas 2000: 15). Growing signs of inept leadership, the return of Marcos-era cronies and nepotism, and the lack of a coherent and comprehensive program addressing poverty, however, eroded Estrada's popularity. On 2 October, Ilocus Sur Governor Luis 'Chavit' Singson, Estrada's former close associate, linked President Estrada to anomalous *jueteng* payoffs of $8 million and $2.6 million from tobacco excise tax (Doronila 2001: 4). [17] In the wake of this exposé, Cardinal Sin (2000) and the Presbyterial Council of the Archdiocese of Manila issued a statement on 11 October declaring that the presidency 'has lost the moral ascendancy to govern'. This statement was the first official position from a national organization. The following day, Vice-President Gloria Macapagal-Arroyo resigned as Secretary of the Department of Social Welfare and Development (DSWD). From then on, she became the unifying symbol of the opposition movement. On 20 October, CBCP President Archbishop Quevedo seconded Cardinal Sin's position (Quevedo 2000). The NCCP and the Council of Ulama (Islamic leaders) added its voice to Cardinal Sin's call for Estrada's resignation (Magno 2001: 259).

The Catholic Church held a mass prayer rally at the EDSA Shrine, Mandaluyong, on 4 November 2000 led by Cardinal Sin and former president Aquino. In his speech, Sin called for Estrada's resignation on the basis of the widespread immorality that had plagued the office of the president (Bordadora, Nazareno and Javellana 2000). Some 80,000 to 100,000 were mobilized making it the largest anti-Estrada rally during his presidency (ibid.). The anti-Estrada civil society forces from the right, centre and left of the political spectrum backed the prayer rally. The CBCP, backing Cardinal Sin's call, issued a statement enjoining the faithful to join prayer rallies which would be staged in the dioceses throughout the country (CBCP-NASSA Press Release, n.d.). In many provinces and cities including Baguio City, Nueva Vizcaya, Pampanga, Bulacan, Bacolod City and Iloilo City, similar prayer rallies were organized by the Church (PDI 2000: 1 and 4).

Nevertheless, cracks within the Church were visible among and between the bishops and lay organizations. CBCP President Archbishop Quevedo's statement supporting Cardinal Sin's appeal was not a collegial statement binding on all members, unlike the CBCP statement issued in February 1986. Only about a third of all the Philippine bishops were actively involved in the campaign to oust Estrada (Carroll 2001: 246). The Archbishop of Cebu, Cardinal Vidal, for instance, remained sympathetic to Estrada and avoided calling for his resignation to the dismay of many parishioners in Cebu (ibid.). Bishop Teodoro Bacani, a Manila Auxiliary bishop and El Shaddai spiritual director,

Bishop Camilo Gregorio, and others supported Estrada. Brother Mike Velarde, leader of El Shaddai, aligned his flock with Estrada although some El Shaddai leaders signed a letter calling for his resignation. By contrast, the Couples for Christ, a middle class Catholic charismatic group, became a key player in the movement to make Estrada accountable. These divisions within the Church affected its internal dynamics and its interaction with civil society. Although many groups in the Church formed partnership with anti-Estrada CSOs, the Church failed to win the support of pro-Estrada organizations and many urban poor communities. Staff of NGOs supporting some urban poor organizations in Manila were seen marching with the anti-Estrada camp while the communities they organized joined the pro-Estrada rallyists.

On 20 January 2001, Gloria Macapagal-Arroyo took her oath of office before Chief Justice Hilario Davide at the EDSA Shrine. In a national survey, 61 per cent accepted Arroyo as the new president while only 22 per cent opposed her (ABS-CBN/SWS 2001: 50). Estrada, however, refused to accept the legitimacy of the Arroyo administration. On 2 March 2001, the legal question was laid to rest by the Supreme Court which voted 13–0 in favour of the legitimacy of the Arroyo administration (Yamsuan 2001). Despite this decision, the legitimacy of the Arroyo administration would continue to be a major issue especially when the 2004 presidential elections raised a host of issues that undermined the credibility of the electoral system. It was alleged that the Vatican was critical of the CBCP involvement in the events leading to the ousting of Estrada. Nonetheless, the Apostolic Nunciature rejected this allegation claiming that 'The Holy See ... is in absolute harmony and solidarity with the Catholic Bishops of the Philippines' ('Press Release of the Apostolic Nunciature' 2001). Vatican support gave legitimacy to the Church leadership involvement, an important recognition that what they were doing was in accord with the thrust of the Vatican leadership.

The CBCP and Macapagal-Arroyo administration

In general, the CBCP backed the Macapagal-Arroyo, but not as much as it did the Aquino administration. There were moments when the CBCP was critical of the administration. One such issue was the president's ambivalence on the death penalty for capital offences. Although President Macapagal-Arroyo had opposed the death penalty while serving in the Estrada administration, shortly after she declared her intention to run for the presidential office, she reversed her position (Aravilla

2004). The CBCP and human rights groups protested her decision not to stand in the way of the execution of convicts found guilty of heinous crimes. The CBCP charged that it was a political move to get more support from the Chinese-Filipino community who were often victims of kidnapping and extortion (ibid.). Before visiting Rome to meet Pope Benedict XVI on 26 June 2006, she pressed Congress to approve legislation ending the death penalty for those convicted of heinous crimes, a step many viewed as resulting from Church pressure.

A more pressing issue was the legitimacy issue hounding her presidency. Following her victory in the May 2004 presidential elections, accusations of electoral manipulation were raised. Macapagal-Arroyo admitted speaking by phone to a member of the Electoral Commission during the election period. This was seen by many as an attempt to use her influence to change the outcome of the election in her favour. Since it was a neck and neck race between Macapagal-Arroyo and Fernando Poe, the opposition and many independent-minded groups, Church leaders and citizens questioned the credibility of the result.

The first impeachment bid against the president was easily rejected by the legislature, a predominantly pro-administration entity. Her government pushed for charter change, seen by many as a search for a graceful exit, but this met with stiff resistance from the opposition, civil society actors and the CBCP. Many view the proposed charter change as an attempt to fuse and strengthen legislative and executive bodies, and perpetuate the interests of the governing elite. Although the CBCP did not join the clamour for her resignation, it was critical of the government's approach to brush aside the legitimacy issue (see CBCP 2006a; 2006b and 2006c). In a SWS survey released on 13 July 2006, 67 per cent of the Filipinos opposed the government's version of charter change (Mangahas 2006). The CBCP declared that while they respect those seeking for her impeachment to ferret out the truth, it opposed the government's proposal to have the charter changed immediately 'without the widespread discussion and participation that such changes require' (CBCP 2006c). Once again, the CBCP took to task the government for lack of accountability.

Conclusion

Based on the foregoing discussion, it appears that the CBCP was and arguably still is a key actor in strengthening democracy through engaged citizenship. Engaged citizenship is not content with the assertion of rights but calls for active engagement in strengthening the 1987 democratic constitution, restoring people's confidence in the electoral system, promoting peace and development, opposing the charter change schemes of Ramos, Estrada and Macapagal-Arroyo, pressing for accountability and transparency during the Estrada administration and pressuring Macapagal-Arroyo to address the legitimacy issue hounding her administration. In these interventions, the CBCP was fashioning a new wave of citizenship that was not merely rights based, but anchored on participation in strengthening and defending democratic institutions (e.g. 1987 Constitution, electoral reform), formulating a comprehensive peace agenda and pressing for State accountability.

The CBCP engagements with post-Marcos regimes showed a keen sense of democratic building through the increasing appreciation and practice of engaged citizenship. During the Aquino administration, the CBCP supported the democratic constitution, defended it from a string of military coup attempts, defined a peace agenda that it hoped would be acceptable to other peace stakeholders and strengthened the electoral system and human rights advocacy. The CBCP's commitment to promote Church-based electoral movements (e.g. VOTE-CARE and PPCRV) demonstrates that electoral reform cannot be left conveniently to the government and political parties. By conducting voter's education, ensuring fair and honest electoral proceeding, enabling people to cast informed political choices and so on, the people were able to exercise responsibly their right to participate in the elections.

During the Ramos administration, the CBCP consolidated its role as a guardian of democracy. Of notable importance here is the role played by the electoral movements to strengthen the electoral system – although this was not as forceful and influential as in the 1992 elections. The most important role of the CBCP as a body and the bishops as individual leaders was the active resistance against charter change that sought to weaken the democratic elements of the 1987 Constitution. The CBCP's position to defend the charter articulated the sentiments of the people who resisted the attempt to change the 1987 Constitution. On a another note, the CBCP's participation (including individual bishops through the BUF) in promoting peace in Mindanao and the realization of the GRP-MNLF peace agreement, although seen by some as a partial success, demonstrated its capacity to mobilize public opinion and voice their concerns in the peace process.

During the Estrada administration, the CBCP continued its mission of instilling engaged citizenship. This can be gleaned from its involvement in the anti-charter change campaign and in pressing accountability and transparency within the Estrada administration. Although it was a player in the ousting of Estrada in the interest of good governance and public accountability, Estrada's removal had an unfortunate effect of denigrating the democratic institutions that have always been fragile in post-authoritarian Philippine society.

The CBCP pursued its task of citizenship formation during the Macapagal-Arroyo administration. Once again, the CBCP has shown its unwavering support for the involvement of citizens in matters of great social and political importance: anti-death penalty campaign and charter change attempt (the third time in post-authoritarian Philippine society). It may be too soon to evaluate the role and impact of the CBCP's engagement with the Macapagal-Arroyo government. The fact, however, is no other single national organization in the Philippine society has paralleled the CBCP's influence to reshape the discourse and practice of citizenship. It remains to be seen though if the CBCP can sustain over the long haul its legacy and momentum in changing the everyday practice of Philippine citizenship.

Notes

1. The BBC is a partnership between the bishops and business people which promotes social reform and generated corporate funds for socio-economic projects. The BCC backed the National Movement for Free Elections (NAMFREL) in the 1980s and 1990s.
2. The NCCP is an aggregation of mainline Protestant Churches.
3. The BUF's role is discussed further below.
4. Conservatives were generally supportive of martial law and hesitant to involve the Church in temporal affairs. Moderates were critical of government policy that threatened the collective interests of the Church but ambivalent with regard to martial law. Progressives were critical of martial law and supportive of groups that struggled for political liberation (Youngblood 1982: 35–36).
5. Nonetheless, the social reform provisions were diluted by a deeply cautious Congress and weak executive leadership (Rocamora 2001: 45, 50–53). A typical example is the Comprehensive Agrarian Reform Law (CARL), a center-piece of the Aquino administration that was emasculated by Congress. On the other hand, the 1992 Urban Development and Housing Act (UDHA) in 1992 indicated that it was possible to pass pro-poor social legislation. In UDHA's case, the key players included the Urban Land Reform – Task Force (ULR-TF), the Institute of Church and Social Issues (ICSI), the BBC through Jesuit priest Joel E. Tabora, Cardinal Sin and influential elements in Congress (Karaos, Gatpatan and Hotz 1995).
6. The INC is a highly organized, secretive and centralized Church founded in 1914 by Felix Y. Manalo. It is vigorously opposed to mainstream Christian Churches. Its fundamentalist positions on Christian doctrines and practices make it difficult for other Churches to engage the INC in meaningful dialogue.

7. Business and professional groups were traditional supporters of NAMFREL since early 1950s (Hedman 1998). NAMFREL, being the only recognized electoral movement in the 1986 elections, was a very broad formation of sectors covering the business people, academic establishments, the Church, civic groups and other private organizations.
8. The CLP is an umbrella organization, comprising 37 national lay associations and 40 diocesan Councils of the Laity.
9. Many of these volunteers were also affiliated with VOTE-CARE. It is very difficult to determine how many members were exclusively under PPCRV or VOTE-CARE.
10. Schaffer (2001) provides a critical review of PPCRV and Church-based electoral movements based on an urban poor community in Manila.
11. Short of mentioning his name, the Church campaigned against Estrada on the basis of his known lifestyle and moral values (Aquino 1998: 8). In Sunday services, priests exhorted the faithful to vote for morally upright candidates. These attempts to erode popular sentiment for Estrada proved unsuccessful. Given his popularity plus a well-oiled political party, *Laban ng Makabayang Masang Pilipino* (LAMMP, Struggle of the Nationalist Filipino masses), he won nearly 40 per cent of the total votes cast in a ten-way contest, largely from poorer classes (Mangahas 1998: 124).
12. Church-linked organizations such as the Peace Promotion and Monitoring Council (PPMC) and the National Citizens' Peace Monitoring Council (NCPMC) were instrumental in providing reports to the NCC on ceasefire violations (Diokno 1994: 70). NASSA served as the NCC secretariat.
13. The Moro Islamic Liberation Front (MILF) is another faction in the Moro struggle for independence. The MILF adopted a more conservative stance than the moderate MNLF.
14. The SPCPD declared 14 (originally 13) provinces and 10 cities as 'Zones of Peace and Development' and 'Consultative and Development Councils' in Mindanao.
15. The 'Filipino-First Policy' ensures that land is predominantly owned by Filipinos. The constitution allowed 60 per cent ownership of land to Filipinos and 40 percent to foreigners. Estrada's CONCORD wanted 100 per cent ownership of land by Filipinos or foreigners.
16. *Pulse* Asia Inc. concluded that 42 per cent were against CONCORD, 32 per cent were agreeable provided only in a 'big crisis or emergency' while only 25 per cent were amenable to constitutional change if the citizens wanted it (see Gonzales 1999: 1).
17. 'Jueteng' is an illegal but widespread lottery game.

Bibliography

ABS-CBN/SWS. 2001. 'Survey on people power 2 and the change in the presidency', 2–7 February.

Abueva, José V. 1992. 'Strengthening the Constituency for Peace.' In *Ending the Armed Conflict: Peace Negotiations in the Philippines*, ed., Emmanuel C. Lallana. Quezon City: University of the Philippines Centre for Integrative and Development Studies and University of the Philippines Press, 9–21.

Abueva, José V. 1997. 'Philippine Democratisation and the Consolidation of Democracy Since 1986 EDSA Revolution: An Overview of the Main Issues, Trends and Prospects.' In *Democratization: Philippine Perspectives*, ed., Felipe Miranda. Quezon City: University of the Philippine Press, 1–81.

Alegre, Alan. 1997. 'Dirty Dancing with Democracy.' *Politik* 4 (2), November, 42–44.

'AMRSP and Mission Partners' Statement against Charter Change.' September 1997.

Aquino, Belinda A. 1998. 'Filipino Elections and "illiberal" Democracy.' *Public Policy* II (3), July/September, 1–26.

Araneta, Sandy. 1999. 'Sin to Join Cory in Aug. 20 Rally.' *The Philippine Star* (TPS), 31 July 1999, 1 and 6.

Aravilla, José. 2004. 'CBCP, Human Rights Group Outraged by GMA Decision on Convicts.' Available from http://www.newsflash.org/2003/05/h1/h1019384.htm, 16 April 2007.

Bagares, Romel. 1999. 'No to Poll Reforms, Yes to Foreign Ownership.' *TPS*, 12 December, 1 and 5.

Baretto-Lapitan, Giselle. 1997. 'The Church and the Philippines.' *Intersect* 12 (4), May, 25.

Bernas, Joaquin G. 1999. *A Living Constitution: The Ramos Presidency*. Pasig City: Anvil Publishing, Inc.

Bordadora, Norman, Rocky Nazareno and Juliet Javellana. 2000. '"Take a vow now": Estimated 80,000 to 100,000 Attend EDSA Shrine Prayer Rally.' *PDI*, 05 November, 1 and 14.

Callahan, William A. 2000. *Pollwatching, Elections and Civil Society in Southeast Asia*. Aldershot and Burlington: Ashgate Publishing Ltd.

Carlos, Desiree. 1986. 'Sin Backs Charter, Peace Talks.' *Malaya*, 05 November, 2.

Carroll, John J. 1999. 'Forgiving or Forgetting? Churches and the Transition to Democracy in the Philippines.' *Pulso*, Monograph no. 20, August.

——. 2001. 'Civil Society, the Churches and the Ouster of Erap.' In *Between Fires: Fifteen Perspectives on the Estrada Crisis*, ed., Amando Doronila. Pasig City: Anvil Publishing Inc., and Makati City: PDI, 236–251.

CBCP. (1990), *Letters and Statements, 1984–1990*. Manila: CBCP.

——. 2003a. 'Statement of the CBCP Administrative Council on Martial Law.' Available from http://www.cbcponline.org/documents/1970s/1972-martial_law.html, 21 February 2007.

——. 2003b. 'A Covenant Towards Peace: A Pastoral Letter of the Catholic Bishops' Conference of the Philippines on the Ratification of the 1986 Constitution of the Philippines.' Available from http://www.cbcponline.org/documents/1980s/1986–1986constitution.html, 21 February 2007.

——. 2003c. 'One Hundred Days of Prayer and Penance for National Reconciliation, Unity and Peace.' Available from http://www.cbcponline.org/documents/1980s/1986-100days_prayer.html, 27 March 2007.

——. 2006a. 'Pastoral Statement on the Alleged 'People's Initiative' to change the Constitution.' Available at http://www.cbcponline.net/html/peoplesinitiative.html, 18 April 2007.

——. 2006b. 'Renewing Our Public Life Through Moral Values.' Available at http://www.cbcponline.net/statements/renewingourpublic.html, 18 July 2007.

———. 2006c. 'Shepherding and Prophesying in Hope: A CBCP Pastoral Letter on Social concerns.' Available from http://www.cbcponline.net/statements/state-mentonsocialconcerns.html 17 July 2007 'CBCP-NASSA Press Release.' n.d.

Claver, Francisco. 1988. 'A History of BCCs: the Philippines.' In *Church of the People: the Basic Christian Community Experience in the Philippines*, eds, Gabino A. Mendoza et al. Manila: Bishops-Businessmen's Conference for Human Development, 18–27.

Claver, Francisco F. 1992. 'Church: Non-partisan but active.' *Intersect* 6(6): 8–9.

Coronel-Ferrer, Miriam Coronel and Antonette Raquiza (eds). 1993. *Options for Peace: Summary of Events Related to Negotiating the Communist Insurgency in the Philippines 1986–1992*. Manila: Coalition for Peace et al.

Diokno, Maria Serena I. 1994. *The 1986–1987 Peace Talks: A Reportage of Contention*. Quezon City: University of the Philippines, Centre for Integrative and Development Studies and the UP Press.

Doronila, Amando. 1997. 'Pulling the Back from the Brink.' *PDI*, 9 September.

———. 2001. *The Fall of Joseph Estrada: The Inside Story*. Pasig City: Anvil Publishing Inc., and Makati City: Philippine Daily Inquirer (PDI).

Gallardo, Froilan and Blanche Rivera. 1999. '58 Bishops Unite, Says No to Erap Charter.' *PDI*, 01 August, 1 and 14.

Go, Miriam Grace A. 1997. 'PIRMA: Dead Three Times Over; Will It Rise Again?' *Politik* 4 (2), November, Quezon City: Ateneo Center for Social Policy, 37–41.

Gonzales, Stella O. 1999. 'Survey Says Erap Popularity Down.' *Philippine Daily Inquirer*, 14 October, 1 and 20.

Guyano, Edilberto Calang. 1995a. 'Citizens for Clean Polls: Partners for Hope.' *NASSA News* XXIII (2), March–April, 16–17.

———. 1995b. 'VOTE-CARE Campaign: Success at the Grassroots' *NASSA News*, XXIII (3), May–June, 10–13, 22–24.

Hedman, Eva Lotta E. 1998. 'Whose Business is it Anyway? Free and Fair Elections in the Philippines' *Public Policy* II (3), July/September, 145–170.

Jones, Emma and John Gaventa. 2002. 'Concepts of Citizenship: A Review.' *IDS Development*, Bibliography 19.

Karaos, Anna Marie A., Marlene V. Gatpatan, and Robert V. Hotz, S. J. 1995. 'Making a Difference: NGO and PO Policy Influence in Urban Land Reform Advocacy.' *Pulso*, Monograph no. 15, January.

Kassimir, Ronald. 1998. 'The Social Power of Religious Organisation and Civil Society: The Catholic Church in Uganda.' In *Civil Society and Democracy in Africa: Critical Perspectives*, ed., Nelson Kasfir. London and Portland, Oregon: Frank Cass, 54–107.

Ledesma, Antonio J. 2005. *Healing the Past, Building the Future: Soundings from Mindanao*. Quezon City: Jesuit Communication Foundation, Inc and Manila: CBCP, Episcopal Commission for Inter-religious Dialogue.

Linantud, John L. 1998. 'Whither Guns, Goons, and Gold? The Decline of Factional Election Violence in the Philippines.' *Contemporary Southeast Asia* 20 (3), December, 298–318.

L'Osservatore Romano. 1986. 'Pope's Letter to Bishops of (the) Philippines: Ministry of Teaching and Guidance at Service of Truth and Justice' 28, 14 July, 5.

Magno, Alexander. 2001. 'Philippines: Trauma of a Failed Presidency.' *Southeast Asian Affairs*, 251–261.

Mangahas, Mahar. 1991. 'Who's Afraid of the Catholic Church?' *Social Weather Bulletin* 91 (4), February, 3.

——. 1998. *SWS Surveys in the 1998 National Elections*. Quezon City: Social Weather Stations.

——. 2000. 'Public Satisfaction with Governance in the Philippines, 1986–99', *SWS Occasional Paper*. June.

——. 2006. 'June 2006 Social Weather Survey: "No" Vote in Cha-cha Plebiscite Rises to 67%; Only 6.8% have Signed an Initiative-Petition.' Available from http://www.sws.org.ph, 17 July 2007.

Mangahas, Malou. 1988. 'Sin Prods Government on Genuine Land Reform.' *The Manila Chronicle*, 26 February, 1 and 8.

Marfil, Martin P. and Nereo C. Lujan. 1999. 'Narvasa Body Open to Junking Cha-cha.' *PDI*, 23 August, 1 and 18.

NCCP-RDO. 1992. 'The Philippine Churches in the Search for Peace.' *Tugon: An Ecumenical Journal of Discussion and Opinion* XII (1), 132–166.

Philippine Daily Inquirer (PDI). 1999a. 'We're Not afraid.' 21 August, 1 and 18.

——. 1999b. '160,000 rally outside Metro.' 21 August, 6.

——. 1999c. 'We Must Never Forget.' 22 September, 1 and 16.

——. 2000. 'Resign Calls Thunder Across Nation.' 5 November, 1 and 4.

Pinches, Michael. 1997. 'Elite Democracy, Development and People Power: Contending Ideologies and Changing Practices in Philippine Politics.' *Asian Studies Review* 21 (2–3), November, 112–113.

PPCRV. 1992. 'Faith and Fire: the PPCRV Way. A Post Election Report of the Parish Pastoral Council for Responsible Voting (PPCRV) to the Catholic Bishops' Conference of the Philippines (CBCP)' 25 July.

——. 'Report of the Parish Pastoral Council for Responsible Voting (RRCRV) to the Commission on Elections and to the Catholic Bishops' Conference of the Philippines on the Conduct of the May 11, 1998 National and Local Elections.'

'Press release of the Apostolic Nunciature.' 2001. Manila, 19 December.

Quevedo, Orlando B. 2000. 'On the Senate Hearing on the Singson Exposé', 20 October.

Quitorio, Pedro C., III, (ed.) 1995. *CBCP: Letters and Statements 1984–1990*. Manila: CBCP.

Ranger, Terence. 1995. 'Conference Summary and Conclusion.' In *The Christian Churches and the Democratization of Africa*, ed., Paul Gifford. Leiden, New York and Köln: E. J. Brill, 14–35.

Riedinger, Jeffrey M. 1999. 'Caciques and Coups: the Challenges of Democratic Consolidation in the Philippines.' In *Democracy and Its limits: Lessons from Asia, Latin America, and the Middle East*, eds., Howard Handleman and Mark Tessler. Notre Dame, Indiana: University of Notre Dame Press, 176–217.

Rocamora, Joel. 2001. *Breaking Through: The Struggle within the Communist Party of the Philippines*. Pasig City: Anvil Publishing Inc.

Santos, Ruperto C. 1997. 'A Short History of the Catholic Bishops' Conference of the Philippines, 1945–1995.' *Philippiniana Sacra* 96, September–December, 395–449.

Schaffer, Frederic Charles. 2001. 'Clean Elections and the "Great Unwashed": Electoral Reform and Class divide in the Philippines.' A Paper delivered at the 2001 Annual Meeting of the American Political Science Association, San Francisco, August 30–September 2, 2001, 09 September.

Sin, Jaime L. Cardinal. 1999a. 'Let us Uphold the Dignity of the Constitution.' In *On the Way of Truth: A Compilation of Pastoral Appeals and Statements during the 25 Years of His Eminence Jaime L. Cardinal Sin as Archbishop of Manila, March 18, 1974 – March 18, 1999*, ed., Nestor C. Cerbo. Manila: Archdiocese Office for Research and Development, 440–445.

——. 1999b. 'Pastoral Invitation: "Collegial Protest Against the Charter Change".' In *On the Way of Truth: A Compilation of Pastoral Appeals and Statements during the 25 years of His Eminence Jaime L. Cardinal Sin as Archbishop of Manila, March 18, 1974 – March 18, 1999*, ed., Nestor C. Cerbo. Manila: Archdiocese Office for Research and Development, 462–463.

——. 2000. 'On the Way of Truth. A Pastoral Statement of the Presbyteral Council of the Archdiocese of Manila.', 11 October.

Sin, Jaime L. Cardinal and the Auxiliary Bishops of Manila. 1989. 'A Pastoral Letter: Seize Power through a Coup d'etat is a Sin.' *TMC*, 13 December, 1 and 13.

'Social Weather Report Survey. Performance Rating of Institutions.' n.d. Social Weather Stations data base.

Tasker, Rodney. 1992. 'Church Militant: Religious Leaders Seek to Influence Vote.' *Far Eastern Economic Review*, 7 May, 18–20.

Thatcher, Jonathan. 1997. 'Church, Business Turn on Ramos.' *The Business Daily*, 08 September, 6.

The CBCP Monitor. 1997a. 'Pastoral Statement on Charter Change', I (5), 16 March, 3.

——. 1997b. 'Laity Also Against Charter Change,' I (5), 16 March, 3.

——. 1997c. 'Addiction to Power is the Real Issue Behind Charter Change moves – CBCP', I (17), 31 August, 12.

—— 1997d. 'People Power Alive in Anti-Cha-Cha Rallies', I(9), 08 September, 3.

——. 1999. 'CBCP President Urges Vigilance, Wisdom in Dissent; Assails New Cha-Cha Moves', III (16), 15 August, 3.

The 1987 Constitution of the Republic of the Philippines. n.d. Mandaluyong City: National Book Store.

Vidal, Ricardo J. Cardinal. 1997. 'Statement Against Charter Change' 5th Visayas Region Pastoral Assembly, September 1–4, 1997, Cebu City, *The CBCP Monitor* I (18), 14 September, 3.

Villacorta, Wilfrido V. 1991. 'Ideological Orientation of Political Forces in the Aquino era.' In *Economy and Politics in the Philippines Under Corazon Aquino*, ed., Berhard Dahm. Hamburg: Institut für Asienkunde, 161–183.

Vitug, Marites Dañguilan and Glenda M. Gloria. 2000. *Under the Crescent Moon: Rebellion in Mindanao*. Quezon City: Ateneo Center for social Policy and Public Affairs and Institute for Popular Democracy.

Wurfel, David. 1988. *Filipino Politics: Development and Decay*. Quezon City: Ateneo de Manila University Press.

Yamsuan, Cathy. 2001. 'It's 13–0 for Gloria: Supreme Court Cites Angara Diary as Basis for Erap Resignation.' *PDI*, 03 March, 1 and 16.

Youngblood, Robert. 1982. 'Structural Imperialism: An Analysis of the Catholic Bishops' Conference of the Philippines.' *Comparative Political Studies* 15 (1), April, 29–56.
—— 1989. 'Aquino and the Churches: A "Constructive Critical Solidarity"?' *Pilipinas: A Journal of Philippine Studies* 13, Fall, 57–71.

7
FBOs and Change in the Context of Authoritarianism: The Islamic Center Charity Society in Jordan

Janine A. Clark[1]

Introduction

Throughout much of the Middle East, faith-based charities affiliated with Islamist groups and/or parties comprise some of the largest and most effective organizations addressing the needs of the poor. Jordan is no exception, with the Islamic Center Charity Society (ICCS), the charity of the Muslim Brotherhood (MB), being the largest in the country other than those established or patronized by members of the royal family. The ICCS forms what most scholars regard as the charitable or social wing of the MB while the Islamic Action Front (IAF), an umbrella party of the MB together with independent Islamists, forms its political wing. Scholars of Islamist movements tend to focus on the political significance of these movements, and specifically their political parties, making reference at best to the recruitment function of the charities (Clark 2004a, 2004b, 1995; Wickham 2002; Wiktorowicz 2001; Wiktorowicz and Farouki-Taji 2000; Kandil and Ben Nefissa 1994; Sullivan 1994).[1] Yet charities affiliated with Islamist movements, such as the ICCS, are integral to the movements within which they are situated, and their presence and activities have implications for the movement's relations to the population at large, the internal politics of the movement and the movement's relationship with the regime and state. The socio-political nature of the ICCS, furthermore, has numerous implications for development. In addressing one of the central themes of this book, the future potential of faith-based organizations (FBOs) as positive and negative drivers of change, this chapter situates the ICCS within the MB and concludes with the argument that the type of change the ICCS can or cannot make, including the degree to which it can fulfil the United Nation's Millennium Development Goals, is intertwined with and contingent upon the future of the authoritarian regime in Jordan and political development in the region at large.[2]

The Muslim Brotherhood: historical background

As stated above, the MB is a multi-faceted social movement with two basic wings. These are its social wing, its social welfare and educational activities conducted under the umbrella of the ICCS, and its political wing, largely its political party, the IAF. The ICCS is one of the largest charities in the country, and the IAF similarly is the largest opposition party. The three organizations are administratively and financially separate, with distinct elections, administrative bodies and sources of revenues. While they overlap significantly in terms of members and/or supporters, decisions technically are made separately and the finances from one organization do not support the others. The success of the MB in its social and political endeavours is to a large extent due to its relationship with the regime in Jordan.[3] For most of its history, the MB has been a protected, indeed privileged, organization allowing it to gain unique advantages over other organizations in civil society. As the following section demonstrates, however, this relationship has changed dramatically since the early 1990s with a growing polarization between the MB and the regime.

The Hashemite Kingdom of Jordan emerged out of the British mandate of Transjordan and achieved independence in 1946 under the rule of the Hashemite family originally hailing from the area now known as Saudi Arabia. While the population is divided along ethnic lines with Jordanians, Palestinians and, to a much lesser extent, Circassians, Chechens, Armenians and Kurds, it is largely united by Sunni Islam. Sunni Muslims comprise approximately 90 per cent of the population, including the monarchy. In addition, approximately six per cent of the population is Christian; there also are limited numbers of Shi'a and adherents to other faiths.

The MB is almost as old as the Kingdom itself. It was established in 1945 and registered as a legal charitable society under the patronage of King Abdullah I (1921–1951). Emphasising education in Islamic (Sunni) principles, the activities of the early MB primarily took place in schools, and the MB founded its first school in the 1950s. The MB became more politicized after the 1948 War with Israel and the massive influx of Palestinian refugees into Jordan and its programme reflected this, calling for the implementation of Islamic law (*shari'a*) and the establishment of an Islamic order. In 1953, the MB was re-designated as a 'general and comprehensive Islamic committee'. With its new designation, it was able to operate freely and be de facto politically active while all other political organizations were banned. Under the protection of the regime and with the expansion of the type and number of its activities, the MB established the ICCS to deal specifically with its charity activities in 1963. The early years of favouritism by the regime were to set a pattern for much of the MB's history. Both Abdullah I and King Hussein (1953–1999) saw it to their advantage to privilege the MB at the expense of other organizations. Legalizing the organization brought it clearly into the open and allowed successive kings to keep an eye on it (Boulby 1999: 46).[4] In addition, the growth of the MB was seen as a means by which the rise and later the popularity of pan-Arab nationalism could be undermined. Finally, royal patronage of the MB indirectly would buttress the monarchy's own Islamic legitimacy based on its descent from the tribe of Prophet Mohammed (Wiktorowicz 2001: 95–101; Boulby 1999:46; Bar 1998: 32; Hourani et al. 1993: 13–14;).[5]

By 1989, when King Hussein liberalized the country politically and re-introduced national elections, the MB had deep and historical ties to the population. Running as independents, the MB won 22 seats which, combined with the 10 seats won by independent Islamists, created a Muslim Brotherhood-dominated Islamist bloc that controlled 40 per cent of the elected lower house (Boulby 1999: 73, 104; Mufti 1999: 110; Freij and Robinson 1996: 1–32). The candidates ran on a platform that largely focused on Jordan's economic problems and corruption. Economically, they called for the protection of private property, reduction of government debt, lowering of inflation, cutting government spending, measures to boost investment confidence, the redistribution of wealth through tax reform, the protection of infant industries, a virtual ban on imports, national self-sufficiency even in sectors where Jordan does not enjoy a comparative advantage, and the elimination of usury. Socially, the Brotherhood condemned moral corruption – alcohol, gambling, drugs, dance halls, bawdiness and the use of makeup. Finally, the platform called for greater democratic freedoms in Jordan, including freedom of expression, movement and worship (Robinson 1997: 377). Shortly after the legalization of political parties in 1992, the IAF, an umbrella party of MB together with independent Islamists, was established.[6]

Throughout the 1980s, the MB was active in elections of the country's professional associations and labour unions. While having electoral successes, it was only after 1989 that the Islamists' popularity soared (Hamayil 2000: 66–67). Since 1989, the MB and the IAF consistently have won council majorities in professional associations elections and student council elections. Despite a national electoral law (enacted in 1993) that discriminates against urban candidates and political parties (as opposed to rural, tribal independents, the backbone of monarchical support), the Islamist bloc attained 22 seats (16 seats went to the newly created IAF) in the 1993 parliamentary elections and 17 seats in the 2003 parliamentary elections.[7]

In its new leadership role, the MB soon found itself in a far more confrontational relationship with the government and regime than it had experienced prior to political liberalization. In 1994, Jordan signed the Washington Declaration and, later that year, the Wadi Araba peace treaty with Israel. The Islamists took the lead in opposing peace with Israel and were soon joined by leftists, Arab nationalist and eventually centrist political forces (Clark 2006). Although each had distinct reasons for opposing the peace, the opposition groups were able to unite under a banner objecting to Jordan's abandonment of the 'Arab camp' in favour of the 'peace camp' that included Israel and the United States (Clark 2006; Abu-Odeh 1999; Hamarneh, Hollis, and Shikaki 1997; Brand 1995). As efforts to prevent the treaty and then to prevent normalization of relations with Israel mounted, the government and regime resorted to increasingly authoritarian measures, further fuelling the flames of Islamist and popular anger. In anticipation of the popular resistance the treaty would face and wanting to ensure its passage in parliament, in 1993, the King initiated what many now see as the beginning of Jordan's process of de-liberalization, the above mentioned electoral laws. Viewed across the political spectrum as a conscious effort by the regime to reduce the number of seats won by Islamists in parliament, the law had its desired effect. The 1993 elections brought to power a parliament of largely tribal MPs loyal to the King that ratified the peace treaty by a vote of 55–23 (Scham and Lucas 2001: 60). As opposition to the normalization mounted, the government roll-back of political liberties further included the regulation of speeches in mosques, laws controlling the freedom of the press and new restrictions on demonstrations.

With international and regional events, such as the September 11, 2001 terrorist attack on the World Trade Center in New York, the US war on terrorism in Afghanistan as well as the US invasion of Iraq and the ousting of Saddam Hussein, the Islamist-led opposition has continued to demonstrate unabated against American and Israeli policies and practices in Iraq and Palestine and against Jordan's relations and/or collaboration with these two states. Oppositional activities furthermore include protests against the authoritarian measures designed to silence the opposition and against domestic policies, such as rising fuel prices. As Jordan began to be rocked by repeated, and increasingly violent, demonstrations, in 2001, King Abdullah II (1999–) suspended parliament and postponed the November elections. National elections were not held again until June 2003.

While the streets of Jordan have been calmer since the resumption of parliament in 2003, the MB/IAF remain the most vocal opposition voice – enough so that the government has continued in its attempts to silence them. In 2005, the government tabled a new professional association's (PA) law which most analysts argue was in direct response to the upcoming elections in Iraq and the Islamist-lead PAs' objections to the US occupation. In addition to restrictions and mechanisms for monitoring PAs, the law proposed the introduction of the one-person-one-vote system in syndicate elections. As in parliament, this electoral system would have a direct impact upon MB electoral success. The proposed PA law followed on the heels of a new non-governmental organization (NGO) law that also continues to be reviewed and revised today. The proposed NGO law clearly reflects the government's post 9/11 security fears and deals with NGOs, and particularly the ICCS, as security threats granting greater powers to the state in terms of NGO registration, monitoring, and dissolution and imposes harsher penalties, including criminal persecution and imprisonment. Finally, in 2006, despite objections by national and international human rights groups, the parliament passed a controversial new anti-terrorism law that allows security forces to put suspects under tight surveillance, to detain suspects without a court order, and to be tried at the State Security Court and to ban them from leaving the country.

Politically, regime repression has had multiple consequences, the most obvious of which has been the alarming re-assertion of authoritarianism in Jordan. Second, it has antagonized relations between the MB/IAF and the regime. Third, it has contributed to a consolidation of the anti-regime opposition polarizing the country's parties into two camps, pro-regime parties and anti-regime parties. Fourth, Islamist activities are fewer in number and size as compared to the 1990s. Indeed, opposition political parties as a whole are weak, activities at the professional associations have been curbed and university student council activities are limited to largely academic and administrative issues. The public, furthermore, is increasingly apathetic.

The ICCS

Within this context of increasing tensions between the regime and the MB, the ICCS remains one of the biggest and most successful NGOs in the country. As was its mother organization, the MB, the ICCS was protected throughout much of its early history. Its comparative advantage was boosted further by the influx of oil revenues in the form of remittances sent back home from the Gulf and customs and transportation taxes after 1973. As increased incomes translated into charitable donations, the ICCS' activities rapidly expanded during the 1970s. By the early 1990s, the revenues and expenditures of the ICCS far exceeded most other NGOs in the country.[8]

The stated goals of the ICCS are the following: education and teaching, through the establishment of schools, kindergartens and other educational organizations; medical and health care through its hospitals and medical centres; productive and training projects to serve local communities; and financial aid to poor families and orphans (www.islamicc.org). Based in Amman, the ICCS runs 4 branches and 55 centres in which it offers the above mentioned services and support.[9] With a budget of over one billion Jordanian Dinar (JD) (*Al-Hayat* 4 July 2006),[10] in 2004–2005, the ICCS spent 9,880,000 JD spent on services and items for the poor, an additional 2,100,000 JD and 815,000 JD on orphans and poor families respectively (both of which are sponsored monthly), and distributed 100,000 JD to 880 university student to help cover their educational fees (*Al-Arab Al-Youm* 1 July 2006). Within its centres, the ICCS runs 2 hospitals, 15 medical clinics, 1 college and 28 schools. The hospital is considered one of the best in Jordan and offers a full array of surgical and other services and is Jordan's only private teaching hospital (www.islamic-hospital.org; Clark 2004a: 93–94, 99–103). The medical clinics alone received 153,819 patients in 2005 and the number of students in the schools was 12,062 (*Al-Arab Al-Youm* 1 July 2006). Finally, the ICCS has a fund for subsidizing the medical costs of poor patients who receive services at the Islamic Hospital; between 1982, when the Islamic Hospital in Amman was founded, and 2006, the Fund for the Sick and Poor subsidized 58,056 cases to a tune of 5,738,197 JD in total (*Al-Arab Al-Youm* 1 July 2006). The sums its deals with and the number of poor the ICCS aids, thus, are enormous by Jordanian standards.

The MB's focus on charity stems from Islam's strong emphasis on social justice and social welfare, including (but not limited to) the giving of alms (*zakat*) as one of the five pillars of Islam. Islamic values, furthermore, are reflected directly and indirectly in the majority of the ICCS' activities. The ICCS schools follow the basic curriculum of the Ministry of Education but offer extra classes in religious education. In addition, teachers integrate an Islamic component into all subjects. Outside the classroom, the students have lectures on topics of social relevancy in the mosque. Both teachers and students must perform noon-time prayers. The aim of the schools is to teach a lifestyle; students are not given an Islamic education in the narrow sense of the word (Clark 2004a: 95; Roald 1994: 173). Similarly, the Islamic Hospital in Amman has strict criteria for the hiring of its employees. All nurses must be practicing Muslims, have high morals, and wear proper Islamic dress – all females must wear the *hijab* and long, modest dress. The hospital furthermore attempts to implement gender segregation with female nurses and doctors treating female patients.[11] The staff is encouraged to discuss Islam with patients, and religious literature is available for patients and Islamic videos and programming are shown on TV (Clark 2004a: 94).

Having stated this, neither the schools nor the hospital promote an Islamic model of education rooted in philosophical pedagogical concepts coming from Islamic scholars. Rather, as Roald points out, the ICCS schools are based on a 'dichotomized understanding of science' – Islamic sciences deal with worship and academic sciences deal with worldly affairs (Roald 1994: 175). The ICCS schools do not reject secular social sciences but seek a greater emphasis on Islamic values of modesty and on political values that emphasize Arabism and pan-Islamism (as opposed to Jordanianism as represented by an emphasis on the royal family in the public schools) (Roald 1994: 172, 175). The ICCS educational institutions, therefore, are neither rigid in their approach towards Islam nor are they anti-Westernization. They largely promote (and are sometimes criticized for) the formalization or practice of outward features of basic Islamic values (such as veiling) (Roald 1994: 172, 175). They furthermore uphold a worldview that is avowedly opposed to the existence of Israel and to Western interference in the region.

In the numerous smaller ICCS centres, those distributing aid and clothing and offering limited medical services, however, there is little to distinguish the ICCS centre from other charities, including state-run *zakat* centres (Clark 2004a: 109, 151–154).[12] The act of giving aid and support is itself the expression of faith. In these centres, Islamic values largely are held up by those who work in the centres and the religious-based motives they may have for working or volunteering there. What differentiates the ICCS is the belief of those who work within the ICCS that they are promoting Islam through their work (Clark 2004a: 153; Wiktorowicz 2001: 65, 67, 85).

As its name and goals state, the ICCS is a charity and engages in poverty reduction and not development or empowerment *per se*. While its educational services may be regarded as empowering, the ICCS is rooted fundamentally in a distributive logic and not an empowerment one. Having stated this, the ICCS does contribute to many of the Millennium Development Goals, including eradicating extreme poverty and hunger, achieving universal primary education, reducing child morality, improving maternal health and combating diseases.[13] Noticeably absent are the two goals of promoting gender equality and empowering women and developing a global partnership for development.[14] The following sections address these two issues.

ICCS and gender

The ICCS is run by an elected board of directors consisting of nine people; a general assembly of 360 members elects the board.[15] The members overwhelmingly are MB supporters albeit not exclusively. As the ICCS is run by and affiliated with the MB, an understanding of its approach towards gender needs to be put within the larger context of the MB and IAF.

The MB, IAF and ICCS all have female members and/or employees and volunteers. While exact numbers are not available, most estimates indicate that as much as 50 per cent of the Islamist movement is female. Within the MB, women are not readily visible and do not have the right to vote nor to nominate candidates within the organization. However, the IAF's political platform clearly acknowledges the legitimate rights of women and their role in the development of society, noting that women have a right to participate in public life, including in leadership roles (Hourani et al. 1993: 32). Theoretically, women may hold any political post except for 'head of state' (Ibid: 21).[16] Although not originally the case when the IAF was created, women are allowed to vote, to stand for elections internally and to run as candidates for the IAF in national elections (Clark and Schwedler 2003; Brand 1998). As a result, there are a handful of women in the IAF's *Shura* (Consultative) Council, and the IAF had its first (and only) female candidate in the 2003 parliamentary elections.[17] The women's sector within the IAF, furthermore, is very active recruiting women to the party. However, the *Shura* Council meets only twice a year (although it can and has been called for extraordinary sessions, sometimes meeting a total of four times per year) and is a relatively weak body. The Executive Council is the most important decision-making body in the IAF; there are no women in it.

Having stated this, the MB and IAF are socially conservative bodies. This is most readily evidenced in the IAF's document in political reform released on its website in October 2005 (www.jabha.net). The document is highly gendered extolling women in their roles as mothers and caregivers. While it further states that women are equal to men except in regards to certain texts (unnamed) issued by wise (but unnamed) judges and have the right to vote, participate in elections and hold official positions, it does little to assuage women activists' concerns regarding MB/IAF actions in the past. These actions include the MB's attempts in the early 1990s to legislate a ban on male hairdressers and on males (including fathers) watching girls' sports.

Within this larger context, the ICCS unsurprisingly is highly gendered in its approach. The ICCS is overwhelmingly run by men (with the exception of the girls' schools and the college teachers) and the services are in keeping with a socially conservative understanding of women's needs. The hospitals, medical centres, college and schools are all segregated, with separate facilities for males and females. Female students and staff in the college and schools are expected to wear the *hijab* (Islamic head-dress).[18] And in some of the centres for orphans, boys receive more classes than girls (for example, twice a week as opposed to once a week) in recognition both of the perceived greater tendency for boys to get into trouble and of their future leadership roles.

With the exception of the all-girls schools and the all-girls college, *Merkaz Nusayba* in the city of Zarka is the only centre in the ICCS run entirely by women and strictly for women and children. Its two main goals are to increase the role of women economically within society and the family and to provide charity for needy families. The centre offers a variety of programmes for women, such as sewing, hair-dressing lessons, handwork and crafts (such as crocheting), sports (there is a sports hall in the basement) and Qur'an singing. It also offers lectures on issues such as health care and child care. They, furthermore, enlist women volunteers to distribute clothing and food to the poor. This conservative approach towards gender is entirely in keeping with other Islamic charities in Jordan; it is markedly different, however, from the country's activist NGOs.

The ICCS and the NGO community in Jordan

Broadly speaking, Jordanian NGOs can be divided into three categories, those that are 'non-governmental', 'semi-governmental' and 'royal'. With a high degree of government regulation and interference, Jordan's NGOs are anything but non-governmental. The term is used here, however, to denote those organizations and associations that are non-profit and, most importantly, are neither established by nor patronized by the government or a royal family member.[19] As distinguished here, NGOs are established and run by members from the general population and can have volunteers, employees, fee-paying members or a combination thereof. Semi-governmental NGOs are those that were established by the government, and as a result have ministerial representation on their boards of directors (and potentially some NGO representatives).[20] Royal organizations or RONGOs, such as the Jordan River Foundation headed by Queen Rania (wife of Abdullah II), are founded by and under the patronage of a member of a royal family member. The ICCS' relationship with Jordan's RONGOs and NGOs is determined both by their respective relationships to the regime and socio-political values reflected in their aims and projects. Based on both these grounds, the ICCS largely operates in isolation from the NGO community at large – an arrangement that neither side finds problematic.

Jordan has a long history of royal family members establishing organizations in the name of specific causes. While they are the projects of individual members of the extended royal family, and not state projects, it is extremely difficult not to view RONGOs as extensions of state or, more accurately, *palace* power in order to ensure the dominance of Hashemite political interests (Brand 2001: 585; Brand 1998: 171). RONGOs can be found in every sector of society demonstrating the benign and paternal face of the monarchy, promoting the monarch's and state's views, and ensuring that civil society activities do not challenge their policies.[21] As such, the underlying power structure and aims of RONGOs place them indirectly at odds with the ICCS. This divide is exacerbated by the differing approaches the respective institutions take. RONGOs and semi-governmental NGOs are development organizations and not charities. The Jordan River Foundation's programmes include assisting communities in establishing business cooperatives. While it works with local religious leaders as part of some of it projects, by the very nature of the political context, the power structures the foundation and the ICCS represent, and the differing philosophies regarding social work (broadly speaking), there is virtually no contact between the two organizations.

The situation is no different when one looks at activist NGOs, such as the Jordan Women's Union (JWU). The JWU focuses on a broad range of projects aimed at economic and political empowerment, including campaigns to amend laws of concern to women, and was the first NGO to start up a help hotline for women who suffer form domestic abuse and a Children's House where divorced parents can visit their children (commonly, the separated parent has to do so at the police station). The leftist orientation of the JWU, as many other activist NGOs, ultimately makes cooperation between the JWU and the ICCS very difficult. While IAF women have approached women in the JWU regarding the prospects of joint participation at opposition rallies related to foreign affairs (and IAF also visited the JWU in order to see the shelter), the two work in isolation from each other.

In contrast to the ICCS, RONGOs and NGOs receive substantial funding from Western donors such as the European Union and the United States Agency for International Development (USAID).[22] The distinctly dissimilar worldviews and, as a consequence, different agendas all mean that RONGOs and the ICCS operate on decidedly different playing fields. RONGOs are predominantly in the business of development and their audience is to a large extent a Western one – it speaks to Western donors, international agencies and agendas. The ICCS does not. It neither requests nor accepts funding from Western donors, preferring to raise money through donations locally and regionally.[23]

The political and social tensions between RONGOs and NGO activists on the other hand and the MB/IAF on the other was most clearly evidenced in the debates over the legal amendments regarding divorce and the honour crimes law (Clark 2006, 2003; Nanes 2003; Brand 1998). An honour crime refers to the killing of a girl or woman in order to cleanse her family's honour as a result of alleged sexual transgressions. A man's right to take action against his wife or female relative is enshrined in Jordanian law via four articles in the Penal Code. Article 340a exempts from punishment a perpetrator who discovers his wife or female relative committing adultery and he kills, injures or harms one or both of them. Article 340b similarly provides a reduced sentence for a man who surprises his wife or other female relative in an unlawful bed and murders, wounds or harms them.[24] The proposed amendment regarding honour crimes (submitted to parliament as a temporary law) abolished Article 340 and introduced tougher punishments for adulterers, for murderers of female relatives who were victims of rape, molestation or abduction, and for rapists. The temporary Personal

Status Law (PSL) introduced a form of divorce (commonly referred to as *khula'*, based on the Arabic word extraction) allowing women divorce on demand.[25] The amendment gives women the same rights to undisputed divorce that Jordanian men possess – with no rights to financial compensation and with the stipulation that they return their dowries.[26]

While various RONGOs, semi-governmental NGOs and NGOs had been active in attempts to amend laws related to honour crimes, as well as pressuring for greater divorce rights for women, the MB and IAF were vitriolic in their opposition to both amendments and to the activists who supported them.[27] In the parliamentary debate surrounding the PSL amendment and Article 340, the MB and IAF railed against perceived Western interference, undemocratic practices and declining morality (Clark 2006, 2003; Nanes 2003). Indeed, the debate soon pitted different worldviews against each other – the Western values the NGO activists presumably represented against supposedly Islamic and Jordanian values – and involved quite caustic attacks against some of the activists supporting the abolition of Article 340 for their Western lifestyle, appearances and values. They were not debates regarding women's rights per se. The IAF argued that abolishing Article 340 would invite immorality and accused the West of pressuring the regime to abolish the article; of eroding Jordanian values and culture. IAF MPs similarly argued that the divorce law was being promoted by wealthy, presumably Westernized 'women of comfort and leisure who don't care about their families' (*Jordan Times*, 28 June 2004). If implemented, *khula'* would encourage moral disintegration and destroy family values. Hayat Musimi, the IAF's sole female MP, predicted the collapse of hundreds of families should the amendment pass (*Al-Dustur*, August 4, 2003; *Jordan Times*, August 4, 2003).

As a charity institution, the ICCS was silent throughout the debate. In fact, the debate was largely between NGO/RONGO activists and the MB and particularly the IAF; not between political parties. However, the two amendments demonstrate not only the institutional and political context within which the ICCS is rooted but also the disparity between the ICCS and the NGO community at large, including RONGOs as the representatives of the royal family. Any global partnership for development would not only be contingent upon an expansion of the ICCS' mandate beyond poverty reduction to encompass other aspects of development, but a sea shift in basic world views; particularly the underlying assumptions regarding liberal democratic rights and freedoms that underlie Western and international development projects.

The ICCS and the middle class

The ICCS' success is not only due to its historically protected status but the strong professional middle-class networks in which it is embedded. These networks include middle-class doctors and teachers who donate to and work for the ICCS. At the same time, they are themselves clients of the ICCS. In fact, ICCS largely is by and for the middle class. This focus on the middle class serves to address the needs of MB supporters (who are middle class), who indirectly recruit greater numbers of supporters, and ensure the viability of the ICCS.

As documented elsewhere, while the ICCS serves thousands of poor, the organizational needs of the ICCS and the social base of the MB necessitate, if not dictate, that the ICCS offer employment and services to the middle class. Without the middle class, the contacts it has, the donations it raises and the professional job skills it provides, the ICCS simply could not maintain the size and level of excellence it does presently. The ICCS has approximately 3,400 employees, most of whom are educated professionals working in the schools, medical clinics and hospitals (*Al-Arab Al-Youm*, 1 July 2006). These middle-class employees provide excellent services, but they also receive employment and working conditions that are superior to those found elsewhere in terms of salaries, hours and vacation time (Clark 2004a: 103, 106; Clark 2004b).

Perhaps most importantly, the question needs to be asked to whom they are providing services. A closer examination of the ICCS reveals that it offers two types of services, charity services for the poor and fee-paying services for the middle class. The ICCS' hospitals, college and schools are cases in point. The Islamic Hospital in Amman, for example, is a '5 star' hospital. According to a 1998 price list, the cost of a natural delivery, one child, no complications and one over-night stay in a third-class room in the Islamic Hospital is 190 JD. This fee is comparable to some of the most expensive private hospitals in the country. If we examine the prices of *al-Bashir* Hospital, a public hospital located in poorer East Amman and catering to lower incomes, the cost of a delivery and over-night stay is only 18 JD! (Clark 2004a: 100–101). A similar situation exists in the ICCS schools. According to the ICCS Executive Report for 1998, out of the ICCS' 11,345 kindergarten, elementary and secondary/high school students, there were only 93 students on scholarships for the poor and orphans. In other words, 11,252 students were paying full-tuition – ranging anywhere from approximately 120 JD per year (kindergarten) to 545 JD per year (grade 10) (Clark 2004a: 103). Yet, according to the World Bank,

Jordan's poor households spend only 19.99 JD per capita per year on education (Clark 2004a: 103).

The ICCS' middle-class bias is reflected in the location of the ICCS centres. In contrast to the charitable NGO community in general, which is evenly distributed between rural and urban communities, the Islamic NGO community tends to be located in urban centres (Clark 2004a: 98–99). An overwhelming number are located in the governorate of Amman, followed by the cities of Zarka and Irbid. In other words, ICCS services are located in urban areas, particularly Amman, where there are more people with the means to donate time and money to ICCS activities.

This focus on urban areas comes at the expense of the country's tribal regions, such as Ma'an, Mafraq, Tafiela, which are the poorest and the least economically developed in Jordan (International Crisis Group 2003). Jordan suffers from significant regional disparities with the 2.02 million citizens who live in Amman scoring the highest levels in the Human Development Index (HDI) while the development status of Ma'an, Mafraq and Tafiela remain relatively weak. Although between 1997 and 2002, Ma'an and Tafiela recorded significant improvements in the HDI, well above national average, they remain the lowest (*Jordan Human Development Report* 2004: 1, 20; Saif forthcoming). Yet, of the 55 ICCS centres, only 2 are located in Ma'an (Ma'an has an education centre and an orphanage) and 1 in Tafiela (the centre hosts an orphanage and a health centre). Amman has 21 centres (2 of these are the Islamic Hospital and the Fund for the Sick and Poor), each of which offer multiple services (www.islamicc.org).[28]

The location of the ICCS centres and the ICCS' focus on the middle class is necessary to attract and maintain a trained workforce; it is vital to the sustainability of the ICCS. The middle-class bias also serves to address the demands and needs of the MB's membership base writ large. Since the late 1940s, the MB leadership has been dominated by professionals – the first generation in Jordan that sought 'to advance itself through their professional skills and talents rather than through the use of wealth and personal connections', and pursued its livelihood through salaries, technical fees, scholarships and professional activities (Boulby 1999: 50–51). These were often the first generation of men to be literate in their families and, most importantly, to 'discover their best friends at school or in a political movement, not among kin. They are the first to trust strangers on grounds of competence or shared ideology' (Boulby 1999: 51). As Marion Boulby states, they were young, usually in their twenties, had attained some degree of post-secondary education, and were professionals or professional-in-the-making. Furthermore, most of the Brethren met while at school in Jordan or abroad (Clark 2004a: 86–87; Boulby 1999: 37–38, 50–58, 103). Almost forty years later, the composition of the members of the IAF's Founding Committee broken down according to profession reveals that a disproportionately high number of members similarly are white collar professionals. Of the 353 founding members of the IAF, in 1992, 37.7 per cent were professionals (this figure excludes business people and salaried employees). This includes 24 university professors, 26 physicians, 22 engineers, 16 pharmacists, 25 lawyers, 17 managers, and 3 journalists (Clark 2004a: 17; Moaddel 2002: 121–122; Azm 1997: 101–103). The middle-class constituency of the MB, furthermore, is located in the country's urban areas. Examining voter behaviour in national elections, it becomes clear that the IAF's power base is concentrated in Amman and Zarqa.[29]

The ICCS thus serves both a political and social purpose. By catering to the middle class it serves to address and integrate the operational dictates of the ICCS as a charity organization and the recruitment and retention logic of the MB as a social-political movement. To a certain extent a tension exists between the ICCS and the MB in terms of goals. The ICCS has not escaped derogatory labels from those clients (and MB members and supporters) who argue that the ICCS is betraying its fundamental purpose and values by offering 'five star' fee-based services (Clark 2004a: 102, 110–110, 113, 159). This tension is highlighted when one examines the ICCS as the politically powerful institution that it is within the MB.

The ICCS within the MB

As stated above, the ICCS is headed by a body of nine individuals (historically, men) which is elected every two years. While the positions are unpaid, they bring with them a great deal of prestige. In fact, the ICCS elections have become a forum of intense competition with important political overtones. Those who win the elections, and the interests they represent, stand to wield great influence within the MB. They, furthermore, have at their disposal thousands of jobs that translate into political and economic tools for the ICCS leadership. The ICCS thus plays an important role in the internal politics of the MB.

While typically not covered by the press or discussed by academics, the ICCS elections can be as significant as those for the MB and IAF leaderships. To a certain extent, more is at stake. The ICCS offers its leadership a degree of clout within the larger MB and, at the same time, access to resources that it can wield at its discretion.[30] The election results have been contested on more than one occasion and the MB leadership has been forced to deny serious signs of divisions and factionalism within the movement as a result of incidents at the ICCS.

Certainly, nepotism has long been a fact of life, with the ICCS privileging MB supporters (regardless of expertise) when hiring for key positions within the ICCS institutions. In an interview, the former Director of the Fund for the Sick and Poor estimated that as many as 90 per cent of the employees at ICCS organizations are members of the MB and that, furthermore, MB candidates are repeatedly chosen over more qualified non-Islamists, thus undermining the quality of services (Clark 2004a: 105; Wiktorowicz 2001: 107–108).[31] By the 1990s, the ICCS was taking concerted efforts to clean its house and ensure that appropriately qualified people were hired.[32] A former general manager of the *Dar al-Arqam* schools was fired for a lack of qualifications and a prominent manager of the ICCS was eventually convicted of embezzlement.[33] Given the significant economic resources at stake and a prevailing attitude that supporters should be rewarded for their sacrifices to the movement, the clean-up job has proven to be an uphill battle. Largely unnoticed is that the nepotism is often reflected in the hiring of supporters of one faction or another within the MB in order to strengthen the clout of the faction or camp.

Contrary to common belief, the MB/IAF are neither monolithic nor static, rather they encapsulate a variety of internal viewpoints, opinions and interests. Decisions within both organizations are the result of the interplay between, on the one hand, various factions within the organizations and, on the other, the context within which the decisions are being made. Indeed, prominent Jordanian political analysts refer to ideological divisions, divisions according to different personalities and the interests or institutions they represent, and generational divisions within the MB/IAF.[34] Members, for example, differ in the degree to which they are pragmatic or reformist as opposed to legalistic in their interpretations of religious texts; in other words, the degree to which they feel religious texts should be re-interpreted in light of changing social and political realities (Clark and Schwedler 2003). Institutional interests include the ICCS and/or its larger constituent institutions, such as the Islamic Hospital. There is, therefore, a great deal of jostling for power within the MB/IAF that makes any clear and easy distinction between moderates and hardliners impossible – these labels change from issue to issue. In a similar vein, it is very difficult to describe the MB or the IAF as becoming more or less moderate as a whole. While a combination of moderate voices may dominate on some issues, they do not dominate on others.

ICCS leaders do not have direct influence in the decision-making of the MB/IAF (they do not, for example, have a reserved spot in the executive councils of either institution). However, they have built up stocks of 'moral capital' through years of working in the MB and ICCS resulting in a wide network of supporters and like-minded colleagues. Upon being elected to the ICCS board of directors (largely as a result of these moral receipts), the director now brings even greater authority and clout (and networks) to the *Shura* Council of the MB. As head of the ICCS or an ICCS institution, representing a network bound together by personal, institutional and financial interests, his voice carries weight within any discussions, regardless of whether or not he is elected to the Executive Council.[35] At stake, therefore, within the ICCS elections is power and prestige. Within the MB/IAF, what is at stake is the creation of coalitions between various groups, based on ideology or interests, to ensure specific policy outcomes.

The politicization of the ICCS was most evident during its 2003 elections. The heated elections brought Daoud Qojak to power as head of the ICCS, a former IAF MP and considered an ideological hawk within the MB. Upon acquiring the reins of the position in January 2004, the newly elected board under Qojak fired 400 ICCS employees, all of whom were hired by the former administration of Kandil Shaker. Shaker, considered an ideological dove, had undertaken the same housecleaning upon his election in 2002, sidelining many hawks from the ICCS (*Al-Majd* 28 January 2004; *Al-Dustur* 29 January 2004).[36] Qojak's 2004 actions ultimately lead to a sit-in of ICCS members protesting the dismissals and demanding that the MB step in.[37] The high stakes at ICCS elections were also evidenced during the 2002 elections. Losing to Ibrahim Masoud by an extremely slim margin of votes, Mahmoud Abu Ghanemeh contested the election results.[38] The case was eventually taken to the Court of Higher Justice where the election results were overthrown and Abu Ghanemah won a seat on the ICCS board.[39] Similarly, the election of several members of the 2006–2008 board was contested in April 2006 based on conflict of interest grounds (due to their business interests). In response, the Ministry of Social Development, with which the ICCS is registered, established a committee together with the Audit Bureau to determine if the accusations were valid.

The heated elections within the ICCS reflect both the high political and economic stakes of the election outcomes. They also further demonstrate the interconnected nature of the ICCS as an institution of the MB. This means that any discussion of the ICCS in the future by necessity involves the MB and by extension the Jordanian regime.

MB, the ICCS and the 'War on Terror'[40]

As stated above, the MB's relations with the Jordanian regime have become strained with the government and regime increasingly viewing the MB as a security threat. Within this context, the financial, political and social clout of the ICCS has made it a target for the government in its efforts to safeguard its policies and, it appears to believe, Jordan. While initial fears of the ICCS' dissolution have been laid to rest, the ICCS now is in the eye of the storm between the regime and the MB and, by extension, the war on terror.

Since 2001, Jordan has been integral to the US war on terror. Though not in favour of the United States invasion of Iraq, Jordan informally provided logistical support to the United States-led campaign to oust Saddam Hussein in spring 2003. Since 2003, Jordan also has conducted training at Jordanian installations for the new Iraqi army, including its police force, and has supplied Iraq with military equipment (Prados and Sharp 2006). Jordan's participation in the war on terror has incurred a substantial increase in US. aid. Following its participation in the war on terror, US aid almost doubled, amounting to JD 250 million in economic and JD 198 million in military assistance in 2003 (not including supplemental funding) (Prados and Sharp 2006: 12, 16). Similarly, trade between the two countries has increased with President Bush ratifying the US-Jordanian Free Trade Agreement shortly after September 11, 2001.

Despite its early involvement, the long-term implications of Jordan's participation in the war on terror only really hit home in November 2005 when Jordan was the target of several terrorist attacks linked to prominent al-Qaeda leader, Abu Musab al-Zarqawi. Suicide bombers attacked 3 hotels, killing 60 people and injuring over hundred. While the MB/IAF were among the first to organize anti-al-Qaeda demonstrations, in the aftermath of the bombings, the MB became one of the leading targets of the new security-conscious regime.[41]

Security fears were raised further with Hamas' victory in the January 2006 Palestinian elections. The victory inspired and emboldened segments of the MB/IAF with IAF leaders asserting the party's strength, articulating their policy priorities and demanding political reforms. More importantly, the Hamas victory and the MB/IAF's new-found confidence raised regime fears of the 'Hamasisation' of the MB/IAF – the growth of a Palestinian-dominated stream in the leadership that advocates the motifs and strategy of Hamas.[42]

Amidst the atmosphere of heightened security tensions and associated rhetoric, al-Zarqawi was killed by coalition forces in Iraq in June of 2006. Referring to al-Zarqawi as a martyr, four prominent IAF MPs went to the family home of al-Zarqawi in the city of Zarka to express their condolences. All four MB members promptly were arrested for fuelling national discord and inciting sectarianism under Jordan's penal code.[43] The member's actions, furthermore, triggered a series of spontaneous unprecedented pro-government demonstrations against the four arrested members and in support of the families of the victims of Amman's hotel bombings by Iraqi terrorists in November 2005. In addition, the parliament's speaker of the house demanded an official apology from the MB to the people of Jordan.

Fearing a growing terrorist element within the MB, the government seized the moment of popular discontent with the MB and struck at the MB's most important tool, the ICCS. In July 2006, the government released a report on corruption in the ICCS, sending it to the prosecutor general for review.[44] The 1,700 page report detailed 'violations, reservations and comments' on the financial performance of the organization citing, among other issues, financial impropriety relating to improper and overpriced equipment purchased for the Islamic Hospital kidney and eye units and to the improper issuance of loans and hiring of consultants. While the MB argued that the report was false and that there is no connection between the ICCS and the political activities of the MB, the four members of the ICCS board are under investigation and were ordered to step down from their positions.[45] All four have been replaced by new representatives elected by the ICCS.[46]

The events of July 2006 exposed serious divisions within the MB. Following a meeting with the prime minister in late July, the MB issued a statement in which it underlined its commitment to national principles, the constitution and laws, prioritization of national interests over all other interests, allegiance to the King, condemnation of terrorism in all forms and rejection of extremist Islamic thought. The internal MB reaction to the statement was profound with 18 out of 40 members of the MB's Shura Council resigning from their posts in protest. While all 18 eventually were convinced to remain in their elected positions, their attempted resignation is a clear indication of the internal debate that has been unleashed within the MB – a debate in which the ICCS, its voice and role, is one of the central issues.

The ICCS, development and future change

This chapter has attempted to demonstrate that the ICCS must be understood as part of a larger socio-political movement and as such, it argues, the type of change the ICCS is driving is intimately related to the MB's relations with the state. The over-riding context of increasing authoritarianism, much of it perceived by the MB (and the opposition writ large) to be the result of efforts to secure foreign policies that are beneficial to and at the behest of Western states, creates clear limits to the extent to which gaps can be bridged between the ICCS and other development NGOs. Today's political situation exacerbates differences between worldviews, all but ensuring the unwillingness and inability of the ICCS and the NGOs community at large, including RONGOs, to bridge their differences and work together in the global fight against poverty and social exclusion.

A closer examination of the differences between the ICCS and the development community indicate that these differences are not fixed but rather are contextually oriented. The examples of the above mentioned temporary laws regarding divorce on demand and honour crimes killings clearly indicate the role regional events and Jordanian authoritarianism played in moulding the debates and the perceived differences between the different sides.[47] As stated above, the debates were about the source of the laws and the presumed underlying values they represented (Clark 2006, 2003; Nanes 2003). Lost in the rhetoric and polarization of voices was the actual debate over women's rights – a debate in which the two sides differed on the nature of the amendments and not on women's rights per se. The MB condemns honour crimes and permits women to divorce.[48] In fact, opponents to the amendment to Article 340 raised several important concerns that were also shared by many lawyers and human rights activists. The first was that cancelling Article 340 would not solve the problem – Article 340 deals with the issue of catching someone in the act of adultery. Many human rights activists and lawyers further argued, in agreement with some MPs, that what is actually being implemented in the courts in the case of honour crimes is Article 98, and not 340. Many of the MPs were in favour of amending of Article 340 rather than replacing it.

Similar to the 'honour crimes law', the IAF came out strongly in favour of a woman's right to divorce but opposed the *khula'* amendment which was supported by Chief Islamic Justice Sheikh Tamimi (the King's advisor on Islamic affairs). At issue was the nature of the divorce procedures and, in particular, the role of the judge (or lack of it). The disagreement between Sheikh Tamimi and the IAF revolved around the interpretation of the *Hadith* in which the justification for *khula'* arises.[49] According to the *Hadith*, a woman approached the Prophet explaining that although her husband is a good man, she would like to end the marriage. In the *Hadith*, the Prophet consulted both sides, received their consent and granted the woman her divorce upon the mutually agreed condition that she return the land her husband gave her when they married. According to the IAF interpretation, the Prophet was acting in the role of a judge; accordingly today a third party must supervise the negotiations between the couple and rule upon the divorce.[50] Sheikh Tamimi's interpretation is that the woman made the decision – that the *Hadith* grants her the right to divorce on demand without the ruling of a judge (*Jordan Times*, June 28 2004; *Al-Dustur*, September 19 2003).[51]

While a full range of opinions were expressed within the IAF regarding the two amendments, the polarized political environment (and the fact that these were some of the first temporary laws to be discussed by the angry parliamentarians upon reconvening after the two year suspension of parliament), largely ensured that reformist voices would not prevail. However, despite their opposition to the amendments, the two issues demonstrate the flexibility and potential areas of convergence between human rights activists and Islamists.

As an integral institution within the MB, the ICCS is directed by the philosophies and values of the MB and its decision-making processes. Any efforts towards working jointly to alleviate poverty and discrimination globally must begin by addressing the authoritarianism in Jordan. Until that point, the social role of the ICCS will be kept hostage to its political role.

Notes

1. One of the few studies to examine Islamic FBOs from a development perspective is Sullivan 1994.
2. This chapter draws on extensive original field research between 1998 and 2006. See, for instance, Clark 2004a.
3. Established in 1921, Jordan is a constitutional monarchy with an appointed prime minister and upper house and an elected lower house.
4. Both kings were concerned that the MB would employ violent methods as its mother organization in Egypt.
5. In return for its protected status, the MB supported the monarchy politically. While the MB criticized various policies, it by-and-large refrained from criticizing the political structure or the legitimacy of the monarchy itself, operated above ground and never espoused violence.
6. Dominated by the MB, the IAF is considered its party.

7. The Islamists managed to hold onto their share of the vote in 1993, 16 per cent as compared to15.6 per cent in 1989. Clark 2004a: 88. The IAF boycotted the 1997 elections.
8. The largest NGOs are some of the 'royal NGOs' (see below) and the General Union of Voluntary Societies (GUVS), a state-created umbrella organization of NGOs that monitors and evaluates NGOs and establishes various development projects.
9. The four branches are in Zarqa, Mafraq, Irbid and Ramtha.
10. 1 JD was the equivalent of approximately 1.41 US dollars.
11. Gender segregation has not been fully implemented in terms of doctors as there are insufficient female doctors. Patients may choose a male or female doctor. Clark 2004a: 94.
12. The Ministry of *Awqaf* has established *zakat* committees throughout the country that are run as community-based NGOs. For a discussion of the monarchy's attempts to assert its vision of Islam and control religious institutions and voices, see Wiktorowicz 2001: chapter 2.
13. There is no reference to HIV/AIDS on the Islamic Hospital website.
14. The environment is not part of the ICCS mandate.
15. *Al-Arab Al-Youm* 1 July 2006. (In Arabic). See also Clark 2004a; Idem, 'Social Movement Theory and Patron-Clientelism.'
16. In Arabic, *hakim 'aam.*
17. In 2003, a female IAF candidate accepted a quota seat in parliament. See Clark 2004c.
18. Females must don the *hijab* even prior to puberty.
19. All NGOs in Jordan are required to adhere to Law 33 of 1966, the Law of Societies and Social Organizations, which establishes the procedures, regulations and enforcement on NGOs, and to register with appropriate ministry. For further details, see Wiktorowicz 2001: 26–33.
20. The National Council for Family Affairs, a coordinating organization for NGOs chaired by Queen Rania, is one example.
21. Critics of RONGOs are less critical of RONGOs' programmes, than their social connections, genesis and relationship to power. Hermann 2000: 94.
22. Only 16 per cent of JWU's funds are raised from self-financing. Similarly, the Jordan River Foundation receives 42 per cent of its funding from national and international public and private sources. Global Development Forum 2000: 36, 41, 45.
23. The ICCS is also independent from other Islamic charities. If coordination between the two occasionally occurs, it is due to the personal friendships of the respective directors and not as part of a larger strategy.
24. By not defining 'unlawful bed', Article 340b expands the crime of adultery (Article 340a) to include other sexually compromising situations. Article 97 reduces the sentence of those who commit a crime in a fit of fury from execution or life imprisonment with hard labour to imprisonment for six months or a year. Article 98 allows for a reduced sentence for a crime committed by a man in fit of fury because of an unlawful or dangerous act committed by the victim. In the latter two cases, no time limit is put on the state of fury.

25. The amendment grants women divorce without evidence of any form of maltreatment, dereliction or improper moral standards on the side of the husband.
26. Jordan's other types of divorce require women to provide evidence justifying the divorce and a judge's ruling.
27. Abdul Latif Arabiyyat, Former Secretary General of the IAF, Interview with author, Amman, 23 November, 2003.
28. Amman suffers from areas of concentrated poverty due, in recent years, to high rates of rural–urban migration. Saif forthcoming.
29. The IAF also has strong representation in the Baqa'a Palestinian refugee camp outside Amman. Clark 2004a: 89.
30. Ra'if Nijim, former Director of the Fund for Sick and Poor, Interview with author, Amman, 25 January 2004.
31. Ibid.
32. Mohamed Abu Ruman, *Al-Ghad* newspaper, Interview with author, Amman, 11 May 2006; Mohammed Najjar, *As-Sabeel* newspaper, Interview with author, Amman, 19 January, 2004; Ibrahim Ghoreibeh, *Al-Ghad* newspaper, Interview with author, Amman, January 12 2004.
33. Najjar, interview, op cit.; Ghoreibeh, interview, op cit.
34. Samih Ma'ita, journalist, Interview with author, Amman, 7 February 2004; Ghoreibeh, interview, op cit.; Hilmi Asmar, journalist, Interview with author, Amman, 15 January 2004.
35. Samih Ma'ita, journalist, Interview with author, Amman, 7 February 2004, 10 January 2004 ; Ghoreibeh, interview, op cit.; Asmar, interview, op cit.
36. Majid Tobeh, *Al-Ghad* newspaper, Interview with author, Amman, 8 February, 2004.
37. Ibid.
38. Ziad Abu Ghanemeh, ICCS, Interview with author, Amman, 20 January 2004; Tobeh, interview, op cit.
39. Ghoreibeh, interview, op cit.
40. This section is based on Clark, 2007.
41. In January 2006, the government charged IAF leader Jamil Abu Bakr with 'harming the dignity of the state', based on articles on the IAF website criticizing the government.
42. In April 2006 tensions between the regime and the MB continued with the Jordanian security forces' discovery of weapons and the arrest of ten Hamas members for allegedly targeting sites throughout the Kingdom. The IAF accused the government of fabricating the event.
43. Three were tried; one was acquitted and two others (prominent IAF MPs) given limited jail sentences.
44. The report done by the MOSD and the Audit Bureau.
45. The MB, along with other opposition parties, issued a statement accusing the government of attempting to eliminate the ICCS (among other charges). *Al-Hayat* 4 July 2006. (In Arabic).
46. Analyst Ibrahim Ghoreibeh argues that by allowing the ICCS to replace the four members, the government has demonstrated that its actions were not politically motivated. *Al-Ghad* 22 June 2006; *Al-Ghad* 28 June 2006.

47. This discussion is based on Clark 2006.
48. Abdul Latif Arabiyyat, Former Secretary General of the IAF, Interview with author, Amman, 23 November, 2003.
49. *Hadith* are traditions relating to the words and deeds of the Prophet Mohammed and are important tools for determining the Muslim way of life.
50. Azzam al-Huneidi, IAF, Interview with author, Amman, 1 December, 2003.
51. As explained by Abdul Latif Arabiyyat to the author, Amman, 23 November, 2003.

Bibliography

Abu-Odeh, Adnan (1999), *Jordanians, Palestinians and the Hashemite Kingdom in the Middle East Peace Process* (Washington, DC: United States Institute of Peace).

Adams, Linda Schull (1996), 'Political Liberalization in Jordan', *Journal of Church and State*, Vol. 38, No. 3 (Summer), pp. 507–528.

Anderson, Betty S. (1997), 'The Status of "Democracy" in Jordan', *Critique*, Vol. 10 (Spring), pp. 55–76.

Azm, Ahmad Jamil (1997), 'The Islamic Action Front Party', In Hani Hourani (ed.), *Islamic Movements in Jordan* (Amman: Al-Urdun al-Jadid Research Center).

Bar, Schmuel (1998), *The Muslim Brotherhood in Jordan* (Tel Aviv: Tel Aviv University/The Moshe Dayan Center for Middle Eastern and African Studies).

Boulby, Marion (1999) *The Muslim Brotherhood and the Kings of Jordan, 1945–1993* (Atlanta, GA: Scholars Press).

Brand, Laurie A. (1995),'Palestinians and Jordanians: A Crisis of Identity', *Journal of Palestine Affairs*, Vol. XXIV, No. 4 (Summer), pp. 46–61.

—— (1998), *Women, the State, and Political Liberalization: Middle Eastern and North African Experiences* (New York: Columbia University Press).

—— (2001), 'Development in Wadi Rum? State Bureaucracy, External Funders, and Civil Society', *International Journal of Middle East Studies*, Vol. 33, No. 4, pp. 571–590.

Clark, Janine (1995), 'Islamic Social Welfare Organizations in Cairo: Islamization from Below?', *Arab Studies Quarterly*, Vol. 17, No.4 (Fall), pp.11–28.

—— (2003), '"Honor Crimes" and the International Spotlight in Jordan', *Middle East Report*, Vol. 229 (Winter), pp. 38–41.

—— (2004a), *Islam, Charity and Activism* (Bloomington, Indiana: Indiana University Press).

—— (2004b), 'Social Movement Theory and Patron-Clientelism: Islamic Social Institutions and the Middle Class in Egypt, Jordan and Yemen', *Comparative Political Studies*, Vol. 37, No.1 (October), pp. 1–28.

—— (2004c), 'Women in Islamist Parties: The Case Study of the Islamic Action Front in Jordan', *Arab Reform Bulletin*, Vol. 2, No.7 (July).

—— (2006), 'The Conditions of Islamist Moderation: Unpacking Cross-Ideological Cooperation in Jordan', *International Journal of Middle East Studies*, Vol. 38, No.4 (November), pp.539–560.

—— (2007), 'Jordan', in Toby Archer and Heidi Huuhtanan (eds), Islamist Opposition Parties of the Potential for EU Engagement (Helsinki: Finnish Institute of International Affair), pp. 43–55.

Clark, Janine Astrid and Jillian Schwedler (2003), 'Who Opened the Window? Women's Struggle for Voice within Islamist Political Parties', *Comparative Politics*, Vol. 35, No. 3 (April), pp. 293–312.

Fathi, Schirin H. (1994), *Jordan: An Invented Nation?* (Hamburg: Deutsches Orient Institute).

Freij, Hanna Y. and Glenn Robinson (1996), 'Liberalization, the Islamists and the Stability of the Arab State', *Muslim World*, Vol. 136, No. 1 (January), pp. 1–32.

Global Development Forum (2000), *Directory of Non-Governmental Organisations in Jordan* (Amman: Global Development Forum).

Hamarneh, Mustafa, Rosemary Hollis and Khalil Shikaki (1997), *Jordanian-Palestinian Relations: Where To?* (London: The Royal Institute of International Affairs).

Hamayil, Umar Khrawish (2000), 'Institutional Characteristics of the Jordanian Professional Association', In Warwick M. Knowles (ed.), *Professional Associations and the Challenges of Democratic Transformation in Jordan* (Amman: Al-Urdun al-Jadid Research Center).

Hermann, Katja (2000), *Aufbruch Von Unten* (Hamburg: LIT Verlag). (In German).

Hourani, Hani, Taleb Awad, Hamed Dabbas, Sa'eda Kilani (1993), *Islamic Action Front Party*. 1st edition translated by Sa'eda Kilani. (Amman: Al-Urdun al-Jadid Research Center, September).

International Crisis Group (2003), Middle East Briefing No. 5, *Red Alert In Jordan: Recurrent Unrest In Maan* (19 February).

Jordanian Ministry of Planning and International Cooperation, the UNDP, JOHUD/Queen Zein Al Sharaf Institute for Development (2004), *Jordan Human Development Report: Building Sustainable Livelihoods* (Amman: Ministry of Planning and International Cooperation, the UNDP; JOHUD/Queen Zein Al Sharaf Institute for Development).

Kandil, Amani and Sarah Ben Nefissa (1994), *Civil Associations in Egypt* (Cairo: Al-Ahram Centre for Political and Strategic Studies). (In Arabic).

Kornbluth, Danishai (2002), 'Jordan and the Anti-Normalization Campaign, 1994–2001', *Terrorism and Political Violence*, Vol. 14, No. 3 (Autumn), pp. 80–108.

Layne, Linda (1994), *Home and Homeland: The Dialogics of Tribal and National Identities in Jordan* (Princeton: Princeton University Press).

Lynch, Marc (1999), *State Interests and Public Spheres* (New York: Columbia University Press).

—— (2002), 'Jordan's Identity and Interests' In Shibley Telhami and Michael Barnett (eds), *Identity and Foreign Policy in the Middle East* (Ithaca: Cornell University Press).

Moaddel, Mansoor (2002), Jordanian Exceptionalism: A Comparative Analysis of State-Religion Relationships in Egypt, Iran, Jordan and Syria (New York and Basingstoke: Palgrave).

Mufti, Malik (1999), 'Elite Bargains and the Onset of Political Liberalization in Jordan', *Comparative Political Studies*, Vol. 32, No. 1 (February), pp. 100–129.

Nanes, Stefanie Eileen (2003), 'Fighting Honor Crimes: Evidence of Civil Society in Jordan', *Middle East Journal*, Vol. 57, No. 1 (Winter), pp. 112–129.

Prados, Alfred B. and Jeremy M Sharp (2006), *CRS Report for Congress* (Jordan: US Relations and Bilateral Issues). (July 14).

Roald, Anne Sofie (1994), *Tarbiya: Education and Politics in Islamic Movements in Jordan and Malaysia* (Stockhom: Almquist and Wiksell).

Robinson, Glen E. (1997), 'Can Islamists Be Democrats?', *Middle East Journal*, Vol. 51, No. 3 (Summer), pp. 373–388.

Saif, Ibrahim (Forthcoming), 'Employment Poverty Linkages and Policies for Pro-Poor Growth In Jordan (1990–2003)', International Labor Organization.

Scham, Paul L. and Russell E. Lucas (2001), '"Normalization" and "Anti-Normalization" in Jordan', *MERIA*, Vol. 5, No. 3 (September), pp. 54–70.

Schwedler, Jillian (2003), 'More Than a Mob', *Middle East Report*, Vol. 226 (Spring), pp. 18–23.

Sullivan, Denis J. (1994), *Private Voluntary Organizations in Egypt: Islamic Development, Private Initiative, and State Control* (Gainesville, Florida: The University Press of Florida).

Tal, Lawrence (1995), 'Dealing with Radical Islam', *Survival*, Vol. 37, No. 3 (Autumn), pp. 139–156.

Wickham, Carrie Rosefsky (2002), *Mobilising Islam* (New York: Columbia University Press).

Wiktorowicz, Quintan (2001), *The Management of Islamic Activism* (Albany: State University of New York).

Wiktorowicz, Quintan and Suha Farouki-Taji (2000), 'Islamic Non-Governmental Association and Muslim Politics', *Third World Quarterly*, Vol. 21, No. 4 (August), 685–699.

8
Who's Afraid of Religion? Tensions between 'Mission' and 'Development' in the Norwegian Mission Society

Ingie Hovland

Introduction

There has been a recent surge of interest in the topic 'faiths and development' in the United Kingdom, at universities and research institutes as well as in the UK Department for International Development (DFID). This interest throws up a series of new questions within development studies and related disciplines: from the perspective of development studies it raises questions about how donors and faith-based organizations (FBOs) can most constructively engage with each other; from the perspective of social anthropology it raises questions about the very different ways that diverse groups relate to that common human experience known as 'faith', and, specifically, how the grand twentieth-century project of development may have more intimate connections to faith and religion than it acknowledges.

More broadly, it feeds into the ongoing debate on 'secularisation' within anthropology and other disciplines. Traditionally, 'secularism' was taken to mean the gradual decline of religion in post-Enlightenment societies. The Enlightenment, it was assumed, had exposed the folly of all 'irrational' elements of human life, such as magic and religion, and instead promoted notions of rationality and a belief in technical progress. It was assumed that (irrational) religion and (rational) progress were directly opposed to each other. This conceptualization of secularism has, however, been recently challenged by scholars who argue it presents an ideological myth rather than social reality. Asad (2003), for example, examines the rise of 'secular' thought and life throughout the period of modernity, and describes the complexity of this process. In finding it to be deeply rooted and intertwined in religious formations, he argues that the secular is not simply an 'opposite' to religion, or even to the 'rational'; it is, rather, a multi-layered category with a complex history. Meyer and Pels (2003) have similarly examined 'secular' modern societies, and present thoughtful descriptions of instances where 'secular' modernity seems to embrace, use, respond to and even depend on 'magical' elements of life. They too conclude that magic and secular modernity are not 'opposites'. Magic is a part of modernity in many ways, even constitutive ones.

Davie (2002) has compared the rise of modernity in Western Europe with other regions in the world. She demonstrates how Western European processes of secularization and de-Christianization accompanying modernization have not occurred elsewhere. The formation of the secular in Europe is, then, a rather particular case. In other regions of the world, including in North America, secular modernity is coupled with religion in different formations – and in some regions, such as sub-Saharan Africa, it is not at all experienced as strange that an increase in modern social structures and experiences can be coupled with an *increase* in religious formations (cf. Chabal and Daloz 1999 on the mutually constitutive bonds between religion and politics in several contemporary African political systems). In sum, the recent debate in this field has made scholars rethink the relationship between secularism and religion, and has given us far more complex descriptions of actual historical and contemporary experiences of how religion, magic, 'secularism' and modernity are entwined and respond to each other, rather than being clearly separate or directly opposed phenomena, despite the Enlightenment's strong desire for this to be true.

This chapter will engage with these broad questions around faith and secularism, and their implications for development, through an examination of an issue that became hotly debated within the Norwegian Mission Society (NMS) around 2003–2004. NMS is a Norwegian Protestant (Lutheran) non-governmental organization (NGO) that carries out both active religious mission work (i.e. evangelization) as well as 'secular' development projects. During this period, the question of the relationship between these two streams of work – evangelization and 'development' – created tensions within the organization and informed debates outside it.

Within NMS, policy staff at the NMS head office in Stavanger, Norway, sought to keep a clear separation between these two work programmes for a range of reasons. First, they had just guided the organization through a restructuring process that focused on three new work programmes (evangelization, development and capacity building), and they wished to encourage organizational loyalty towards these three distinct programmes. Second, they wished to signal to the outside world that they had a functional and thought-through organizational structure, and identified clearly defined work programmes as a means of achieving this. Lastly, having received funding from the Norwegian government's bilateral aid organization, the Norwegian Agency for Development Cooperation (NORAD), NMS needed to be able to demonstrate how NORAD funds were being spent on development work and *not* on mission. They therefore required separate budget lines for these two types of work. During the research period NMS policy staff discussed why and how a clean separation between 'evangelisation' and 'development' should be maintained, and all field staff – known as 'missionaries' in NMS – were duly instructed from the head office on how to maintain a separation between 'religious evangelising' activity and 'development' activity, to prevent a mix-up between the two.

Coinciding with this internal discussion, external critics of NMS claimed that the distinction between 'religion' and 'development' meant nothing in practice and that the result of NMS' work was a dangerous convergence of mission and development. For example, NMS was attacked in the media for using NORAD funding to pay the salaries of religious missionaries overseas. In short, NMS was felt to be a significant and provocative threat to the 'secular' basis of the Norwegian development project, because of the perceived collapse of the boundary between mission and development – which NMS in turn was quick to deny.

This chapter will explore this tangled issue more closely by first turning to the historical background of NMS and how the relationship between religious mission and development has changed over the past 160 years of the organization's history. It will then turn to a brief sketch of the secular context in Norway in which Norwegian development aid has been embedded, and which NMS continuously positions itself in relation to. This will set the stage for introducing the criticisms that were lobbied against NMS, and how NMS responded to these – as well as the tensions that these criticisms uncovered within NMS' own organizational structure. In conclusion, it will suggest that it is important for FBOs in development to become better at dealing with faith, and to be able to engage with donors in a clear way on this issue; but it is equally important for 'secular' development organizations to become better at dealing with the interconnections between religion, secularization, modernity and development, rather than blindly assuming that development, as a 'secular' project, is opposed to religion.

Religion and development in NMS

NMS has around 70 staff at their head office in Stavanger, Norway, and around 100 Norwegian missionaries based in 12 countries around the world, mostly in sub-Saharan Africa and South East Asia. NMS exclusively recruits staff who profess a personal Christian faith and who are willing to be loyal to the organization's overarching purpose of 'spreading the gospel', as they put it in interviews with me. For NMS this encompasses a belief that Christianity is the only true faith, and to try to convert non-Christians to the same belief. NMS has an annual budget of around 190 million Norwegian kroner (NOK, around £16.5 million), distributed across their three work programmes: (1) Church and Christian evangelization work – where the aim of conversion is strongest; (2) development work – mostly carried out through micro-level projects dealing with, for example, health, agriculture, education or water; and (3) capacity development – undertaken mostly in collaboration with NMS' local partner churches. NMS policy emphasizes that their work is 'holistic', in the sense that they try to take into account both the material and the spiritual dimensions of people's lives. This is reflected in their work, which seeks to link faith as well as health, education, livelihoods and gender issues.

This 'holistic' policy dates back to the foundation of NMS in 1842. Religious mission and development have always been undertaken side by side by NMS missionaries and historically have not been separated into different 'work programmes' within the organization. (such division is a recent trend). Although there has always been debate within NMS about which 'types' of work should take priority, this ongoing and unresolved debate around priorities and resources has never detracted from the broad range of work that has been carried out in practice.

NMS' first missionaries, sent to Zululand (in what is now South Africa) after it was established in 1842, are hard to compartmentalize in terms of their function (see e.g. Jørgensen 1990, Myklebust 1980, Nome 1943–1949). H. P. S. Schreuder had completed a degree in theology at the University of Christiania and was ordained as a pastor. He also had basic training as a medical doctor and treated those who sought his assistance whether Christian or not (including the Zulu king on his arrival). In addition, he was a self-trained carpenter, and coordinated the building of several churches in Zululand that are still standing today. He also enjoyed crafting objects, and had acquired sufficient knowledge of linguistic principles to be able to write and publish the first Zulu grammar and reading book (Schreuder 1848, 1850). Nor was he alone in undertaking multiple tasks. Add to this the skills he acquired in political negotiation, Zulu folklore and horse-riding, and it becomes increasingly clear that for him, and his first missionary colleagues, their missionary existence was part and parcel of the life that they built among the Zulus. In practice, there was no separation between their religious mission and the other aspects of their life and work.

Throughout the history of NMS, this tendency to engage with people on both 'spiritual' and 'development' matters at the same time, as two sides of the same coin, continued until very recently. But the precise balance between the two has been subject to long-standing debate within the organization, as various debates and arguments in the pages of the organization's magazine, *Misjonstidende*, attest. Some missionaries have felt that 'secular' development work detracted from the aim of religious conversions, while others argued that if health, agriculture and education were not considered priorities, then they would never be able to show people the love of God in practice. The debates have also focused on the blend of staff needed to improve engagement with local communities. Whilst some called for more pastors, others suggested those with more practical skills were required, such as experts on cattle. However, it is only in the recent period that debates have focused on whether 'secular' activities should be seen as 'separate' from more explicitly church work.

This new debate emerged in the 1990s with the publication by NMS of a policy document (Kristensen, Sandsmark and Aano 1995). It was felt necessary in this document to clarify that 'secular' work was never used as bait for religious conversion. It was seen as important to clearly distinguish NMS from other mission agencies who were perceived to be using the promise of food and medicines as leverage for religious conversions. NMS has always opposed such a strategy as a result of its Lutheran roots which criticises such an approach. Lutheran understandings of conversion suggest that anyone who converts because of exterior, material desires, has not undergone a genuine conversion. Thus, any conversion that occurs because material goods have been used as 'bait' will be perceived as resulting in a 'nominal' (rather than a sincere and genuine) believer, which in effect often amounts to a nonbeliever. The process of baiting is also regarded as a mockery of the seriousness and depth of sincerity that religious conversion entails within NMS. One missionary noted in the research that he had once been planning the distribution of some project materials together with a local member of staff in Madagascar. When the local staff member indicated that they might use these materials to gain converts, the missionary replied 'We don't want any "rice Christians"!' (a term used to refer to people who called themselves Christian because they were offered food, often rice, in return for a conversion). However, despite this aversion to using material goods as bait for religious conversion, NMS had previously never explicitly condemned such an approach in any policy document. By the mid-1990s, it became apparent that it was, indeed, necessary to make this position clear to rule out misunderstandings over the relationship between religion and development in NMS.

By the 1990s NMS found themselves in a thoroughly secularized Norway. During the century and a half following NMS' establishment, secularization in Norway had taken place in a similar pattern to that elsewhere in Western Europe. In this regard, Norway is part of the 'exceptional' countries in the world that have produced a type of modernity that sees itself as opposed to religion (Davie 2002). However, the secularization process was complex, as Asad (2003) has pointed out. Whilst folk traditions involving the church are still decidedly alive, for example, most couples who decide to get married, still get married in church, the Church itself has been subject to changing attitudes and beliefs. Many members of the Lutheran Church of Norway today, for example, are open to a religious dimension of life, yet sceptical to any religious mission activity (Jørgensen 1995); many Norwegians are open to the idea of spiritual experiences, but shy away from the idea that there is only one religious truth. NMS have increasingly been confronted (in some cases aggressively) with these changing attitudes, as will be explored in the following section.

The legitimacy of FBOs in a secular society

In 2004, NMS and other religious mission organizations in Norway became caught up in a hostile debate in the Norwegian media over the legitimacy of faith-based development NGOs (for contributions to the debate, see e.g., *Dagens Næringsliv* 07.02.04; Magnus, Reinlund and Persen 2004; and Tvedt 2004; Bolle and Meland 2003). There was a highly critical TV documentary and several newspaper commentaries over the question of whether Norwegian faith-based NGOs – specifically, the Norwegian Christian mission organizations – should receive funding from the Norwegian government's aid budget. Eighteen Christian mission and development organizations in Norway have come together under the umbrella organization Norwegian Missions in Development (*Bistandsnemnda*), and as a group receive around 140 million NOK each year (around £12 million) from NORAD, around 1 per cent of NORAD's total aid budget, which complements the organizations' own fundraising networks.

This prompted some provocative questions in the media debate: can organizations that officially aim to carry out Christian mission activity, that is, to convert people, be asked to implement development projects funded by government aid money? And if so, under what conditions? NORAD funds some of the development work of Norwegian Christian faith-based NGOs, but this is done on the clear premise that this funding should only go to *development* work and not to religious evangelization or *mission*; the Norwegian government does not wish to use the aid budget to fund religious conversion activity. This distinction between 'development' and 'mission' is clearly marked by the perception of 'faith' that has come to the fore in post-Enlightenment secularized societies such as Norway. Faith is seen as a separate (and declining) compartment of life, distinct from other areas such as education, health, or family. While this compartmentalization is debatable even in highly secularized societies such as Norway (cf. the debates around whether secular modernity is really as opposed to religion as it claims, Asad 2003; Meyer and Pels 2003), it is certainly not tenable in many other societies around the world, where modernity goes hand in hand with religious convictions, experiences and arguments (Davie 2002). The NORAD request for separation between 'development' and 'mission' seems to be based on the Western European assumption that development is a secular project; and, moreover, that secularization is 'separate' from religion. Given the tenuous nature of these assumptions, it comes as no surprise that it is far easier to draw the line between *development* and *mission* in theory than in practice, and during the media debate, the question was raised as to whether it was, indeed, possible to make the distinction at all, as NORAD claimed.

Norway's most vociferous development studies academic, Terje Tvedt, contributed to the debate by stating in a newspaper comment that the development/mission distinction did not hold in practice:

> What would the Storting [Norwegian Parliament] say if the Indonesian or Saudi Arabian state funded fundamentalist Muslim organisations that carried out charity work among street children in Oslo, but primarily were concerned with Islamising all of Norwegian society? ... The Norwegian faith communities have

invested in local church development [abroad,] based on their own understanding of the Bible, and with support from the Ministry of Foreign Affairs they have managed to establish a series of what we in development jargon call 'local partners'. These are often churches that carry out mission work ... The parliamentary papers on aid and foreign policy have maintained that the state only supports development work. They clearly emphasise that the state does not support evangelising activity abroad. Undoubtedly, secularly oriented politicians have believed in this formal distinction between development and evangelising, but it goes against the mission commission and does not take the mission project seriously (and regardless of will, it is an almost impossible distinction to maintain in practice). (Tvedt 2004, my translation)

In effect, Tvedt was saying publicly that government money was being misspent when it was assigned to the development work of Norwegian mission organizations, because they were lying when they said that they kept a distinction between their development work and their evangelizing work. Several of the mission organizations and other faith-based NGOs, including NMS, were exasperated by this attack, and felt a strong need to reply to it and to point out why they thought it was both erroneous as well as largely missing the point. In fact, the General Secretary of NMS, Kjetil Aano, was sufficiently provoked to write a reply entitled 'The fear of religion', which was sent to the same newspaper the following week (Aano 2004). I want to pick up on one of the points he made in this reply.

The fear of religion

Aano suggested that this debate should not be reduced to scepticism of religion per se, but should rather be centred on an informed discussion around the role of value-based development work: 'much of what the mission organizations represent actually constitutes an added value in relation to aid through the government apparatus – and the two sides complement each other. Engagement and popular support on both sides is one such added value' (Aano 2004, my translation). Value-based development is not only carried out by faith-based organizations, he went on to say, but also by labour movements, organizations working on physical integrity (such as sports or disability movements) or development organizations that base their work on an explicitly humanitarian ethos. NORAD, for example, today acknowledges that development is never 'neutral'. The argument over the role of value-based development therefore fits well in the Norwegian context at the moment: it is possible to argue that the question is not whether development should be based on values, because it always is anyway, but rather *which* values it should be based on, and how these values should shape implementation. NMS argued that the fact that they are value based does not make them any less legitimate as an NGO. On the contrary, it means that they are willing to acknowledge the basis for their work. It even means, Aano indicated, that having an explicit basis is exactly what can give them a niche within the larger development project, and that this is the added value that they can bring.

At the same time, NMS reiterated its division of activity, justifying its continued receipt of NORAD funds. They used the NORAD funds for purely *developmental* projects which benefit local communities regardless of their religious beliefs and which do not include any Christian conversion activity. The *conversion* activities and *development* activities, NMS argued, were kept in clearly separate work programmes and on strictly separate budgets.

It gradually becomes clear that there is a certain tension for NMS here. On the one hand, they wish to work in an integrated way, ('holistic', as they say), which takes people's material *and* spiritual life dimensions into account – and this forms part of their value base, or faith base. Arguably, this value base is what enables them to add value to the development project as a whole, since it clarifies their position and suggests a niche that they can fill – for example, in civil society work with local churches, or in HIV/AIDS work in Christian youth groups, or in gender projects among church women groups, to name just a few examples from the work NMS is currently engaged in. On the other hand, NMS have to split this value base off and draw up a separation between the explicitly 'religious' part of their work and the so-called pure 'development' part of their work as a condition for administering funding from NORAD. This means, for example, that the gender project among church women groups was classified as 'religious', and was thus kept separate from NORAD-funded projects. Despite the fact that this type of project was a direct result of NMS' value base, that this value base and these types of projects, were arguably what they could claim to be their added value, they could only do so when they were speaking to NORAD in abstract terms. When it came to discussions about funding they had to leave it out. In this way they are splitting the very integrated value base that could be their niche in the broader picture of NORAD funding policy – and they are splitting it in response to NORAD policy. One could say that NORAD throws them into a somewhat schizophrenic mode here.

Let me return at this point to the title that the NMS General Secretary chose for his reply 'The fear of religion'. In many ways, he has identified the critical problem. In the development field – and NORAD is not alone here – there often seems to be a vague, undefined fear of religion. Religion is split off. It is not trusted. It is frequently ignored, and sometimes it even seems as if people pretend it is not there at all. In many ways it has become a taboo (Ver Beek 2000). Paradoxically, whilst there is this scepticism of religion and religious mission, development itself has a mission – or even *is* a mission – in the way that it is conceptualized and practiced. Development also has a grand utopian vision that needs to be taken largely on faith. (For a tongue-in-cheek analysis of the missionary zeal of the World Bank, for example, see Mihevc 1995.) The extensive and imposing 'secular' development project that has taken such hold during the last half of the twentieth century has grown its own creeds, visions and prophecies. As 'secular' development strives to forget about its own religious forms, then, it is easy to turn around and attack the organizations that most visibly manifest the very forms it is trying to hide, namely the faith-based NGOs.

This anxiety about religion – amongst those outside the faith-based community – means that organizations like NMS find themselves in the ironic position of having to *acknowledge* their value base and *split it off* at the same time. But what does the broader development mission gain by such a split? All that NORAD gains, for example, is the opportunity to fund an additional number of standard 'secular' development projects that are by passable but very rarely innovative. Some of the most interesting work in NMS is now not funded by NORAD, since it integrates both the 'religious' and 'development' realms of people's lives, and the potential synergy effect between religion and development is in theory lost to the bilaterally funded projects – thanks to the fear of religion.

But those in the development funding world are not the only ones who are afraid of religion. In many cases, the FBOs themselves are strikingly anxious of religion too.

The fear of religion (part ii)

In his reply 'The fear of religion', Aano also pointed out that we need an informed debate about *the role of religion* in development processes – and in political and social processes more broadly.

the question of the increasing role of religion as a conflict factor ... is an important discussion. But precisely because religion is so important, it also has great potential as an agent of peace and reconciliation .... This is an area that we as Christian organisations know. And we can clearly get much better at developing and using this potential. But precisely as religious organisations who know the worth, depth and significance of religion, we are able to play an important role as a central actor in such work. (Aano 2004, my translation)

In other words, it is imperative today to engage with the question of when and under what circumstances religion incites violence, and what FBOs can do to minimise this risk and to draw on the reconciliatory dimensions of religion instead.

Like any organization, NMS has the potential both to exacerbate religious difference and to engage with it. NMS' religious projects are exemplary 'success stories' when they are done well. As mentioned already, this can be the case, for example, in gender projects with church women groups; while I was doing research on NMS, the NMS missionaries in Ethiopia worked with their partner church (the Lutheran Mekane Yesus Church) to identify the position and role of women within the church, and I was told about subsequent church leadership meetings where the 'Women's Secretary' of the church was able to query the (minimal) size of her budget, and where women were able to come together to raise the issue of female genital mutilation as a serious concern to them in a clear challenge to some (male) leader's tacit endorsement of this practice. This is briefly mentioned here to highlight the fact that NMS does indeed negotiate the religion–development interface with integrity and thoughtfulness in projects such as this one. However, at this religion–development interface, tensions and problems arise for NMS staff. The tensions that occur are important entry points into understanding how to come to grips with the role of religion and religious difference, when faith and development come together.

During my research on NMS I conducted formal interviews with many of the organization's staff. In one of these interviews, a particular side of the tension caused by the programmatic split between 'religion' and 'development' emerged – despite the fact that it was not supposed to. I had asked the interviewee what the term 'missionary' meant to him. He answered that while the term 'missionary' might primarily be associated with someone who works to 'get more Christians', this does not necessarily hold in all situations. He explained what he meant by using the example of one of NMS' development projects which is partly funded by NORAD. The project combines education, health, livelihoods and community work. The Norwegian NMS staff on this project are called 'missionaries', but because of the NORAD funding, their objective is *not* to convert people to Christianity, but instead to contribute to improved education opportunities, improved health opportunities, and more democratic structures for local decision-making in the project villages.

The interviewee's next comment as he was describing this particular project to me, however, was 'Of course, they [the project staff] still hold Christian devotions in the villages'. At the moment of saying this, real-ising perhaps that such revelations were not appropriate since the project – as he himself had just informed me – was not supposed to include active Christian evangelizing activity, he quickly backtracked. He stated first that 'Well, they [the Christian devotions] don't show up in the NORAD budgets', (perhaps not such a wise choice of words either). But he then found a better tack, and started to explain to me how he pictured the role of Christian evangelizing in development. He was very careful, clearly not wishing to appear disrespectful of other religions, while at the same time also clearly wanting to communicate to me that he felt people who hold, for example, African traditional beliefs would on the whole gain a much better life if they converted to the beliefs and norms of Christianity instead. In his opinion, Christianity would enable them to make use of health care in a better way, gain more education, improved job prospects and, most importantly, a different mindset – in short, 'development'. In extension of this logic, therefore, he felt that it was in fact directly counterproductive to run development projects without also changing people's (traditional) religious beliefs to (Christian) beliefs that were more amenable to a host of modern social processes and progress.

Now, let me first make it clear that I do not think that all NMS devel-opment project staff carry out Christian evangelizing activity in this way when they are aware that they are not supposed to, or that all NMS staff would support this breach of their own organizational policy. But I do think that this case illustrates well the difficult tension that many NMS staff find themselves caught up in when their devel-opment work is supposed to be split off from their religious work. At the most fundamental level, they may not recognize their own God within this split framework, and if they feel they cannot carry out a 'split-up' development project with any integrity, then it becomes dif-ficult for them to buy into the organizational separation between 'religion' and 'development'.

Or consider a second case: the example of an NMS health clinic partly funded by NORAD. The work at this clinic is officially supposed to be clearly separate from attempts at religious conversion, and people of all faiths are supposed to be able to use the clinic freely. In practice, however, the NMS staff at the clinic find it difficult to maintain this policy. For example, clinic staff come together to pray to the Christian God – not just in private, but in the middle of the clinic itself, once a day, in a very visible way. Anyone inside or outside the clinic is welcome to join in. To the staff, this seems very natural; after all, this is where they are carrying out their work. Conversely, I was told by one of the missionaries that if visitors to the clinic start chanting so-called traditional religious incantations for the patients they are accompanying, then they are told in no uncertain terms by clinic staff that this cannot be done in the clinic; they either have to stop the religious incantation, or leave.

Thus, while NMS' official organizational policy and NORAD reports and all budgets indicate that the clinic is not dominated by any one faith but is open to all, it is in practice a Christian space. Again, the missionaries see the Christian God as being 'pro-development', and thus the best God for the clinic, while the other gods, spirits or ancestors who are evoked are perceived to be potentially undermining, as they do not always seem to support the 'secular' aims of the clinic regarding the need for diagnosis, vaccination, medication, nutrition, check-ups and so on. And, quite understandably, as long as NMS project staff hold this view, they are anxious about other religions, and act accordingly. In this way, the staff at the clinic attempt to maintain their own sense of meaning and integrity. At the same time, of course, they are completely subverting the official organizational policy of NMS that has been so carefully constructed in Stavanger and presented as a sign of legitimacy to NORAD in order to gain funding for the clinic.

One of the crucial factors in this picture is the way the NMS staff relate to their own religious faith. As mentioned earlier, they have to be willing to be loyal to the aim of converting non-Christians to Christianity in order to be employed by NMS. People who apply to NMS are, therefore, often people who see the aim of witnessing about their Christian faith as one of the underlying reasons not only for their job, but for their whole life. And this in turn means that even though the organization might retain its organizational integrity in relation to NORAD by stating in official policy that evangelization and development work is separate, this is, in certain situations, a difficult distinction to make in the minds and practices of many of its staff. In certain situations, in fact, individual members of staff – like the staff at the clinic – may quickly find their own ways of adapting and destabilizing the official NMS policy, so that they can maintain their own individual integrity and be true to their own relationship to their faith; the very relationship to their faith that made them apply for a job in NMS in the first place.

In sum, then, the theoretical separation between 'religious' activity and 'development' activity in NMS causes particular tensions for the organization as a whole as well as for individual members of staff. For the organization as a whole, this separation forces a certain split between their value base on the one hand, including the value this can bring to the broader development project, and on the other hand, the basis on which they apply for government funding. Moreover, it splits off NORAD-funded projects from some of the more innovative projects that are happening at the religion–development interface. For individual members of staff, the split can be experienced as a requirement that in certain situations threatens to undermine both the development work that they are involved as well as their personal integrity.

In conclusion: who's afraid of religion?

In conclusion, let me return to the question in the title of this chapter: Who's afraid of religion? In different ways, we all seem to be somewhat afraid of religion, both outside and inside faith-based organizations. More specifically, we are afraid of *other people's* religion: those in development funding circles are often anxious about the religion of the missionaries, and those in Christian missionary circles are often anxious about the religion of the non-Christians. How can we deal with this?

First, it is important to deal explicitly with these issues. We must explicitly include religion to a far greater extent as part of the field of development studies – because so often it is a very important dimension of life for so many of the people concerned, both among staff and so-called 'beneficiaries'. At the same time we should be aware of the tensions and dilemmas that the explicit handling of religion creates, both for development policy in funding agencies, and for staff in the very organizations that should in theory be best equipped to deal with this topic, namely staff in faith-based NGOs.

Second, it might be advantageous for bilateral organizations to find more constructive funding mechanisms to channel funds to faith-based NGOs rather than making these funds conditional on a supposedly clean *separation* between church work and development work. This separation does not seem to stand much chance of being anything more than an exceptionally theoretical exercise in any case. In addition, it can make faith-based NGOs lean slightly towards a schizophrenic nature in their negotiations with funding agencies.

And third, returning to some of the false pretences of development 'secularism', we must challenge the assumption that secularism is inherently separate from or opposed to religious thought and practice. Given the broader academic debate around the complex formations of 'secularism', including the intertwined relationships of secularism, modernity and religion, it is pertinent to ask what implications this will have for the development project. More work may be needed on how best to acknowledge the actual role of religion in social processes that have 'secular' development aims, and on how faith-based NGOs might best be included in the broad landscape of aid policy. It seems appropriate to ask whether these organizations can take on some of the important role of including religion in development without further deepening religious divisions and potential conflict; and whether they can take seriously the religious dimension of people's lives and integrate this into development work even in those cases where people's religion is different from the faith of their own staff. Is it possible to enable faith-based NGO staff to deal with faith differently than in the example from the clinic above? Is it possible for them to explicitly include the question of God *in* development without assuming that there is only one possible God, whether secular or religious, *of* development?

Open discussion around these questions might equip FBOs to become even better at dealing with faith, and it might equip 'secular' development organizations to become even better at dealing with the fact that development is not necessarily a 'secular' activity, in the traditional sense, at all. Which in turn might alleviate some anxiety all around.

Bibliography

Aano, Kjetil (09.03.2004) 'Angsten for religion' ['The fear of religion'], *Dagbladet*, www.dagbladet.no/kultur/2004/03/09/392859.html, accessed 28 August 2007.

Asad, Talal (2003) *Formations of the Secular: Christianity, Islam, Modernity*, Stanford University Press, Stanford.

Bolle, Tor Aksel and Øystein Meland (2003) 'Bistand, bønn og bibler' ['Development, prayer and Bibles'], *Verdensmagasinet X* No 6/2003.

Chabal, Patric and Jean-Pascal Daloz (1999) *Africa Works: Disorder as Political Instrument*, The International African Institute, in association with James Currey, Oxford, and Indiana University Press, Bloomington and Indianapolis.

Dagens Næringsliv (07.02.2004) Editorial.

Davie, Grace (2002) *Europe, the Exceptional Case: Parameters of Faith in the Modern World*, Darton, Longman & Todd, London.

Jørgensen, Tor Berger (1995) 'Misjon i fornyelse – NMS mot år 2000' ['Mission in renewal – NMS towards 2000'], *Norsk Tidsskrift for Misjon* [*Norwegian Journal of Mission*] 49 (2) 114–126.

Jørgensen, Torstein (1990) *Contact and Conflict: Norwegian Missionaries, the Zulu Kingdom, and the Gospel 1850–1873*, Solum, Oslo.

Kristensen, Anne Karin, Jan Sandsmark and Kjetil Aano (1995) 'Prinsippdokument om NMS' diakonale profil: Kristen livspraksis i møte med vår tids utfordringer' ['Position paper on NMS' diaconate profile: Christian lifestyle in encounter with the challenges of our time'], NMS, Stavanger.

Magnus, Per Christian, Robert Reinlund and Kjell Persen (01.03.2004) 'De norske statsmisjonærene' ['The Norwegian state missionaries'], *Dokument 2* (TV programme).

Meyer, Birgit and Peter Pels (eds)(2003) *Magic and Modernity: Interfaces of Revelation and Concealment*, Stanford University Press, Stanford.

Mihevc, John (1995) *The Market Tells Them So: The World Bank and Economic Fundamentalism in Africa* Zed Books, London.

Myklebust, Olav Guttorm (1980) *H. P. S. Schreuder; Kirke og Misjon* [H. P. S. Schreuder; Church and Mission], Gyldendal Norsk Forlag, Oslo.

Nome, John (ed.)(1943–1949), *Det Norske Misjonsselskaps Historie i Hundre År* [The Norwegian Mission Society's History over One Hundred Years], vols 1–5 Dreyers Grafiske Anstalt, Stavanger.

Schreuder, H. P. S. (1848) *Læsebog i Zulu-Sproget* [Reading Book in the Zulu Language], Christiania.

—— (1850) Grammatik for Zulu-Sproget [A Grammar for the Zulu Language], Christiania.

Tvedt, Terje (01.03.2004) 'Utenrikspolitikk og statsmisjon' ['Foreign policy and state mission'], *Dagbladet*, www.dagbladet.no/kultur/2004/03/01/392248.html

Ver Beek, Kurt Alan (2000) 'Spirituality: A Development Taboo', *Development in Practice*, 10 (1) 31–43.

9
Saudi Arabian NGOs in Somalia: 'Wahabi' Da'wah or Humanitarian Aid?

Mohammed R. Kroessin with
Abdulfatah S. Mohamed

Religious and secular missionaries: the politicization of aid

In the Western world, both the Geneva Conventions and the Red Cross-sponsored 'Code of Conduct for NGOs in Disaster Relief' are seen to provide the mandate and operational framework for humanitarian action. However, a renewed linking of aid and broader political goals, common during the Cold War, can now be observed. Even before the war on terror, questions as to the usefulness of a separation of aid from politics were being raised (cf. Duffield 2001). The distinguished journalist David Rieff in, *A Bed for the Night: the Crisis of Humanitarianism* (2002) went further, pronouncing the death of pure humanitarianism, viewing it cynically as an extension of the foreign policy of Western governments. The picture today remains mixed and the NGO community continues to be the main vehicle for humanitarian aid, calling into question how 'non-governmental' many NGOs can actually be. As Joanna Macrae (2002: 53) puts it, ' [it] is not whether humanitarian aid is political, but how.'

The discourse on the role of NGOs in humanitarian aid emphasizes that there is a mixture of religious and 'secular missionaries' that make up the NGO sector.[1] They have a range of philosophical or ideological underpinnings and objectives depending on whether they subscribe to a human rights-based approach to development, or are borne out of a traditional faith-based agenda. Alex de Waal (1997) coined the term the 'humanitarian international' as a descriptor for Western-funded liberal interventions where NGOs are perceived wrongly or rightly as 'neo-colonial vanguards – the missionaries of Western neo-liberalism' (Slim 2004: 6). Further projected on the relationship between the West and the Muslim world in 'Huntingtonian' fashion,[2] it could be perceived as a struggle between 'Jihad and MacWorld' (Donini 2004). At an abstract level of analysis, all humanitarian and development actors ought, therefore, to be regarded as 'missionaries', although not necessarily in a religious sense. They are underpinned by a particular value set that drives them to promote social change and to shape the world in their image.

This analysis will show that Saudi-Arabian relief and development organizations are in this respect not entirely different from Western humanitarian agencies. From a secular Western perspective, however, their worldview is perceived to be different, if not antagonistic. They are deeply rooted in an Islamic humanitarian tradition which is related to, yet different from, Christian notions of compassion. Almost 1,500 years of Islamic charitable practices such *Zakat* (obligatory alms) and *Awqaf* (charitable trusts), often but not always coupled with *Da'wah* (inviting to Islam), serve both as a philosophical and organizational backbone of these organizations. The new-found wealth of Gulf states, generated by the oil crises of the 1970s and 80s, have made Saudi NGOs a significant 'missionary' force. Their particular focus has been on areas where Muslim communities were seen as under threat, as in the Balkans, as a counter-balance to Christian missionary work in Asia and Africa or to bring back those who are regarded as deviant Muslims to the puritan teachings of the 'Wahabi' interpretation of Islam and turn them into 'Good Muslims' just as many Evangelical missionary organizations seek to create 'Good Christians'. As the case study of Somalia emphasizes, this is often done on the back of humanitarian or developmental projects, though within Islamic teachings a distinction is not necessarily made. A closer look at three different Saudi NGOs also shows that a high degree of diversity exists in the way in which this sense of mission is operationalised.

The Saudi enigma – 'Wahabi' reformers or extremists?

Post-9/11 books from academics and investigative journalists are filled with writings that seek to elucidate the post-modern resurgence of religion. One of the biggest conundrums within this discourse is subsumed in the catchphrases 'Islamic fundamentalism' (Choueiri 1997) and 'Wahabism', concepts which are often equated uncritically. The term 'Wahabism' has been increasingly used in public rhetoric – by politicians and particularly the media – to describe what is perceived as an ultra-conservative and puritan, and thus extreme and unacceptable, form of Islam. However, these allegations need careful unpacking. Whilst many have written on the topic, most were assessing 'Wahabism' from a particular vantage point. Some of the strongest ideological attacks have come, for example, from Daniel Pipes (2002) and Stephen Schwartz (2004), both of whom contend that Wahabism's core message espouses intolerance, violence and terrorism. Their analyses coincides with a neo-conservative agenda that sees Islam, and especially political Islam, as the new enemy of the West. In the case of Schwartz (who runs the 'Wahabi Watch' website[3] as part of his role as the Director of the Centre for Islamic Pluralism), this is compounded by his fervour for Sufism, which sees itself as advocating the true, peace-loving nature of Islam and is, thus, apparently diametrically opposed to 'Wahabism'. Clifford Geertz (2003), however, contends that Schwartz's aptly titled *Two Faces of Islam: Saudi Fundamentalism and Its Role in Terrorism*, is founded upon a conflation of Wahabism and Islamism in general. In similar vein, Algar 2002, Lewis 2003 and Ali 2003 whilst offering a poignant analysis of particular aspects of 'Wahabism', are more typically ideologically driven and reductionist. They call to mind Edward Said's (1991) critique of Western 'orientalism' as a fear of the 'other'.

Therefore, an ideologically more neutral approach is necessary to provide a deeper understanding of the complex issue of "Wahabism'. More historically rigorous accounts (e.g. Rentz 2005; DeLong-Bas 2004) help to clarify some of the basic facts. In general terms, 'Wahabism' constitutes an orthodox Islamic theology,[4] named after Muhammad ibn Abd al Wahab (1703–1792), and dominates the Saudi religious establishment, due to a historical link between Abd al Wahab and the House of Saud.[5] Significantly, the term 'Wahabi' is used derogatively by opponents whilst the group itself prefers the term 'Salafism', due to associations with the 'Salaf as-Salih', the 'pious predecessors' or the first three generations of Muslims who succeeded the Prophet Muhammad and who sought to protect this legacy. This term was constructed by the Iraqi scholar Ibn Taymiya (1263–1328) and adopted later by Muhammad ibn Abd al Wahab and his followers. In this context, the group views itself as a reform movement, rescuing Islam from what they perceive to be religious innovations (in Arabic, *Bid'ah*) such as deviations from the ideal of the sacred past in the form of heresies, superstitions and idolatry. Its reformist approach led some to oppose it, often because they felt their own bases of power and prestige were threatened. In the cases of the Shi'a and the Ottoman Empire, these negative perceptions stemmed from armed conflicts in which military forces claiming adherence to 'Wahabism' were victorious (Delong-Bas 2004).

'Wahabism' or 'Salafism' focuses on the *Qur'an* and *Hadith* (narrations from the Prophet Muhammad) as fundamental texts, as interpreted by the first three generations of Muslims. Matters of belief and religious practice are further expounded in commentaries such as Ibn Abd al Wahab's book *Kitab al-Tawhid* (Book of Monotheism), and *Ibn Taymiya's Al Aqeedah Wasitiyah* (lit. Tenets of Faith written in [the small Iraqi town] Wasit) which are theological in nature and do not espouse what would nowadays be regarded as political Islam.[6] This theology advocates a puritanical and legalistic stance in matters of faith and religious practice and puts the purification of *aqeedah* (tenets of faith) to the fore, thus rejecting Shi'a and Sufi interpretations which in 'Wahabi' thought are essentially polytheist doctrines in sacrilegiously placing Ali (the grandson of Prophet Muhammad), Imams, Saints or the Prophet himself as intermediaries between God and man.

The impact of 'Wahabi' theology is, however, inextricably linked to the power of the House of Saud (Lewis 2003), the ruling clan of the Najd area in central Arabia and cemented by the marriage of the son of Muhammad ibn Saud with the daughter of Muhammad ibn Abd al Wahab in 1744. On the basis of Abd al Wahab's religious verdicts, Ibn Saud provided the Saudi military with the power to both purify the central and eastern Arabian region from what they regarded to be religious abominations[7] and to unify it under his leadership. After the death of Abd al Wahab at the turn of the nineteenth century, the Saudi dynasty incorporated rulings stemming from Ibn Taymiya's justification for a rebellion against the nominally Muslim Mongols who had usurped the Abbasid Caliphate in the thirteenth century, into 'Wahabi' doctrine, legitimizing armed conflict against the Ottoman Empire (Delong-Bas 2004). Raids also took the Saudi army into Iraq where the Shia holy city of Karbala was sacked, defining the relationship between Shiism and 'Wahabism' ever since. The Hijaz, along with the Muslim holy places of Makkah and Madina, was conquered in 1804. Their loss represented for the ruling Ottomans a fundamental challenge to their claim of religious leadership and they declared war against al-Saud who was in turn conveniently labelled as a 'Wahabi' 'infidel' and crushed in 1818 with the execution of Abdullah Ibn Saud. This signified the end of the first Saudi state (Delong-Bas 2004); the Saudi dynasty, however, and thus the 'Wahabi' theology, continued to exist mainly in the Central Arabian Najd region well into the beginning of the twentieth century, after successfully recapturing Riyadh from the Ottomans and their Egyptian troops.

A later successor, Abdul Aziz Ibn Saud (1880–1953), aided by the British agent St John Philby,[8] who switched camps and became his Chief Adviser, was skilful in his dealings with the British Empire and won their support in overthrowing the Turkish rulers. With the eventual demise of the Ottoman Empire, the al-Saud dynasty resumed power and re-conquered Makkah and Medina in 1925–1926. This gave them control over the annual pilgrimage, with Abdul Aziz declaring himself king and the custodian of the holy sites. The Hijaz became the heartland of the Kingdom of Saudi Arabia, with Riyadh as its political and Jeddah its commercial capital. Within global Islam, the 'Wahabi' strand remained limited to Arabia and the Gulf and was, thus, a minor current. There were only few avenues to engage a broader audience, although the annual pilgrimage exposed the Muslim world to some 'Wahabi' teachings, e.g. the decree that a unified congregational prayer should be held at the Ka'bah in Makkah instead of different services by the worshippers of the different schools of Islamic jurisprudence[9] as was the case under the Ottomans (Yamani 2001; Phillips1996). The discovery of oil in Arabia in the early 1930s, however, created new dynamics that catapulted Saudi Arabian 'Wahabism' to the forefront of state-sponsored Islamic missionary work. Philby undermined British influence in the region, however, by facilitating the entry of United States commercial interests, followed by a political alliance between the United States and the Saud dynasty. In 1936, Standard Oil of California (SOCAL, also known as Chevron) and Texaco pooled their assets 'East of Suez' into what later became ARAMCO (Arabian–American Oil Company), perhaps the richest commercial prize in the history of the planet (Yergin 1991). These vast oil revenues gave an immense financial impetus to the spread of 'Wahabism'.

Vehicles for Islamic charity: Zakat, Sadaqah and Awqaf

While oil wealth was central to the rise of Saudi charitable and development organizations, the traditional vehicles of charity have been instrumental. Islam has a rich 1,400-year tradition of charitable giving in the form of *Zakat* (obligatory charity), *Sadaqah* (voluntary charity) and *Awqaf* (charitable trusts often set up through endowments) that continue to the present day. The redistribution of wealth in the form of charitable giving is central to the Islamic faith and an obligation upon every believer. This importance is highlighted by the term 'financial worship' used by Benthall in his exposition of Islamic charity (1998). The basic mechanism for this is 'Zakat' which became a mandatory act of worship when the Islamic State was established by the Prophet Muhammad in 622 CE; many Qur'anic verses revealed in Madinah deal with the topic (al-Qardawi 1999).[10] The word *Zakat* is mentioned in the *Qur'an* 30 times in different contexts and is derived in Arabic from the verb *'Zaka'*, meaning to 'grow' and 'become better'. *Zakat* consequently means *purification of wealth* (al-Qardawi 1999: xliii).

In Islamic doctrine, *Zakat* is one of the 'five pillars' and must be given by every Muslim at a rate of 2.5 per cent of any disposable wealth at the end of each year. Beneficiaries of this obligatory charity are detailed in the Qur'an, '*Zakah expenditures are only for the poor and the needy, and for those employed to collect [Zakah] and for bringing hearts together and for freeing captives and for those in debt and in the way of Allah and for the traveller – an obligation imposed by God and God is Knowing and Wise*' (Qur'an Surah 9, verse 60). In modern terms this could be translated into the following areas of public expenditure:

poverty reduction,
administrative overheads for civil servants dealing with public welfare,
peace-building and community cohesion,
promotion of freedom, basic human rights and civil liberties,
personal insolvency settlements,
public works, particularly security and defence,[11]
homeless, refugees and migrants.

Furthermore, voluntary charity, in Arabic *Sadaqah* (meaning 'to give away' and 'realising one's faith by action') is also strongly encouraged. It is regarded as individual devotion that is given directly to the destitute beneficiary without the need for state administration or intermediation (al-Qardawi 1999). Other Islamic teachings also stress particular seasons for giving, such as the month of Ramadhan where Muslims are encouraged to feed the destitute whilst fasting themselves. A special contribution also has to be made at the end of the fasting month called *Zakat al-Fitr*, an amount of food or the monetary equivalent to feed one person in need. Similarly, during the *Hajj* period, the fifth pillar of Islam, Muslims whether performing pilgrimage or not are expected to sacrifice a cow, goat or camel to feed the needy, a practice known as *Qurbani*. Alms-giving occupies a central role in Islamic doctrine; as Benthall (2003: 15) underlines, 'Islam is the only one of the three Abrahamic religions that explicitly urges the believer not only to be generous but also to persuade others to be charitable.'[12] Strikingly, orphans are often the focus of many charitable activities, again based on a saying of the Prophet.[13]

In the modern era, Muslims have dispersed across the globe and no central Islamic administration exists, except in countries such as Pakistan, Sudan or Saudi Arabia where the collection of *Zakah* is organized by the Government but also channelled through private charitable organizations. As a result, *Zakah* and *Sadaqah* in Muslim and increasingly non-Muslims countries are collected by Islamic charities and distributed around the world in similar fashion to Western relief and development NGOs which raise funds directly from the public or through government grants. *Zakah* and *Sadaqah* can be given in kind or, nowadays predominantly, in cash with donation boxes often found in mosques and community centres whilst Islamic charities may also have offices and charity shops where donations can be deposited. This may create a lack of accountability and transparency, given donors' anonymity on the basis of an Islamic sentiment that 'alms given discreetly are better than those that are publicised' (Benthall 2003c: 39). As a consequence, where Islamic NGOs have been criticized for the inappropriate use of funds, they have often found themselves unable to effectively counter these allegations. Nevertheless, due to the obligatory nature of *Zakat* and the admonishment of the Prophet to be charitable, the momentum of Muslims donating to Islamic charities – both regulated and informal – is unabating, despite the enormous scrutiny to which Muslim agencies are currently exposed.

From Saudi petro-dollars to 'Wahabi' 'Dawah'

In general terms, *'Da'wah'* means 'invitation' and is often equated with proselytizing, although it 'has historically encompassed a wide range of meanings' (Hirschkind 2004: 190). The invitation can be extended by word but also through personal example (e.g. virtue and piety). Furthermore, in Arabic the word *Da'wah* can have non-religious meanings, yet primarily it carries the connation of 'preaching'. In many ways, inviting to Islam is regarded both as a collective and individual duty on the basis of some of the key themes in Qur'an.[14] However, perhaps in contrast to a Christian or secular understanding of proselytization, *Da'wah* is the invitation in itself, whilst the desired outcome is held to be entirely in the hands of God. In fact, *Da'wah* organisations have a distinct history from those of Christian missionaries. Most modern *Da'wah* related activities are based on the distribution of information (both passively through pamphlets or the relatively new medium of the

Internet and actively through preachers). Service provision, including the building and running of mosques, particularly where emerging civil society groups inspired by political Islam compete with the state in many of the autocratic and secular regimes of the Muslim world (Hirschkind 1997) has also become an integral part of the 'invitation'. Moreover, a lot of *Da'wah* is also intra-communal with a focus on calling fellow Muslims to increased piety as is the case with the prolific *Tablighi Jamaat* movement. Originating in the Indian subcontinent in the 1920 and theologically unconnected to Saudi Arabia, it is seen as an apolitical movement promoting internal grassroots missionary renewal (Metcalf 2004), though it has millions of activists worldwide.

Post World War II ,'Wahabism' remained relatively isolated within the Arabian peninsula. From the late 1950s to the 1970s, however, the Middle East was gripped by political turmoil and military conflict that had major impact on geo-political stability amid the ensuing oil crisis. In particular, the struggle ruling monarchies and revolutionary forces espousing secular pan-Arabism, led by Gemal Abdul Nasser, was regarded by the Saud dynasty as an existential threat. 'Wahabism' was promoted as a pan-Islamic third force. By embracing pan-Islamism, Saudi King Faisal could counter the idea of pan-Arab loyalty around Egypt with a larger transnational loyalty centred on Saudi Arabia (Al-Rasheed 2002). *Da'wah* or preaching Islam, with a strong 'Wahabi' theological flavour and funded by the Saudi state, became a counter current to the threat perceived from Arab socialism and Arab nationalism. Hence, the first evidence of Saudi-funded 'Wahabi' missionary work can be traced to 1962 when the Saudi government established the Muslim World League to 'promote Islamic solidarity' as a means of strengthening its legitimacy in (or hegemony over) the Muslim world. The 1967 Arab defeat at the hands of Israel and Gemal Abdul Naser's death in 1970 pushed King Faisal of Saudi Arabia to affirm his claim to leadership of the Muslim World. Thus, the political rationale for promoting 'Wahabism' as the only viable alternative to secular pan-Arab socialism was born. 'Wahabi' state-sponsored *Da'wah* projects began to sprout throughout the Muslim world, with oil wealth funding the construction of mosques and the printing of religious pamphlets. Many such *Da'wah* projects were run by Islamist activists, often from Egypt's Muslim Brotherhood (*al-Ikhwan al-Muslimeen*) who emigrated to Saudi Arabia *en masse* as a result of Nasser's crackdown in the 1960s.

Arguably, Saudi 'Wahabi' *Da'wah* is now more grounded in regional *real politik* and is utilized as a tool to provide further legitimacy to the custodians of the two holy sites of Islam. In this context, Jonathan

Benthall (2003) underlines the Saudi dynasty's fear of Gaddafi's rise to power in 1969. The ensuing competition for moral–spiritual authority and political leadership in the Islamic world and the spread and influence of Gaddafi's 'Green Book' in Africa further fuelled 'Wahabi' missionary activities. The Muslim World League (MWL, or *Rabita* from *Rabita al-Alam al-Islami*) was set up by Muslim religious figures from 22 countries in Makkah in Saudi Arabia in 1962 as an umbrella and representative body for Muslim believers, although Sunni Saudi Arabia dominated and funded it. As an overall vehicle for pan-Islamic political leadership, King Faisal encouraged the establishment of the inter-governmental 'Organization of Islamic Conference' (OIC) set up in Rabat, Morocco in 1969 but headquartered in Jeddah, Saudi Arabia. Subsequently, the Islamic Development Bank (IDB) was founded by the first conference of OIC Finance Ministers in 1973, potentially adding a regional financial institution to the Saudi missionary 'arsenal'.

A renewed catalyst for the spread of 'Wahabism' was the Islamic Revolution in Iran led by Ayatollah Khomeini in 1979 with the Shi'a version of Islam subsequently actively promoted across Africa throughout the 1980s and 1990s. Scholarships for African students to pursue their studies in Iran were widely used to spread the message. The Saudis, however, regarded themselves as the guardians of Islamic revival and did not want to loose out to their competitors in Tehran, thus further driving 'Wahabi' *Da'wah* activity (cf. Burr and Collins 2006). The fall of the Shah also increased the Saud dynasty's sense of uncertainty and led to political and economic instability in the Gulf region. This, in turn, created global instability with the US military presence in the region wavering temporarily (Pollack 2002). The relationship between Saudi Arabia and the United States of America was mainly driven by mutual interest in oil extraction and cemented by the United States opposition to British, French and Israeli intervention in the 1956 Suez conflict of 1956 and by Saudi (i.e. 'Wahabi') conservatism and its staunch opposition to communism. The Palestinian cause, interestingly, was not the key driver for the establishment of Muslim or Saudi NGOs as Jonathan Benthall (2003) argues, with modern welfare organizations barely dating back to the Arab defeat of 1967. The Palestinian cause did, however, strain relationships between Saudi Arabia and the United States (Pollack 2002). Matters came to a head when the United States supported Israel during the 1967 conflict with Egypt, and the Saudis declared that oil supplies would be cut off to those aiding Israel. When the Egyptian–Israeli conflict again flared up in 1973 this threat became reality, and the Saudi-dominated Organisation of Petroleum Exporting Countries declared a 70 per cent oil price hike. The 'oil weapon' (Yergin 1991: 554) was born, and although it was not used again, it created the foundation for the unprecedented wealth of the Kingdom.

Subsequently, 'black gold' became a key funding source for the work of Saudi Arabian governmental and non-governmental organizations in the field of humanitarian aid and development assistance. According to the Saudi Arabian government, its aid to the developing world since the mid-1970s puts it among the largest donors in the world, both in terms of volume and ODA/GNP ratio with disbursements of $48 billion from 1975 to 1987 (or $4 billion a year, the second largest disbursement after the United States).[15]

In this context it is important to distinguish between Saudi private charity and government-led charitable work, although the dividing line is sometimes unclear. Although much of the funding comes from *Zakat* and *Sadaqah* collected through a network of fundraising branches within Saudi Arabia, NGOs also enjoy a close relationship with the Royal family, into whose coffers the oil revenue flows and which acts as patron or donor (Barasi 2005). The phenomenon of the Saudi NGO is a relatively recent one and Saudi NGOs operating as organizations similar to Western NGOs working outside Saudi Arabia during emergency or crisis can be attributed to the early 1980s and the 'Afghan Jihad' (Ottaway 2004; Bellion-Jourdan 2000).

Saudi NGOs involvement during the Afghan Jihad was initially seen as solidarity with Afghan refugees in Pakistan and response to needy 'Muslim brothers' and only then extended to humanitarian assistance to the *mujahideen*. Whilst the degree of the humanitarian nature of this support may be debatable, it is often forgotten that both Saudi and American administrations at that time were supporting the *mujahideen* against the Russian invaders. Western media referred to the *mujahideen* positively, as freedom fighters although the term *mujahideen* has now taken on a negative connotation, as the equivalent of terrorists. Hence, Saudi support is being revaluated in terms of its role in spreading violent beliefs (cf. Burr and Collins 2006).

The range of Saudi organizations shaped by these historical developments, however, was diverse, as highlighted by the case studies that follow. Some were purely humanitarian, for instance, the Saudi Red Crescent (Benthall 2003; Ghandour 2003); others engaged in spreading the Islamic message, inevitably with 'Wahabi' undertones due to the nexus between the religious establishment and state funders, on the back of development work and others again supported what they perceived to be freedom fighters in, for example, Bosnia, Chechnya and Iraq. The last category is particularly difficult to assess since academic research is virtually non-existent; analysis is limited to 'grey' or rather 'shadowy' literature coming from the counter-terrorism establishment and the outcome of many legal cases, if indeed still in place, is unclear. However, although Saudi NGOs are part of a rich tradition of Islamic humanitarianism, many are closely linked to broader political objectives. As Benthall notes, ' The political intentions of many Islamic humanitarians seem obvious to non-Muslim observers. At the same time, Islamic humanitarianism cannot be reduced to politics alone. Traditions such as Zakat, sadaqa and waqf, and the rich verbal imagery of the Quran, constitute a form of social capital' (Benthall 2003a: 4).

These objectives are either necessitated by Muslim *real politik* or by a social change agenda which within a puritan 'Wahabi' understanding could mean the espousing of conservative Islam to stem what may either be perceived to be a tide of secularization, syncretic forms of Islam or other types of political Islam. In this sense, most Islamic organizations carry an element of *Da'wah*, that is, they see their work as contributing to an overall invitation to Islam – subject to their own interpretation. This could either be through direct propagation and proselytization, often of 'stray' or non-practising Muslims, or through charity with an emphasis on particular forms of Islamic compassion. Even in making humanitarian work accessible to people from all faiths, Bellion-Jourdan (2000: 15) argues, 'the da'waist attitude towards aid is always present: it justifies the universality of aid by the universal ambition of Islam as a religion destined for the whole humanity'. Conversely, whilst *Da'wah* in the vast majority of instances involves preaching and other missionary-type activities (Hirschkind 1997), alms-giving, providing medical care, mosque building, publishing and generally promoting what is considered to be public virtue through community action could also legitimately be seen as a practical application of that invitation. Whilst this approach may throw up ethical questions within a Western humanitarian framework, Saudi organizations do not necessarily see a distinction between humanitarian work and 'Wahabi' *Da'wah*. In modern terms it could cynically be labelled 'aid conditionality', with a focus on saving lives as per an often quoted Qur'anic verse,[16] but also with the intention of saving souls.

Case studies: the work of IIRO, WAMY and Al-Haramain in Somalia[17]

Very little research has been carried out on the work of NGOs in Somalia since the failure of the US-led United Nations Operation in Somalia

(UNOSOM) missions with the notable exceptions of the work of Andre Le Sage (2004) and an International Crisis Group study (2005). Nevertheless, many assertions are made about the impact of Islamist groups in Somalia and the alleged role of Saudi Arabia in fuelling their activities.

In Saudi Arabia, government funding for international relief and development is complemented by the work of diverse community of Saudi NGOs with over 250 organizations reportedly in operation nationally, regionally and internationally (Burr and Collins 2006: 38). Not very much, however, is known about their actual humanitarian and developmental activities apart from the work of the Saudi Red Crescent Society which is relatively well documented (cf. Benthall 2000) and a number of NGOs under the media spotlight since allegations about links of such organizations to 9/11 and support for violent extremism (cf. Burr and Collins 2006). The apparent lack of transparency and accountability in such organizations which gives rise to concern in the West could be explained by the traditions of anonymous giving in Islam discussed above, though a number of Saudi government departments have responsibility for the work of NGOs with the Saudi royal family being a large contributor (Burr and Collins 2006; Barasi 2005). Amid pressure from the United States, the Saudi government has clamped down on public fundraising activities including a ban of charity collection boxes in mosques and the shutting down of some leading charities. The Saudi Ministry of Information announced in July 2003 that all NGOs are barred from sending funds abroad. The subsequent establishment in 2004 of a National Commission for Relief and Charity Work Abroad was meant to introduce more accountability, but it also increased government control over the activities of NGOs, heavily funded by the Saud dynasty yet enjoying a degree of freedom (Barasi 2005).

Even less is known of their work in Somalia. Within this context, it is important to understand the wider regional picture with Somalia as a Muslim country which has a long history of cultural, religious and trade ties with the Arabian Peninsula. The vast majority of Somalis are Sunni Muslims,[18] following the Shafi'i school of Islamic jurisprudence. Less than one per cent of ethnic Somalis are Christians. Allegiance to the Muslim faith reinforces distinctions that set Somalis apart from their immediate African neighbours, most of whom are either Christians or adherents of traditional African belief systems. At the same time, all of Somalia's neighbours have Muslim minority communities, often ethnically Somali, as in Ethiopia's Ogaden region or in Kenya's northern Mandera district, stimulating regional tensions. According to the International Crisis Group (ICG), for instance, 'the Government of Ethiopia [...] fears that Somalia may eventually fall outside its direct political influence' (ICG 2002: 12), a concern heightened by suspected support from arch enemy Eritrea for Islamic groups. Although Somalis are ethnically not Arabs, they identify more with Arabs than with their fellow Africans, and Somalia joined the Arab League in 1974 as the first non-Arab member during Siad Barre's presidency. There was no specific history or presence of Gulf-based or Saudi NGOs in Somalia at that period of time. However, many Somalia students were studying in Islamic Universities in Saudi Arabia.

Throughout the 1980s, Somalia became increasingly dependent upon economic aid from the wealthy oil-exporting states of Kuwait, Qatar, the United Arab Emirates and Saudi Arabia. Since the demise of the Barre regime in 1991, and Somalia's descent into anarchy, these countries have continued to support Somalia through NGOs. The Somalia NGO sector, in the absence of a functioning government providing basic education and health to its citizens,[19] plugged this considerable gap (cf. Le Sage 2004). Over the past 15 years, Somalis have come to rely on non-state provision of food and social services such as health and education. Foreign donors, from both the 'West' and the Arab world, have rushed in to meet these needs. Arab Islamic charities have contributed significantly to service delivery but as part of their problem analysis also tend to espouse social change on the basis of their faith, to overcome the evils of 'clannism'. This does not automatically imply, however, that Somalia has been a fertile ground for political Islam or extremism. As Le Sage argues, for instance, 'to directly equate Islamic charities with Islamist political agendas would be simplistic' (2004: 8). Perhaps contrary to the ICG (2002) assessment that Islamic charities in Somalia 'proselytise', it is clear that 'Wahabi' missionary objectives are focused on preaching the tenants of their theology and providing support to local Qur'anic schools and madrassahs. These limited objectives stem in large part from the nature of Somalia as a conservative Muslim country. Almost by definition, direct proselytization of large numbers of non-Muslims cannot be found. Moreover, even within the context of 'Wahabi' organizations preaching their ultra-conservative message and seeking to win over followers, Somalia's conservative Muslim society provides little scope for antagonistic proselytization between different camps. Syncretic forms of Islam exist and are firmly rooted; yet, the Islamic practices overall are more based on Arab rather than on African Islamic interpretations. However, allegations have been made about support for subversive activities and almost by default Islamic charities have been implicated *en masse*. As the ICG notes, however, '[t]he term 'Islamic charities' implies a distinction from NGOs assisted by Western donors that is in reality not so clear cut at the interface with the beneficiary community. Many Somali organizations are simply committed to providing a service that is consistent with their beliefs and practices as Muslims' (ICG 2005: 22).

Interestingly, Saudi NGOs in Somalia are to some extent passive or reactive contributors to development, waiting for local communities to come forward and request assistance for projects, instead of pursuing their own development agenda. One important reason is Saudi and other Gulf NGOs look for counter-part funding from the local community (Le Sage 2004). *Awqaf* (charitable trusts) set up to manage service delivery are often fee-based, that is, the initial set up cost will be met by external donors whereas the revenue generated from service fees will continue to finance the project. This coupled with the fact that they are almost entirely staffed by Somali nationals (Novib/WAMY 2004) makes them both relatively responsive to local needs or to the prevailing 'market' conditions. It also adds to their sustainability – local people are more in control than through other service delivery models, creating buy-in and protecting it from clan politics.

A closer look at three prominent Saudi NGOs working in Somalia will help to paint a differentiated picture of the phenomenon. All have a strong Islamic identity, both in terms of names or imagery used and in their utilization of *Zakat* or *Sadaqah*, the setting up of *Awqaf*, support for religious (madrassah-based) education and for orphan care. By virtue of understanding the motivation of the often private funders for such work, this utilization of religious concepts in themselves do not make these organizations automatically outright 'missionaries'. A comparison will, therefore, demonstrate that some of the organizations perceived in the West as promoting 'Wahabi' missionary activity are very similar to Western humanitarian organizations (e.g. the International Islamic Relief Organization). Others are clearly seeking to win over either non-practising Muslims or Muslims of other (e.g. Sufi) orientations, to their world view (e.g. the World Assembly of Muslim Youth), whilst another type may have overstepped the dividing line between relief and support for subversive political activism in their social change agenda (the case of Al-Haramain).

The International Islamic Relief Organization (IIRO)

The IIRO was established in Mekkah in 1978 as the relief arm of the Muslim World League and is one of the largest Muslim relief agencies in the world. Its humanitarian activities became widely known within Saudi Arabia and abroad during the Afghan Jihad during the 1980s, emphasizing the importance of understanding the historical context which in turn becomes a political driver. IIRO's stated mission[20] is 'to provide [medical, educational and social] assistance to victims of natural disasters and wars all over the world', evolving from the early focus on the refugee crisis in Pakistan stemming from the Russian invasion of Afghanistan. Today, IIRO is headquartered in Jeddah and has field offices in more than 20 countries in Asia, the Middle East and Africa, including Somalia. Its service delivery function is split between different departments, ranging from urgent relief and refugees to health care, orphans and social welfare, education, agricultural assistance and architectural and engineering consultancy. Most of IIRO's funding is derived from private donations in Saudi Arabia, and it has close links with the Saudi Government through members of the royal family. In 2001, it is reported to have carried out 2,800 projects worth $33 million in 95 countries (Benthall 2003a). By 2004, according to its latest annual report, its spending had grown to over $35 million.[21] The fact that such reports exist counters, at least to some degree, the commonly held belief that there is there is little transparency on the part of Saudi NGOs, although independent verification through independent auditors and transparent governance systems are also desirable.

For all that is known publicly,[22] IIRO is a mainstream faith-based relief agency. It is one of the few Muslim members of the influential Geneva-based global NGO umbrella body the International Council for Voluntary Agencies (ICVA) and has consultative status with the Economic and Social Council (ECOSOC) of the United Nations. Some analysts have even likened IIRO to a secular agency with 'activities, structure, mode of operation and development programmes [...] not different from that of secular transnational NGOs' (Salih 2002: 20).

IIRO has been operational in Somalia since the early 1990s with an office in Mogadishu and sub offices in southern Somalia. It focuses on food aid (including Ramadan meals and the distribution of Qurbani meat), and the provision of shelter and medical care, particularly to the internally displaced. It also supports a number of educational projects, namely the computer and sewing training centres 'Taiba' and 'Um Al Qora'. Together with its Qur'an memorization programme – religious education in the Somali cultural context is considered part of mainstream education – IIRO's Somalia programme is one of its largest. This makes IIRO primarily a humanitarian NGO. Its emphasis on Islamic projects is partly due to donor preferences – funds flow in when religious rewards are promised to those who donate to the building of mosques and to support the memorization of Islam's holy scripture in madrassahs and mosques. At the same time, Somali beneficiaries request IIRO support for religious activities, for instance, support of local madrassah-based education in the absence of other forms of education. Moreover, there have been no allegations or evidence that IIRO has been involved in 'Wahabi'-based *Da'wah*, let alone complicity in supporting subversive or extreme activities in Somalia.

World Assembly of Muslim Youth (WAMY)

In similar vein, WAMY was established in Riyadh, Saudi Arabia in 1972 by a Royal Decree of the late King Faisal. The stated purpose of the organization[23] is to 'help and empower Muslim Youth in the Muslim World'. The main activity of WAMY in the past three decades has been the youth educational camps. WAMY has regional as well as local branches in and outside Saudi Arabia, North America, Europe, Asia and Africa with a presence in 55 countries and an associate membership of over 500 youth organizations around the world. In the early 1980s WAMY extended its work to collect aid for emergency relief and to help Muslim communities in social welfare and community development. Part of WAMY's stated mission of empowerment is also the provision and dissemination of Islamic information through leaflets, posters, exhibitions and so on, and its *dawa'ist* objectives are also underlined by a strong presence in the Western non-Muslim world unlike, for example, IIRO which only has fundraising offices in America and Europe. This makes WAMY in many ways unique and different from the archetypical 'Wahabi-da'wah organization which focuses on producing primarily 'better Muslims' in the Muslim world by preaching adherence to theological precepts. This has primarily to do with the way that WAMY is practically influenced by the teachings of the Muslim Brotherhood (al-Ikhwan al-Muslimeen) by virtue of internal staff dynamics – many WAMY activists were of Egyptian origin having fled Naser's reign. Their focus on unity between Muslims and raising political awareness, rather than theological purity, lends itself better for an operation within diverse cultural environments. Moreover, WAMY's operational strategy to a good extent seems to be inspired by a study of Western models both from the Christian missionary and the youth movement realm like the Scouts and is more modern in its methodology. Particularly its significant work of supporting young people in their physical, mental and also spiritual development aims to shape them as constructive contributors to Islamic society. Thus their outlook is reformist within the context of political Islam whilst *Da'wah* is realized within the modern context of a secularizing Muslim world.

WAMY also has consultative status at the United Nation's ECOSOC and spent reportedly $28m during 2004 on Islamic and humanitarian work.[24] But WAMY has experienced a considerable 40 per cent drop in their fundraising income compared to the period before 9/11 due to restrictions and 'fear of Muslims falling foul of strict US efforts to monitor terror funding', stated Saleh Wohaibi, WAMY's Secretary General, in a rare interview with Western media. (Reuters 2006).

In Somalia, it has established various humanitarian and youth educational projects including the building of hospitals and schools, orphans' sponsorship, community development projects, building mosques, digging wells and the provision of food aid during Ramadan and Qurbani.[25] The distribution of Islamic information, that is, *Da'wah*, in the form of Somali-language copies of the Qur'an and theological pamphlets – including copies of Abd al Wahab's writings although not exclusively – is an integral part of WAMY's work, which makes it in essence a missionary organization in its literal meaning. However, the focus is not on Wahabi theology but the creation of a social order, informed by Islam, as its 'lax' attitudes – in the 'Wahabi'/Salafi understanding – towards gender segregation in its Somali schools demonstrates. *Da'wah* and school curricula which are Arabic based and contain Islamic studies as the case in most Muslim schools (Novib/WAMY 2004) is limited to what is acceptable to Somalis thus creating opportunities for horizontal peace among, for example, students in WAMY funded schools which come from different clans within the country.

Al-Haramain Islamic Foundation (AHIF)

The history of AHIF is slightly different from the previous examples. The organization is both younger and more non-governmental as it was initiated in Peshawar towards the end of Afghan War. In 1988, AHIF was endorsed as a relief organization working under the Muslim World League and was operating in many countries worldwide. Its founder, Sheikh Aqeel Al-Aqeel, who previously worked for the Saudi Red Crescent was also believed to have close relationships with Saudi Ministries of Interior and Islamic Affairs. The organization's name refers to the two holy sites, Makkah and Madinah, and thus has a highly religious appeal as well as an indirect link to the King of Saudi Arabia, custodian of the holy sites.

In the backlash post 9/11, many Muslim NGOs in the United States of America such as Global Relief, Benevolence International and Holy

Land Foundation were designated as terrorist organizations or deemed to be supporting terrorism. AHIF's Somalia and Bosnia branches were also designated.[26] In Somalia itself, AHIF is the only Saudi charity that has been directly linked to terrorism and listed and designated as a terrorist organization by the Office of Foreign Assets Control (OFAC). The designation of AHIF Somalia, however, was mainly based on circumstantial evidence, including the employment of individuals linked to terrorism.[27] First, it seems, AHIF Somalia staff had links to *Al Itihad Al Islami*, which had resisted the American mission 'Restoration Hope' in Somalia and was considered by US intelligence sources as the East African branch of Al-Qaeda. Yet, according to the ICG (2005), Al-Qaeda is not regarded to have such tangible infrastructure or branches, whilst others (Moeller 2006) argue that a failed state does not offer the protection a terrorist group requires. Second, according to US Security sources, those who carried out the 1998 bombing of the US embassy in Nairobi came from Somalia and were funded by Saudi NGOs. In what was perhaps a pre-emptive strike to stem Western criticism of other Saudi NGOs, the Saudi Government suspended the work of AHIF and dissolved the organization in 2004.

When Sheikh Aqeel Al-Aqeel was interviewed by the Washington Post, he argued that 'The mistakes of individuals should not be attributed to the whole institution' (Ottaway 2004). Furthermore, extensive research by Le Sage (2004) could find no further evidence of AHIF Somalia relations with terrorists known in Somalia. In many ways, AHIF's Somalia branch had low visibility and AHIF like many other Saudi NGOs lacked transparency. There is no conclusive evidence, however, for AHIF's involvement in terrorism (Moeller 2006), and the absence of an independent judiciary in Somalia or Saudi Arabia makes it extremely difficult to prove or rebut such allegations.

In general, AHIF was not uniquely different in its activities from the other Saudi or Gulf-based NGOs when it first came to Somalia in 1992. However, it did adopt a more 'fundamentalist' attitude as a religious organization. As Le Sage points out (2004: 25), women were required to wear the full hijab and to cover their faces, circumstantial evidence perhaps, but pointing to a different approach to organizations such as WAMY. Nevertheless, AHIF provided a welfare service, operating orphanages and financing Qura'nic schools, as well as building mosques in Somalia. This latter programmatic focus, however, suggests that AHIF was primarily a religious organization and less a charitable or development organization. AHIF operated a total of eight orphanages – according to Le Sage (2004) five of these orphanages were in Mogadishu whilst the other orphanages were in Merka in southern Somalia, and Burao and Hargeysa in Somaliland – caring for about 3,500 children throughout the country.[28] The closure of AHIF, thus, had an impact on supporting the fragile social welfare system in Somalia and as a former Somali employee of AHIF said, 'This is like taking food from the mouths of children...These children did not have much but they had a roof over their head, three meals a day and schooling. Now they have nothing. Will those responsible for the closure of AHIF take care of these children or is it that the lives of 3,000 Somali children are of no consequence?' (UN-IRIN 2003).

Saudi charities in Somalia: a converging Islamist agenda?

Clearly, the above discussion of three charities emphasizes that whilst there is a number of key areas of programmatic overlap, that is, Islamic education, Ramadan food aid or Qurbani programmes, this convergence is primarily donor driven. Arguably the support given by Saudi NGOs to Somali communities leads to a notable effect in strengthening social, economic and political linkages with the Arab World, yet it is evident that a number of international state and non-state actors vie for political influence. But more importantly, it also underlines the distinctions between different nuances of what from the outside appears to be a uniform entity. Islamic charities, particularly so-called 'Wahabi' organizations, are in the case of Somalia responsive to the needs of the local people and make a substantive contribution to the delivery of public services (e.g. education and healthcare) in the absence of state provision. However, they have different visions as to how best to achieve their social agenda.

WAMY represents perhaps the strongest case for a primarily missionary-type organization, with its focus on education and youth camps clearly informed by Christian missionaries and the scout movement. However, Al Haramain's programmatic focus and the way puritan beliefs like the strict covering of women were adopted throughout their programmes, suggests a strong eagerness to convert beneficiaries to the ultra-orthodox Saudi interpretation of Islamic law. IIRO, on the other hand, can be classified primarily as a humanitarian or social welfare organization, despite the donor-driven religious elements within the range of programmes carried out.

In the Somali context none of them were found to be proselytizing (i.e. seeking to convert), yet a varying degree of *Da'wah* to Muslims of other persuasions is omnipresent. However, through an appeal at a commonly accepted platform, that is, that of Islam, Saudi NGOs together with other Islamic charities seem to have overcome obstacles related to 'clannism' in their service delivery. According to Le Sage (2004), in Somalia it appeared to be acceptable for Islamic NGOs to stipulate conditions, for example, that beneficiaries must adopt basic Islamic practices as they discourage communities from resorting to violence and can transcend clan boundaries. The recent rise of the Union of Islamic Courts is possibly a case in point that may suggest that advocating the adherence to an arguably strict form of Islam may increase a sense of social stability among Somali society, whose social fabric has been riddled with clan fighting for decades.

Conclusion

In the complexities of the post 9/11 world, Islamic non-governmental organizations figure amongst the global casualties of the war on terror, particularly Saudi 'Wahabi' organizations. And so have the beneficiaries of humanitarian and social welfare programmes previously implemented by such organizations. A perceived lack of transparency, ideological affiliations and speculation about association with Al-Qaeda are equated with support for terrorist activities and in the process, the work of those carrying out genuine humanitarian activities has come under threat. This chapter illustrates the need for a greater understanding of the underlying principles and practices of 'Wahabism' – so often portrayed as 'extreme' and a deeper understanding of their important work in the field of humanitarian activity.

The analysis offered here, based on a historical (re-)evaluation of the phenomenon of 'Wahabism' and brief operational profiles of Saudi NGOs at work in Somalia, serves to illustrate what we currently know, vis-à-vis the existing literature. We have sought to provide some insights into the origins of Wahabism and its underlying principles, particularly as they relate to the central concepts of charity and humanitarian action in Islam. We have seen that Saudi Arabia and its NGOs are significant players in the global humanitarian field, carrying out billions of dollars worth of humanitarian work around the world, second only to United States in global spending in this arena. The profile of three key organizations operating in Somalia has illustrated the diversity in nature of Saudi NGOs operating in the country combining humanitarian and proselytizing activity to varying degrees, the final example illustrating how ideology and perceived association can lead to the closure of a humanitarian organization. Even collating the brief overview of organizational work in this chapter was difficult, and given the perceived lack of transparency with which Saudi NGOs currently operate, and the current global climate, it is perhaps not surprising that Saudi NGOs are unable to respond to intense scrutiny. In order to persevere in the vast and vital field of humanitarian work, greater efforts will need to be made on the part of Saudi NGOs to display transparency and accountability in the international arena, based on commonly held standards beyond what is perhaps acceptable in the Muslim world. This can be achieved through building on the rich Islamic tradition of humanitarianism which in many ways precedes both Christian and modern Western secular concepts of relief and development.

The Islamic counter-part to social change is represented in the concept of *'Daw'ah'*. The example of Saudi NGO working in Somalia has shown that they are carrying out what could be perceived as 'missionary' type of activities, to varying degrees, alongside their humanitarian activities. Each organization has a distinctive interpretation of the philanthropic message of the Qu'ran and how the responsibility of *Da'wah* is to be operationalised. Each constitutes a significant humanitarian and development organization, playing an important role in supporting the poor in Muslim countries afflicted by conflict and state failure. Some openly seek to win followers to their 'Wahabi' understanding of Islam, while others seek to demonstrate the compassion of Islam and the generosity of the Kingdom of Saudi Arabia. In the case of Somalia, the call is made to Muslims to 'purify their practice', rather than to those of other faiths to embrace Islam. Whether we view Saudi charities in as vehicles of state-sponsored proselytization or whether they are more benignly viewed as non-governmental organizations pursuing their own social change agenda, it is evident from this and other studies that all NGOs and missionary organizations carry varying levels of ideological baggage and in this respect the Saudi NGOs are no different. However, 'Wahabi' or Salafi-inspired organizations are less committed to securing converts to the Muslim faith then they are in working with existing Muslims and winning them over to a more puritan interpretation of Sunni Islam – with creating 'Good Muslims' just as many missionary organizations seek to create 'Good Christians'.

Western and Arab organizations work side by side in many cases yet separately – many Western organizations remain ignorant of their Arab counterparts and Arab organizations have found it difficult to secure recognition from Western organizations, for instance, invitations to participate in dialogue among the leading donors working in the country. This chapter has argued that there is a clear need to avoid media-driven stereotyping of organizations which seem at odds with Western cultural values and to reach beyond these generalizations to explore the similarities between these and many Western organizations. It demonstrates the need for Western donors to engage in dialogue with their Gulf state counterparts who make a considerable contribution to global humanitarian action, to involve them in networks and to coordinate aid efforts on the basis of a robust understanding of complementarities rather than differences.

Notes

1. Cf. Martens 2002, Edwards and Hulme 1996. The term 'secular missionaries' is used in *The Economist* (2000).
2. After Samuel Huntington's 'Clash of civilizations' thesis.
3. http://www.islamicpluralism.org/wahhabiwatch/ww2006.htm
4. Orthodox here refers to 'Wahabism' espousing only the traditional foundation of Islamic legal and theological thought (the Qur'an and the sunnah of the Prophet) (Eliade and Adams, *Encyclopaedia of Religion*, 1987).
5. This link has continued for over 250 years with descendants of Abd al Wahab's who take the name Ahl al-Shaykh (literally the 'family of the religious scholar') and take high positions in the religious establishment of the country as 'vital partners to the House of Saud, crucially conferring Islamic legitimacy on its rule' (Henderson 2003).
6. Abd al Wahab was not necessarily a prolific writer and many of his works are actually short treatises like 'Kitab al-Tawhid'. Salafis like Oliver (2004) argue that Abd al Wahab never espoused extremism, violence or terrorism.
7. The main targets were shrines and the graves of saints, which play a major role in Sufism but are held in Wahabi doctrine as *shirk* (polytheism). Both theologies are highly antagonistic to the present day.
8. Philby's vivid accounts (1928) provide some interesting historical and ethnographic insights into the al-Saud dynasty and 'Wahabism'.
9. Within Sunni Islam, there are four schools of jurisprudence which are: Hanafi (predominant in non-Arab areas within the former Ottoman Empire and in South East Asia); Maliki (mainly in West Africa); Shafi'i (mainly in north and east Africa including Somalia); and Hanbali (predominant in Saudi Arabia and the Gulf) (cf. Philips 1996).
10. The translation of Yusuf al-Quardawi's book entitled 'Fiqh az-Zakat' is possibly one of the most comprehensive compilations of Islamic sources and scholarly verdicts on the topic available in the English language.
11. Al-Qardawi mentions that 'in the way of Allah' is regarded by the majority of Islamic jurists as referring to 'jihad' (Arabic for 'struggle') although he argues that a contemporary interpretation could include state expenditure on defence (coupled with revenue from land tax, kharaj), or even the financing of the establishment of an Islamic state. He refers to cultural, educational and informational jihad which includes Da'wah (al-Qardawi: 427–428) which would suggest that jihad is not understood as a purely military struggle. Other analyses from a counter-terrorism perspective (e.g. Burr and

Collins 2006) argue that actual practice is often the opposite and hint at an 'alms for jihad' paradigm. Benthall's elucidations (2003a and b), based on both historical and ethnographic research, offer a more nuanced analysis.

12. Surah al-Ma'un (A Small Kindness, Qur'an Chapter 107): 'Have you seen the one who denies the Recompense? For that is the one who drives away the orphan, and does not encourage the feeding of the poor.'

13. The Prophet Muhammed stated in a well-known Hadeeth: 'I and the one who looks after an orphan will be like this in Paradise', putting his middle and index fingers together. (Sahih Bukhari, *Volume 8, Book 73, Number 34*).

14. The Qur'an relates the stories of the Biblical prophets as a reminder to the community of believers to invite to the truth. Individual Muslims are called to give Da'wah, in for example, Surah An-Nahl (16: 125): 'Call unto the way of thy Lord with wisdom and fair exhortation, and reason with them in the better way. Lo! thy Lord is best aware of him who strayeth from His way, and He is Best Aware of those who go aright.'

15. Source: official Saudi information website http://saudinf.com/main/l102.htm [accessed 12/12/06]

16. 'and who so saveth the life of one, it shall be as if he had saved the life of all mankind.' (5: 32)

17. The case studies is mainly based on a survey of academic literature and information available from brochures and the websites of the organizations in question. Benthall underlines that this 'lack of financial transparency also makes studying Islamic humanitarianism particularly difficult' (Benthall 2003c: 43).

18. However, Somalis have introduced local ritual and custom into Islam, for example, with reference to the social significance of 'baraka', the blessings from heads of Sufi orders or clan leaders (see I. M Lewis 1998). Thus, a degree of conflict between these syncretic local traditions and the puritan version of Islam espoused by 'Wahabism' results.

19. With the partial exception of the Republic of Somaliland, and the neighbouring regions to the north-east which have declared the autonomous state of Puntland, no state-supported welfare system exists.

20. Further information can be found on IIRO's website http://www.iirosa.org/web/index.php

21. see IIRO Annual Report for the Fiscal Year 2003/2004. http://www.iirosa.org/web/index.php

22. However, on 3rd August 2006 the U.S. Department of the Treasury designated the Philippine and Indonesian branch offices of IIRO for facilitating fundraising for al Qaida and affiliated terrorist groups. Treasury additionally designated Abd Al Hamid Sulaiman Al-Mujil, the Executive Director of the Eastern Province Branch of IIRO in the Kingdom of Saudi Arabia. For further information see http://www.ustreas.gov/press/releases/hp45.htm

23. For further details see http://www.wamy.org (in Arabic).

24. WAMY Annual Report 2003.

25. see WAMY Annual Report 2003. http://www.wamy.org

26. The process of designation has been criticized by civil rights lawyers in the United States and an umbrella group for Saudi charities called 'Friends of Charities Association (FOCA) is exploring legal options to challenge it – see www.foca.org for details.

27. The briefing provided by the US Treasury on Al-Haramain Somalia branch almost praises the Saudi Arabia-based Al-Haramain International Foundation as a 'charitable and educational organization', although it alleges that the Somalia office is linked to Al-Qaeda. The evidence made publicly available, that is, the payment of salaries through Al-Barakaat Bank, however, appears to be rather scant. See http://www.treasury.gov/offices/enforcement/key-issues/protecting/charities_execorder_13224-a.shtml#ahsom
28. See http://www.orphanages.jeeran.com/somalia.htm

Bibliography

Ahmad, K. (1978), *Economic Development in an Islamic Framework*, Leicester: The Islamic Foundation.
Algar, H. (2002), *Wahhabism: A Critical Essay*, New York: Islamic Publications International.
Ali, T. (2003), *The Clash of Fundamentalisms: Crusades, Jihads and Modernity*, London: Verso.
Al-Mundhiri, Z. A. A. (trans.) (1998), *Summarized Sahih Muslim*, Riyadh: Dar-us-Salam Publishers.
Al-Rasheed, M. (2002), *A History of Saudi Arabia*, Cambridge: Cambridge University Press.
Al-Qardawi, Y. (1999), *Fiqh az-Zakat: A Comparative Study*, London: Dar Al Taqwa.
Barasi, L. (2005), 'Saudi Arabia's Humanitarian Aid: a Political Takeover?' ODI Humanitarian Practice Network, *Humanitarian Exchange*, No 29, London, pp. 41–43.
BBC News Online (2003), 'War on Terror Hits Somali Orphans', 20 May 2003, available online http://news.bbc.co.uk/2/hi/africa/3044485.stm [accessed 10/06/06].
Bellion-Jourdan, J. (2000), 'Islamic Relief Organizations: Between 'Islamism' and 'Humanitarianism'', *ISIM Newsletter*, No. 5.
Benthall, J. (1998), *The Qur'an's Call to Alms: Zakat, the Muslim Tradition of Alms-Giving*, *ISIM Newsletter*, No.1, p. 1.
—— (2003a), 'Humanitarianism, Islam and 11 September', *ODI HGP Briefing*, No 11.
—— (2003b), 'Raising the Red Crescent', *New Humanist*, 1 November, Vol. 118, Issue 4 (November/December) http://newhumanist.org.UK/660 [accessed 28/08/07].
—— (2003 c), 'Humanitarianism and Islam after 11 September', In Joanna Macrae and Adele Harmer (eds), *Humanitarian Action and the 'Global War on Terror': A Review of Trends and Issues*, HPG Report 14.
Benthall, J and Bellion-Jourdan, J. (2003), *The Charitable Crescent: Politics of Aid in the Muslim World*, London/New York: Tauris.
Bryden, M. (2003), 'No Quick Fixes: Coming to Terms with Terrorism, Islam, and Statelessness in Somalia', *Journal of Conflict Studies*, Vol. XXII, No. 2, pp. 24–56.
Byman, D, Lesser, I. O., Pirnie, B., Benard, C. and Waxman, M. (2000), *Strengthening the Partnership: Improving Military Coordination with Relief Agencies and Allies in Humanitarian Operations*, Santa Monica, CA: RAND Co-operation.
Choueiri, Y. (1997), *Islamic Fundamentalism* London/Washington: Pinter, revised edition.
Cragg, K. (1986), *The Call of the Minaret*, London: Collins, 2nd ed.

Delong-Bas, N. J. (2004), *Wahhabi Islam: From Revival and Reform to Global Jihad*, London/New York: Tauris.

De Waal, A. (1997), *Famine Crimes: Politics in the Disaster Relief Industry in Africa*, London: James Curry Publishers.

De Waal, A. (ed.) (2004), *Islamism and Its Enemies in the Horn of Africa*, London: Hurst.

Donini, A. (2004), *Western Agencies don't have a Humanitarian Monopoly*, *Humanitarian Affairs Review*, October, available online http://www.human-rights.unisi.it/h2006/allegati/universality.pdf [accessed 28/08/07].

Duffield, M. (2001), *Global Governance and the New Wars: The Merging of Development and Security*, London and New York: Zed Books.

The Economist (2000), 'Sins of the Secular Missionaries', Jan 27th 2000.

Edwards, M. and Hulme, D. (1996), *Beyond the Magic Bullet: NGO Performance and Accountability in the Post-Cold War World*, West Harford: Kumarian Press.

Esposito, J. (1997), *Political Islam: Revolution, Radicalism, or Reform?* Boulder, Colo./London: Lynne Rienner.

Geertz, C. (2003), 'Which Way to Mecca? Part II', *New York Review of Books*, Vol. 50, No. 11, available online http://www.nybooks.com/articles/16419 [accessed 28/08/07].

Ghandour, A-R (2003), 'Humanitarianism, Islam and the West: Contest or Co-operation', ODI Humanitarian Practice Network, *Humanitarian Exchange Magazine*, No 25, pp. 14–17.

Henderson, S. (2003), *Institutionalised Islam: Saudi Arabia's Islamic Policies and the Threat They Pose*, Testimony given to the US Senate Judiciary Committee, Subcommittee on Terrorism, London 10th September 2003.

Hirschkind, C. (1997), *What is Political Islam?*, The Middle East Research and Information Project (MERIP) Middle East Report 205.

—— (2004), 'Civic Virtue and Religious Reason: An Islamic Counter-Public' In Drobnick, J. (ed.) *Aural Cultures*, Toronto: YYZ Books.

Holden, D. and Johns, R (1982), *The House of Saud*, London: Pan Books.

Huntington, S. P. (1996), *The Clash of Civilizations and the Remaking of World Order*, London: Simon and Schuster.

Ibn Abd al Wahab, M. (1996), *Kitab at-Tawhid*, Riyadh: Dar-us-Salam Publications.

International Crisis Group (2002), *Somalia: Countering Terrorism in a Failed State*, Africa Report No.45.

International Crisis Group (2005), *Somalia's Islamists*, Africa Report No.100.

Khan, M. M. (trans.) (1997), *Sahih Bukhari*, Riyadh: Dar-us-Salam Publishers.

Le Sage, A. (with Menkhaus, K.) (2004), *The Rise of Islamic Charities in Somalia: An Assessment of Impact and Agendas*, Paper presented at 45th Annual International Studies Association Convention, Montreal, 17–20 March 2004.

Lewis, B. (2003), *The Crisis of Islam: Holy War and Unholy Terror*, London: Phoenix.

Lewis, I. M. (1998), *Saints and Somalis: Popular Islam in a Clan-based Society*, Lawrenceville, N. J.: Red Sea Press.

Macrae, J. (2002), 'The Political Dimension', ICRC Forum, available onlinehttp://www.icrc.org/Web/ara/siteara0.nsf/htmlall/5LWFE4/$FILE/Political_dimension.pdf [accessed 20/05/2006].

Manji, F. and O'Coill, C., (2002), 'The Missionary Position: NGOs and Development in Africa', *International Affairs*, Vol. 78, No 3, pp. 567–583.

Metcalf, B. D. (2004), *Islamic Contestations: Essays on Muslims in India and Pakistan*, New Delhi: Oxford University Press.

Moeller, B. (2006), Religion and Conflict in Africa: with a Special Focus on East Africa, Danish Institute for International Studies, DIIS Report No. 6.

Millard Burr, J. and Robert O. Collins (2006), *Alms for Jihad: Charity and Terrorism in the Islamic World*, Cambridge: Cambridge University Press.

Novib and WAMY (2004), Arab Donor Policies and Practices on Education in Somalia/land.

Oliver, H.J. (2004), *The 'Wahhabi' Myth*, Toronto: T.R.O.I.D. Publications.

Ottaway, D. B. (2004), 'US Eyes Money Trails of Saudi-Backed Charities', *Washington Post*, Thursday August 19 2004, available online http://www.washingtonpost.com/wp-dyn/articles/A13266-2004Aug18.html [accessed 05/05/06].

Philby H. St. J. (1928), *Arabia of the Wahhabis*, London: Constable Publishers.

Philips, B. (1996), *The Evolution of Fiqh: Islamic Law and the Madhabs*, Riyadh: International Islamic Publishing House.

Pickthall, M. M. (1996), *The Meaning of the Glorious Qur'an*, Beltsville, MD: Amana Publications.

Pipes, D. (2002), *In the Path of God: Islam and Political Power*, Somerset, NJ: Transaction Publishers.

Pollack, J. (2002), 'Saudi Arabia and the United States 1931–2002', *Middle East Review of International Affairs*, Vol. 6, No. 3, http://meria.idc.ac.il/journal/2002/issue3/jv6n3a7.html [accessed 28/08/07].

Rahman, F. (1987), 'Islam: An Overview', In Eliade, M. and Adams, C. J. (eds) *Encyclopaedia of Religion*, London: Macmillan.

Rentz, G. S. (2005), *Birth of the Islamic Reform Movement in Saudi Arabia: Muhammad B. 'Abd Al-Wahhab (1703/4–1792) and the Beginnings of Unitarian Empire in Arabia*, London: Arabian Publishing Ltd.

Reuters (2006), 'Saudi Charity Spending Down 40 pct on "Terror" Fear', available online www.alertnet.org/printable.htm?URL=/thenews/newsdesk/L29179051.htm [accessed 12/11/06].

Rieff, D. (2002), *A Bed for the Night: Humanitarianism in Crisis*, New York and London: Simon & Schuster.

Royal Embassy of Saudi Arabia (2004), *Initiatives and Actions Taken by the Kingdom of Saudi Arabia to Combat Terrorism*, Information Office briefing, Washington, DC.

Royal Embassy of Saudi Arabia (2006), *Initiatives and Actions Taken by the Kingdom of Saudi Arabia to Combat Terrorism*, Information Office briefing, Washington, DC.

Said, E.W. (1991), *Orientalism: Western Conceptions of the Orient*, London: Penguin.

Salih, M. A. M. (2002), 'Islamic NGOs in Africa: The Promise and Peril of Islamic Voluntarism', Occasional Paper, Centre of African Studies University of Copenhagen, March 2002.

Schwartz, S. (2004), *The Two Faces of Islam: Saudi Fundamentalism and Its Role in Terrorism*, London: Random House.

Slim H. (2004), *How We Look: Hostile Perceptions of Humanitarian Actions*, Presentation at the Conference on Humanitarian Co-ordination, Geneva, 21st April 2004.

UN-IRIN (2003), 'Somalia: Orphans Facing Street Life After Saudi NGO Pulls Out' Nairobi, 21 May 2003, available online http://www.irinnews.org/report.asp?ReportID=34225&SelectRegion=Horn_of_Africa&SelectCountry=SOMALIA [accessed 10/06/06].

US Treasury (2002), Fact Sheet: Designations of Somalia and Bosnia-Herzegovina Branches of Al-Haramain Islamic Foundation, http://www.ustreas.gov/press/releases/po1086.htm [accessed 25/01/07].

Yamani, M (2001), *The Saudi Time Bomb*, Interview with Frontline, 5th November 2001, available online http://www.pbs.org/wgbh/pages/frontline/shows/Saudi/interviews/yamani.html [accessed 10/05/2006].

Yergin, D. (1991), *The Prize: The Epic Quest for Oil, Money and Power?*, New York and London: Simon & Schuster.

Zarabozo, J (2003), *The Life, Teachings and Influence of Muhammad ibn Abdul-Wahhaab*, Riyadh: Ministry of Islamic Affairs, Endowments, Dawah and Guidance, KSA.

10
Faith-Based Organizations as Effective Development Partners? Hezbollah and Post-War Reconstruction in Lebanon

Mona Harb

Introduction

Defining Hezbollah as a faith-based organization (FBO) may seem unusual as it is normally labelled by many Westerners as a terrorist organization and is thus rarely examined as an 'ordinary' or legitimate political player. Yet, this is the position I adopt here. This chapter considers Hezbollah as a Lebanese political party which has been in charge of the elaboration and implementation of development policies for middle and lower-income Shi'i groups for over 25 years. I will also analyse the role of Hezbollah's affiliated institutions as FBOs and will argue that their successes in service provision and management makes them, in certain conditions, effective and accountable partners for development stakeholders. Before proceeding, I will briefly relate Hezbollah to the Lebanese political context.

The Lebanese political system distributes positions according to a religious community's size as calculated in the 1932 census: the Presidency is allocated to a Christian Maronite, the Executive is led by a Sunni Muslim, while the legislative is directed by a Shi'i Muslim.[1] First introduced in the 1943 National Pact, this allocation of positions extends throughout Lebanon's system of public administration. In 1989, following 15 years of civil war, the Pact was revised by the Taïf agreement under the auspices of Syria and Saudi Arabia: the allocation of key political positions among religious communities remained but powers were redefined to decrease the authority of the Maronite President in favour of the Shi'i head of parliament and the Sunni Prime Minister. Since the withdrawal of Syrian troops in Spring 2005 (following the uprising generated by the assassination of ex-prime minister Rafic Hariri) and the Israeli war waged on Lebanon in 2006, this political system is undergoing serious challenges and severe turmoil, fuelled by regional and international tensions.[2]

Shi'i groups in Lebanon represent an interesting case study of how political players organize the affairs of their constituency in the context of a weak laissez-faire state. In place of the broad Shi'i social movement of the 1960s, Shi'i political mobilization triggered a split into two groups in the early 1980s which gradually matured during the 1990s: the Amal movement, led by Nabih Berry, head of the parliament and Hezbollah, led by Sayyed Hassan Nasrallah.[3] Amal is embedded in public institutions and channels state resources to its constituency, echoing the clientelistic relations between the state and other sectarian political leaders. Conversely, Hezbollah prefers to operate autonomously from state agencies and, to this end, has established its own network of organizations responsible for service provision in the fields of education, health, urban development, micro-credit, agriculture, religion, culture and sports. Moreover, while Amal's commitment to a strict Shi'i theology is rather passive and left to individual discretion, Hezbollah encourages its constituency to adhere to a particular form of Shi'i piety, strongly linked to the Iranian concept of *wilayat al-faqih*.[4] Historically, Amal and Hezbollah have adopted rival approaches to the role of the Shi'i within the Lebanese system, approaches which are beyond the scope of this discussion: suffice to mention that they engaged in violent conflict in 1989, resulting into a geographic-based subdivision of power over Shi'i regions and neighbourhoods. The enmity remained but was transformed into less violent forms until 1996 when Syria forced Hezbollah to ally with Amal over legislative elections.[5] Since 1996, the 'rival brothers' have adopted a strategic alliance, brokered by Syria and Iran, which was further consolidated after the Syrian withdrawal in Spring 2005, and which is stronger than ever today. At the grassroots level, Hezbollah has displaced Amal and become the favoured representative of the Shi'i community. Clientelistic practices earned Amal a reputation for corruption and the movement progressively lost its popularity to Hezbollah as the latter won the respect and allegiance of many Shi'i thanks to its reputation for accountability as well as to its success in resisting the Israeli occupation of South Lebanon – which ultimately resulted in the withdrawal of Tsahal (Israeli forces) in May 2000.

Hezbollah's role has drastically changed since its emergence in 1982: it has abandoned its revolutionary ideals and chosen instead the pragmatic path of reforming the system from within. This choice, referred to by some authors as the 'lebanonization' of Hezbollah (Hamzeh 1993) materialized in 1992, for the first post-civil war legislative elections. Since then, Hezbollah has increasingly solidified its representation within parliament and the cabinet in addition to establishing a significant presence in local governance through its representation in municipal councils. Hezbollah's parliamentarians have led the largest legislative blocs in the Assembly (with 12, 10, 12 and 14 seats respectively in 1992, 1996, 2000 and 2004, out of a total of 128 seats). Its success in municipal elections, since their resumption in 1998, has confirmed the party as a 'dominant political force' (Hamzeh 2004: 131), at the expense of Amal. For example, in the municipalities contested by Hezbollah and Amal in Shi'i regions during the local elections of 2000, Hezbollah won 87 municipalities out of 142 in the South (61.2 per cent), 36 municipalities out of 38 in the Beqaa (94.7 per cent) and all of the six municipalities in the suburbs of Beirut (100 per cent) (Hamzeh 2004: 132–133). Hezbollah joined the cabinet with two ministers for the first time in July 2005, a couple of months after the Syrian withdrawal. After long years of evolution to become a 'constructive opposition [critiquing] the government and its policies in a responsible manner, with the general interest in mind' (Saad-Ghorayeb 2002: 30), Hezbollah has now left this rather comfortable external position and is now taking sides within the Lebanese quagmire – the outcome of which is still unclear at present.

How does Hezbollah operate as a FBO? How could it appeal, as a development partner, to other stakeholders? The chapter answers these questions in two parts: In the first, I argue that Hezbollah's network of organizations is characterized by two interdependent features which largely explain its success and durability. On one hand, service provision relies on a diversity of institutions operating as a holistic policy network characterized by (1) responsiveness and accountability, (2) professionalism and leadership and (3) effectiveness and performance. On the other hand, service provision has produced its own social and cultural environment, referred to as the Islamic sphere or the Resistance society, which conveys faith-based meanings and values to its beneficiaries. In the second part, I illustrate my argument by focusing on a case study of the summer 2006 war in which I explain how particular Hezbollah's institutions have dealt with the reconstruction challenge. I focus on *Jihad al-Bina'*, the party's construction non-governmental organization (NGO), and on the Consultative Center for Studies and Documentation (CCSD), the party's think tank, to show how Hezbollah has been able to position itself as a key interlocutor with the government on reconstruction matters, and how it has been able to successfully elaborate a reconstruction strategy to rebuild the neighbourhood of Haret Hrayk in Beirut's suburbs. The chapter closes with reflections on the role of faith within Hezbollah's institutions and on the implications of the different usages of faith for donors and other development stakeholders.

A note on methodology: the discussion of Hezbollah as a FBO largely stems from my PhD research which examined Hezbollah as a political stakeholder elaborating and implementing social and local development policies in the context of the southern suburbs of Beirut, Hezbollah's stronghold in the Lebanese capital (Harb 2005). The discussion of Hezbollah's role in the ongoing reconstruction efforts uses data collected in Beirut's suburbs during September and October 2006. For this chapter, I engaged in participant observation and conducted about 25 semi-structured interviews with key stakeholders in Hezbollah's institutions, supplemented by informal conversation. My recent research confirms the findings of my earlier PhD research concerning the party's accountability vis-à-vis its constituency and the enduring vigour of its legitimacy. It reveals new findings in relation to Hezbollah's capabilities to operate independently from state institutions in a complex situation such as post-war reconstruction, which normally would require extensive resources and innovative tools of intervention. It also reveals the weakness of the Lebanese 'state' which actually operates as a political system that has paradoxically reinforced the persistence of FBOs such as Hezbollah.

Hezbollah as a faith-based organization

It is crucial to go beyond the terrorism label of Hezbollah and understand the organizational structure of the party as well as the various features that characterize its functioning as a holistic policy network. In what follows, I unravel Hezbollah's black box and look at its main core and at an array of institutions active in Beirut's suburbs, the Beqaa and South Lebanon as well as the specific sectors in which it's active; education, health, research, development, sports and so on. I also discuss the objectives guiding those institutions, highlighting the material and symbolic values they promote and the contribution made to producing a faith-based society.

A holistic policy network

Hezbollah is headed by a Decision Making Council (the *Shura* Council),[6] composed of seven members, including the organization's Secretary General, Sayyed Hassan Nasrallah and Vice-president, Sayyed Naim Qassem. The *Shura* Council oversees five councils, each presided over by the five other members: (i) the Executive Council, (ii) the Political Bureau, (iii) the *Jihad* Council, (iv) the Judicial Council and (v) the Parliamentary Council.[7] The Executive Council, also named the General Convention, elects the members of the *Shura* and defines the party's policies, including foreign policy. It is formed of 12 members responsible for specific policy areas (education, health etc.) and for selected Lebanese regions (Beirut, the southern suburbs, South Lebanon and the Bekaa). The Political Bureau groups 11 members and operates as an advisory body to the *Shura* Council. The *Jihad* Council is in charge of the military resistance against Israel while the Judicial Council is responsible for conflict resolution in accordance with religious laws. Finally, the Parliamentary Council coordinates the works of Hezbollah's parliament representatives.

Hezbollah's Executive Council serves as an umbrella to what I refer to as 'satellite organizations': these form what is commonly named the Islamic sphere (*al-hala al-islamiyya*). There are about ten such satellite organizations. They are all non-governmental organizations (NGOs), registered with the Ministry of Interior. However, their administrative and financial relationships to the party vary: some are local branches of Iranian organizations and do not report directly to the party while others have been established by Hezbollah and report directly to its ruling bodies. Others are managed by party cadres but are financially and administratively autonomous. In turn these organizations fall into two main groups, those that provide services to users directly or indirectly involved in the military resistance and those that manage social, religious, financial and urban services oriented for a larger audience.

The first group includes (i) the Martyr organization (*al-Chahid*, established in 1982) and (ii) the Wounded organization (*al-Jarih*, established in 1990). The former is the local arm of an Iranian organization of the same name, while the latter was founded by Hezbollah. *Al-Chahid* takes care of about 2,500 families; it manages a hospital, dispensaries and schools. *Al-Jarih* helps more than 3,000 wounded and their families. Within the second group, two organizations, both founded by Hezbollah and dependent on its structure, provide education and micro-credit services. The Educational Institution (*al-Muassasa al-Tarbawiyya*, founded in 1991) manages the education sector: it is responsible for 9 schools in Lebanon, grouping about 5,300 students.[8] The Good Loan (*al-Qard al-Hassan*, established in 1984) specializes in micro-finance and distributes an average of 750 micro-credit loans per month, following Islamic rules of borrowing.[9] Four other satellite organizations are administratively autonomous from Hezbollah's, though they are managed by Hezbollah cadres and employees are affiliated to the party. Three are local branches of Iranian institutions: The Support (*al-Imdâd*, established in 1987) distributes social services to the needy and to the poor. The Islamic Health Society (*al-Hay'a al-Suhiyya*, founded in 1984) supervises 46 health centres and a hospital.[10] Jihad for Building (*Jihad al-Bina'*, founded in 1988) operates in the building sector, especially in South Lebanon and in the Beqaa. The fourth organization, the Consultation Center for Studies and Documentation (CCSD, established in 1988), is a think tank that prepares policy reports and studies: it handles a database of more than 500,000 articles, has published around 300 reports on Lebanon's public policies, and has organized dozens of local and regional conferences.[11]

These satellite organizations are amongst the most prominent service providers in Lebanese Shi'i regions.[12] Since the 1998 municipal elections, these organizations have acted as partners of local governments led by Hezbollah-backed councils who rely on their social work expertise for implementing local development strategies. Indeed, most of these organizations have more than 15 years of professional experience. Hezbollah's satellite organizations can be labelled as 'faith-based socio-political organizations' described by Clarke (in Chapter 2) as those 'which interpret and deploy faith as a political construct, organizing and mobilizing social groups on the basis of faith identities but in pursuit of broader political objectives', rather than 'faith-based terrorist organizations which promote radical or militant forms of faith identity, engage in illegal practices on the basis of faith believes or engage in armed struggle or violent acts justified on the grounds of faith'.

In addition, I suggest equating Hezbollah's FBOs with policy institutions because this association will help us further evaluate their role in development. Muller and Surel (1998: 16–23) suggest three indicators to identify policy institutions: first, organizations should have norms guiding their actions which need to be planned; second, they need to pursue a policy agenda which has some relationship to public authorities; third, they need to have their own distinct audiences. Hezbollah's organizations fit this framework well: (i) the norms guiding their policy stem from the mission of resistance and the religious model of *wilayat al-faqih*; (ii) they develop their policy agenda in accordance with Lebanese public agencies' existing strategies and (iii) they have local audiences, or 'publics', composed primarily of pious Shi'i who adhere to their norms and values. Moreover, using Gaudin (2004: 116–117), one can suggest that Hezbollah's FBOs operate as a policy network. Gaudin posits three indicators for the existence of a policy network: first, there needs to be a hierarchy in the decision-making process; second, the institutions forming the network need to have some durability; third, they need to be able to adapt to change over time. All characteristics are found within Hezbollah's organizations: (i) the institutions abide by internal regulations that define and organize responsibilities according to a specific hierarchy (ii) Hezbollah's institutions have been operating in the policy sector for over 13 years: more than 65 per cent of the party's institutions have experience of more than 15 and act as partners of international agencies, such as the United Nation Development Programme (UNDP) and UNICEF; and (iii) the party's institutions have a particular propensity to learning and an impressive ability to adjust to new norms of action.

Organizational features

Hezbollah's FBOs are thus characterized by their holistic approach: they form a network of organizations that provide a comprehensive set of policies framing diverse components of daily life. Several organizational features explain why these institutions have been successful over the past two decades and have been able to mobilize such a large base of beneficiaries. It is difficult to quantify this social base: journalists estimate the number of Hezbollah's cadres and members at between 30,000 and 40,000.[13] With an average family size of 5, and a fair assumption that these individuals' families are sympathetic to the party, this number can easily reach 200,000. In addition to these direct allegiances, previous studies have shown that users of Hezbollah's social services amount to several thousands: Hamzeh (2004: 54–56) estimates the yearly beneficiaries from Hezbollah's educational services at 25,500 students and the yearly users of medical services at 409,281; Harik (2004: 92) claims that Hezbollah's micro-credit organization distributes 7,500 loans annually. Another significant indicator is the number of votes collected by Hezbollah's candidates: during the parliamentary elections of 2000, Hezbollah's candidates scored the highest votes in the South of Lebanon, 201,901 votes, while in Baalbek, they reached 56,926 (Hamzeh 2004: 117–119): that is, a total of 268,827. In sum, low estimates of Hezbollah's social base would be 300,000.

The organizational features of Hezbollah can be grouped under three categories: (1) responsiveness and accountability; (2) professionalism and leadership; and (3) effectiveness and performance. First, let us look at responsiveness and accountability. Hezbollah's institutions are eager to provide services that cater to local needs. For that purpose, institutions operate in a decentralized manner, enabling them to identify local needs and priorities. The system operates on two levels:[14] one is spatial and subdivides neighbourhoods into zones managed by 'geographic leaders'; the other is functional and designates 'service representatives' for each service sector. Both types of leaders supervise a network of volunteers whose responsibility is to identify potential beneficiaries. Most of these volunteers are women. Beneficiaries are then matched with the concerned service institution. This dual system maximizes the outreach of Hezbollah's networks and ensures its responsiveness to local needs while disseminating participatory values. Moreover, it ensures regular feedback to the service providers, enabling them to adapt their services. This 'embeddedness' also helps in developing trust between service users and Hezbollah's institutions, enhancing their accountability.

Second, Hezbollah's institutions are distinguished by their professionalism (*itqan*), characterized by dedicated personnel and by charismatic leadership. This feature is especially salient when compared to public service providers renowned for bureaucracy and corruption. Both females and males occupy key positions in each institution, except for the leadership which is reserved for males. The institution's leader is typically a charismatic male, a professional and/or educated, often with past experience in militant work, calm and composed, able to act as a role model for employees and to project the institution's professional image. Everyone seems to have a clear understanding of the institution's goals and strategies. The institutions' directors rotate on a regular basis, building their managerial capacities across policy sectors. Thus, they are knowledgeable about an array of services provided by different institutions.

Third, I turn to effectiveness and performance. Hezbollah's institutions are keen on scientific knowledge, rational thinking and technical expertise as these are believed to produce effective and 'modern' outputs.[15] The leaders of these institutions care about quantitative studies and statistical information: they rely on experts to produce such knowledge. In addition, Hezbollah's institutions trust learning from experience; they evaluate their work regularly and revise their policy agendas accordingly. A prime example can be found in the work of Hezbollah-controlled municipalities in the suburbs of Beirut as illustrated by the Best Practices UN Award awarded to Ghobeyri municipality (Harb 2001).

These organizational features are not the only features explaining the successes of Hezbollah's institutions. Upon closer examination, these features are closely associated with specific religious ideals, as illustrated by the following quote from one Hezbollah organization's brochure:

> Our work in the Islamic Health Society forms a *jihad* for God, and a modern challenge (*tahaddi hadâri*) through the creation of medical institutions on Islamic bases, where values of honesty, good will, excellence, modesty and service are developed. This proves the capacity of Islamic reason (*al-'aql al-muslem*) of managing medical work and leading it to the required objective. [extracted from the Islamic Health Society's, *Al-Hay'a al-Suhiyya* newsletter, no.0, w.d., p. 44.]

Hence, responsiveness is grounded in the concept of social justice (*'adala*) and participation (*ishrak*), professionalism is rooted in excellence (*itqan*) and effectiveness is embedded in modernity (*hadara*). Indeed, Hezbollah's organizational structure incorporates a range of pious beliefs and faith values that I will now explore.

The production of a faith-based society

Hezbollah's institutions disseminate codes, norms and values that produce a particular type of social and cultural environment, structuring daily life practices, as well as subjective and collective identities. This environment, or Hezbollah's reference group, is referred to as the Islamic sphere (*hala islamiyya*) or the 'Resistance society' (*mujtama' al-muqawama*). Before discussing how this society is produced and consolidated by what I term 'faith-propagation institutions', I will briefly examine the paradigms characterizing the Islamic sphere, namely resistance, martyrdom and piety.

The Islamic sphere aggregates different groups around Hezbollah, irrespective of the religious reference by which they abide.[16] It proposes one common denominator for these groups: obedience to Shi'i faith as promoted by Hezbollah or what they term 'authentic' piety (*iltizam*). Those who commit to the Islamic sphere are referred to as *multazimin*, which literally means 'those who are committed to authentic faith'. Over the years, an increasing number of Shi'i have progressively adapted their daily practices to the norms and values of this type of piety.

Hezbollah's networks played a key role in producing what Deeb (2006) refers to as 'a social and religious transformation' in Lebanon.

For pious Shi'i, faith is naturally experienced and lived on a daily basis, through a variety of social and cultural practices: 'religion penetrates everything; it has a conspicuous but discrete presence' (Deeb 2006). Indeed, in Lebanese Shi'i neighbourhoods today, religion is highly visible in the streets (marked with wall inscriptions, streamers, signs), on the balconies of houses or apartment blocks (covered by curtains to hide women from eyesight), in homes (decorated by religious objects and images) and in shops (selling religious garments and objects). Religion is also read on bodies (hidden by dark veils and robes for women, covered with tie-less costumes for men who also wear a light beard). And religion is translated in sounds and language (religious greetings and language, specific types of songs).

Being a *multazim* 'naturally' means adhering to the Islamic concept of *jihad*, materialized in the mission of resistance (*muqawama*), which ultimately leads to martyrdom (*shahada*). In Hezbollah's view, resistance is not only military, but is foremost political, social and cultural: resistance is conceptually both a spiritual *jihad* and a military *jihad*. Resistance is thus promoted as a liberation journey, freeing the individual from a life of oppression and humiliation equivalent to death. Failing to resist means submission to injustice and inequality which not only means disgrace in this life but in the afterlife (Qassem 2002: 58–29; Saad-Ghorayeb 2002: 125). Consequently, resistance is perceived and experienced as a mission, a duty and a way of life. It goes beyond combat and becomes an individual process, carried out through daily practices related to body, sound, signs and space, transmitting 'religious and community knowledge' (Deeb 2006).

Interestingly, over the past decade, Islamic sphere narratives have increasingly borrowed national references and symbols from Lebanese folklore (the cedar tree, the flag, tourist sites etc.), proposing a hybrid type of national discourse, mixing secularism with religiosity. This is particularly evident in songs about the resistance, which evolved over time to accommodate a youth audience attracted by popular tunes. Such hybrid national narratives are also materializing physically in cultural arenas such as martyr museums, commemorative resistance sites as well as entertainment places which are respectful of religious codes (cafés, restaurants, beaches, fitness clubs etc.). These days, the nationalism of Hezbollah is scaling new heights; in early 2007 its constituency occupied Martyr's Square, demanding the resignation of the government, the same square which witnessed demonstrations two years earlier by other nationalist Lebanese groups. Without falling into binary readings of religious nationalism versus secular nationalism (which does not really apply in Lebanon), what seems to be important here is how Hezbollah is negotiating its place in an imagined nation by developing hybrid narratives, combining its pious representations with depictions of a 'Lebanon' associated with other sectarian groups and national discourses.

Several Hezbollah institutions are directly responsible for promoting and disseminating the narratives of the Islamic sphere and for constantly mobilizing the resistance society. Varying strategies have been elaborated by these 'faith-propagation institutions' for this purpose: (a) media strategies; (b) commemorations and spatial markings; and (c) volunteering and solidarity networks. First, *al-Manar* television and *al-Nour* radio station[17] play a key role in diffusing the vocabulary and the imagery of the Islamic sphere through shows, documentaries and games addressing themes of resistance, Islam, Palestine and Zionism. No shows are purely about entertainment – they all have some educational and/or pious dimension. Advertisements also promote Hezbollah institutions and Islamic NGOs appealing for donations. As it presents itself, *al-Manar* is committed 'to confirm to the world the role of resistance and to work on establishing a resistance nation'.[18]

Second, commemorations and spatial markings contribute to the dissemination of faith messages in everyday life. In addition to the historical commemoration of Ashura, Hezbollah has introduced the commemoration of Qods Day, Martyrdom Day and Liberation Day, with the aim of consolidating Shi'i identity. Commemorations have an important spatial dimension as places are transformed by a variety of signs and objects, displaying particular writings, images and symbols which have developed over the years into public art. Imagery translates visually the paradigms of the Islamic sphere and its associated themes: martyrdom, the liberation of Palestine, United States and Israeli enemies and religious leaders. The commemorations are managed by an Information Unit which defines its role as follows: 'we want to transmit the [Islamic] sphere in the streets, to express what urban space is about, what are its characteristics, [we want] to convey this sphere's identity'.[19] The Information Unit cooperates with elected local governments in (re)naming streets and open spaces. Through these territorial markings of space, Hezbollah manages to create an environment, or milieu, for the Resistance society and the Islamic sphere. In Beirut, the party's stronghold in the southern suburbs is increasingly known as *Dahiyet* Hezbollah – the suburb *of* Hezbollah.

The third mechanism through which the Islamic sphere is produced is less visible to the observer, though it nevertheless complies with institutional regulations. It relies on networks of women volunteers as well as neighbourhood clerics (*sheikhs*) who operate in mosques and in *hawzat* (religious institutes) – key places through which mobilization and recruitment take place (Charara 1996: 215). Sheikhs train other sheikhs who become their employees and whose role is to propagate support for the Islamic sphere and the Resistance society. Within the *hawzat*, women and men are (separately) trained in the Shi'i religion. An increasing number of individuals have been joining these *hawzat* in recent years, to transmit this knowledge to the immediate and extended family unit. Female volunteers are referred to as 'volunteer sisters' (*akhawat muttatawi'at*), emphasizing the intimacy and the trust involved in their community role. Fawaz shows how they act as the 'informal liaisons between the social leaders inside the organizations and the beneficiary families': each area is directed by a woman who coordinates the work of her peers and reports to the organization with which she is associated (Fawaz 2004b: 14). Thus, 'volunteer sisters' have at least three functions: (i) recruitment; (ii) follow-up and evaluation of the service provided and (iii) building durable ties with beneficiaries and ensuring their piety and political commitment. Because they reside in the neighbourhood, women are able to identify through interpersonal contacts the families that need aid and to match it with the concerned Hezbollah organization. Thus, they act as relays: they inform the families of available services, maintain a regular relationship with the family (through visits, correspondence, outings etc.), and make sure the service has been provided to a high standard, evaluating its impact and reporting back to the organization concerned. Hence, even if they do not appear in the formal apparatus of the party, women conscientiously and effectively participate in Hezbollah's social policy making and implementation.

Such networks differ from the formal organizational ones previously examined as they rely on interpersonal relationships, on kinship and on neighbourhood ties. They contribute to the dissemination of an array of bodily and linguistic codes, signs and paraphernalia, as well as to the (re)production of cultural practices that structure the daily existence of pious Shi'i. They allow Hezbollah to ground its social work in kinship and family networks revolving around pious practices. The Islamic sphere thus operates as a cognitive framework which nourishes a Shi'i consciousness: pious Shi'i strongly identify with the collective whole upon which their individual identity depends. This consciousness, fortified by Hezbollah's political leaders and clerics, by martyrdom imagery and by commemorations and a variety of informal institutions and networks as examined above, maintains the social bonds that are essential for the preservation of pious norms and rules. The relationship of the individual to the whole is mediated by the daily choices of pious individuals, and embeds within it a feeling of solidarity: the pious work together to build the Resistance society and the Islamic sphere. Moreover, collective consciousness generates a feeling of pride and self-worth, especially powerful in a context where Shi'i are constantly victimized as being poor and underdeveloped.[20] Building on Bourdieu's views of society 'as a mechanism for the generation of meanings for life,' I contend that Hizballah's Islamic sphere has succeeded in giving social importance to Shi'i individuals, and in providing them with reasons for life and death, thus endowing their lives with meaning (cf. Hage 2003: 78). In summary, Hezbollah's holistic policy networks not only provide material resources to their beneficiaries, they also define a world of social meanings.

Hezbollah under challenge: FBOs and reconstruction

The previous section demonstrates how Hezbollah's institutions operate as effective policy makers in the context of local development, disseminating policy norms that can be easily related to international development paradigms, namely economic growth, modernity and progress, and using policy tools rooted in participatory and community-based practices. In this sense, Hezbollah is not very different from other FBOs that carved themselves a political space within the national state by promoting what Renders (2002) terms 'faith-based development'.

Since its decision to participate in mainstream Lebanese politics in 1992 (and until Syrian withdrawal from Lebanon in May 2005), Hezbollah progressively transformed its political agenda, diversified its social base and increased its popularity. Hezbollah played the role of an opposition party,

> an opposition [which] was an 'inclusionary' and 'issue-based' social, economic and political critique of the government, which pursued the implementation of such secular issues as the abolition of political sectarianism, social justice for the oppressed, public freedoms, the diffusion of political power and political transparency [...]; [i]ts castigation of the government revolved around the popular themes of political corruption, administrative inefficiency, overspending on

large-scale reconstruction projects and the underdevelopment of deprived areas (Saad-Ghorayeb 2002: 30).

In this respect, Hezbollah was viewed sympathetically by the less pious and even by some secularists as many of its demands and positions were not faith-dependent: according to Harik, 'Hezbollah's fundamentalist ideology is neither overwhelmingly important in creating [...] [electoral] lists nor greatly off-putting to those espousing secular and leftist views' (Harik 2004: 109). Thus, by the late 1990s, local NGOs, academics and donors found Hezbollah increasingly more palatable and their trials at partnering with its municipal councils or FBOs for research and/or development projects often left them with positive impressions.[21] As one UNDP official told me during an informal conversation, 'we really like working with Hezbollah's organizations as they are professional and animated by the willingness to help; they believe in development and progress; they want to learn and are eager to hear from them on how to improve livelihoods'.

To further illustrate Hezbollah FBOs' potential role in development, I will now explain how particular party organizations have addressed the extraordinary challenge of rebuilding following the destruction caused by the Israeli war in Lebanon (July–August 2006). This conflict led to 1,183 dead (of whom 30 per cent were children) and 4,054 injured; the destruction of thousands of housing and commercial units and extensive infrastructure damage caused by Israeli aerial and naval raids.[22] Most of the destruction was concentrated in the southern Beirut suburbs (*Dahiye*), in South Lebanon and in Baalbeck, though raids also targeted factories, warehouses, dams, schools, hospitals, bridges, roads, highway sections, gas stations and other vital nodes. The Lebanese government estimates that 30,000 homes and 92 bridges were destroyed and the total cost of the damage to reach US\$3.1 billion. Hence, post-war reconstruction requirements are enormous, involving tens of thousands of Lebanese civilians who need to be housed immediately. What has been the government response to such dire needs? How is Hezbollah mobilizing its networks to face such challenges: what policies are its FBOs elaborating and for what ends? How is faith deployed within these policies?

The government: subcontracting reconstruction

Perhaps unsurprisingly to the usual observers of the Lebanese quagmire, the government's response has been sluggish and unhurried, leading many to interpret this delay as a conspiracy to increase pressure on Hezbollah and to shake its foundations.[23] I will not discuss the context of such accusations. Suffice to say that the government response to the ominous needs of reconstruction have been, at best, insufficient and, at worst, seriously flawed. The government agency in charge of reconstruction is the High Relief Council (HRC), under the supervision of the Prime Minister, Fuad Siniora. The HRC has been centralizing early recovery actions and coordinating foreign financial assistance. In mid-August 2006, the PM announced a two-tier reconstruction policy: the rebuilding of destroyed towns and villages in Lebanon and the reconstruction of the southern suburbs of Beirut. In towns and villages, compensation will be paid according to the extent of damage: completely destroyed buildings will receive $40,000, partially destroyed buildings 70 per cent of that sum, major damages 40 per cent and minor damages 10 per cent . Institutions involved in the payment of compensation include the HRC, the Council of the South, the Ministry of the Displaced the Central Fund of the Displaced, and the Council for Development and Reconstruction. The reconstruction process specifies that rebuilding will occur

> according to a mechanism that will be adopted by the donor, who will have the following obligations: (a) rebuilding the town or village infrastructure according to the general master plan; (b) pledging to build a public building for the use of the municipality...; (c) pledging to pay compensations to the stricken population according to the same norms adopted by the state.[24]

For the southern suburbs of Beirut, the government formed a 'reconstruction committee' with an advisory role, including representatives from various public institutions, professional syndicates and delegates from Hezbollah and other political groups. The government issued its reconstruction policy for the southern suburb, based on the committee's recommendations, in November 2006. Decision no. 146/2006 states that the reconstruction of *Dahiye* will be funded through a separate compensation scheme, more generous than that proposed for the rest of the country: $55,000 per destroyed housing unit and up to $30,000 per partially damaged home.

Government policies regarding post-war reconstruction are characterized by three striking features: first, they exclusively rely on compensation as a strategy for rebuilding; second, they rely on existing public agencies which are renowned for their opaque and corrupt practices and on existing legal mechanisms with clear limitations.[25] Third, they are remarkable for their omissions and their vagueness: they say that villages and towns will be rebuilt according to the master plan, but what happens when there is no master plan, which is the case for the majority of towns and villages? Also how will the reconstruction of the southern suburbs occur? Are previous building laws still operational? What happens when people want to rebuild according to the infractions previously regularized?[26] These are only some of the numerous unanswered questions that complicate the lives of citizens who lost their houses and their sources of revenue, and who are at a loss on what will happen to them.

By reducing the task of reconstruction to monetary compensation, by transferring it to institutions which provoke popular mistrust and by reusing controversial laws for rebuilding, the government ignores what one may call the 'opportunity' of destruction to boost its political legitimacy and to induce a state-building process in a war-torn country. Against this background of government incompetence, Hezbollah is trying to rapidly define a reconstruction policy. Indeed, during the war, Nasrallah asked people not to worry about reconstruction costs, and pledged that their homes will be rebuilt 'better than before'.[27]

Hezbollah: attempting to envision and organize reconstruction

As soon as the war ended on August 13, 2006, Nasrallah announced the first component of Hezbollah's reconstruction program: 'the sheltering policy' (*siyasat al-iwaa'*), which provides each family which lost its home a sum of $12,000, in addition to furniture compensation, meant to help in renting and furnishing an alternative house for a year. Nasrallah hoped that, during that year, the reconstruction process would be well underway and people would be able to reoccupy their residences. Within days, Hezbollah distributed millions of dollars in cash to thousands of families. The distribution was managed by the party's Executive Council and took place in offices located in schools and other buildings throughout the bombed neighbourhoods in the southern suburbs, in South Lebanon and in the Beqaa. Hundreds of volunteers helped expedite the process, covering '75% of the requests in 48 hours'.[28]

Simultaneously, two Hezbollah FBOs are actively dealing with the challenges of reconstruction: Hezbollah's think tank, the Consultation Center for Studies and Documentation (CCSD) and Hezbollah's construction FBO, *Jihad al-Bina'*. I will now turn to their role in reconstruction of *Dahiye*, in the suburbs of Beirut which used to house the headquarters of Hezbollah. *Jihad al-Bina'* is in charge of engineering, infrastructure and architecture projects, as well as rural development and agriculture policies and programs.[29] Between 1988 and 2002, it was responsible for the construction of 78 buildings and the rehabilitation of another 10,528 (including homes, schools, shops, hospitals, infirmaries, mosques, cultural centres and agricultural cooperatives), most of them in South Lebanon (Hamzeh 2004: 50–51). *Jihad al-Bina'* relies on financial assistance from its Iranian sister organization as well as from Islamic charitable sources.

As soon as the ceasefire went into effect, *Jihad al-Bina'* asked architects and engineers to volunteer their services to help conduct damage assessments. I went to that first meeting where hundreds of volunteers gathered in a large room on the ground floor of al-Mehdi school. *Jihad al-Bina'* officials distributed caps and jackets marked with its logos, and samples of a survey questionnaire prepared by the institution. The questionnaire, with more than 40 questions, sought information on damage in striking detail. A large, multi-coloured map showing the bombed neighbourhoods of *Dahiye* was pinned on the wall: dark red for buildings razed to the ground, light red for those heavily damaged and structurally unsound, and pink for those badly damaged but in need of further assessment. These were the results of a preliminary assessment begun by *Jihad al-Bina'* engineers during the war. Now what was needed was a more precise assessment to assess the extent of damage to each residential unit, to guide compensation in the first stage and reconstruction in the second. The *Jihad al-Bina'* delegate explained that they had divided the neighbourhoods shown on the map into 75 subsections for the survey: he asked volunteers to form groups of four to five individuals, and to agree a team leader who would report back to him. He then explained the questionnaire and emphasized the need to fill it completely and accurately. It took ten days to complete the survey and enter it into a computer database. The survey was then distributed to concerned Hezbollah institutions and to *Dahiye's* local governments. Simultaneously, *Jihad al-Bina'* worked on removing the rubble from the *Dahiye's* streets in an effort to facilitate traffic circulation. Government trucks and bulldozers were late, so *Jihad al-Bina'* started work with equipment rented from private enterprises in *Dahiye*. Engineering teams worked in coordination with other Hezbollah institutions, checking the rubble for unexploded ordinance as people returned to their homes and shops.

Hezbollah's think tank, CCSD, produced a working paper on reconstruction options and convened an informal meeting with researchers and experts to brainstorm the next steps. The possible planning tools that could be used within the framework of Lebanese law were examined (real-estate, company, public agency, land grouping and subdivision, building cooperatives) – their pros and cons were discussed, along with the possible stakeholders who could lead the reconstruction process (local governments, Hezbollah FBOs and/or private enterprises). This working paper also contains an interesting discussion which reveals the think tank's vision of reconstruction – a vision presented to the public in a seminar organized by the American University of Beirut.[30] During this discussion, the CCSD vice-president argued that the physical reconstruction of *Dahiye* should be combined with social and economic development, should recreate the pre-war social fabric and restore the social heterogeneity that characterized the destroyed neighbourhoods. He highlighted how reconstruction could encourage change and progress while preserving the social identity of the neighbourhood. He also insisted on thinking of reconstruction within a development context which integrated housing needs with economic policies. Indeed, and as explained in a separate interview, the CCSD is currently in the process of suggesting to Hezbollah's leadership a set of economic strategies which could help the owners of commercial, industrial and other enterprises to restart their businesses. The CCSD is also in the process of investigating micro-credit options and economic incentives that could support enterprises in re-launching their activities as rapidly as possible, with the aim of building a 'productive' society.

Hence, while *Jihad al-Bina'* was focusing on the residential survey, the CCSD directed an economic survey. Both surveys provided Hezbollah with information required to evaluate the needs of the population. The reconstruction policy as elaborated by Hezbollah seems to allocate specific roles to different FBOs while encouraging flexibility and exchange amongst institutions. FBOs with extensive experience, such as *Jihad al-Bina'* and the CCSD, are in charge of central functions like studies, surveys and planning, leading to specific strategies (e.g. financial aid, compensation). The execution of these strategies is then allocated, via the Executive Council, to the FBOs that have a 'closer relationship to the people' and to local governments.[31]

The second phase of Hezbollah's reconstruction policy is still not officially announced but preliminary investigations show that it will proceed as follows: first, Hezbollah will complement the compensation payments of the government to fully refund all losses. Already, the Executive Council has reimbursed sums below $5,000. Second, they will decide on the legal framework through which the reconstruction project will be executed, and how roles will be distributed between main stakeholders. Time will reveal more information, but at this stage what is significant is how Hezbollah's FBOs managed to position themselves as essential interlocutors with the government and how the organizational features I discussed in the first section were fully displayed in the aftermath of a war that aimed to annihilate it. Some see this subdivision of roles between the state and Hezbollah as an interesting complementarity,[32] while others are wary about the relationship linking 'a state to a failed state' (Saad-Ghorayeb 2006). Without going into this discussion, what is interesting here is that both Hezbollah FBOs, *Jihad al-Bina'* and the CCSD, and under the most difficult circumstances, proved their abilities to be responsive (they answered the needs of planning, studies and research), professional (they produced maps, conducted surveys and appealed to needed expertise) and effective (they provided rapidly the needed information for compensations to take place and for policy decisions to be made). These FBOs' showed that they can be held accountable, that their leadership was solid and that their performance was relatively respectable and of good quality.

The uses of faith in policy making

The role of faith was central to the success of Hezbollah-associated FBOs in the reconstruction process. Indeed, faith was the main driver behind the mobilization of volunteers and in attracting financial donations. Faith thus becomes the motor of public participation and the basis for community-based policy making. Concurrently, faith enhances feelings of self-worth, dignity and belonging amongst Hezbollah's constituency. Also, as noted above, faith promotes moral values that have individual and collective meanings. Indeed, narratives justifying Hezbollah's policy choices are grounded in faith values and have long lives: they are not easily challenged in contemporary Lebanese society. For instance, few within the Islamic sphere really question the sources of Hezbollah's finances and wonder how the party is able to pay billions of dollars in cash to beneficiaries: the rhetoric of '*shar'i* money' or '*zakat* money' (i.e. money collected as part of the due Islamic taxes) is overpowering, implying that there are thousands of Islamic benefactors around the world contributing generously to the resistance. This rhetoric can be further explained when we relate it to how other believers perceive their role vis-à-vis the needy: 'for believers, to be a Jew or a Muslim or a Christian, implies a duty to respond to the needs of the poor and the marginalized' (Ferris 2005: 316). Thus, for Hezbollah, as for other FBOs, faith leads to solidarity and to collective action which produces fertile prerequisites for effective policy making – centrally elaborated but implemented via decentralized institutions building on existing local participatory processes (at least partially).

In Chapter 2, Clarke distinguishes between four different uses of faith in the work of FBOs: the expression of faith in the work of a FBO can be passive, active, persuasive or exclusive. In the case of Hezbollah, faith is mostly persuasive, though it can become active in some situations and exclusive in others. Faith is persuasive when

> it is an important and explicit motivation for action and in mobilizing staff and supporters; [when it] plays a significant role in identifying, helping or working with beneficiaries and partners and provides the dominant basis for engagement; [when it] aims to bring new converts to the faith [and] to advance the faith at the expense of others. (Chapter 2: 32)

Faith becomes active in the case of some Hezbollah services: technical (infrastructure management, policy advice) and financial (the recent 'sheltering policy').[33] Faith is also active when it comes to partnerships in the field of research and/or development: Hezbollah's institutions cooperate easily with UN agencies and with academic institutions such as the American University of Beirut; some Hezbollah-controlled local governments also benefited from United States Agency For International Development (USAID) grants. Faith becomes exclusive, however, when it is about providing a service within which religious and spiritual commitment is mandatory, such as an educational service.

In the context of post-war reconstruction, several international donors are mobilizing to help Lebanon. Several articles highlight how they will have to deal with the reality on the ground if they want to carry out effectively their assistance programs, that is, they will have to work with Hezbollah's institutions.[34] However, due to the labelling of Hezbollah as a terrorist organization by the United States and other countries (Harb and Leenders 2005), many of these donors are reluctant to cooperate with its institutions and choose instead to ally with other NGOs, more often than not unrepresentative of prevailing needs. But, if Hezbollah is perceived as a 'faith-based socio-political organization', in charge of policy making and managing a network of institutions that service a wide constituency with dire socio-economic needs, then foreign assistance to its institutions could make sense. Indeed, Hezbollah FBOs use Shi'ism for mobilizing their social base just as Christians, Jews, Hindus or others use their faith for recruiting their members: in each case, faith operates as a set of 'strong ethical principles' that are 'essential prerequisites for long-term economic progress' (Tyndale 2000).

Although Hezbollah's use of faith includes persuasive and exclusive practices, several of its institutions promote an active type of faith and thus represent potential foci for donor funding. Specifically, in the case of FBOs like *Jihad al-Bina'* and the CCSD where deliverables are technical and directly linked to policy making, there is significant overlap between their paradigms of development and those of international donors, and they are open to learning and improvement. Indeed, although Hezbollah's institutions are well-positioned to take action and have proven their ability to address effectively policy issues and challenges,[35] the current situation requires a totally different type of knowledge, one which is able to grasp holistically the extensive needs caused by a post-war situation and to elaborate integrated and sustainable planning policies – a type of knowledge which goes beyond the current scope and concern of Hezbollah's institutions.

Conclusion

In this chapter, I have argued that Hezbollah's abilities to successfully dominate the Shi'i political scene for the past two decades and to operate as a key service provider can be explained by its holistic policy network organized around an array of FBOs. Hezbollah's FBOs are distinguished by their organizational features (responsiveness and accountability, professionalism and leadership, effectiveness and performance) which sustain a distinct 'Islamic sphere' in which specific paradigms and meanings are circulated (including resistance, martyrdom and piety). I illustrated my argument by examining the ongoing performance of two Hezbollah-associated FBOs operating in the post-war reconstruction sector. In the context of a slow and inadequate government response where reconstruction is subcontracted to the market, a construction institution (*Jihad al-Bina'*) and a think tank (the Consultation Center for Studies and Documentation) are addressing reconstruction challenges by surveying and assessing needs, thinking of potential reconstruction tools and mechanisms and envisioning reconstruction goals. Faith plays a central role in this process, as it governs solidarity networks and generates mobilization, volunteering and collective action. Faith is also deployed in several guises as it shifts between being active, persuasive or exclusive guises.

The multiple ways in which faith is used by Hezbollah FBOs opens up opportunities for foreign donors to consider cooperation – especially in the present situation where needs are beyond the capabilities of the government. Indeed, one can imagine institutional setups in which foreign assistance programs target FBOs such as *Jihad al-Bina'* and the CCSD as key developmental partners. These institutions have significant professional experience, they have strong ties to local communities, they believe in participatory processes, and their concepts of development are in line with donor' agendas. Indeed, as the CCSD specifies

> we want our society to be a productive society, we would like reconstruction to lead to social development and to economic growth; the Islamic specificity of our developmental vision is its benevolent dimension: our society believes in solidarity, in participation, in the Islamic concept of *shura*, in cooperation; you can say that our developmental vision is market-based but has a participatory edge: it is capitalistic and relies on the private sector for economic development but within a collective vision of society.[36]

We are thus not so far away from donor narratives which give pre-eminence to the market in the quest for economic growth and to participatory approaches in implementing developmental policies. With this in mind, such partnerships could be beneficial to all parties. Foreign donors could be confident their grants will be spent effectively and will reach the neediest. Hezbollah's FBOs could acquire new tools and mechanisms through which they can enrich their practice. The government would be thankful to have the challenge of reconstruction partially taken off its tired shoulders. The ensuing interactions would probably and subtly lead to exchanges of ideas and knowledge which could in turn generate more appreciation and tolerance for what is too often perceived as the 'distinct other'.

Notes

1. The Lebanese population consists of 18 groups, of which Christian Maronites, Sunnis and Shi'i are the most prominent. Lebanon has a population of 4 million, with 26.5 per cent Sunni, 26.2 per cent Shi'i, 22.1 per cent Maronites and 18.7 per cent other Christians (See Mark and Prados 2005, p. 7 and *an-Nahar* local newspaper of 10/02/2005).
2. On Lebanese politics since Rafic Hariri's assassination, see Middle East Report, *Inside Syria and Lebanon*, fall 2005, no.236; and MIT-EJMES,

The Sixth War, summer 2006, vol. 6 (http://web.mit.edu/cis/www/mitejmes/intro.htm).

3. For more on the history of Amal, see Norton 1987.
4. On *wilayat al-faqih*, or the concept of 'the guardianship of the jurisprudent' within Hezbollah, see chapter 3 in Saad-Ghorayeb 2002.
5. A strategy often used by Syria in Lebanon: breaking sectarian groups into several leaderships and fueling this division by supporting both sides and maintaining a subtle power balance amongst them.
6. *Shura* is an Islamic concept which means consultation: it promotes governance through debate and dialogue.
7. See Qassem (2002: 86) and ICG (2003: 2–3). The voting members who select the *Shura* members range between 250 and 300 individuals (see *The Daily Star* of 01/08/01 and *an-Nahar* of 16/08/04).
8. Interview with the director of *al-Muassassa*, 08/09/1999.
9. Interview with director of *al-Qard*, 02/03/2000.
10. *Al-Hay'a al-Suhiyya* brochure, without date.
11. CCSD brochure, 2002.
12. Unfortunately, no figures are available to backup this claim apart from my field observations. Other authors, however, have highlighted the ability of Hezbollah to mobilize a varied audience, largely composed of Shi'i, but grouping different socio-economic groups, pious and less pious individuals, and rural and urban populations (Saad-Ghorayeb 2002; Abi-Saab in LCPS 1999; Harik 1996: 62–63).
13. See as-Safir local newspaper, 18/05/2004.
14. Author's interviews with Hezbollah's social services director, 25/08/1998.
15. Here, the understanding of modernity has to be related to the Arabic, where modernity (*hadâtha*) is often associated with notions of civilization (*hadâra*), progress (*taqaddum*), development (*inma'*) and urbanization (*tamaddun*). Also, the idea of modernity is linked to rationality and reason (*al-'aql*), to knowledge (*ma'rifa*) and to science (*'ilm*). Often, in our interviews, our informants refer to the Quran or to *Hadith* to justify a 'desire' for modernity as inherent to Islam.
16. Shi'i faith allows believers to select their religious reference (*marja'iyya*). In Lebanon, pious Shi'i emulate either Sayyid Fadlallah, the Lebanese cleric based in the southern suburbs, or Sayyid Khamenei, the Iranian cleric whose local representative is Sayyed Hassan Nasrallah, or Sayyed al-Sistani, the Iraqi cleric who also has a local representative.Other believers follow the Quran rather than emulating particular clerics.
17. Hezbollah owns one radio station, (*al-Nour*, The Light, founded in 1989), one TV station (*al-Manar*, The Beacon, operating locally since 1991 and via satellite since 2000) and one monthly magazine (*Al-Intiqad*, The Critique).
18. In English, see http://www.dm.net.lb/almanar/about.htm
19. Author's interviews with Hizballah director of the Information Unit, 07/10/2004.
20. Shi'i political and social history has generated imagery in which Shi'i are represented as victims persecuted by oppressors. Thus, Shi'i are often compared to the 'deprived'(*mahrûmin*). Conspiracy theories are rooted in religious practices, such as Ashura.

21. Amongst the notable experiences are research cooperation between the Islamic Health Society and the American University of Beirut's Faculty of Public Health, as part of a US grant; and UNDP and USAID/Mercy Corps support to a number of municipalities in the South of Lebanon of which several are headed by Hezbollah's members, in the fields of infrastructure and rural development. In addition, the European Union and the Agence Universitaire de la Francophonie have also endowed several Hezbollah's municipalities with aid.

22. See the Lebanese government's website: www.rebuildlebanon.gov.lb.

23. See, for instance, 'Examples of how Siniora is Stalling the Reconstruction of the South', *al-Akhbar* local newspaper, 06/11/06, no.71. http://www.al-akhbar. com/ar/node/5399

24. Information here comes from the HRC's website www.rebuildlebanon.gov. lb. See in particular 'Rebuilding process of the destroyed towns and villages (with the exception of Beirut southern suburb)'.

25. On corruption during the first post-war reconstruction (1990–2006), see Leenders 2004, Dagher 2002 and Wakim 1998. One of the main building laws during that period allowed residents to build without permit, producing a built environment of poor quality.

26. In Haret Hrayk, as in other Beirut's neighbourhoods, during the civil war (1975–1990), most buildings were built without reference to existing building laws. In the early 1990s, a series of regularization laws normalized the legal status of these buildings.

27. See Nasrallah's speech of 14/08/2006.

28. Interview, CCSD vice-president, 11/10/2006.

29. The organization 'provides technical assistance to farmers in land reclamation and cultivation, opening agricultural roads and installing irrigation networks. Moreover, it supports agricultural production by providing farmers with credit facilities. It has also established a tomato processing and canning industry and a number of dairy farms in the Biq'a region'; UN-ESCWA categorizes Jihad al-Bina' as 'one of the best-equipped organizations' operating in the field of rural development in Lebanon (Hamzeh 2004: 51–53).

30. 'The Socio-Politics of Reconstruction', a discussion organized by the Sociology Café of the Department of Sociology, American University of Beirut, 30/10/2006.

31. Interview, CCSD vice president, 11/10/06.

32. Discussion with World Bank experts working on the reconstruction file for the government, September 2006.

33. Hezbollah provided compensation for all residents who lost their houses, including non-pious Shi'i, Sunnis and Christians.

34. See for instance Worth R. and Fattah H., 'Relief Agencies Find Hezbollah Hard to Avoid', *The New York Times*, 23/08/2006 which argues that 'Hezbollah has been the fastest and, without a doubt, most effective organization doling out aid to the shattered towns and villages of southern Lebanon'.

35. As Ferris (2005: 325) argues: 'local faith communities are among the first to respond to the immediate humanitarian needs of affected people – long before international organizations are able to move relief assistance in'.

36. Interview, CCSD vice president, 11/10/2006.

Bibliography

Bahout J., 1994, 'Deux ans après les élections législatives de l'été 1992, où en est le parlementarisme libanis ?', *Revue Internationale et Stratégique*, 16, pp. 57–66.

Charara W., 1996, *Dawlat Hezbollah* [The Hezbollah State], Beirut: Dar an-Nahar.

Dagher A., 2002, 'L'administration libanaise après 1990', unpublished paper presented at the conference *Le modèle de l'Etat développemental et les défis pour le Liban*, LCPS, Beyrouth, 15–16 February.

Deeb L., 2006, *An Enchanted Modern: Gender and Public Piety in Shi'i Lebanon*, Princeton: Princeton University Press.

European Commission – Joint Research Center, 2006, *Rapid Preliminary Damage Assessment, Beirut and South Lebanon*, August, p. 3, available online at www. rebuildlebanon.gov.lb, accessed 22 August 2007.

Fattouh B. and Kolb J., 2006, 'The Outlook for Economic Reconstruction After the 2006 War', *The MIT Electronic Journal of Middle-East Studies*, 6(1), pp. 96–114.

Fawaz M., 2004a, *Strategizing for Housing: An Investigation of the Production and Regulation of Low-Income Housing in the Suburbs of Beirut*, unpublished PhD dissertation in Urban Planning, Boston: MIT.

Fawaz M., 2004b, 'Action et idéologie dans les services: ONG Islamiques dans la banlieue sud de Beyrouth', In Ben Nefissa S. et al. (eds), *ONG et Gouvernance dans le Monde Arabe*, Paris: Karthala and CEDEJ, pp. 341–367.

Ferris E., 2005, 'Faith-Based and Secular Humanitarian Organizations', *International Review of the Red Cross*, 87(858), pp. 311–325.

Gaudin J.-P., 2004, *L'Action Publique. Sociologie et Politique*, Paris: Presses de Sciences Po et Dalloz.

Haddad S., 2006, 'The Origins of Popular Support for Lebanon's Hezbollah', *Studies in Conflict and Terrorism*, 29(1), pp. 21–34.

Hage, G., 2003, ' "Comes a Time We Are All Enthusiasm": Understanding Palestinian Suicide Bombers in Times of Exighophobia', *Public Culture*, 15(1), pp. 65–89.

Hamzeh N., 1993, 'Lebanon's Hizbullah: From Islamic Revolution to Parliamentary Accommodation', *Third World Quarterly*, 14(2), pp. 321–337.

Hamzeh N., 2004, *In the Path of Hizbullah*, New York: Syracuse University Press.

Harb M., 2001, 'Pratiques comparées de participation dans deux municipalités de la banlieue de Beyrouth: Ghobeyri et Bourj Brajneh', In A. Favier (ed.), *Municipalités et Pouvoirs Locaux au Liban*, Beirut: CERMOC, pp. 157–177.

Harb M., 2005, *Public Action in a Multi-Confessional Political System: Shi'i Political Movements in Post-War Lebanon*, PhD in Political Science, Institut d'Etudes Politiques, University of Aix-en-Provence.

Harb M. and Leenders R., 2005, 'Know Thou Enemy: Hezbollah and the Politics of Perception', *Third World Quarterly*, 25(5), pp. 173–197.

Harik J., 1996, 'Between Islam and the System: Sources and Implications of Popular Support for Lebanon's Hezbollah', *Journal of Conflict Resolution*, 40(1), pp. 41–67.

Harik J., 2004, *Hezbollah: The Changing Face of Terrorism*, London: IB Tauris.

ICG/Middle-East Briefing, 2003, *Hizb'Allah: Rebel Without a Cause?*, Bruxelles: ICG.

LCPS, 1999, *Al-intikhabât al-baladiyya fi Loubnân 1998, makhâd al-dimoukratiyya fil moujtama'ât al-mahalliyya* (*The Municipal Elections in Lebanon in 1998 and the Democracy Process in Local Communities*), Beirut: LCPS.

Leenders R., 2004, 'Nobody having too much to answer for: 'laissez-faire', networks and post-war reconstruction in Lebanon', In Heydemann S. (ed.), *Networks of Privilege: The Politics of Economic Reform in the Middle East*, New York: Palgrave, pp. 169–200.

Mark C. A. and Prados A. B., 2005, *Lebanon*, CRS Issue Brief for Congress, Washington: Congressional Research Service. IB8911B.

Muller P. and Surel Y., 1998, *L'Analyse des Politiques Publiques*, Paris: Montchrestien.

Norton A. R., 1987, *Amal and the Shi'a: Struggle for the Soul of Lebanon*, Austin: University of Texas Press.

Norton A. R., 1998, 'Hezbollah: From Radicalism to Pragmatism?', *Middle East Policy*, 5(4), pp. 147–159.

Picard E., 1995, 'Les habits neufs du communautarisme libanais', *Cultures et conflits*, 15–16, pp. 49–70.

Qassem, N., 2002, *Hezbollah: al-manhaj,al-tajriba, al-mustaqbal* (Hezbollah: Method, Experience, Future), Beirut: Dar al-Hadi.

Renders M., 2002, 'An Ambiguous Adventure: Muslim Organizations and the Discourse of Development in Senegal', *Journal of Religion in Africa*, 32(1), pp. 61–82.

Saad-Ghorayeb A., 2002, *Hezbollah: Politics and Religion*, London: Pluto Press.

Saad-Ghorayeb A., 2006, 'Hizbollah's Outlook in the Current Conflict, Part One: Motives, Strategy and Objectives', Carnegie Endowment for International Peace, *Policy Outlook*.

Tyndale W., 2000, 'Faith and Economics in "Development": a Bridge Across the Chasm?', *Development in Practice*, 10(1), pp. 9–18.

Ver Beek K. A., 2000, 'Spirituality: A Development Taboo', *Development in Practice*, 10(1), pp. 31–43.

Wakim N., 1998, *Al-ayâdî al-soud (Les mains noires)*, Beyrouth: Charikat al-matbu'at lil tawzi' wal nachr.

11
Hindu Nationalism and the Social Welfare Strategy

Christophe Jaffrelot

Introduction

The rise of Hindu nationalism has been one of the most significant developments in Indian politics over the past 20 years. It is a recent phenomenon in terms of election results: the party most representative of this political trend, the Bharatiya Janata Party (BJP–Party of the Indian People) increased its number of seats from 2 out of 542 in the general elections of 1984 to 85 in 1989, 120 in 1991, 160 in 1996, 178 in 1998 the year when it rose to power as the leading force of the ruling coalition. Though it lost the 2004 election it remained only seven seats behind the Congress party.

Since the late 1980s, the movement largely owes its success to its ability to mobilize support in the streets on ethno-religious issues and to make alliances with regional partners, but also to earlier grassroots work by its network of activists. Its on-the-ground activities are mainly centred on a strategy of social welfare work to which few observers have paid attention, doubtless because such a concentration on social work is unexpected on the part of a movement dominated by a high-caste elite–or else because of an unwillingness to recognize that social work is a factor contributing to its success at the local level, which is something the Indian (left-wing) intelligentsia finds hard to accept.

Ethno-religious nationalism

Though some seeds of Hindu nationalism were sown by socio-religious reform movements in the nineteenth century, Hindu nationalist ideology

---

First published in a shorter version (Dieckhoff and Guiterrez 2001: chapter 10).

was first thoroughly codified in 1923 by Vinayak Damodar Savarkar (1883–1966) in *Hindutva, Who is a Hindu?* In this work, Hinduness (*Hindutva*) is considered as membership of an ethnic community possessing its own territory and sharing the same racial characteristics (Savarkar 1969: 32). For Savarkar, a Hindu is primarily someone who lives in the land beyond the Indus, between the Himalayas and the Indian Ocean, an area 'so strongly retrenched that no other country in the world is so clearly designated by the finger of nature as a geographical unit' (Savarkar 1969: 82). This is why the first Aryans, in Vedic times, developed there 'a sense of their nationality' (Savarkar 1969: 5). Here we have an ethnic rationale in the sense that the enclosed character of what Savarkar calls 'Hindustan', the land of the Hindus, is described as a factor conducive to unity of the population through intermarriage: 'All Hindus claim to have in their veins the blood of the mighty race descended from the Vedic fathers' (Savarkar 1969: 85). Focusing on the racial criterion, postulating the existence of an invisible yet potent bond, that of blood, is a way of de-emphasizing the internal divisions in Hindu society.

Though the pillars of Hinduness are, according to Savarkar, geographical and ethnic unity, *Hindutva* also allegedly meets all the criteria of national unity – cultural, religious and linguistic unity (the latter because Sanskrit is set up as the referent of all Indian languages) – that Savarkar had read about in the European authors on whom he had been nurtured.[1] Thereafter, every political programme based on Hindu nationalist ideology would call for recognition of Sanskrit or Hindi – the vernacular language closest to Sanskrit – as the national language.

The tenets of Hindu nationalist ideology were subsequently revised by the Rashtriya Swayamsevak Sangh (RSS–Association of National Volunteers), which was founded in 1925 by an admirer of Savarkar, Keshav Baliram Hedgewar (1889–1940). The RSS soon became the leading organization in the Hindutva movement.

Golwalkar, who succeeded Hedgewar as chief of the RSS in 1940, gave the movement its ideological charter in 1938 with his book *We, or Our Nationhood Defined*. In this book, religious minorities were called upon to pledge allegiance to Hindu symbols of identity as the embodiment of the Indian nation. Hindu culture being the essence of Indian identity, religious minorities were requested to limit expressions of community distinctiveness to the private sphere.

The concept of 'Chiti' or 'Race-spirit' in the writings of Savarkar and later of Golwalkar conveys the idea of the soul of the nation rather than biological conceptions (Jaffrolet 1995). This is doubtless the aspect of

German-style ethnic nationalism – in which the 'nation-spirit' idea is central – which was most attractive to the ideologues of Hindu nationalism. This conception allows – in fact insists upon – integration of minorities by means of acculturation and at a subordinate level, whereas the tenets of biological racism, reasoning in eugenic terms, could well have incorporated an idea of total exclusion. This difference reflects the importance of social categories in Hinduism, a civilization which has always been characterized by an ability and a determination to assimilate the Other at a subordinate level as part of the organicist, hierarchical rationale of a caste-based society.[2] Golwalkar considered as *mlecchas* (barbarians) foreigners 'who do not subscribe to the social laws dictated by the Hindu religion and culture' (Golwalkar 1947: 62), a definition which closely coincides with the traditional usage of this term. In ancient India, a *mleccha* was someone on the fringe of the orthopraxy specific to the caste society dominated by Brahminical values.[3] Gyanendra Pandey has described Hindu nationalism as 'upper caste racism' (Pandey 1993: 252), and this neatly sums up the ambivalence of this ideology.

Hindu nationalism clearly grew up as a form of ethnic nationalism based on a certain social organicism. It owes its relative distinctiveness to the influence of the caste system, which accentuates its hierarchical aspect (minorities only being allowed to exist at a subordinate level) but – in theory – steers it clear of eugenics. These tenets continue to form the basis of the Hindu nationalist movements.

The Hindu nationalist network first spread among the high castes of northern India and is still largely confined to this area. This geographical situation can be explained in two ways. First, the Sanskrit Great Tradition on which their ideology is based is closely related to the Hindi-speaking north; second, this is a region inhabited by a large proportion of high-caste Indians who are attracted by Hindu nationalism because the movement seems well equipped to protect them from the rising power of the low castes.

The Hindu nationalist network

The Hindu nationalist movement, especially the RSS which is its main organ, has always regarded itself as destined to encompass the whole of India; this being so, it determined at a very early stage to spread throughout Indian society. First, it developed a network of *shakhas* (local branches), which organized daily physical training and Hindu nationalist propaganda sessions in urban neighbourhoods and villages. The RSS's ultimate ambition was to reach all the cities and villages of

India in this way. Its membership rose from 10,000 in 1932 to 600,000 in 1951 and today stands at around 2 millions, divided among 25,000 branches (*shakhas*) and 31,000 sub-branches (*upshakhas*). The *upshakhas* are the RSS's real basic units since the number of *shakhas* simply indicates the places where the movement is present. A town or village may contain several sub-branches.

After independence, this coverage of the Indian territory was supplemented by an effort to develop a network of sectoral affiliates: the aim was not to penetrate society directly by means of *shakhas*, but to set up unions or organizations to defend specific social categories. In 1948, Delhi-based RSS officials founded the Akhil Bharatiya Vidyarthi Parishad (ABVP–the Association of Students of India), a students' union which was primarily intended to counter communist influence on university campuses. A few years later, in 1955, the RSS set up a trade union, the Bharatiya Mazdoor Sangh (BMS–the Indian Workers' Association) primarily to oppose the 'Red unions' in the name of Hindu nationalist ideology, which attaches greater importance to social cohesion than to the class struggle, in line with organicist principles incorporating some Gandhian features (Jaffrelot 2005: 355–370). By the early 1990s, the BMS had become India's biggest trade union.

Alongside these unions, the RSS developed a number of more specialized organizations. In 1952, it founded a tribal welfare movement, the Vanavasi Kalyan Ashram (VKA–Centre for Tribals' Welfare[4]) whose purpose was primarily to counter the influence of the Christian missionaries among the tribals of central India where their evangelization and social work had led to many conversions. The VKA imitated the techniques of the missionaries and brought about a number of 're-conversions'.

In 1964, in association with Hindu religious figures, the RSS launched the Vishva Hindu Parishad (VHP–World Hindu Council), a movement designed to bring together the different Hindu sect leaders and provide this loosely organized religion with some kind of centralized structure. Hindu nationalists took Christianity as their model, especially its concept of the consistory. For a long time, the VHP attracted only gurus who had founded their own ashram and who saw the VHP as a platform for improving their public exposure. However, the leaders of the major sectarian orders remained steadfastly outside. The Ayodhya movement, in which it played a leading role, enabled the VHP to broaden its recruitment and to win over many religious figures to the cause of militant Hinduism, though without necessarily recruiting them into its ranks (Jaffrelot 1999).

These organizations give the Hindu nationalist movement a foothold in most sectors of society, where they work hand in glove with the *shakha* network. All these bridgeheads are presented by the mother organization as the 'Sangh parivar', 'the family of the Sangh', that is, the RSS. However, this designation obfuscates the tensions at work in this ideological movement, which have grown since the increase in popularity of the Bharatiya Janata Party.

From working on society to working 'for society'

The prime function of the RSS was to work on Hindu society in order to rid it of caste and sect divisions and to forge a nation (Jaffrelot 1996). Alongside the network of *shakhas*, the RSS also exploited the readiness of the local notables to support publicly its activities: at the local and regional levels the *pracharaks* (propagandists) in charge of an area work under the patronage of a leading citizen known as a *sanghchalak* (director) who provides guidance. Many *sanghchalaks* are merchants or industrialists.

Social welfare work for Hindus is one of the main activities of the RSS. Its first action of this type, in 1926, was to provide essential supplies (especially drinking water) for the devout in the Nagpur region who were taking part in the festival to mark the birth of Ram and were being exploited by priests (Andersen and Damle 1987: 34). It later often intervened in this way when natural or political disasters occurred. To take one example, it set up a Hindu Sahayata Samiti (a Hindu mutual aid society) in Delhi in 1947 to house, clothe and even find work for the millions of refugees who were fleeing West Pakistan.[5] Similar efforts were deployed on behalf of Hindu refugees in the Srinagar valley who were housed in camps under canvas at Jammu and Delhi. RSS volunteers invariably distinguish themselves by aiding victims of floods and earthquakes.[6] This 'social welfare strategy' has, however, been implemented more systematically since 1989 when the RSS set up a new affiliate known as Seva Bharti (Service of India).

This movement's founder, Vishnu Kumar, is a former RSS *pracharak*. The official objectives of Seva Bharti, whose motto is 'social welfare is my duty', are

(1) to eradicate untouchability, (2) to imbue people with the spirit of service and unity [social and national], (3) to promote and perform literary, cultural, social and charitable activities among the poor and our underprivileged brothers who live in rundown districts,

and (4) to serve the economically needy and socially backward sectors by contributing to their physical, educational, social, moral and economic development without distinction of caste, language or region, so that they gain self-confidence and are integrated into society.[7]

Seva Bharti's ideological purpose is, clearly, to assimilate marginal populations which are naturally appreciative of charitable work, into a Hindu nation, the model and spearhead of which is the RSS. This scheme has proved particularly worthwhile for the Hindu nationalists since these social groups have been growing rapidly and neither the RSS nor its affiliates had ever succeeded in putting down roots within them. It was difficult for a movement dominated by high castes to reach this working-class population set apart by many socio-cultural features (caste awareness and social habitus, and in some cases a language, which, in the case of Hindi, for example, contains very few Sanskrit elements).

For the moment Seva Bharti is concentrating its activities in northern India. In Delhi it has opened 12 dispensaries and runs an ambulance service in twenty-odd slum areas, providing virtually free medical assistance. Strong emphasis is placed on all forms of education. A van with video equipment visits needy neighbourhoods and slums to promote 'moral and cultural education': 'Education does not end with the eradication of illiteracy' explains the secretary of Seva Bharti when talking about these video films. 'We want to instil in slum-dwellers national awareness and a sense of hygiene, to teach them what is good, what is good for society and how they can be useful to society'.[8]

Naturally enough, in order to attract 'customers' the films shown are sometimes the *Ramayana* and *Mahabharata* epics which were tremendously popular when broadcast on nationwide television. Significantly, the van used is referred to as Samskar Rath. *Rath* is the word used to designate the vehicles which transport divinities in processions; the use of the word *samskar* conjures up a cluster of far richer meanings.

The term *samskar* designates rites of passage but also, more generally, everything that shapes the personality of the individual from childhood on (Kapani 1992: 43). In Hindu tradition, 'to have good *samskar*' usually means having no vices (not smoking or drinking alcohol, for example), having very polished manners, even following a vegetarian diet, in short, imitating Brahmins, which is what the term Sanskritization implies.[9]

The RSS's uses of the term *samskar* reflects its aspiration to reform mentalities in line with the high Hindu tradition and, more specifically, to infuse Hindu awareness and national discipline. It reinterprets the concept of *samskar*, which it adapts to its own needs, presenting it as a vector of Sanskritization for the low castes. Many untouchables enter *shakhas* to learn how to live a disciplined life, in which they recognize good *samskar*.

In keeping with the RSS's approach, Seva Bharti's concentrates on low-caste children, to whom they offer the free education. A reception centre for abandoned children was opened in 1987, there are 15 Sanskrit Kendra (Sanskrit learning centres) and 129 Bal and Balika Samskar Kendras (*samskar* learning centres for boys or girls) attended by 19,304 children supervised by 352 teachers, many of whom are voluntary workers connected with the RSS. The organization emphasizes that in these centres 'children learn not only to read the alphabet and books but also receive *samskars* (moral education)'.[10] Seva Bharti has set up 26 tutorial centres for students from needy families and 3 electricity and electronics apprenticeship courses for adolescents who have dropped out of the school system. A reported 2,550 girls were attending 63 dress-making centres with the goal of making their families 'economically self-sufficient'. Brochures published by Seva Bharti add that its activists 'regularly visit them to instil in them a spirit of devotion and love of the motherland'.

All these activities are made possible by gifts, either in rupees or in kind (one donor has given the organization a large area of land south of Delhi for an orphanage). Benefactors, as the Secretary General of Seva Bharti admits, are mainly recruited from the merchant castes, in keeping with their tradition of patronage of charitable works with religious overtones: 'Gifts from merchants cover around half our expenses. We go to see trades people in the bazaars. We talk to them about our work, they come and see our centres and show their approval. They make gifts. These gifts are the foundation of all our work.'[11] The fact that a substantial proportion of Seva Bharti's resources comes from these philanthropic practices is essential to the effectiveness of its social welfare strategy in terms of instilling and diffusing Hindu nationalist ideology. However, this effectiveness, of which the figures published by the organization are not a reliable indicator, also needs to be tested on the ground.

Ideology in schools for the poor

Motia Khan is a slum squashed between the approaches to Connaught Place (which opens on to New Delhi) and the Jhandewalan neighbourhood (built after Partitition to house refugees from western Punjab). It comprises some 600 *Jhuggi Jhonpri* (rundown dwellings) housing 3,000 or so people mainly from Bikaner district in Rajasthan. Most of these people are *Sassi* (untouchables) the first of whom settled there in the early 1980s and were afterwards joined by other caste members. Most of them have no permanent employment but do odd jobs which are sometimes remunerative, like selling maps of India to tourists. Some inhabitants of Motia Khan get by fairly well, but because of the high cost of building land in Delhi they are frequently threatened with 'expropriation' by the municipality to which the land belongs[12], and in addition they can never escape their condition as untouchables. They complain of the humiliating treatment meted out to them by the teachers in the state schools where they have tried to enroll, and of their failure to keep up with lessons.

Thanks to its 'social welfare strategy' the RSS has managed to put down roots in this slum area by responding to the demand for education on the part of the Sassis. The RSS's second headquarters – the main one being in Nagpur – is at nearby Jhandewalan and one of the *pracharaks* who live there permanently makes regular visits to Motia Khan. This man, Virendra Bhatnagar, is a Brahmin from Uttar Pradesh whose family was affiliated to the Arya Samaj, a Hindu socio-religious reform movement (Jones 1974). He joined the RSS at the age of eight at his schoolteacher's instigation and decided at a very early age to become a *pracharak*; he left school in order to start out on this 'career' and was posted by the leadership of the movement to the BMS. From 1963 to 1986, he worked for the organization as a local then a regional secretary in Uttar Pradesh and finally in Delhi. This unbroken commitment was a reflection of his 'deep-rooted choice', his liking for 'the service of the underprivileged'.[13]

In 1989, on the occasion of the centenary of the birth of Hedgewar the RSS launched a far-reaching programme called Naran Seva (For the Service of Man). Virendra Bhatnagar was chosen to coordinate its activities in Delhi. He immediately gave priority to the development of schools and personally took charge of the school at Motia Khan which he named Vivekananda Shishu Mandir, Temple of the pupils of Vivekananda, from the name of one of the late nineteenth century precursors of militant Hinduism in Bengal. The school, which opened in July 1991, soon had 120 pupils aged from 4 to 20 divided into three classes, all at elementary level, not even basic education being available in the slum.

In August 1992, a year after its foundation, women teachers at the school claimed that it comprised three classes of 60 pupils, including adult women. In fact there has probably been a downturn in numbers since UNICEF set up a rival school in the same slum area with more substantial resources. The RSS is clearly focusing on the same populations as this international organization[14] but for imbuing them with its ideology.

A little textbook distributed to pupils includes many patriotic poems, starting with the RSS prayer which includes the statement that the national flag is none other than the flag of the organization which is saffron, the colour of Hinduism. Another song, entitled 'Our dear country', ends with this couplet: 'Once it was happy and prosperous, today it is shattered into a thousand pieces and unhappy. But look, now it is reborn, our dear country'.

A song entitled 'We must have pride' is more insidious as it is implicitly directed against minorities. It goes as follows:

> Every inhabitant of this country must have pride,
> *Bande Mataram*

[*Salute to the Mother*, the first anthem of the independence movement should be sung every day.]

> The country is not made of earth but of feelings.
> If it breaks, we must take stock of the break. [...]
> The tie of blood must be recognized.
> The enemy has infiltrated his way among us and is
> fomenting a plot.
> Now we must be heedful of the fear that possesses households.
> Fearful is he who pretends to ignore the problem .
> We must be on the watch for the smoke that comes before fire. [...]
> How much longer shall we go on doing nothing?
> We must launch a campaign from a high platform.
> Our sole desire is to bear the country to the pinnacle of greatness[15]

The enemy mentioned can only be the Muslims – 12 per cent of the Indian population – regarded by Hindu nationalists as a fifth column linked to an Islamic International of which Pakistan is the main component. The image of the smoldering fire clearly refers to the communal riots that sporadically erupt throughout northern India and for which the Hindu nationalists recommend people to be ready.

It is hard to assess the impact of such propaganda on the school's pupils. One might simply suppose that if they are faced with it over a long period their outlook is bound to change. The teaching is not restricted to this kind of indoctrination, however. Seva Bharti tries to dilute ideology by giving prominence to noble and virtuous themes which are easily incorporated into ideology while flattering youthful idealism, which is particularly strong among the low castes seeking respectability. The women teachers insist that their main concern is to instil into children born into a dirty, rough and violent world habits of basic hygiene, better manners and respect for their elders and for society.[16] The nationalist, hierarchic and even organicist connotations of this socialization are found in the cult of Saraswati, the goddess of learning. Each lesson begins and ends with a Sanskrit prayer to Saraswati, with a strong ideological content:

Oh she whose vehicle is the wild duck
Oh knowledge bearer [gyandayini]
Oh mother, give us a pure thought [amba vimal]
Let us make India the diadem of the world
Give us this heroic strength, give us a pure thought,
Fill our hearts with courage and virtue,
Make our lives full of renunciation and asceticism,
Grant us temperance, truth and love,
Fill us with pride.

This prayer explicitly combines emphasis on *samskars,* whose appeal is of a type to encourage children to attend school, with overt nationalism. The children recite the prayer – clumsily, because of the difficulty of the language – facing the image of the goddess and with their hands clasped together. When Virendra Bhatnagar and the schoolmistress talk to the pupils they make it a point of honour to bring in the few words of Sanskrit the pupils know, doubtless because the pupils consider this a mark of prestige.

The school owes some of its appeal to the fact that it is an instrument of Sanskritization. But other factors are also involved. Schooling is free and the modest equipment the pupils need (textbook, pencils, exercise books and slate) is provided by the organization. The schoolmistresses are unpaid volunteers; they give two hours a day to the organization, a service they present as the highest form of sacrifice (a cardinal notion in Hinduism, together with renunciation). One teacher, a Brahmin, is the wife of a singer who is popular for his renderings of religious texts, and is an active RSS member; the other is the wife of the head of a local RSS *shakha,* who is a member of a commercial caste. Another of the school's strong points is that the teachers have been specially trained not to humiliate the children. Last but not least, the school offers vocational training for girls via dress-making classes. Seventeen girls assiduously follow this course for which the school possesses seven sewing machines. Those who complete the course receive a certificate of qualification. A competitive mood was created when the first shirt made by a pupil was sold, for 25 rupees. The same shirt, bought from a tailor, would have cost at least 40 rupees.[17]

Study of the Motia Khan school leads to the conclusion that the 'social welfare strategy' really does provide the RSS with new outlets for its ideas. Indeed, Virendra Bhatnagar also points out that though there is still no *shakha* in Motia Khan, a few boys attend the *shakha* at the Jhandewalan headquarters. I saw the same mechanisms at work in a rural environment in the village of Piparsod in central India (Madhya Pradesh) near the town of Shivpuri.[18]

Ideology in the village, via the school

Shivpuri is a district capital with some 80,000 inhabitants located 120 km south of Gwalior on the Delhi-Bombay road. Its literacy rate is 47.84 per cent compared to 16.48 per cent for the district as a whole. These figures were linked to the percentage of untouchables in the town, 15.6 per cent, which is comparable to the national average, but which is exceeded in 667 of the district's 1,300 villages (Government of India: 15–22).

In this district, the main RSS affiliate which seeks to meet local educational needs is not Seva Bharti but Vidya Bharti (Indian knowledge). This is an organization which was founded in 1977 to coordinate the network of some 700 Saraswati Shishu Mandir schools (Temples of Saraswati' Children) which the RSS has been developing since the 1950s. Fifteen years or so later, Vidya Bharti had 40,000 teachers and 1.2 million pupils in 5,000 schools (including 1,325 in Uttar Pradesh and approximately a thousand in Madhya Pradesh), more than a third of them providing education up to higher secondary level.[19]

At Shivpuri are one of the 5,000 Saraswati Shishu Mandirs and one of the 40 Vidya Bharti boarding schools. Vidya Bharti defines its goal as training 'children full of self-confidence, proud of their religion and showing respect and love for the glorious past [of their nation]'.[20] This ideological slant is apparent in the timetable of the 130 boarders: from 5:30 to 8 a.m., they pray together, then they do yoga exercises and recite the *Bhagavad Gita*, which the Hindu nationalists are attempting to set up as the Book of Hinduism. A leaflet describing the boarding school presents it as a modern form of the ancient *gurukuls* (traditional teaching places centred on a *guru* where young Brahmins learned *Veda* – literally 'Knowledge').[21]

The school, thus, claims a place within the Great Hindu Tradition but it does not fit readily into the rationale of a 'social welfare strategy': the annual fees for a boarder are 8,000 rupees, plus the cost of two uniforms, one for winter, one for summer. Nevertheless, in line with current trends, a kindergarten has been opened there which is free for untouchables from the mainly low-caste neighbourhood where the school is located. Despite the high standard of the state school in the sector – which is recognized by those responsible for the boarding school – 40 young untouchables come to the Ambedkar Saraswati Shishu Mandir to learn 'the *samskars,* how to behave, etc.'.[22] It was opened in July 1991 in the aftermath of celebration of the centenary of Ambedkar, the untouchable leader, when there was strong collective mobilization on the part of the low castes.

This social welfare strategy and the very existence of the boarding school are the result of philanthropic initiatives, since the enrolment fees are not sufficient to cover maintenance costs. While the principal is an RSS cadre, the school is supported by leading local citizens sympathetic to the RSS, a landlord and the head of a small carrier firm with two trucks. The Shivpuri population, from whom gifts were solicited, had an objective interest in the development of the school in their town since 200 day-pupils attend it in addition to the 130 boarders and the education has a high reputation. Brochures about the school emphasize its discipline, the teaching of English, which the Hindu nationalists regretfully accept as indispensable, and selection on the basis of merit. Shivpuri's upper-middle class has thus helped to finance the school, with its own young people in mind. However, the principal explains the amount of funds collected (several hundred thousand rupees) in terms of the socio-ritual implications of gift-making rather than in terms of this less praiseworthy transactional motivation: 'People give to build a temple, people give to build a school'.[23]

Until independence, Shivpuri (located on a plateau with a more temperate climate) was the summer capital of the reigning dynasty, the Scindias. Patronage of religious foundations and festivals (e.g. the Kumbh Mela at Ujjain, one of the seven holy cities of Hinduism) formed part of the Scindia dynasty's traditional attributions and duties. In the 1950s, a son of the Angre family became the private secretary of the deposed Maharajah and, more importantly, of his wife, whose political career he furthered. Her affinities with the Hindu nationalists led the Rajmata Scindia to join the Jana Sangh and then the BJP, to which since 1967 she has brought a considerable 'vote bank'. She also actively supports the RSS's 'religious' affiliate, the VHP. She has given part of her palace at Gwalior to this organization. It is as though she had simply shifted her religious patronage to a more ideological ground.

These acts of generosity go hand in hand with a skill in managing the family fortune which has made it possible for the Rajmata and her secretary Angre to invest in merchant shipping and the popular press. The Rajmata Scindia officially presents herself as an 'industrialist'.[24] The VHP leadership team, to which the Rajmata belongs, consists, in addition to cadres detached from the RSS, of Marwaris who have done very well in business, such as president V. H. Dalmia.[25] Support by industrialists for the VHP is also found at local level: for example, the president of the Madhya Pradesh branch is a Marwari and the president of the Bhopal branch is a Jain.[26] Naturally enough, the RSS galaxy thereby gains respectability.

Patronage of a 'religious charity', which generally involves philanthropy designed to win merit, also exists at village level where any attempts by the RSS to put down roots are usually hampered by a number of factors that are less marked in the urban environment. First, the farmers do not have enough free time to assemble each day for physical exercise or for an ideology session. Second, they are too divided to envisage collective activity of this kind. At Piparsod (a village 17 km from Shivpuri), the Brahmins and the *kirar* (a farmer caste dominant in the region[27]) compete for pre-eminence (Chambard 1980). RSS *pracharaks* have tried to develop a *shakha* in the village from their base at Shivpuri but have always given up after a few weeks' effort. During the summer of 1991, the new *pracharak* tried a new tactic and opened a Saraswati Shishu Mandir.

This was an extremely astute move because, despite its 2,500 inhabitants, Piparsod had no school. The result is a real 'hunger for education'. (The only school to open there was sabotaged by the Brahmins who were loath to see the low castes getting an education).[28] Furthermore, the Shishu Mandir was able to charge affordable registration fees – 30 rupees per pupil per month – because the two teachers accepted low pay (600 rupees per year) saying they were motivated by a spirit of devotion. One teacher, who has a B.Sc. in maths and trained at Shivpuri where he still lives, seemed, however, not to be much of an ideologue though the *pracharak* intimated that he would soon be joining the RSS, thus becoming 'one of us'.[29] His colleague – and superior – Madan Lal Pandey was also the RSS secretary in the area and responsible for developing *shakhas* there. Born in a neighbouring village, Madan Lal Pandey was preparing his B.A. at Shivpuri when he encountered the RSS for the first time.

Apart from teaching arithmetic and spelling, these teachers seemed very keen to get the children to recite the *Gayatri Mantra*. This is a Sanskrit prayer which is in theory a high-caste prerogative but the Shishu Mandir are open to all and are an instrument of Sanskritization for the low castes. The father of one girl pupil from the very impure barber caste emphasized that the children learn good manners there, implying these are Brahmin manners.[30]

So this Shishu Mandir – whose single class contains some forty pupils aged around six – owes its success to the appeal of Sanskritization and inexpensive education. Here too, the 'social welfare strategy' is made possible by resources obtained via an important aspect of the Hindu economic ethos – religious gifts. The school's main asset is the building it occupies, one of the village's few two-storey houses, which was given to the Sishu Mandir by a Gwalior doctor who was born in Piparsod (Chambard 1994). After this man's death, his widow gave the building to the school, and in the same spirit, the village notables founded an association bearing her husband's name in order to perpetuate his memory and to run the school.[31]

A few months after its opening, the school was being used in the evening for a new RSS *shakha*: Madan Lal Pandey was assembling twenty-odd villagers there for a physical and ideological training session.[32]

Conclusion

The Hindu nationalist movement obviously owes its recent successes not only to the radical and populist mobilization strategies it has deployed, but also to its excellent local roots linked to its network of activists and its social welfare strategy, regarding schooling especially. This strategy exploits the philanthropy of patrons wishing to gain merit by their gifts.

In spite of certain limitations, this strategy seems to be sound for two reasons. First, it facilitates an approach to families whose political culture is not Hindu nationalist. When the organizations concerned are distinctively not the RSS, the BJP or any other well identified offshoots of the Sangh parivar, the project's affiliations are concealed, prominence being given to its right-thinking Hindu aspect alone, notably via emphasis on *samskar*. In answer to one of my questions, the Piparsod barber mentioned above stressed that the Sishu Mandir is separate from the BJP for which, as a Congress voter, he had no respect. In other words, this method of proceeding allays the ideological susceptibilities of parents the better to shape the political culture of their children.

The second asset of the Hindu nationalist social welfare strategy lies in the goodwill shown to it by some official bodies, even before the BJP took over in 1998. The public authorities, under pressure because of the economic crisis, are cutting investment in the social sphere and are very willing to pass on their responsibilities to private organizations. This is happening particularly quickly in the federal states where the BJP came to power in 1990–1991 (Madhya Pradesh, Rajasthan, Himachal Pradesh, Uttar Pradesh, Delhi, Gujarat and Maharashtra) whose governments are clearly supporting RSS projects;[33] but this encouragement – sometimes associated with financial aid – was already perceptible within central government dependent bodies before the BJP came to power. In 1991, the government awarded Seva Bharti the 'Certificate of Merit' and a 50,000 rupee reward. The Minister of Health and the Family pays Seva Bharti an annual subsidy of 6,000 rupees and the Delhi Development Authority has provided them with eight offices in the capital.[34] This evolution may reduce the RSS's dependence on philanthropists.

The main handicap the RSS social welfare strategy will have to overcome is connected with the social categories it targets, the most underprivileged strata. In India these are the low castes whose culture is often far removed from the Great Tradition which the RSS seeks to instill in them. The cleavage can be perceived in the language – often a dialect – used by these strata of society, and in their clothes and dietary habits, in short their whole ethos: this may constitute a barrier. It is true that their desire for Sanskritization is conducive to the diffusion of RSS ideology, but militant associations of untouchables and the Bahujan Samaj Party (the party of the majority of society) are actively engaged in a counter-political conscientisation programme. According to their logic, the untouchables need not imitate the Brahmins but stand on their own and eradicate the caste system. In the long run, this egalitarian agenda is more likely to make inroads among the Dalits (the broken men), to use these activists' terminology.

Postscript

The fieldwork research on which this chapter is based was conducted in the early 1990s. Fifteen years later the *modus operandi* of the Sangh parivar has not changed, so far as its strategy of social welfare in India is concerned. In 2004, a visit to the headquarters of Seva Bharati in Delhi showed that the organization was continuing to grow in the same directions as before. Five hundred and ninety-seven Bal and Balika Samskar Kendras were functioning with 20 to 25,000 pupils; 14 mobile and 10 permanent dispensaries treated about 100,000 people every year; 200 cutting and tailoring centres benefited 20–25,000 girls every year, and 7 computer centres were attended by 800–1000 students every year (based on the archives of the organization I was given access to by Dharam Vir Kohli in February 2004).

Over the past 15 years, the only really new development came from the outside support the Sangh Parivar received from the diaspora. In the 1980–1990s, the Indian diaspora gained momentum in many different ways. Its 2 million members or so became one of the richest minority in the United States, asserting themselves politically through the creation of an Indian caucus in the Congress. It also benefited from the growing interest of the government of New Delhi which after creating a special status for the overseas Indians (Non Resident Indians) started to organize every year a big symposium in the Indian capital in the honour of those who had left India but maintained some relation with the country (Therwath 2005: 411–435).

The Sangh parivar was prompt to exploit the rise of the Indian diaspora which was largely made of Hindus, especially in the United States. The RSS and the VHP were already active overseas, among them, since the 1950–1960s in order to maintain a cultural link between these Indian abroad and their homeland. But the leaders of the parivar realised that they could also tap this source of income on behalf of their social work because the rich Indians who had succeeded abroad may well feel the need to do something for their country of origin as charities. As in India, the RSS created new branches without publicizing their ideological affiliation: people were supposed to give money for financing philanthropical activities.

In the United Kingdom the Sangh parivar created Bharat Sewa – a synonym for Seva Bharati – and in the United States, in 1989, the India Development and Relief Fund. Both were directly related to the 'charity branch' of the RSS (Sewa Vibhag – the service division). These organizations have been very successful. From 1990 to 1998 the India Development and Relief Fund (IRDF) has collected 2 million dollars and the Hindu Heritage Endowment, which the Fund had created in 1994, 2.6 million dollars in four years (Bhatt, 2000; Mathew 2000: 529; Rajagopal, 2000). According to another source, the IRDF has raised

5 millions dollars between 1995 and 2000, a huge sum of money that it has distributed to 184 associations involved in social work in India (Sabrang Communications 2002). The Constitution of the IRDF disposes that 20 per cent of the money collected should go to organizations that the donor himself has chosen, but that left 80 per cent to the discretion of the Fund. Now, out of the 75 associations which benefited from the support of the IRDF between 1995 and 2000, 60 belonged to the Sangh parivar, including Sewa Bharti and the VKA.

These revelations created some commotions in the United States, but most of the donors knew already that they were supporting a Hindu nationalist organization. In fact, they had been very much upset to learn that the IRDF had sent money to the victims of a fire in a mosque in Mecca – so much so that the director had to apologize.[35] Their Hindu chauvinism offers a remarkable illustration of what Benedict Anderson has called 'long distance nationalism' (Anderson 1998). Unsurprisingly, the leaders of the BJP, the political party of the Sangh parivar, have started to make tours in the United States to raise money in order to finance their election campaigns in the 1990s.

The same scenario unfolded itself in United Kingdom. After the Gujarat earthquake in 2003, Bharat Sewa – rechristened 'Sewa UK' – collected £2.3 millions, out of which £1.9 million have been sent to the Gujarat branch of Sewa Bharti. Allegedly, one third of this money has been used to build Hindu nationalist schools, especially in the tribal belt, whereas it was supposed to help villagers to rebuild their houses. These malpractices have been exposed by activists of AWAAZ, a human rights movement working in South Asia (AWAAZ 2004).

Notes

1. He was thoroughly acquainted with the writings of J. S. Mill, Spencer, Darwin, Tyndals, E. Haeckel, T. H. Huxley, Carlyle and Emerson (Savarkar 1984: 269–270).
2. Hindu nationalist cadres often describe Muslims as 'salt in the dal' : they make no harm so long they remain in a (dominated) minority.
3. Romila Thapar explains that this exclusion is not based on a racial criterion; it is social and ritual and hence can be overcome via acculturation and recognition of the superiority of the Brahmin (Thapar 1978: 165, 169, 179). Even today, the common assumption among the Hindu nationalists is that the brahminical values are superior, including that of repression that is equated with samyan (self-control). They would disapprove of the low castes' spontaneity. (I am grateful to Jayati Chaturvedi for this piece of information).

4. The Hindu nationalists translate 'indigenous peoples' by 'vanavasi', literally 'those of the forest', and not, as is generally the case in India, by 'adivasi', that is, 'those who were there before', because from their point of view, the country's first inhabitants were the 'Aryans' and not the autochthonous populations, which were driven back or conquered by the Aryan invaders, from whom today's tribes are descended.

5. This organization was under the patronage of the *sangchalak* of Delhi, Hans Raj Gupta (*Organiser*, 21 August 1947, p. 16).

6. After an earthquake that claimed some 3,000 victims in northern India, the RSS sent 500 volunteers to the scene and distributed clothing and medicine valued at 400,000 and 250,000 rupees respectively (*Organiser*, 8 December 1991).

7. A tract entitled *Seva Bharti*, New Delhi, [undated].

8. Interview with R. Atri on 12 August 1992 in New Delhi.

9. This concept was introduced by M. N. Srinivas to designate all the practices used by low castes to improve their social status, which consist of copying certain distinctive traits of the Brahmins (Srinivas 1965: 214–215).

10. Duplicated document entitled 'Introduction-Seva Bharti: Delhi' obtained from the movement's headquarters, p. 2.

11. Interview with R. Atri.

12. *Times of India*, 10 October 1992, p. 4.

13. Interview with Virendra Bhatnagar, 7 October 1991 at Jhandewalan.

14. Seva Bharti states in its typewritten newsletters that it wishes to be associated with UNICEF programmes in order to benefit from foreign funding. This goes counter to the RSS claim to indigenous self-sufficiency, the notion of svâvalmban (self-dependency).

15. Duplicated Hindi textbook giving no details of publisher, place or date.

16. Interview with Sadhana Ojha and Gita Goyal on 14 August 1992 at Motia Khan.

17. The sewing machines are an instance of a classic ploy in the Hindu nationalist social welfare strategy. The way in which they are acquired illustrates an important aspect of the Hindu economic ethos, the making of gifts with religious overtones. The machines are supplied by merchants or bought by private individuals and then given to the school during a ceremony, which invests the gift with its full significance. At the Jhandewalan headquarters, panels of photos illustrating RSS activities (rather like those used in catechism groups) are displayed: there are photos of gleaming new Singer sewing machines covered with *mala* (garlands of flowers, often saffron yellow French marigolds). Another important factor is the presence of a local religious figure, the head of the Udaisin ashram (a sect mainly found in the Punjab and relatively open to the low castes). This holy man, Sw ami Raghavanand, performs for Seva Bharti the rites that consecrate the gift, especially *havan* (Vedic sacrifices). He is even willing to teach the low castes the technique involved in doing the *havan*, and also Sanskrit – indispensable for uttering the sacred formulas. He explains that Westernized politicans are destroying Hindu traditions and that it is, therefore, essential to go out of the ashrams and regenerate society on its most ancient foundations. Swami Raghavanand and Virendra Bhatnagar, the *pracharak*, represent two variants of the same ideological project. Their strength lies in their ability

to expound this project in terms of the protection of Hinduism, thereby attracting to themselves a flow of gifts.

18. I am grateful to Jean-Luc Chambard for inviting me just at the time when the 'social welfare strategy' was starting to be in evidence there and for helping me to carry out my survey.

19. N. Khanna, 'Education: the RSS way' *Sunday* 1 December 1991, pp. 22–23.

20. *Saraswati Vidyapith Avasiya Vidyalaya-Vivarnika*, 1985 [brochure without indication of place] (Hindi).

21. Saraswati Vidyapith Avasiya Vidyalaya – Shivpuri [undated].

22. Interview with Ram Hari Pandey, secretary of the boarding school, 18 August 1992, at Shivpuri.

23. Interview with Kamal Kumar Pandey, 16 August 1992, at Shivpuri.

24. This is the profession she gives in the biographical notices published by the secretariat of the Lok Sabha (the lower house of Parliament, to which she has been a candidate since 1957, except in 1977, till she died in 1999).

25. The Vice-Presidents, B.P. Toshniwal and S.K. Somaiya, are also Marwaris.

26. Interview with B. G. Toshniwal on 27 August 1992 at Indore and with A. Ajmera on 13 November 1990 at Bhopal.

27. The dominant caste – another concept we owe to Srinivas – is that which is most numerous and owns most land. The village leaders traditionally come from its ranks.

28. I am grateful to Jean-Luc Chambard, the instigator of this initiative, for this piece of information.

39. Interview with Vivek Joshi, 27 October 1991, at Piparsod.

30. Interview with Sarvan on 27 October 1991 at Piparsod, carried out in collaboration with Jean-Luc Chambard.

31. Interview with H.S. Sharma, 17 August 1992, at Piparsod.

32. Interview with M.L. Pandey, 17 August 1992, at Piparsod.

33. In Madhya Pradesh, 2,005,000-square-metre plots, total value 100 million rupees, have been turned over to Vidya Bharti schools for a trifling sum (*India Today* 31 October 1992, p. 43).

34. Ghinurie, Y. 'Altruistic expansion' India Today, 31 July 1992, p. 27.

35. www.swordoftruth.com/sworoftruth/archives/oldarchives/bjprss.html

Bibliography

Andersen, W. and Damle, S. (1987), *The Brotherhood in Saffron. The Rashtriya Swayamsevak Sangh and Hindu Revivalism* (New Delhi: Vistaar).

Anderson, B. (1998), *The Spectre of Comparisons: Nationalism, Southeast Asia, and the World* (London and New York: Verso).

AWAAZ-South Asia Watch Limited, *In Bad Faith? British Charity and Hindu Extremism*, London, 2004. http://www.awaazsaw.org, accessed 26 February 2004.

Bhatt, C. (2000), 'Dharmo rakshati rakshitah : Hindutva Movement in UK', *Ethnic and Racial Studies*, 23, 3, pp. 559–593.

Chambard, J.-L. (1980), *Atlas d'un village indien* (Paris: EHESS).

Chambard, J.-L. (1994), 'Les violences d'un village hindou. Suicide de femme chez les barbiers et "violences légitimes" des dominants au Madhya Pradesh', In D. Vidal, G. Tarabout and E. Meyer (eds), *Violences et Non-Violences en Inde* (Paris: EHESS), *Purusharta* 16.

Dieckhoff, A. and Guiterrez, N. (eds) (2001), *Modern Roots: Studies of National Identity* (Aldershot: Ashgate).

Golwalkar, M. S. (1947), *We, or Our Nationhood Defined* [fourth edition] (Nagpur: Bharat prakashan).

Government of India (undated), Census of India 1981 – Series II – Madhya Pradesh District Census Handbook Part XIII-B – Shivpuri District, Bhopal, State Government Publications.

Jaffrelot, C. (1995), 'The Idea of the Hindu Race in the Writings of Hindu Ideologues in the 1920s and 1930s: A Concept between Two Cultures', In P. Robb (ed.), *The Concept of Race in South Asia* (Delhi: Oxford University Press).

Jaffrelot, C. (1996), *The Hindu Nationalist Movement and Indian Politics, 1925 to the 1990s: Strategies of Identity-Building, Implantation and Mobilisation* (New York: Columbia University Press), pp. 327–354.

Jaffrelot, C. (1999), 'The Vishva Hindu Parishad – Structures and strategies', In J. Haynes (ed.), *Religion, Globalization and Political Culture in the Third World* (Basingtoke and New York: Palgrave McMillan), pp. 191–212.

Jaffrelot, C. (2005), *The Sangh Parivar: A Reader* (Delhi: Oxford University Press).

Jones, K. (1974), *Arya Dharm – Hindu Consciousness in 19th Century Punjab* (Berkeley: University of California Press).

Kapani, L. (1992), *La Notion de Samskara* (Paris: Collège de France – De Boccard).

Khanna, N. (1 December 1991), 'Education: the RSS way' *Sunday*, pp. 22–23.

Mathew, B. and Prashad, V. (2000), 'The Protean Forms of Yankee Hindutva ', *Ethnic and Racial Studies*, 23, 3.

Pandey, G. (1993), 'Which of Us are Hindus?', In G. Pandey (ed.), *Hindus and Others – The Question of Identity in India Today* (New Delhi: Viking).

Rajagopal, A. (2000), 'Hindu Nationalism in the US: Changing Configurations of Political Practice', *Ethnic and Racial Studies*, 23, 3, pp. 467–496.

Sabrang Communuications (2002), *The Foreign Exchange of Hate: IRDF and the American Funding of Hindutva* (Bombay: Sabrang Communications).

Savarkar, V. D. (1984), *My Transportation for Life* (Bombay: Veer Savarkar Prakashan).

Savarkar, V. D. (1969), *Hindutva; Who is a Hindu?* (Bombay: S.S. Savarkar).

Srinivas, M. N. (1965), *Religion and Society Among the Coorgs of South India* (London and New York: Oxford University Press).

Thapar, R. (1978), *Ancient Indian History* (New Delhi: Orient Longman).

Therwath, I (2005), '"Far and wide". The Sangh parivar's global network', In C. Jaffrelot (ed.), *The Sangh Parivar: A Reader* (Delhi: Oxford University Press), pp. 411–435.

12

Conclusion: Faith and Development – of Ethno-separatism, Multiculturalism and Religious Partitioning?

Michael Jennings and Gerard Clarke

At the heart of this collection is a discussion of the role of faith in modern society. What can faith-based organizations (FBO), communities and leaders contribute to social, economic and political development, in the contemporary world? In particular, what are the links between faith and modernity? Does religion speak to what is often presented as a secular mission, the eradication of poverty and the empowerment of the poor? For much of the twentieth century, the answer from social scientists was that faith and religion were increasingly irrelevant. And taking its lead from such analyses, the donor community similarly failed to see faith communities as partners in development. The past century, it appears, has seen the victory of the secular, at least in Western Europe and North America. At the beginning of the twentieth century eminent thinkers across Europe believed that faith, at least in its organized form, was losing the battle against an encroaching secularism. Durkheim saw the rise of science as the greatest threat to religion: 'it seems natural that religion should lose ground as science becomes better at performing its task' (Durkheim 1995: 431). And whilst the new gods of science had not been fully born, 'the former gods are growing old or dying' (ibid.: 431). Secularism was given political form in France, with its 1905 law separating the Church and State. Religion was banished from public space: state-funding for religion was ended, and the use of religious symbols and signs on public buildings prohibited. The republic, it was declared, 'neither recognizes, nor salaries, nor subsidizes any religion.'[1] The advances of the European Enlightenment had, it appeared, rendered precarious the foundations of the old religions, leading towards a more rationalist and avowedly secular society.

A century on from the 'victory' of French secular instincts, and the predicted secularization of modern society still looks far from complete. Over the past decade a global resurgence of religion, especially conservative religion, has transformed national and international politics (see Bergen 1999; Sahliyeh 1990). Within the international arena, religion and faith appear to have renewed their claim to authority and power, but in ways that are largely characterized as negative. The resurgence of religious affiliation has been linked to a rise in conflict centred on identities such as culture, ethnicity and religion. According to the author of the 'clash of civilizations' paradigm, international politics is no longer based on rivalry between the proponents of Western economic liberalism and communist economic autarky. 'In the post-Cold War world', Samuel Huntington argues, 'the most important distinctions among peoples are not ideological, political or economic. They are cultural' (Huntington 1997: 21). In Huntington's post-Cold War world, nine culturally defined civilizations compete for influence and power, six of them based on current nation state formations ('Western', Latin American', 'African', 'Sinic' and 'Japanese') and four based on religious identities – 'Islamic', 'Hindu', 'Orthodox' (Christian) and 'Buddhist'. In so doing, Huntington gave birth to apocalyptic predictions of a world plagued by religious conflict or by conflict between civilizations defined in religious and non-religious terms. 'In this new world', he argued, 'the most pervasive, important and dangerous conflicts will not be between social classes, rich and poor or other economically defined groups but between peoples belonging to different cultural entities' (ibid.: 28). Huntington recognized that the world's major religions could play a positive role in promoting the common values of a universal civilization. But at heart, he predicted a bleak world in which the United States laboured against underground or subversive 'ethno-separatists', pulling the strings of a united front of 'multiculturalists' (Huntington 1997: 305).

In this vein, those who promote engagement and dialogue between 'development' organizations (multilateral, bilateral and non-governmental) and faith-based organizations and leaders may well be regarded as naïve multiculturalists, or worse still, the supplicants of ethno-separatists bent on the destruction of Western civilization. Harsh criticism perhaps and yet Amartya Sen's critique of the 'clash of civilizations' thesis represents as significant a critique of the 'faith and development' interface as that implied by Huntington. Sen attacks the 'imagined singularity' behind Huntington's culturally defined civilizations and the 'civilizational incarceration' to which it leads (Sen 2006: 10–11). Are we to believe, Sen asks rhetorically, 'that the relationships *between different human beings* can somehow be seen, without serious loss of understanding, in terms of relations *between different civilizations*' (Sen 2006: 11. Italics from the original). While the answer may be clear, Sen clouds matters with his criticism of a putative religious partitioning of the world, of a 'reliance on religion-based classification of the people of the world' (ibid.: 12, xv–xvii), and of the government policies that result. Sen, 'a strong believer in secularism and democracy' (and what he implies is an intrinsic link between them) (ibid.: 19) finds common cause with Huntington when he bemoans the 'confounded view of what a multiethnic society must do', for instance, support faith-based (and state-financed) schools (ibid.: 13). To this end, he issues a significant warning to advocates of the 'faith and development' interface;

> Trying to recruit religious leaders and clerics in support of political causes, along with trying to redefine the religions involved in terms of political and social attitudes, downplays the significance of non-religious values that people can and do have in their appropriate domain whether or not they are religious...The efforts to recruit mullahs and the clergy to play a role outside the immediate province of religion could, of course, make some difference in what is preached in mosques or temples. But is also downgrades the civic initiatives people who happen to be Muslim by religion can and do undertake (along with others) to deal with what are essentially political and social problems. (Ibid.: 78)

Interviews with officials of the UK Department for International Development (DFID) suggest a similar concern within many 'development' organizations (cf. Clarke 2007). Some of those interviewed voice significant concerns about the erosion of DFID's traditional secularism and the conceptual separation of Church and state on which it is based. They fear donor entanglement in sectarian or divisive agendas. They argue that the faith identities of the poor should not be privileged over their other myriad identities, that the assertion of class or gender identities, for instance holds more promise to empower the poor. Some argue that faith is mixed up inextricably with culture and is difficult to isolate in any useful sense, that organized religion promotes social exclusion, that most world religions, for instance, have played a critical role in the social encoding of male and female roles to the detriment of women and girls.

And yet, Sen's critique of 'imagined singularity' is at odds with the striking neglect for most of the twentieth century of religion as a variable in the promotion of 'development', in the daily struggles of the poor and in the concern of the well-off. The reality is, of course, that faith and religion were at the heart of the 'development' experience throughout the twentieth century. The predictions of Durkheim, Weber, Marx and others predicting a new secular future were based on a narrow Eurocentric vision that ignored trends in three continents – Africa, Asia and the Americas – and focused almost entirely on the experience of Christianity in western Europe. Far from representing an ever smaller proportion of the world population, membership of organized faith groups has increased in the latter half of the twentieth century.[2] Religion and faith has not given way to secularism, but maintained, if not extended, its reach into society at large (Barrett and Johnson 2007: 8). The presence of a powerful social, political, economic and cultural faith-based discourse at local, national and international levels is a reality that cannot be ignored or dismissed as the dying gasp of a pre-modern relic.

The notion that faith organizations function within a set of reactionary parameters, or working against notions of human rights, does not stand up to historical examination. Religious leaders and organizations have for centuries fought against the tyranny of Leviathan, as much as they have formed part of the Establishment. In 1985, for example, the Church of England published its report, *Faith in the City*, criticizing government policy on urban poverty and social exclusion. A response to simmering urban tensions in the early 1980s (notably the Brixton and Toxteth riots of 1981), and to Lord Scarman's report into the violence in the south London area of Brixton, the report criticized government policy on social deprivation in the cities of Britain. The government response was furious. One of the report's leading advocates, the late Right Revd Lord Sheppard of Liverpool, was denounced as a Marxist, and the government condemned what they considered an unwarranted and overtly political intrusion into public life by the Church (Webster 2005).

It appeared, or rather was suggested by the government, that this attack on government policy represented something new. Faith was seemingly shifting outside its natural home, the spiritual zone, and moving into the political. Yet the assertion that the Church had no place in political debate was as historically misplaced as it was futile. It was no surprise that Andrew Hake, one of the report's authors, had been a champion of the Kenyan nationalist campaign in the late 1950s, and an architect of policies to combat urban poverty in Kenya in the 1960s. In South Africa, Archbishop Desmond Tutu led global condemnation of the apartheid regime. Trevor Huddleston similarly campaigned against apartheid and other injustices in southern Africa. In Zimbabwe the Christian Churches played a key role in the independence movement; European missionaries took sides in the Biafran conflict. Across Africa anti-colonial struggles were led by traditional religious leaders; In Afghanistan and Palestine, mosques and imams campaigned against Soviet and Israeli occupation respectively. The British Conservative government of the 1980s, reflect as it might a wider feeling amongst Western governments in particular that religion should not involve itself in politics, was misreading the history of faith-based public action. The Anglican Church in 1985 was not entering new and dangerous territory in questioning the policies of an elected government, but acting according to a long-standing tradition of engagement in social, political and economic affairs.

These tensions lie at the heart of much of the current engagement of Western donor organizations with faith groups both in their home countries and in the developing world. The governments of secular nations have simultaneously sought to co-opt the participation of faith-based organizations in social welfare provision, and to keep 'faith' and 'society' separate and distinct as analytical categories. Donor wariness of faith-based organizations reflects deeper unease over potential synergies between the (self-defined) cosmopolitanism of development, and the perceived sectional, narrower doctrines of faith. Despite the emergence of civil society as a central focus (ideologically as well as materially) of donor action from the 1980s, faith-based organizations remained largely sidelined in terms of both analysis and resources, until the early 2000s. This despite the prominent social activism of the Catholic Church in Latin America in the 1960s and 1970s, and the Church and Mosque in pro-democracy movements in sub-Saharan Africa and South-East Asia. The long-term trend towards the secular state over the century did not diminish the role faith played in political discourse and social life, but rather transformed it both conceptually and organizationally. Continuity *and* change characterized the relationship between faith and society in this period. Increasingly excluded from a formal relationship with the state,[3] religions still participated in activities closely related to the functioning of that state, not least in the realm of social welfare, 'charity', and, through this, international development.

Faith and modernity

In his 1689 *A Letter Concerning Toleration*, John Locke outlined the responsibilities of the Church and the civil authority: 'The commonwealth', he wrote,

> seems to me to be a society of men constituted only for the procuring, preserving, and advancing their own civil interests. Civil interests I call life, liberty, health, and indolency of body; and the possession of outward things, such as money, lands, houses, furniture and the like. It is the duty of the civil magistrate, by the impartial execution of equal laws, to secure unto all the people in general and to everyone of his subjects in particular the just possession of those things belonging to this life.[4]

The care of souls, in contrast, was vested in the spiritual domain, the Church: civil power 'neither can nor ought in any manner to be extended to the salvation of souls'.[5] In drawing such distinctions, the association of Enlightenment rational thinking with secular progress and rationality was forged, creating sharp Manichean distinctions between the realm of the spiritual and that of civil authority. In the latter was invested notions of progress, of development, of securing the tangible assets of improved living conditions; whilst the former was given domain over the intangible inner world of the human – the soul. The rise of a distinct development discourse in the twentieth century fitted into this pattern. Development would look after the body, entrusting the soul to the wide range of faiths.

The importance of the clash of civilization discourse in this debate is critical. For whilst it correctly recognises the importance of religion in contemporary global politics, it posits it first as a *resurgence* of religion (an 'unsecularization of the world', as George Weigel describes it (cited in Huntington 1993: 26) and second in the form of *fundamentalist* forms of global religion. The discourse suggests that faith has become something dangerous, running counter to Western civilization which remains centred on post-Enlightenment secular rationality.

This de-coupling of religion from modernity has been noted throughout the collection. As Inge Hovland suggests, 'progress' has tended to be counter-posed with 'religion', with the latter conceptualized as functioning in a separate realm from the secular development project. The conceptualization of modernity, drawing on sociological traditions that sought to present a decline in adherents of the main organized religions in twentieth century Europe as a normative global experience, linked the tropes of 'progress' and 'modernity' with that of 'rationalism', thus in effect serving to exclude the religious dimension from this space. It is a discourse that speaks directly to the notion of 'development', seeking as it does to promote the securing and protection of 'civil interests'. But the notion of a fundamental cleavage lying between the secular and the religious, lying along the fault-line of Lockean self-interest, does not reflect the social realities of how faith, spirituality and religion operate across large swathes of the world. Accepting even for a moment that this does reflect modern European social models (and it is doubtful that this model does function even in the supposed bastion of secular public space in Western Europe), the extent to which it can be extended beyond those narrow parameters is doubtful.

Moreover, such distinctions bring their own dangers. In identifying secularism as the normative rational position, the secular space is in effect laying claim to the legacy of the European Enlightenment. Such claims risk essentializing a Eurocentric perspective that fails to account for the richness of faith's engagement with society elsewhere. As Peter van der Veer notes, 'the very distinction between religious and secular is a product of the Enlightenment that was used in orientalism to draw a sharp opposition between irrational, religious behaviour of the Oriental and rational secularism, which enabled the westerner to rule the Oriental' (van der Veer 1993: 39). The attempts to link progress/ rationalism and secularism, and the exclusion of the religious from that sphere, push organizations, individuals and societies in which faith plays a critical role into the sphere of the irrational and superstitious. And in doing so, it allows donors, analysts and others to effectively ignore this sphere, as constituting little that might be of real interest or significance to development objectives.

These artificial divisions have been compounded in recent discourses over cosmopolitanism. Here, 'development' functions as a cosmopolitan force: inclusive and diverse, eschewing a strict Western blinkered-approach for an embracive approach. It conceptualizes itself as functioning in 'a single moral realm' (Held 2003: 469–470), contrasted against a particularist identity and mode of operation characterized by non-cosmopolitan forces. The language sets up a clear moral distinction between the two. Mary Kaldor, for example, contrasts the 'values of civility and multiculturalism' with those of tribalism and violence. Cosmopolitanism, or the 'politics of ideas', is integrative, forward-looking, in contrast to the backward-looking, and fragmentative 'politics of identity' (Kaldor 1999: 9, 78). Faith, within this paradigm, is a function of a politics of identity, thereby excluding itself from the cosmopolitanism of modern development, and hence from its place at the policy-making and aid-disbursement table.

In the case of faith-based organizations operating in an active and passive capacity (see Chapter 2), 'faith' is presented as an underlying foundation rather than the dominant form of identity and ideology. They have sought to develop a corporate image that avoids characterization by secular donors and governments as agencies that place conversion as a higher priority than development or relief. However, tensions remain within these organizations, hidden behind the corporate image of professional development organizations, over how the two can be separated. Nevertheless, for donors, such organizations present little challenge, operating as they do within the comfort zone. But what of those organizations that present greater difficulties to donors, that espouse more orthodox versions of a faith, or seek to prioritize proselytizing above development? More significantly, how can donors engage with organizations that have real or alleged links to organizations accused of terrorist activity?

In the case of faith-based organizations based upon more radical, perhaps chauvinist forms of religious discourse (operating as persuasive or exclusive organizations), these are generally, cast as regressive ideological forms. As Jaffrolet's chapter shows, however, the apparent exclusivity of Hindu nationalism does not match up to donor attempts to cast it as such. Social welfare in the Indian slums functions on more inclusive terms. Similarly, whilst Islamic groups such as Hezbollah are frequently interpreted through their political Islamic form, in their welfare and anti-poverty work they have sought to present themselves in distinctly modernist forms as the chapters by Mona Harb and Janine Clark showed respectively.

A particular conceptualization of faith is critical to these organizations, but not the sole driving force. Hezbollah is typically interpreted through a security-based prism that essentializes its politics and military structure. Such a narrow gaze fails to account for the breadth of its operations, or its popularity amongst the civilian population. These interpretations also show the apparent cosmopolitanism of 'development' for what it really is: conceived largely in secular terms, and reflecting a Western-centric model that excludes ideologies that challenge its central tenets. In particular, its assertion that it functions within a single moral sphere can serve to exclude faith-based organizations that reject elements of that moral code.

At the heart of this understanding is the belief that the universalism of human rights is enshrined in a secular legal framework, protected by secular governments. But the idea that faith-based organizations operate outside rights-based discourses, or cosmopolitan paradigms, simply does not accord with the actual role of religious discourse in socio-political and moral debates during the past century and even further back. Indeed, underlying William Wilberforce and Thomas Clarkson's campaign to abolish the slave trade was their evangelical Christianity. The wider campaign in Britain owed even more to the campaigning efforts of the Quakers, who organized boycotts and protests from the end of the eighteenth century.[6] In this collection, Linden explains how Roman Catholic theology came to embrace a distinct human-rights approach in its language and contributed to the framing of the Universal Declaration of Human Rights. This tradition of engaging with the great moral questions of the age on the basis of human equality (rather than exclusivity of particular groups) has long featured throughout the twentieth century and (as Linden shows), before. In Kenya during the 1990s, it was the Christian leadership which led criticism of government human-rights abuses. Antonio Moreno's chapter on the Catholic Church in the Philippines shows how religious ideas and values led the Church to promote multi-party democracy as a moral system of governance. Jennings' chapter similarly reveals the determination of the Christian churches in Tanzania to adopt a new approach that recognized the shift from colonial to postcolonial worlds, and find a set of shared values with the state. In neither case were the leadership or organization as a whole speaking for a narrow sub-section of society, but for their interpretation of the good of society in general. In neither case were all elements within the leadership as equally committed to the same goals, and inevitably internal dissent and conflict emerged over the interpretation of new policies. But to assume such discussions reflect a lack of commitment to a universal understanding of particular rights, of modernity, or notions of 'progress', is to assume similar debates are absent from their secular counterparts.

There is an undeniable dark side to the FBO that makes it hard for donors to engage with some as partners. Whilst Hezbollah's welfare activity makes it a significant, if not sole in some areas, source of support for the poor and marginalized, its presence as a military organization within Lebanon and stated political aims inevitably raises real and important questions about its credibility as a partner. As Harb shows, it is important not to simply label it as a terrorist or Islamist organization. But neither can this dark side be ignored. Similarly, the discussions over women's rights within the organizations studied by Clark show that conceptions of human rights, enshrined in international legal instruments, remain subject to cultural debate. Pearson, too, shows how dialogue between faith and development communities can potentially serve to undermine gender equity principles.

But faith-based organizations are not alone in having their values, motives and actions questioned by outside observers. Faith-based organizations do not form a 'sector' in the sense of all agencies adopting a single, shared value system, in the same way that secular development organizations take a myriad of forms and adopt a wide range of values.

Moreover, the faith-based organization does not operate in a separate realm from principles of social justice, human rights, notions of equity and equality. Just as those principles and ideas are debated within explicitly secular organizations, so too FBOs engage with, rather than reject, those debates. Far from being relics of the past, organizations emerging from and linked to religious communities are increasing their role in social and economic development and relief activity. Yet despite their centrality to the welfare of millions across the world, donors remain wary of actively engaging with them.

Faith-based organizations and international development

Why this conceptual and resource gap? The question of whether faith-based organizations *should* have a role in development is redundant. There is now a broad-based agreement that the world's faith communities have an important role to play in the pursuit of the Millennium Development Goals. Jim Wallis, for instance, argues in *God's Politics*, that 'only a new moral, spiritual and even religious sensibility' can underpin 'the struggle to eliminate the world's worst poverty'. 'It is social movements', Wallis writes, 'which change history, and the best movements are the ones with spiritual foundations' (Wallis: 270–271). Similarly, 'Voices of the Poor' a World Bank study documenting the views and experiences of more than 60,000 men and women from sixty countries, (Narayan 2003: 222) notes that FBOs

> emerge frequently in poor people's lists of important institutions. They appear more frequently as the most important institutions in rural rather than in urban ones. Spirituality, faith in God and connecting to the sacred in nature are an integral part of poor people's

lives in many parts of the world. Religious organisations are also valued for the assistance they provide to poor people. (Ibid.: 222)

This acknowledgement of faith and associated organizations in the lives of the poor was largely unprecedented in the discourse of major donor agencies such as the World Bank and signalled a significant shift in thinking. Britain's DFID similarly signalled a shift following its creation in 1997, engaging with faith communities within Britain (and increasingly overseas) (cf. Clarke 2007)). In the United States the Bush administration, not unproblematically, signalled a marked shift towards the faith sector (see Chapters 2 and 3). Between 2001 and 2005, some $1.7 billion was channelled through FBOs by the United States Agency for International Development (USAID).[7]

But in shifting towards a closer relationship with faith communities, donors have acknowledged the potential negative impact of faith on the lives of the poor. 'Voices of the Poor' notes that the role of the FBO:

varies from being a balm for the body and soul to being a divisive force in the community. In ratings of effectiveness in both urban and rural settings, religious organisations feature more prominently than any single type of state institution but they do not disappear when ineffective institutions are mentioned. (Ibid.: 222)

FBOs, the Bank suggests, can be a potent force in the lives of the poor where they focus on material as well as spiritual poverty, avoid divisive or sectarian agendas, and become more involved in the daily struggles of the faithful. FBOs, the Bank concludes, 'must become agents of transformation, using their influence to demand better governance and public accountability' (Narayan 2001: 47). Clare Short, the British Minister for International Development between 1997 and 2003, echoed this call. If faith-based organizations became more engaged in public policy debates, more embedded in pro-poor alliances and networks at national and international level and more active in representing faith-based constituencies, she argued, the potential for positive catalytic change would be enormous (Short 2003: 8–9).

But donor wariness of faith-based organizations runs significantly deeper than concern over issues of their effectiveness, or their potential for division and exclusion. As this collection has demonstrated, the development project is defined primarily as a secular one through a process of de-linking faith-values from broader developmental ones that, as Linden notes, some FBOs have colluded in. Arguably, the term 'faith-based organization' contributes to the conceptualization of development as a secular process. Why not simply include faith organizations in the taxonomy of 'development organizations'? The answer may lie in American political discourse where the rise of the Christian right and the recent reform of welfare legislation has made the term 'faith-based organization' politically salient yet contentious. And the term loses little of this salience and contentiousness when imported into development discourse.

The analytical framework presented by Clarke in Chapter 2 points to other obstacles to donor engagement with faith-based organizations. To the extent that Western donors (multilateral, bilateral and non-governmental) support FBOs, they currently focus on *charitable and development organizations*, yet as Chapter 2 argues, a wide range of FBOs act as drivers of change in the developing world, including *representative organizations and apex bodies, socio-political organizations* and *missionary organizations*.

FBOs also differ enormously in the way they deploy faith in their pursuit of developmental, humanitarian, or broader political, objectives. Donors have traditionally engaged with FBOs that deploy faith in a *passive* or *active* manner. Donors now face the challenge of selectively engaging with FBOs that use faith in a *persuasive* or *exclusive* manner, given their importance in channelling funding to developing countries, in providing services to the poor and in representing them. Whether European donors in particular can engage with evangelical or Wahabi/Salafi organizations that straddle the *active/persuasive/exclusive* divide, or with the representatives of political Islam such as Hezbollah, remains to be seen. Whether donors can work with state or federal governments in India to support moderate forms of *Hindutva* through associated FBOs or support moderate Hindu FBOs that respect minority faiths and challenge caste-based social exclusion is similarly unclear.

And yet, donors themselves face an equivalent challenge in embracing a less secular and technocratic vision of development in favour a more socially and culturally inclusive approach to partnership, of acknowledging the cultural as well as the material dimensions of poverty, based on a broader conception of *well-being*. The *Human Development Report 2004*, for instance, identities two distinct forms of cultural exclusion which compound material poverty: *living mode exclusion*, where a state or social custom denigrates or suppresses a group's culture, including its spiritual beliefs, and *participation exclusion*, where cultural identities, including faith-based identities, give rise to discrimination or disadvantage which leads to social, economic or political exclusion

(UNDP 2004: 27).[8] Within this new conception of well-being, faith is a key aspect of cultural identity and FBOs important institutional expressions.

FBOs, the chapters in this collection demonstrate, have a number of characteristics that distinguish them from their secular peers. They draw on elaborate spiritual and moral values that represent an important and distinct adjunct to secular development discourse. As a result, they have a significant ability to mobilize adherents otherwise estranged by secular development discourse. They are highly networked both nationally and internationally and are highly embedded in political contests and in processes of governance in both horizontal and vertical terms. They are less dependent on donor funding and they have well-developed capacity and expertise in key areas of development practice. As such, they are important actors in the development process and warrant commensurate attention in development policy. In this sense, its worth remembering that 'development' is itself a normative ideal and moral cause, and as such has much in common with the faith discourses from which it has traditionally remained aloof. The challenge posed by the convergence of faith and development is to engage with faith discourses and associated organizations which seem counter-development or culturally exotic to a secular and technocratic worldview, in building the complex multi-stakeholder partnerships increasingly central to the fight against global poverty.

A story is told of a young doctoral researcher in Tanzania looking for a local NGO to study. Finding it difficult to identify anything that might qualify, his supervisor told him to look out for the spire and the minaret, for the Church and the mosque were the only organizations that could genuinely claim a presence in nearly all areas of the country, from the policy chambers of central government to the smallest village in the remotest parts of Tanzania. Modern political and social rhetoric has sought to divide the secular and the sacred, present them as entirely separate spheres with separate concerns. The social reality suggests something different, something much more than a Venn diagram of some shared interests. The place of religion in society is complex, dense and difficult to pin down precisely. But it is real.

Notes

1. Government of France, 1905 Law, available at http://www.assemblee-nationale.fr/histoire/eglise-etat/sommaire.asp#loi accessed on 15 February 2007.
2. For estimates over time, see Barrett and Johnson (2007: 8).

3. Although many avowedly 'secular' democracies still have formal religious representation in the instruments of state: the House of Lords in the United Kingdom, for example.
4. John Locke, *A Letter Concerning Toleration*, first published in 1689. Available at http://etext.lib.virginia.edu/toc/modeng/public/LocTole.html, accessed 14 February 2007.
5. Ibid.
6. The role of the Quakers in modern development is an interesting, if ignored, history. Many modern British NGOs, for example, owe their early shifts to development activity in the 1950s and 1960s to pioneering work done by the Quaker Friends Service Committee.
7. 'Bush Brings Faith to Foreign Aid', *Boston Globe*, 8 October 2006. Available at http://www.boston.com/news/nation/articles/2006/10/08/bush_brings_faith_to_foreign_aid/, accessed on 23 March 2007.
8. The report suggests that faith is the most important element in cultural exclusion, citing evidence that some 359 million people are disadvantaged or discriminated against on the basis of their faith, or 70 per cent of the estimated 518 million people worldwide who belong to groups that face some form of cultural exclusion (pp. 32–33).

Bibliography

Barrett, D. B. and Johnson, T. M. (2007), *International Bulletin of Missionary Research*, 31, 1.

Bergen, P. L. (ed.) (1999), *The Desecularization of the World: Resurgent Religion and World Politics* (Washington DC: Ethics and Public Policy Center, Washington DC and Grand Rapids MI: William B. Eerdmans Publishing Company).

Clarke, G. (2007), 'Agents of Transformation? Donors, Faith-Based Organisations and International Development', *Third World Quarterly*, 28, 1, pp. 835–848.

Durkheim, E. (1995), *The Elementary Forms of Religious Life*, Translated by Karen E Fields (New York: Free Press).

Held, D. (2003), 'Cosmopolitanism: Globalisation Tamed?', *Review of International Studies*, 29, 4, pp. 465–480.

Huntington, S. (1993), 'The Clash of Civilisations', *Foreign Affairs* 72, 3, pp. 22–49.

—— (1997), *The Clash of Civilizations and the Remaking of World Order* (London: Simon & Schuster).

Kaldor, M. (1999), *New and Old Wars: Organised Violence in a Global Era* (Cambridge: Polity Press).

Narayan, D. (2001), 'Voices of the Poor', in D. Belshaw, R. Calderisi and C. Sugden (eds.), *Faith in Development: Partnership Between the World Bank and the Churches in Africa* (Oxford: Regnum Books and Washington DC: the World Bank).

Sahliyeh, E. (ed) (1990), *Religious Resurgence and Politics in the Contemporary World* (New York: State University of New York Press).

Sen, A. (2006), *Identity and Violence: The Illusion of Destiny* (London: Allen Lane).

Short, C. (2003), 'After September 11: What Global Development Challenges Lie Ahead?', in Katherine Marshall and Richard Marsh (Eds.), *Millennium Challenges for Development and Faith Institutions* (Washington DC: The World Bank).

UNDP (2004), *Human Development Report 2004: Cultural Liberty in Today's Diverse World* (New York: United Nations Development Programme and Oxford University Press).

van der Veer, P. (1993), 'The Foreign Hand: Orientalist Discourse in Sociology and Communalism', in Carol A. Breckenridge and Peter van der Veer (eds), *Orientalism and the Postcolonial Predicament: Perspectives on South Asia* (Philadephia: University of Pennsylvania Press).

Wallis, J. (2005), *God's Politics: Why the American Right Gets It Wrong and the Left Doesn't Get It* (Oxford: Lion).

Webster, A. (2007), 'The Right Rev Lord Sheppard', Obituary, *The Guardian*, 7 March.

Index

Printed in the United States
149138LV00003B/34/P